F. David Martin
Lee A. Jacobus

THE HUMANITIES THROUGH THE ARTS

THE
HUMANITIES
THROUGH
THE ARTS

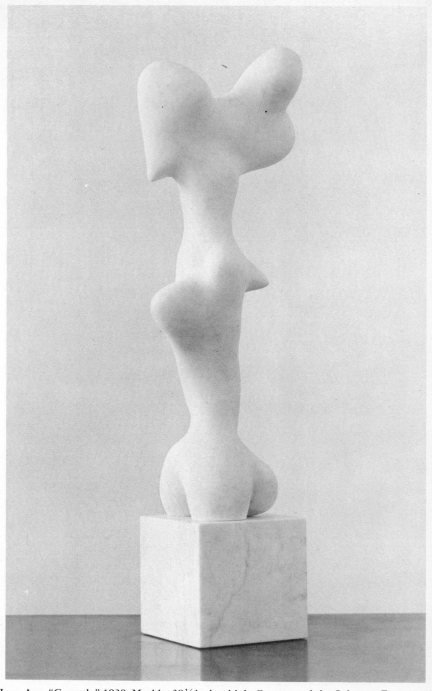

Jean Arp, "Growth." 1938. Marble, 39½ inches high. Courtesy of the Solomon R. Guggenheim Museum.

THE HUMANITIES THROUGH THE ARTS

F. David Martin
BUCKNELL UNIVERSITY

Lee A. Jacobus
UNIVERSITY OF CONNECTICUT

McGraw-Hill
Book Company

New York
St. Louis
San Francisco
Düsseldorf
Johannesburg
Kuala Lumpur
London
Mexico
Montreal
New Delhi
Panama
Paris
São Paulo
Singapore
Sydney
Tokyo
Toronto

This book was set in Patina by University Graphics, Inc.
The editors were James F. Mirrielees, Alison Meersschaert,
and Susan Gamer;
the designer was J. E. O'Connor;
the production supervisor was Sam Ratkewitch.
Von Hoffmann Press, Inc., was printer and binder.

Cover :
Lincoln Center Reclining Figure by Henry Moore,
Lincoln Center for the Performing Arts, New York.
Photograph by Roger Phillips and Dianne Arndt.

THE HUMANITIES THROUGH THE ARTS

1234567890VHVH 7987654

Library of Congress Cataloging in Publication Data

Martin, F   David, date
    The humanities through the arts.

    1. Arts—Psychology. 2. Art appreciation.
I. Jacobus, Lee A., joint author. II. Title.
NX165.M37   701'.15   74–6347
ISBN 0–07–040612–X

FA
777

CONTENTS

PREFACE

The Humanities through the Arts is an exploratory approach to the humanities that focuses on the special role of the arts. The relation of the humanities to values—objects and events important to man—is emphasized; and a basic distinction is made between the role of artists and that of other humanists. Artists reveal values; the other humanists study or reflect upon values. This book provides a self-contained program for studying values as revealed in the arts and reflected upon in the other humanities.

Revelatory aesthetics, the basic theory that organizes the presentation of material in this study, offers a relatively uncomplicated basis for understanding and appreciating the arts. Our approach is one which should be especially welcome to the student, for whom an explicit concern about values is usually central to his education. Teachers, for their part, while respecting the usefulness of formal analysis, are aware of the limitations of separating art from the larger concerns of human values.

While most humanities texts study the arts chronologically within the frameworks of their social and stylistic environments, we have not organized our study historically, except incidentally. The book begins with a general introduction to the humanities, focusing on what they are and the basic importance of the arts to the other humanities. The next two chapters, devoted to definitions of art and varieties of critical approaches to the arts, establish a foundation for critical response. Then the various arts are explored individually in chapters on painting, sculpture, architecture, literature, music, dance, and film, with the relationships of subject matter, form, and content in each of these arts supplying the framework of the analyses.

The emphasis throughout the text is on participation and involvement with maximum understanding and thus maximum intensity of enjoyment — allowing each work of art to unfold its fullness. To help the reader sharpen his perceptive responses to the work of art, we have provided "perception keys," making this book unique among humanities texts. Concentrating on specific works of art, the perception keys include questions and suggestions designed to elicit more sensitive perception. The student is enabled to see immediately the extent or limit of his understanding of any given example. The perception keys also encourage both critical and creative activities by the student. Through genuine participation and involvement, the student is prevented from being a passive receptor of absolute value statements about the arts. The perception keys invite the student to question and test virtually all statements of interpretation and value — whether implicit or explicit — throughout the text as well as in the classroom and in his own general experience. Our analyses, which usually follow rather than precede the keys, are offered not as *the* way to perceive a given work of art, but rather as one possible way. We avoid dogmatic answers and explanations; our primary interest is in exciting our readers to perceive for themselves a specific work of art in all its specificity.

In the final chapter, the relationships of values in the arts to the other humanities — especially history, philosophy, and religion — are explored with the help of "conception keys." Similar in format to the perception keys, they involve the student in conceptual problems and explore the distinctions between perceiving and conceiving. Through its use of perception and conception keys, *The Humanities through the Arts* comes as close to being self-instructional as a humanities book can be.

We believe that the arts and the other humanities are a commonwealth, that they comment on and complement each other just as the sciences do. By deepening our understanding of the revelations and reflections about values that the humanities provide, we deepen the foundations for our value decisions. We also strengthen our powers to endure and to enjoy life; for the humanities, perhaps more than any other civilizing activity, satisfy our insistent zest for existence.

ACKNOWLEDGMENTS

A book of this nature must always be indebted to far more people than can be properly credited. Yet some names must be mentioned. A number of anonymous reviewers read the manuscript at various stages, and for their help we are indeed grateful. Harrison Davis, of Brigham Young University, had some important suggestions and valuable criticisms which led to revisions that strengthened the book.

The critical eye of such people as Selma Jeanne Cohen, editor of *Dance Perspectives,* led to changes and refinements which might not have been made otherwise. Conversations with numerous people involved in the humanities all led, in one way or another, to adjustments or insights that helped during the formulative phases of this book. Such people as Gerald Eager of the art department of Bucknell University; Deborah Jowitt, dance critic of the *Village Voice;* the dance critic Marcia Segal; Martha Myers, chairman of the Department of Dance at Connecticut College; Joanna J. Jacobus, dance teacher; Walter Wehner of the Music Faculty of the University of North Carolina at Greensboro; Marceau Myers, Dean of the Music Conservatory at Capitol University; Jackson Hill of the Music Faculty of Bucknell University; Cheryl Mehalik of McGraw-Hill; and many more besides them, all made contributions of one kind or another which found their way into our book. Naturally, we also want to express gratitude to our students, whose insights and whose needs are reflected here. And we wish to thank Mrs. Nancy Johnson, who scrupulously cared for the manuscript and the frequent overhauls it sustained. Finally, we would like to thank the Bucknell University Press for permission to paraphrase and quote from *Art and the Religious Experience,* 1972, F. David Martin. We would like to dedicate this book to humanities teachers and their students.

F. David Martin
Lee A. Jacobus

1 THE HUMANITIES: AN INTRODUCTION

THE HUMANITIES AND THE SCIENCES

Not too many centuries ago the word "humanities" distinguished that which pertained to God from that which pertained to man. Mathematics, the sciences, the arts, and philosophy were humanities: they had to do with man. Theology and related studies were the subjects of divinity: they had to do with God. This distinction does not have the importance for most of us that it once did. Today we think of the humanities as those broad areas of human creativity and study that are distinct from mathematics and the "hard" sciences, mainly because in the humanities strictly objective or scientific standards are not usually dominant.

The separation between the sciences and the humanities is illustrated by the way in which values work differently in the two areas. Consider, for example, the drinking of liquor: a positive value for some people, a negative value for others. The biologist describes the physiological effects. The psychologist describes the psychological effects. The sociologist takes a poll tabulating people's value preferences concerning drinking. These scientists study values, but they are concerned with "what is" rather than "what ought to be." That is why they can apply strictly scientific standards to their investigations. If they make a value judgment, such as that liquor ought to be banned, they will tend—as scientists—to make it clear that their pronouncements are personal value judgments rather than scientific statements. With humanists, on the other hand, the sharp separation between the "is" and the "ought," between scientific statement and value judgment, is usually not so evident, primarily because the scientific method is not so basic to their work. Most scientists and humanists will agree that we must all make value judgments and that often the sciences can provide important information that helps us make sound decisions. If, for example, the biologists discovered that liquor shortens the life span significantly, this would indeed be relevant to a value judgment about banning liquor. On the other hand, such consensus seems to be lacking with respect to the relevance of the humanities to value judgments. Scientists, more than humanists, probably would be dubious about an assertion that novels such as Dostoevski's *Brothers Karamazov* contribute important information for making sound value judgments about the banning of liquor.

The discoveries of the scientists—for example, the bomb and the pill— often have tremendous impact on a society's values. Yet more than one scientist has declared that he merely makes the discoveries and that others— presumably politicians—must decide how his discoveries are to be used. Perhaps it is this last statement that brings us closest to the importance of the humanities. If many scientists feel they cannot judge how their discoveries are to be used, then we must try to understand why they give that responsibility to others. This is not to say that scientists uniformly turn such decisions over to others, for many of them are humanists as well as scientists. But the fact remains that governments—from that of Hitler to that of Churchill and those of such nations as China, the Soviet Union, and the United States—have all made use of great scientific achievements without pausing to ask the "achievers" if they approved of the way their discoveries were being used. The questions are: Who decides how to use such discoveries? On what grounds should their judgments be based?

Studying the behavior of neutrinos or ion-exchange resins will not help get us closer to the answer. Such study is not related to the nature of man but to the nature of nature. What we need is a study that will get us closer to man himself. It should be a study which explores the reaches of human feeling in relation to values—not only our own individual feelings and values, though that is first in importance, but also the feelings and values of others. We need a study that will increase our sensitivity to ourselves, others, and the values in our world. To be sensitive is to perceive with insight. To be sensitive is also to feel and believe that things make a difference. It involves, furthermore, an awareness of those aspects of values that cannot be measured by objective standards. To be sensitive is to respect the humanities because, among other reasons, they help develop our sensitivity to values—to what we as individuals place importance on. Values are strictly in the domain of the humanities because they are strictly relative to man and his condition.

There are numerous ways to approach the humanities. The way we have chosen here is the way of the arts. The arts clarify or reveal values. As we deepen our understanding of the arts, we necessarily deepen our understanding of values, for that is what the arts are about. We will study our experience with works of art as well as the values which others associate with those works. We will look at the "whys and whats" of art by examining why certain kinds of values are associated with certain kinds of art. And in the process of doing this we will also be educating ourselves about the nature of our own values.

TASTE

This brings us to a crucial issue. Most people have already made up their minds about what art they like and what art they do not like. There are opera buffs who think opera in English is necessarily inferior to opera in Italian, French, or German. In fact, because we have so long listened to opera in foreign languages, the odds are that an American opera lover will find it difficult to accept any opera whose words he can understand. People have various kinds of limitations about the arts. Some cannot look at a painting or sculpture of a nude figure without smirking. Some think any painting is magnificent as long as it has a dog in it, or a horse, or a sunset, or a rolling sea, or a battle, or—and this is an extreme but not impossible case —no recognizable figures at all. And we know people who will read any book that has automobile racing as part of its subject, or that has a scientific angle to it, or that is about something they are already deeply interested in. By watching the local papers we can see how the taste of the mass public shifts. Movies, for example, survive or fail commercially on the basis of the number of people they can appeal to. Consequently, films change periodically in subject matter and kind in order to "cash in" on current popular tastes; and the film, of course, is only one form of commercial art in our time.

Tastes change, and as anyone who has lived in the Western world knows, they change with alarming rapidity. What this means is sometimes difficult to assess; but one thing it certainly means is that the arts, by playing on popular tastes, can also play on our limitations. It means that commercially successful arts can play upon values in such a way as to give us what we think we want rather than what we really need with reference to insight. Also, we all have limitations as viewers of art; most of us defend ourselves against stretching our limitations by assuming that we have developed our taste and that any effort to change it is "bad form." An old saying—"Matters of taste are not disputable"—can be credited with making many of us feel very righteous about our own "taste." What the saying means is that there is no accounting for what people like in the arts, for beauty is in the eye of the beholder. Thus there is no use trying to do anything that might help someone change his mind about the arts. Or, to put it still differently: there is no use in trying to educate anyone about the arts.

Obviously we do not feel that way about the arts ourselves. We believe that all of us can and should be educated about the arts and should learn to respond to as wide a variety of the arts as possible: from rock, to jazz, to string quartets; from Charlie Chaplin to Ingmar Bergman; from Lewis Carroll to T. S. Eliot; from primitive folk art to Picasso. "Taste," in other words, is a word we sometimes use to approve our limitations. And we must admit, since we all have limitations, that the word sometimes comes in handy. But we also realize that we can do without the word in that narrow sense—and happily so if doing without it can help us discover something new and really exciting in the arts we might otherwise have missed.

Most of us use the word "taste" defensively for a good reason. Anyone who tampers with our taste is tampering with our deep feelings. Anyone who tries to change our responses to art is really trying to get inside our minds. This kind of education, if we fail to understand its purpose, naturally arouses resistance in us—unlike the kinds of education that entail gathering facts or learning specific skills.

There are many facts involved in the study of the arts and the humanities. We can verify the dates of Beethoven's birth and death and the dates of his important compositions. We can investigate the history of jazz and consider the claims of Jelly Roll Morton for having been its "inventor." We can decide who was or was not part of the Barbizon school of painting in nineteenth-century France, when Corot and Manet were painting. There are oceans of facts associated with every art. But our interest is not in facts alone.

What we mean by a study of the arts is something that penetrates beyond facts to the values that evoke our feelings—the way a succession of guitar chords can be electrifying or the way song lyrics can give you a chill. In other words, we want to go beyond the facts *about* a work of art and get to the fact *of* the work itself, to the values working in the work. This means we want to learn how to "come to" the work of art itself, to get as close as possible to what is there. This is the meaning of "education" in the sense that we have been using the term. The problem with taste and concepts like it is that they get in the way of our education. We all know some people we do not bother to talk to about the kind of music we like. We do not worry much about it, but we all think that what we like is pretty good and that other people could benefit from paying attention to it—maybe. And the "maybe" is usually connected with two things: whether or not we can get those other people to listen to what we think is good, and then whether or not the experience these other people have is a full and fair one. That last point is crucial: even though a person is exposed to a work of art, the experience may not "take" unless he perceives as much as possible of what is there. A failure of perception is precisely what happens to us when we experience a work of art we are told is good (presuming it actually is good) and we are unable to appreciate it. How many times have we all found ourselves liking something which, years or months before, we could not stand?

RESPONSES TO ART

Our responses to art usually involve processes so complex that they can never be fully tracked down or analyzed. They can only be hinted at when we talk about them. Let us begin by looking at a painting by David Alfaro Siquieros, a contemporary Mexican painter, called "Echo of a Scream" (Figure 1-1).

FIGURE 1-1   David Alfaro Siquieros, "Echo of a Scream." 1937. Duco on wood, 48 by 36 inches. Collection, The Museum of Modern Art, New York; gift of Edward M. M. Warburg.

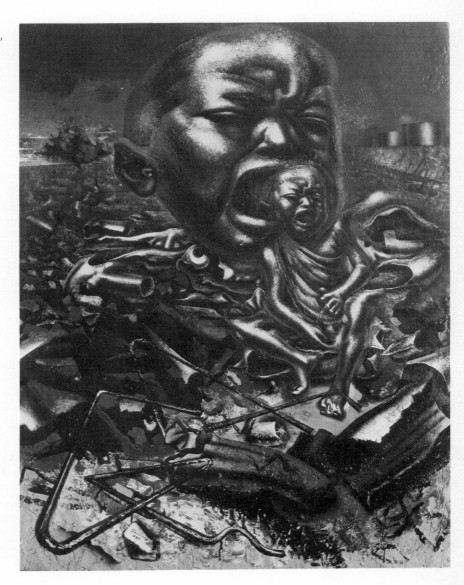

This is a highly emotional painting—in the sense that the work seems to demand a strong emotional response. What we see is the huge head of a baby crying, and then, as if issuing from its own mouth, the baby himself. What kinds of emotions do you find stirring in yourself as you look at this painting? What kinds of emotions would you expect your friends to be having when they look at it? You will not find, under any conditions, that the emotions you might be able to isolate—such as shock; pity for the child; irritation at a destructive, mechanical society; or any other nameable emotion—will sum up the painting or be equivalent to it. This is natural and desirable. If Siquieros could have gotten the same effect in words, he would need no painting.

PERCEPTION KEY "ECHO OF A SCREAM"

1. Identify the objects in the painting.
2. What is the condition of the objects? What is their relation to the baby?
3. What is the meaning of those strange round forms in the upper right corner?
4. How would your response differ if the angular lines were smoothed out?
5. How does Siquieros establish the relative importance of shapes in the composition?
6. Discuss the function of the distortions of natural shapes in the painting. Is awareness of these distortions crucial to a sensitive response to the painting?

Consider another work, very close in temperament to Siquieros's painting—"Eternal City" by the American painter Peter Blume (Figure 1-2; see also Color Plate 1 following page 86).

PERCEPTION KEY "ETERNAL CITY"

1. What common ingredients do you find in the Blume and Siquieros paintings?
2. Do you have a similar reaction to each painting?
3. Is the effect of the distortions similar or different?
4. In terms of the objects and events represented in each painting, do you think the paintings are comparable? Give reasons.
5. Can you think of other works of art in other media—such as sculpture, architecture, literature, music, dance, and film—that represent objects and events similar to those represented in "Eternal City"?
6. Of the other arts mentioned in the fifth question, which one or ones seems most capable of representing the objects and events of "Eternal City"? Will these other media, nevertheless, represent them differently? And if so, what significance may this have for our study of the arts?

FIGURE 1-2   Peter Blume, "Eternal City." 1937. Oil on composition board, 34 by 47⅞ inches. Collection, The Museum of Modern Art, New York. Mrs. Simon Guggenheim Fund. (*See also Color Plate 1.*)

Having attended carefully to the kinds of responses awakened by "Eternal City," take note of some information about the painting which you may not have known. The date of this painting is the same as that of "Echo of a Scream": 1937. "Eternal City" is a name reserved for only one city in the world: Rome. In 1937 the world was on the verge of an enormous war between the fascist nations of Italy and Germany and the democratic nations of Europe and America. In the center of the painting is the Roman forum, close to where Julius Caesar, the alleged tyrant, was murdered by Brutus. But here we see Fascist Black Shirts beating people. At the left is a figure of Christ and beneath him is a beggar woman—a cripple. Near her are ruins of classic Roman statuary. The enlarged and distorted head, wriggling out like a jack-in-the-box, is that of Mussolini: the man who invented the Black Shirts and fascism. Now look at the painting closely again. Do you now respond differently to the painting?

Before going on to the next painting, which is quite different in character, we should pause to make some observations about what we have done. With added knowledge about its cultural and political implications—what we shall call the background of the painting—your responses to "Eternal City" perhaps have changed significantly. Ideally they should have become more focused, intense, and certain. Why? The painting is surely the same physical object you looked at originally. Nothing has changed in the object. Therefore something has changed because something has been added to *you:* information which the general viewer of the painting in 1937 would not only have had right at his fingertips but probably would have responded to

FIGURE 1-3   Pablo Picasso, "Guernica." 1937. Oil on canvas, 11 feet 6 inches by 25 feet 8 inches. On extended loan from the artist to The Museum of Modern Art, New York.

much more emotionally than we do now. Consider how a Fascist or an Italian humanist and lover of Roman culture would have reacted to this painting in 1937. Obviously the experience of this painting is not one thing or one system of things but an innumerable variety of things. Moreover, knowledge *about* a work of art can often help give you knowledge *of* the work of art, a deeper experience of that work. This is important as a basic principle, since it means that we can be educated about what works in a work of art, not just about the things which are external to a work, such as its historical background. It means we can learn to respond more sensitively than we do. It also means that painters like Peter Blume sometimes produce works of art that we must know something about if we are to appreciate them fully. This is particularly true of literature, since most literature assumes that we can fit ourselves into the psychological framework of the characters and the sociological framework of their society as well as the cultural framework of the story. Therefore there are times when we cannot respond very deeply to a work of art simply because we do not have the background knowledge the artist presupposes.

Picasso's "Guernica" (Figure 1-3) is one of the most famous paintings of the twentieth century. It was painted in 1937, like the other paintings. Its title comes from the name of an old Spanish town which was bombed during the Spanish Civil War—the first aerial bombing of noncombatant civilians in modern warfare. Examine this painting carefully.

1. Distortion again is powerfully evident in this painting. Is its function similar to that of the distortion in Blume's or Siquieros's paintings?

2. Describe the objects in the painting. What is their relationship to each other?

3. Is there a clear distinction between the way the animals and the human beings are represented? What does your observation imply?

4. If you were not told, would you know that this painting was a representation of an air raid?

5. Is the subject matter—what the work is about—of this painting war? Death? Suffering? Can you relate the subject matter of "Guernica" to the subject matters of the other paintings we have just discussed? Are these subject matters the same? Could sculpture, architecture, literature, music, dance, and film have the same kind of subject matter as "Guernica"? Be as specific as possible.

6. What kinds of responses does the painting evoke in you?

The next painting—"Composition in White, Black and Red" (Figure 1-4, page 10, and Color Plate 2)—was completed by Piet Mondrian, a very influential Dutch painter, in 1936.

PERCEPTION KEY "COMPOSITION IN WHITE, BLACK AND RED"

1. If you were to comment on "distortion" in this painting, what would that imply about what the painting represents?

2. What are the objects represented in the painting? Do they have anything to do with life outside the painting? What?

3. How would your response differ if all the black areas were repainted orange? Would the balance of the painting be disturbed?

4. Suppose the horizontal black line running across the width of the painting were raised nearer to the top. Would the balance of the painting be disturbed?

5. Suppose the little rectangle at the upper left-hand corner were enlarged. Would the balance of the painting be disturbed?

6. Is balance an especially important factor in this work? Explain.

7. Suppose you noticed, upon entering a room, that the picture frame of the Mondrian had been hung so that its horizontal and vertical lines were not parallel to the wall. Do you think you would have any need to straighten the frame? Suppose you found "Echo of a Scream" similarly awry. Would you have as strong a need to straighten its frame? Explain.

8. Do you need any historical background to appreciate Mondrian's painting? Is what we have said about world conditions in 1937 irrelevant to this

painting? Soon after that date, Mondrian's country, Holland, partially destroyed itself by opening its dikes in an attempt to keep Hitler out. Does this fact influence the way you look at this painting?

9. Does the painting evoke strong responses in you? Do you have more difficulty articulating your responses to it than to the paintings by Siquieros, Blume, and Picasso? If so, how is this to be explained?

10. Is the painting by Mondrian more like music than the paintings by Siquieros, Blume, and Picasso? Explain.

ARTISTIC FORM

The Mondrian obviously is very different from the other paintings in subject matter and style. The responses you have when you look at it are probably quite different from those you had when you were viewing the other paintings, but why? You might reply that the Mondrian is pure form, nothing but a sensuous surface. Unlike the other paintings, no objects or events are represented. And yet this painting can be very exciting. Form—the interrelationships of lines, colors, light, textures, and shapes—can be very moving. Most of us have the capacity to respond to pure form, even in paintings which have a subject matter that distracts us from pure form. Thus, for most people, responding to "Eternal City" involves responding not just to a painter's interpretation of fascism taking hold in Italy but also to the shapes, colors, and proportions of things in the painting. This is certainly true of "Echo of a Scream"; if you look back at that painting you will see that the distortions and placement of figures are calculated to help our responses become deeper than they would be if the crying baby and the destruction of war were represented without distortion. Form, in the hands of a good painter (or any artist), is a weapon for getting inside our minds without our necessarily being aware of it. Or, as the great twentieth-century composer Arnold Schoenberg put it: "The principal function of form is to advance our understanding. It is the organization of a piece which helps the listener to keep the idea in mind, to follow its development, its growth, its elaboration, and its fate."

Every painter uses form, but every painter does not necessarily call attention to it the way Mondrian does. And since we often respond to form without even being conscious that it is affecting us, it is of the first importance that a painter make sure his form is successful. Study the composition of "Eternal City." Figure 1-5 is a tracing of the basic form.

In the "center stage" of the composition is the scene of Fascist Black

FIGURE 1-5   Line tracing of Blume's "Eternal City."

Shirts brutalizing citizens: the government in its forum. To one side is Christ, not only removed but bricked off. Moreover, Christ is smaller and less important to the composition than Mussolini's head—the largest figure —close to the action and in control. The black forms at the foot of the composition represent the smiling common people—middle-class citizens who helped Mussolini gain power and who thought they would benefit from his government.

The form of any painting can be analyzed because any painting has to be organized: parts have to be interrelated. Moreover, it is very helpful to look closely and think carefully about the form of individual paintings. This is particularly true of paintings one does not respond to immediately—to "difficult" or apparently uninteresting paintings. Often the analysis of form can get us into such paintings and open them up so that they become genuinely exciting.

PERCEPTION KEY ANALYSIS AND RESPONSE

Analyze the form of some paintings—"Echo of a Scream," "Guernica," or any other painting you see in this book. Do the same with works of art in other media. Do you find that after such analyses your responses to these works are more satisfactory?

PERCEPTION

We cannot respond properly to a work of art that we do not perceive properly. What is less obvious is what we referred to previously: the fact that we can often give our attention to a work of art and still not really perceive very much. The reason for this should be relatively clear from what we have already said: there are frequently things we do not know about the background of a work of art that would aid our perception of it. If we do not know that background, we may not be able to perceive what is there. Anyone who did not know who Christ was, what fascism was, and what Mussolini meant to the world would have a difficult time making much sense of "Eternal City." But it is also true that anyone who could not perceive the form of Blume's painting might have a completely superficial response to it. Such a person could indeed know all about the background and understand the more or less symbolic statement being made by the painting —but that is only part of the painting. From seeing what Mondrian can do with lines and color, you can understand that the formal qualities of a painting are neither accidental nor unimportant. In Blume's painting, the form acts in such a way as to focus attention and organize our perceptions by establishing the relationships between the elements of the composition.

Form is basic to all the arts and to everything that is organized by man (as well as everything organized by other forces). To perceive any work of

art adequately, we must perceive form. Examine the following poem—
"l(a"—by E. E. Cummings, a contemporary American. It is unusual in
looks, just as it is unusual in its form and its effects upon most of us.

l(a

le
af
fa

ll

s)
one
l

iness

[Copyright © 1958 by
E. E. Cummings. Reprinted
from his volume, COM-
PLETE POEMS 1913–1962,
by permission of Harcourt
Brace Jovanovich, Inc.]

This poem looks at first like a strange kind of code, like an Egyptian hiero-
glyphic. But it is not a code—it is more like a Japanese haiku poem, a poem
which sets a scene or paints a picture and then waits for us to "get it." And
to "get it" requires sensitive perception.

PERCEPTION KEY "l(a"

1. Study the poem carefully until you begin to make out the words. What are
   they?

2. One part of the poem is a general term; the other is the name of an event.
   What is the relationship between them?

3. Is the shape of the poem important to the poem's meaning?

4. Why are the words of the poem hard to perceive? Is that difficulty important to the poem?

5. Once you have perceived the words and imagery of the poem, is your response to it different?

6. Compare your analysis of the poem with ours, which follows.

In this poem there is a word interrupted by parentheses. The word is simply "l one l iness"—"loneliness"—a feeling which we have all experienced and which we can all bring to mind at will. Because of its isolating, biting power, we ordinarily do not like this feeling. Then, inside the parentheses, there is a phrase, "a leaf falls," which is a description of an event: a leaf falls. In poetry such a description is usually called an "image." In this poem the image "illustrates" the idea, or theme, of loneliness. The image reinforces the idea and gives us something we can all imagine to make us feel more deeply the idea of loneliness. But that is not all Cummings has done to help us get a deeper, more intense feeling from the poem. Notice the devices that symbolize or represent oneness, which in a way is what loneliness is. The poem begins with the letter "l," which in the typeface used in the original poem looks like the number "one." Even the parenthesis separating the "a" from the "l" helps the image. Then there is the "le," which is the singular article in French. The idea of one is repeated, doubled, in the "ll" figure. Then Cummings brazenly writes "one" and follows it by "l" and then the ultimate "iness." Furthermore, in the original edition the poem is number one of the collection. By now we should indeed have perceived what Cummings is getting at. But it takes very close looking at this poem to observe that much. And there is more to it even than this. As you look at the poem you will notice that your eye follows a downward path which swirls in a pattern like that of the diagram in Figure 1-6.

This is merely following the parentheses and the consonants. If you follow the vowels as well, you will see that the curves become spirals, and the figure is indeed much like that of a leaf actually falling; this accounts for the long, thin look of the poem. Now, go back to the poem and reread it. Has your response changed? How?

Of course, most poems do not work in quite the way this poem does. Most poems do not rely on the way they look on the page, though this is

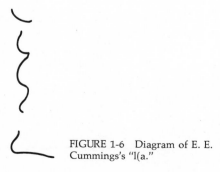

FIGURE 1-6   Diagram of E. E. Cummings's "l(a."

one of the most important things to Cummings. But what most poets are concerned with is the way the images or verbal pictures fit into the totality of the poem, how they make us experience the whole poem more intensely. In Cummings's poem the single, falling, dying leaf—one out of so many—is virtually perfect for helping us understand loneliness from a dying person's point of view. People are like leaves in that they are countless when they are alive and together. But like leaves, they die singly. And when one person separates himself from the community of his friends, he is as alone as the separate leaf.

ABSTRACT IDEAS AND CONCRETE IMAGES

Cummings's poem presents an abstract idea fused with a concrete image or word picture. It is concrete because what is described is a physical event: a falling leaf. Loneliness, on the other hand, is abstract. Take an abstract idea: love, hate, indecision, arrogance, jealousy, ambition, justice, civil rights, prejudice, the generation gap, revolution, coyness, insanity, or any other. Then link it with some physical object or event which you think illustrates the abstract idea. By "illustrate" is meant simply to make us feel that the object or event is bringing the abstract idea to life, to a life that is important to us: a value. If it doesn't make any difference to us, then it is not "working" right: fusion has failed. You need not, of course, follow Cummings's exact way of splitting the word and using parentheses for the event. You may use any way of lining the words up that you think is interesting. You may find that when you have really suited yourself with a satisfactory connection, you will have suited other people as well.

In *Paradise Lost*, usually thought to be a difficult poem, John Milton describes hell as a place with "Rocks, Caves, Lakes, Fens, Bogs, Dens, and shades of death." Now, neither you nor the poet knows precisely what a "shade of death" is—though the idea is in Psalm 23, ". . . the valley of the shadow of death." Milton gets away with it because he has linked this abstract idea to so many concrete images in this single line. He is talking about the *mood* of hell just as much as about the specific landscape, and we realize that he gives us so many topographic details in order to get us ready for the last detail—the abstract idea of shades of death—which in many ways is the most important.

Poetry worked in much the same way in seventeenth-century England as it does in twentieth-century America. The same principles are at work: the described objects or events are used as a means of bringing abstract ideas to life. In turn, the descriptions take on a wider and deeper significance— wider in the sense that the descriptions are connected with the larger scope of abstract ideas; deeper in the sense that because of these connections the descriptions elicit more sensitive responses from us.

The following poem is particularly telling for us because its theme is highly complex: the memory of an older culture (simplicity in this poem) and the consideration of a newer culture (complexity). It is an African poem by the Nigerian poet Gabriel Okara; and knowing that it is African, we can begin to appreciate the extreme complexity of Okara's feelings about the clash of the old and new cultures. He symbolizes the clash in terms of music and he opposes two musical instruments: the drum and the piano. They stand for the African and the European cultures. But even beyond the musical images that abound in this poem, look closely at the images of nature, the pictures of the panther and leopard, and see how Okara imagines them.

PIANO AND DRUMS

When at break of day at a riverside
I hear jungle drums telegraphing
the mystic rhythm, urgent, raw
like bleeding flesh, speaking of
primal youth and the beginning,
I see the panther ready to pounce,
the leopard snarling about to leap
and the hunters crouch with spears poised;

And my blood ripples, turns torrent,
topples the years and at once I'm
in my mother's lap a suckling;
at once I'm walking simple
paths with no innovations,
rugged, fashioned with the naked
warmth of hurrying feet and groping hearts
in green leaves and wild flowers pulsing.

Then I hear a wailing piano
solo speaking of complex ways
in tear-furrowed concerto;
of far-away lands
and new horizons with
coaxing diminuendo, counterpoint,
crescendo. But lost in the labyrinth
of its complexities, it ends in the middle
of a phrase at a daggerpoint.

And I lost in the morning mist
of an age at a riverside keep
wandering in the mystic rhythm
of jungle drums and the concerto.

[From *The African Assertion*,
Austin J. Shelton (ed.), Odyssey, N.Y.,
1968—originally in *Black Orpheus* #6,
1959, p. 33.]

PERCEPTION KEY "PIANO AND DRUMS"

1. What are the objects of most importance in the poem? Do they have significance beyond their existence as observable or useful things?

2. What are the two conflicting forces in the poem? Why are they symbolized by the drum and the piano?

3. Why do you think Okara chose the drum and the piano to help reveal the clash between the old and new cultures?

Such a poem must speak directly to legions of the current generation of Africans. But consider some points in light of what we have said earlier. In order to perceive the kind of emotional struggle which Okara talks about and which is in fact the subject matter of the poem, we need to know something about Africa and the struggle new nations in Africa are having bringing their technology into line with that of more advanced nations. We also need to know something of the history of Africa and the fact that European nations, such as Britain in the case of Nigeria, once controlled much of Africa. Knowing these things, we know then that there is no thought of the "I" of the poem accepting the "complex ways" of the new culture wholeheartedly. The "I" does not think of the culture of the piano as manifestly superior to the culture of the drum. That is why the labyrinth of complexities ends at "a daggerpoint." The new culture is a mixed blessing.

Perception of a work of art, we have argued, is aided by background information, and sensitive perception must be aware of form at least implicitly. But there is much more, we believe, to sensitive perception than that. Somehow the form of a work of art clarifies or reveals values, and our response is intensified by our awareness of those revealed values. But how does the form do this? And how does this awareness come to us? In the next chapter we shall consider these questions, and in doing so we will also raise the question: What is a work of art? As in this chapter, the emphasis will be on painting, though only for the convenience of illustration. Once we have examined each of the arts, it will be clear, we hope, that the principles developed in these opening chapters are equally applicable to all the arts.

2 WHAT IS A WORK OF ART?

Many ways of defining a "work of art" have been proposed. But no definition seems to be completely adequate and none is universally accepted. Thus we shall not propose a definition here but rather attempt to clarify some criteria or distinctions which can help us identify works of art. Since the term "work of art" implies the concept of making in two of its words— "work" and "art" (short for "artifice")—we frequently find it proposed that a work of art is something made by man. Hence sunsets, beautiful trees, "found" natural objects like lovely grained driftwood, "paintings" by insects or birds, and a host of other natural phenomena cannot be considered works of art. You may not wish to accept the proposal that a work of art is man-made. However if you do accept it, consider the "construction" below, Jim Dine's "Shovel" (Figure 2-1).

"Shovel" is part of a highly valuable collection of art and was first shown at a respectable art gallery in New York City. Dine, furthermore, is widely recognized as an important American artist. He did not himself make the shovel, however. It was, like most shovels, mass-produced. Dine mounted it on a painted panel and presented it for serious consideration as an artistic construction. Given these credentials, is it then a work of art?

We can hardly discredit it as a work of art simply because Dine did not

FIGURE 2-1   Jim Dine, "Shovel." 1962. Mixed media. "Sonnabend Gallery." Photograph by Eric Pollitzer.

make the shovel, since we often accept works of sculpture manufactured to specification by factories as genuine works of art. We accept collages by artists like Picasso and Braque, which include objects such as paper and nails that have simply been mounted on a panel. Museums have even accepted such objects as a signed urinal by Marcel Duchamp, a Dadaist artist of the 1920s, who in many ways anticipated the works of Dine, Warhol, Oldenburg, and others in the recent Pop Art movement. Thus it is not the novelty of Jim Dine's use of a ready-made object that appeals to art collectors but rather apparently something about the way he used the shovel.

IDENTIFYING ART CONCEPTUALLY

Three of the most widely accepted criteria for determining whether or not something is a work of art are (1) that the object or event should be made by an artist, (2) that the object or event should be intended to be a work of art by its maker (thus apparently ruling out the shovel, which was intended to be a tool), and (3) that important or recognized "experts" consider it art. Unfortunately, these considerations rely upon information that is not always ascertainable by looking at the work in question. This creates difficulties. In many cases, for instance, we may confront an object like "Shovel" and not know whether Dine may possibly have himself constructed the shovel very carefully in imitation of the mass-produced object, thus satisfying the first criterion that the object be made by an artist; or whether Dine intended it to be a work of art; or whether experts agree that it is a work of art. Dine, in fact, did not make this particular shovel; but since this fact cannot be established by ordinary perception, one has to be told this. Obviously we might have a long wait before getting the information needed to classify "Shovel" as a work of art.

PERCEPTION KEY IDENTIFYING A WORK OF ART

1. If Jim Dine actually made the shovel in his construction by hand, would "Shovel" then be unquestionably a work of art?

2. Suppose Dine made the shovel himself and it was absolutely perfect in the sense that it could not be readily distinguished from a mass-produced item. Would that kind of perfection make the piece any less a work of art?

3. Find people who hold opposing views about the question of whether or not "Shovel" is a work of art. Ask them to argue the point in detail, being particularly careful not to argue simply from personal opinion. Ask them to point out what it is about the object itself that qualifies it for or disqualifies it from being identified as a work of art.

IDENTIFYING ART PERCEPTUALLY

Perception and conception are closely related: we are often led to see what we expect or want to see; we recognize an object because it answers our conception of it. The ways of identifying a work of art mentioned above depend very heavily on the conceptions of the artist and experts on art and perhaps not heavily enough on the viewer's perceptions of the work itself. Objects and events do have qualities that can be perceived without the help of artists or experts, although this is not to say that these specialists cannot be helpful. If we wish to consider the artistic qualities of objects or events, we can easily do so. Yet to do so implies an attitude or an approach. We are going to suggest an approach here which is simple and flexible and which depends on perception—though not so exclusively as to rule out important conceptual aspects. The distinctions of this approach will not lead us to a definition of art, but they will offer us a way to examine objects and events with reference to whether they possess artistically perceivable qualities. And in some cases at least, it should bring us to reasonable grounds for distinguishing certain things as art and others as nonart. We will consider three terms related primarily to the perceptual nature of the work of art:

1. Artistic form
2. Content
3. Subject matter

A fourth term,

4. Participation

relates primarily to what our perception of the work of art does to us.

ARTISTIC FORM

All objects and events have form. They are bounded by limits of time or space, and they have structural (large) and textural (small) elements which bear distinguishable relationships to one another. Form is the interrelationships of part to part (texture) and part to whole (structure). To say something has *form* may mean no more than that some object or event is indentifiable because it has some degree of perceptible unity. Thus a single isolated tone played on a piano has form, although it is probably not very significant. To say that something has *artistic form*, however, usually implies that there is a strong degree of perceptible unity. Artistic form is one of the things we expect to find in a work of art as a way of distinguishing it from objects or events that are not works of art (and we do so no matter what the problems of definition may be).

"Artistic form" is a term which implies that the elements we perceive —lines, colors, and shapes, for example, in a painting—have been organized for the most profound effect possible. The word "organized" implies a structuring which is related to organic or living order. However, not all works of art have organic form in this sense, for example, Mondrian's "Composition in White, Black and Red" (Figure 1-4). Not all works need it. Yet the idea of organicism also suggests unity: the way an object or event takes on a distinct quality because its elements function together in such a way that the object or event is an identity. All works of art possess unity.

Nature provides the artist with innumerable models of unity—small pebbles, conglomerations of stone and mud and sand, flowers, trees, animals, man, the heavens. However, our experience is usually characterized more by disunity than by unity. Consider, for instance, the order of your experiences during a typical day or even a segment of that day. Compare that order with the order most novelists give to the experiences of their characters. One impulse for reading novels is to experience the tight unity which artistic form usually imposes, a unity almost none of us come close to achieving in our daily lives. Much the same is true for music: noises and random tones in everyday experience lack the order that most composers impose. Indeed, even nature's models of unity are usually far less strongly perceptible than the unity of most works of art. Consider, for example, birdsongs, which are clearly precursors of music. Even the song of the meadowlark, which is longer than most birdsongs, is fragmentary and incomplete. It is like a theme that is simply a statement and repetition, lacking development or contrast. Thus the composer, finding the meadowlark's short theme monotonous when repeated again and again, enriches it by adding notes to those already sounded, by varying the basic melody or theme through alternation of rhythm or changing the pitch of some of the notes to higher or lower positions on the musical scale, or by adding a completely different theme to set up a sense of contrast and tension with the initial theme. These developments help us understand the resources of the theme, and this, in turn, helps us grasp its identity. Its individuality comes forth more distinctively. Since strong, perceptible unity appears so infrequently in nature, we tend to value it highly when it appears, as it usually does, in art.

Artistic form, then, refers to a high degree of perceptible unity. That means the elements must work together for a purpose which establishes the singularity of the work itself. Works of art differ, of course, in the power of their unity. If that power slackens too much, then the question arises: Is this a work of art? Consider the Mondrian (Figure 1-4) with reference to its artistic form. If its textural shapes were not carefully proportioned to the overall structure of the painting itself, the tight balance that produces a strong unity of structure would be lost to us. Mondrian was so concerned with this problem that he worked out the areas of lines and rectangles almost mathematically to be sure they had a clear relationship to the total structural area.

Of course, disunity or establishing an "almost unity" can be artistically useful at times too. Some artists realize how strong, in those of us who have viewed many works of art, the impulse toward unity is. Consequently some artists will aim for intense responses by playing against our need for and expectation of unity in works of art. This is particularly true in modern art and especially in the dance. For some people the modern attitude toward unusual or loose organization of formal elements is something of a norm, and the highly unified work of art is thought of as old fashioned. However, it seems that the effects achieved by a lesser degree of unity succeed only because we recognize them as departures from or variations upon well-known, highly organized forms.

Artistic form as distinct from non-artistic form, we have suggested, involves a high degree of perceptible unity. But how do we determine what is a "high degree"? And if we cannot be clear about this, how can this distinction be of much help in distinguishing works of art from things that are not works of art? Consider, for example, the following news photograph—taken on one of the main streets of Saigon in February 1968 by Eddie Adams, an Associated Press photographer—showing Brig. Gen. Nguyen Ngoc Loan, then South Vietnam's National Police Chief, killing a Vietcong captive (Figure 2-2).

Adams stated that his picture was an accident, that his hand and camera moved reflexively as he saw the General raise the revolver. The

FIGURE 2-2 Eddie Adams, "Execution in Saigon." Wide World Photos.

lens of the camera was set, either by chance or by a rapid flick of the hand, in such a way that the background was thrown out of focus. This blurring of the background helped bring out the foreground scene. Does this photograph have a high degree of perceptible unity? Is it a work of art? Certainly the skill and care of the photographer are evident. Not many amateur photographers would have had enough skill to catch such a fleeting event with such stark clarity. Even if an amateur had accomplished this, we would be inclined to believe that he was more lucky than skilled. The care of the photographer for his photograph is even more evident. To get this photograph he risked his life. If his photograph had not been widely publicized and admired, we can imagine the dismay he would have felt. But do we admire this work the way we admire Siquieros's "Echo of a Scream" (Figure 1-1)? Do we experience these two works in the same way? If you think so, why is it that no one, as far as we know, has proposed that this photograph be hung in a museum of art as part of a permanent collection? Was it more appropriate to display this photograph, as was the case, in newspapers and magazines? Such display served a useful purpose as news. Was this its only proper function?

Compare a painting of a somewhat similar subject—Goya's "May 3, 1808" (Figure 2-3 and Color Plate 3).

FIGURE 2-3   Francisco Goya, "May 3, 1808." 1814–1815. Canvas, 8 feet 9 inches by 13 feet 4 inches. The Prado, Madrid. (*See also Color Plate* 3.)

1. Is the painting different from Adams's photograph in the way the details—the textures—work together? Be specific.

2. Could any detail in the painting be changed, moved, or removed without weakening the unity of the structure, the total design? What about the photograph?

3. Is there anything that you could do to the painting that would increase the power of what it reveals—man's barbarity to man?

4. Is it as easy to sustain your attention on the photograph as on the Goya?

5. Are there details in the photograph that distract your attention?

6. Do the buildings in the background of the photograph add to or subtract from the power of what is being presented here too—man's barbarity to man? Compare the looming architecture in the painting.

7. Do the shadows on the street add anything to the significance of the photograph? Compare the shadows on the ground in the painting.

8. Does it make any significant difference that the Vietcong prisoner's shirt is checkered? Compare the white shirt on the gesturing man in the painting. Would you have explicitly noticed the checkered shirt on the Vietcong prisoner if it had not been called to your attention? Did you particularly notice the white shirt in the painting before your attention was called to it?

9. Is the expression on the soldier's face, along the left edge of the photograph, appropriate to the situation? Compare the facial expressions in the painting.

10. Would the theme of man's barbarity to man have been emphasized if General Loan's arm were stiff—just on the point of firing—rather than just reflexing from the shot?

11. What are basic differences between seeing a real man being killed, a photograph of that event, and a painting of that event?

Goya chose the most terrible moment, that split second before the crash of the guns. There is no doubt that the executions will go on. The desolate mountain pushing down from the left blocks escape, while from the right the firing squad relentlessly hunches forward. The soldiers' thick legs —which are planted wide apart, strictly parallel—support like sturdy pillars the blind, pressing wall formed by their backs. These are men of a military machine. Their rifles, flashing in the bleak light of the ghastly lantern, thrust out as if they belonged to their bodies. It is unimaginable that any of these men would defy the command of their superiors. In the dead of night, the doomed are packed up against the mountain like animals being slaughtered. One man alone flings up his arms in a gesture of utter despair—or is it defiance? The uncertainty increases the intensity of our attention. Most of the rest bury their faces, while a few, with eyes staring out of their sockets, glance out at that which they cannot help seeing. The sprawling dead lie smeared in blood. Only the monk seems to be seeing beyond the moment.

With the photograph of the execution in Vietnam, despite its immediate and powerful attraction, sustained attention seems hardly necessary. It takes no more than a glance or two to grasp what is presented. *Undivided* attention, perhaps, is necessary to become aware of the significance of the event, but not *sustained* attention. In fact, to take careful notice of all the details—such as the patterns on the prisoner's shirt—does not add to our reading of the photograph. If anything, our awareness will be sharper and more productive if we avoid such detailed examination. Is such the case with the Goya? We believe not. Indeed, without sustained attention to the details of this work, most of what is revealed would be missed. For example, block out everything but the dark shadow at the bottom right. Note how differently that shadow appears when it is isolated. We must see the details individually and collectively, as they work together. Unless we are aware of their collaboration, we are not going to grasp fully the structure or total design.

We are suggesting that the Goya has a much higher degree of perceptible unity than Adams's photograph—that perhaps only the Goya has artistic form. We base these conclusions on what is given for us to perceive: the fact that the part-to-part (textural) and the part-to-whole (structural) relationships are much stronger in the case of the Goya. Now you may, of course, disagree. No judgment about such matters is indisputable. Indeed, that is part of the fun of talking about whether something is or is not a work of art; we can learn from each other.

PARTICIPATION

Both the photograph and the Goya painting tend to grasp our attention. Initially for most of us, probably, the photograph has much more pulling power than the painting. Both are exhibited and preserved for us to perceive with undivided attention. But the term "participate" is much more accurately descriptive of what we are likely to be doing in our experience of the painting. With the painting, we must not only give but also sustain our undivided attention. If that happens, we lose our self-consciousness, our sense of being separate, of standing apart from the painting. We participate. And only by means of participation can we come close to a full awareness of what the painting is all about. On the other hand, participation is not as obviously required for a full awareness of what the photograph is all about. This difference suggests another key distinction in helping to identify works of art—*participation*. Works of art are created, exhibited, and preserved for us to perceive with not only undivided but also *sustained* attention. Artists, critics, and philosophers of art generally are in agreement about this. Thus if, in order to understand and appreciate it fully, a work requires our participation, we have an indication that the work is art. Therefore—unless our analyses have been incorrect, and you should satisfy yourself about this—the Goya would seem to be a work of art. Conversely, the photograph would seem not to be a work of art. Or at the very least, the photograph is not as obviously a work of art as the painting, and this is the case despite the fascinating impact of the photograph. Yet these are highly tentative judgments. We are far from being clear about why the Goya requires our participation and the photograph apparently does not. Until we are clear about these "whys," the grounds for this judgment remain shaky.

Goya's painting tends to draw us on until, ideally, we become aware of all the details and their interrelationships. For example, the long dark shadow at the bottom right underlines the line of the firing squad, and the line of the firing squad helps bring out the shadow. Moreover, this shadow is the darkest and most opaque part of the painting. It has a forbidding, blind, fateful quality that, in turn, reinforces the ominous appearance of the firing squad. On the other hand, the dark shadow on the street just below the forearm of General Loan takes us nowhere. It is just there. It might as well not be there. The photograph is full of such meaningless details. Thus our attempts to keep our attention on the photograph tend to be forced—which is to say that they will fail. Sustained attention or participation cannot be achieved by acts of will. What we are attending to must fascinate and control us to the point where we no longer need to will our attention.

We can make up our minds to give our undivided attention to something. But if that something lacks the pulling power that holds and draws our attention, we cannot participate with it. A boring or disunified something will keep us aware of ourselves as separate from that something. Participation cannot be forced.

Adams's photograph does not lend itself to participative experiences or even to repetitive experiences. Once we have seen it—despite the intense interest it arouses at first—we have no strong desire to see it again and again. If we were to see it again and again (try this yourself), we would probably find our viewings increasingly boring. No demands that require either our participation or repeated viewings are made upon us by the photograph. The Goya, conversely, tends to defy boredom from repetition. This, of course, is far more true of the actual painting than of even the best reproductions. Many experiences of the painting are necessary before we begin to come close to what it offers. The Goya keeps drawing us back to it. There is an inexhaustibility about the Goya that the photograph seems to lack. That is the basic reason why we appreciate having the Goya exhibited on a permanent basis.

PARTICIPATION AND ARTISTIC FORM

The participative experience—the undivided and sustained attention to an object or event which makes us lose our sense of separation from the object or event—is induced by strong or artistic form. Participation is not likely to develop with weak form because weak form tends to allow our attention to wander. Therefore one of the indications of a strong form is the fact that participation occurs. Another indication of artistic form is the way it clearly identifies a whole or totality. In the case of the visual arts, a whole is a visual field or design framed by boundaries that separate that field from its surroundings. Both Adams's photograph and Goya's painting have visual designs, for both have forms that produce boundaries.

PERCEPTION KEY   ADAMS'S PHOTOGRAPH AND GOYA'S PAINTING

Does the photograph have a more sharply delineated boundary than the painting? Why?

No matter what wall these two pictures are placed against, the Goya probably stands out more distinctly and sharply from its background. Both works are helped by frames, but the photograph seems to need a frame more than the Goya. This is because the form of the Goya is much stronger and thus outlines itself more surely. No detail in the Goya fails to play a part in the total design. To take one further instance, notice how the lines of the soldiers' sabers and their straps reinforce the ruthless forward push of the firing squad. The photograph, on the other hand, has a weak form because a large number of details fail to cooperate with other details. For example, running down the right side of General Loan's body is a very erratic line. This line fails to tie in with anything else in the photograph. If this line were smoother, it would connect more closely with the lines formed by the Vietcong prisoner's body. The connection between killer and killed would be more vividly established. But as it is, and after several viewings, our eye tends to wander off the photograph. The unity of its form is so slack that the edges of the photograph seem to blur off into their surroundings. That is another way of saying that the form of the photograph fails to establish a clear-cut whole or identity.

Artistic form normally is a prerequisite if our attention is to be grasped and sustained. Artistic form makes our participation possible. Some aestheticians, or philosophers of art, such as Clive Bell and Roger Fry, even go so far as to claim that the presence of artistic form—what they usually call "significant form"—identifies a work of art. And by "significant form," in the case of painting, they mean the interrelationships of elements: line to line, line to color, color to color, color to shape, shape to shape, etc. The elements make up the artistic medium, the "stuff" which the form organizes. Any reference of these elements and their interrelationships to objects or events should be basically irrelevant in our awareness.

According to the proponents of significant form, if we take notice of the executions as an important part of Goya's painting, then we are not perceiving properly. We are experiencing the painting not as a work of art but rather as an illustration telling a story, thus reducing a painting that is a work of art to a level of commercial communications. When the lines, colors, etc., pull together tightly, independently of any objects or events they may represent, there is a significant form. That is what we should perceive when we are perceiving a work of art, not some portrayal of some object or event. Anything that has a significant form is a work of art. If you ignore the objects and events represented in the Goya, significant form is evident. All the details jell together; the textures create a strong structure. Therefore the Goya is a work of art. If you ignore the objects and events represented in the Adams photograph, significant form is not evident. The organization of the parts is too loose. The textures create a weak structure. Therefore the photograph is not a work of art. "To appreciate a work of art," according to Clive Bell, "we need bring with us nothing from life, no knowledge of its ideas and affairs, no familiarity with its emotions."

Does this theory of how to identify a work of art satisfy you? Do you find that in ignoring the representation of objects and events in the Goya much of what is important in that painting is left out? For example, does the line of the firing squad carry a forbidding quality partly because you recognize that this is a line of men in the process of killing other men? In turn, does that line's close relationship with the line of the long shadow at the bottom right depend to some degree upon that forbidding quality? If you think so, then it follows that the artistic form of this work legitimately and relevantly refers to objects and events. Somehow artistic form, at least in some cases, has a significance that goes beyond just the design formed by elements such as lines and colors. Artistic form somehow goes beyond itself, somehow refers to objects and events from the world beyond the design. Artistic form informs us about things outside itself. These things—as revealed by the artistic form—we shall call the *content* of a work of art. But how does the artistic form do this?

CONTENT

Let us begin to try to answer this question by examining more closely the meanings of the Adams photograph and the Goya painting. Both basically, although oversimply, are about the same abstract idea—man's barbarity to man. In the case of the photograph, we have an example, an instance of this barbarity. This instance, since it is very close to any knowledgeable

American's interests, is likely to set off a lengthy chain of thoughts and feelings. These thoughts and feelings, furthermore, seem to "lie beyond" the photograph. Suppose a debate developed over the meaning of this photograph. The photograph itself would play an important role primarily as a starting point. From there on the photograph would probably be ignored except for dramatizing points. For example, one person might argue, "Remember that this occurred during the Tet offensive and innocent civilians were being killed by the Vietcong. Look again at that street and think of the consequences if the terrorists had not been eliminated." Another person might argue, "General Loan was one of the highest officials in South Vietnam's government, and he is taking the law into his own hands like a Nazi." What would be very strange in such a debate would be a discussion of every detail or even many of the details of the photograph.

In a debate about the meaning of the Goya, on the other hand, every detail and its interrelationships with other details becomes relevant. The meaning of the painting seems to "lie within" the painting. And yet paradoxically, this meaning, as in the case of the Adams photograph, involves ideas and feelings that "lie beyond" the painting. How can this be? Let us first consider the basic background information. On May 2, 1808, guerrilla warfare had flared up all over Spain against the occupying forces of the French. By the following day, Napoleon's men were completely back in control in Madrid and the surrounding area. Many of the guerrillas were executed. And, according to tradition, Goya represented the execution, on May 3 near the hill of Principe Pio just outside Madrid, of forty-three of these guerrillas. This background information is important if we are to understand and appreciate the painting fully. Yet notice how differently this information works in our experience of the painting compared to the way background information works in our experience of the Adams photograph.

With the photograph, the background information is essential because it calls up important questions about the involvement of the United States in Vietnam. It is these questions that make us take such special interest in the photograph. A century from now, the photograph probably will be largely ignored except by historians of the Vietnamese war. If you are dubious about this, consider how quickly most of us pass over photographs of similar scenes from World War I and even World War II. The value of Adams's photograph seems to be closely tied to its historical moment. We pay attention to the photograph mainly because the information it conveys suggests, in turn, important considerations. For example, if General Loan's behavior was representative of the behavior of the Saigon government, should American soldiers have died in support of that government? This kind of consideration, rather than the photograph itself, rapidly becomes the center of our attention. A division develops between the photograph and its meaning. The photograph is *here*; the ideas and feelings it arouses are *over there*. The *here* and the *over there* are not fused in our experience. This happens because the form of the photograph fails to draw us into participation (or at least prolonged participation) with the photograph. There is not much to be gained by continuing to focus on the photograph, and so we turn to what does concern us—its meaning. And the more we do this, the more the photograph fades away. The abstract idea (man's barbarity to man) and the concrete exemplification or specific image of this idea (General Loan executing his captive) are related to each other— the specific image of the photograph calls up the abstract idea. But they are not likely to be fused in our experience. This would be likely only if the photograph had artistic form. Only a powerful form is likely to fuse meaning.

With the Goya, the background information, while helpful, is not as essential. Test this for yourself. Would your interest in Adams's photograph last very long if you completely lacked background information? In the case of the Goya, the background information helps us understand the where, when, and why of the scene. But even without this information, the painting probably would still grasp and hold the attention of most of us because it would still have significant meaning. We would still have a powerful image of man's barbarity to man, and the artistic form would hold us on that image. Adams's photograph is also a powerful image, of course— initially far more powerful probably than the Goya—but the form of the photograph is not strong enough to hold most of us on that image for very long. And so, as we think about the background information, we are led beyond the boundaries of the photograph. The background information of the Goya, on the other hand, comes into our experience in such a way that it merges with our awareness, which stays within the painting's boundaries. The form of the Goya controls our awareness of the background information so that it is not allowed to escape from the image. With the Goya, the abstract idea (man's barbarity to man) and the concrete image (the firing squad in the process of killing) are tied tightly together because the form of the painting is tight, i.e., artistic. We see man's barbarity to man *in* the lines, colors, masses, shapes, groupings, and lights and shadows of the painting itself. The details of the painting keep referring to other details and to the totality. They keep holding our attention. Thus the ideas and feelings that the details and their organization awaken keep merging with the form. We are prevented from separating the meaning or content of the painting from its form because the form is so fascinating. The form constantly intrudes. It will not let us ignore it. We see the firing squad killing, and this evokes the idea of barbarity and the feeling of horror. But the lines, colors, mass, shapes, and shadowings of that firing squad form a pattern that keeps exciting and guiding our eyes. And then that pattern leads us to the pattern formed by the victims. Ideas of fatefulness and feelings of pathos are evoked, but they too are fused with the form. The form of the Goya is like a powerful magnet that allows nothing within its range to escape its pull. Strong or artistic form fuses its meaning with itself.

In addition to participation and artistic form, then, we have come upon another basic distinction—*content*. Unless a work has content—meaning fused with its form—we shall say that the work is not art. Content is the meaning of artistic form. If we are correct (for, of course, our view is by no means universally accepted), artistic form always informs, i.e., has meaning or content. And that content, as we experience it when we participate, is always ingrained in the artistic form. We do not perceive an artistic form *and then* a content. We perceive them as inseparable. We can, of course, separate them analytically. But that is also to say that we are not having a participative experience. Moreover, when the form is weak—i.e., less than artistic—we experience the form and its meaning separately. We see the form of Adams's photograph and it evokes thoughts and feelings—indeed, a very powerful meaning. But the form is not strong enough to keep its meaning fused with itself. The photograph lacks content, not because it lacks meaning but because that meaning is not merged with a form. Idea and image break apart.

PERCEPTION KEY ADAMS'S PHOTOGRAPH

We have argued that the painting by Goya is a work of art and the photograph by Adams is not. Even if the three basic distinctions we have made so far—artistic form, participation, and content—are useful, we may have misapplied them. Bring out every possible argument against the view that the painting is a work of art and the photograph is not a work of art.

SUBJECT MATTER

The content is the meaning of a work of art. The content is embedded in the artistic form. But what is the content giving meaning about? We shall call it "subject matter." Content is the interpretation—by means of an artistic form—of subject matter. Thus subject matter is the fourth basic distinction that helps identify a work of art. Since every work of art must have a content, then every work of art must have a subject matter, and this may be any aspect of experience that is an object of some human interest. Anything that is related to a human interest is a value. Some values are positive, such as pleasure and health. Other values are negative, such as pain and illness. Man's barbarity to man and executions are very unpleasant. But they are values because they are related to human interests. These values are the subject matter of both Adams's photograph and Goya's painting. They are what both the photograph and the painting *are about*. But the photograph, unlike the painting, has no content. The less than artistic form of the photograph simply presents its subject matter. The form does not transform the subject matter, does not enrich the meaning of the subject matter. On the other hand, the artistic form of the painting enriches or interprets its subject matter, says something significant about it. In the photograph you see the subject matter. It is directly given. But the subject matter of the painting is not just *there* in the painting. It has been transformed by the form. What is directly given in the painting is the content. You can see the content. But you can only imagine the painting's subject matter, for this is not directly given.

The meaning or content of a work of art is what is *revealed* about a subject matter. But in that revelation you must imagine the subject matter. If someone had taken a news photograph of the May third executions, that would be a record of Goya's subject matter. The content of the Goya is its interpretation of man's barbarity to man in those executions. Adams's photograph lacks content because it merely shows us an example of this barbarity. That is not to disparage the photograph, for its purpose was news, not art. A similar kind of photograph—i.e., one lacking artistic form—of the May third executions would also lack content. Because both photographs lack artistic form, they directly present their subject matter. Goya's painting has artistic form and content directly presented, whereas its subject matter is only indirectly presented. Now, of course, you may for very good reasons disagree with these conclusions. You may find more transformation of the subject matter in Adams's photograph than in Goya's painting. In any case, such disagreement can help the vision of both parties provided the debate itself is focused. It is hoped that the basic distinctions we are making—subject matter, artistic form, content, and participation— will aid that focusing.

SUBJECT MATTER AND ARTISTIC FORM

Whereas a subject matter is a value that we may perceive before any artistic interpretation, the content is the significantly interpreted subject matter as revealed by the artistic form. Artistic form is the means whereby values are threshed from the husks of irrelevancies. Whereas nonartistic form merely presents a subject matter, artistic form informs about that subject matter, makes it clearer. Artistic form draws from the chaotic state of life, which—as Van Gogh describes it—is like "a sketch that didn't come off," a distillation. Adams's photograph is like "a sketch that didn't come off" because it has a significant number of meaningless details. Goya's form eliminates meaningless detail. That is why it is so much clearer than the photograph. Artistic form is an economy that produces a lucidity which enables us to understand and cope better with important values. Thus the informing must be about subject matter with value dimensions that go beyond the artist's idiosyncrasies and perversities. Whether or not Goya had idiosyncrasies and perversities, he did justice to his subject matter: he revealed it.

PARTICIPATION, ARTISTIC FORM, AND CONTENT

Participation is the necessary condition that makes possible our insightful perception of form and content. Unless we participate with the Goya, we will fail to see the power of its artistic form. We will fail to see how the textures work together to form a structure. We also will fail to grasp the content fully, for artistic form and content are inseparable. Thus we will have failed to gain insight into the subject matter. We will have collected just one more instance of man's barbarity to man. The Goya will have basically the same effect upon us as Adams's photograph except that it will be less important to us because it happened long ago. But if, on the contrary, we have participated with the Goya, we probably will never see such things as executions again in quite the same way. The insight that we have gained will tend to refocus our vision so that we will see similar subject matters with a heightened awareness. Look, for example, at the photograph by Ronald L. Haeberle (Figure 2-4), which was published in *Life*, December 5, 1969.

In an interview that accompanied the photograph when it was first published in *The Cleveland Plain Dealer* on November 20, 1969, Haeberle reported that he took this picture in March 1968 while following American troops in an attack upon the South Vietnamese village of Mylai. This incident is much more closely related geographically and historically to Adams's photograph than to Goya's painting.

PERCEPTION KEY PHOTOGRAPHS BY ADAMS AND HAEBERLE AND GOYA'S PAINTING

1. Does Adams's photograph refocus your vision in any important way upon Haeberle's photograph?
2. Does Goya's painting refocus your vision in any important way upon Haeberle's photograph?
3. Why are your answers to these questions fundamentally important in determining whether Adams's photograph and Goya's painting are works of art?

PARTICIPATION AND THE WORK OF ART

The ultimate test for recognizing a work of art is how it works in us, what it does to us. A work of art, provided we are able to participate with it,

changes our lives. By its revelation of some subject matter, we now are able
to experience similar subject matter with more sensitivity and understanding. Does Cummings's "l (a" heighten your perception of falling leaves and
deepen your understanding of loneliness? Do you *see* shovels, perhaps, for
the first time after experiencing "Shovel" (Figure 2-1) by Dine? If not, pre-

sumably they are not works of art. But this assumes that we have really participated with these works, that we have allowed them to work properly in our experience, so that if content were present it had a chance to come forth into our awareness. Of the four basic distinctions—participation, artistic form, content, and subject matter—the most fundamental is participation. We must not only *understand what it means* to participate but also *be able* to participate. Otherwise the other basic distinctions, even if they make good theoretical sense, will not be of much practical help in making art more important in our lives. The central importance of participation requires further elaboration.

Participation involves undivided and sustained attention. When attention is sustained, it becomes participative with that which we are attending. Then we no longer *look at* the Goya. We *become* the Goya in the sense that we are not explicitly aware of ourselves standing outside it. Someone watching us would say we are looking at the Goya. But we are so caught up by the power and control of its artistic form that we are unaware of our looking. The subjective and objective sides of experience merge into unity. When we fail to participate, we are spectators. We are aware of ourselves as separate from that which we are attending. In most of our experience of works of art we begin as spectators. Thus, as we settle into our seats and the film begins, we are quite conscious of our place in the theater. But as the film grasps and holds our attention, we lose awareness of such things as our spatial location. Or, as the record begins to play in our living room, our minds and bodies are full of the day's anxieties, but then, as the music catches us up, our feet may even begin tapping, and we "become" the music.

Spectator attention dominates most of our experiences. Spectator attention is more commonsensical, and it works much more efficiently than participative attention in most situations. We would get nowhere changing a tire if we only participated with the tire. We would not be able to use the scientific method if we failed to distinguish between ourselves and our data. Practical success, on every level, requires problem solving. This requires distinguishing the means from the end, and then we must manipulate the means to achieve the end. In so doing, we are aware of ourselves as subjects distinct from the objects involved in our situation. Thus the habit of spectator attention gets deeply ingrained in all of us because of the demands of survival. That is why, especially after we have left the innocence of childhood, participative attention is so rarely achieved. A child who has not yet had to solve problems, on the other hand, is dominated by participative attention. In this sense, to learn how to experience works of art properly requires a return to the open, receptive attitudes of childhood. For in childhood we were more likely to think *from* things than *at* things. Then, we did not always try to dominate things but rather let them reveal themselves to us. Watch a young child at play. Sometimes he will just push things around, but often he will let them dominate him. If he is looking at a flower, he will follow with his hands the curves and textures of the flower, be entranced with its smell, perhaps even its taste—so absorbed that he seems to listen, as if the flower could speak.

Mark Twain tells how, as he learned the functions of a steamboat pilot, the Mississippi River became like a book:

> Now when I had mastered the language of this water, and had come to know every trifling feature that bordered the great river as familiarly as I knew the letters of the alphabet, I had made a valuable acquisition. But I had lost something, too. I had lost something which could never be restored to me while I lived. All the grace, and beauty, the poetry, had gone out of the majestic river! . . . All the value any feature of it had for me now was the amount of usefulness it could furnish toward compassing the safe piloting of the steamboat.[1]

In other words, Twain had become so obsessed with using the river that he could no longer participate with it.

Participative experiences of works of art are communions—experiences so full and final that they enrich our entire lives. Such experiences are life-enhancing not just because of the great satisfaction they may give us at the moment but also because they make more or less permanent contributions to that part of our life which is yet to be. Compare, for example, a photograph of Mont Sainte Victoire (Figure 2-5) and Cézanne's painting (Figure 2-6). It is unlikely that the photograph will be memorable. But if you participate with the painting, you are likely to see the rhythm and the massiveness of similar mountains with, as Bernard Berenson put it, a "higher coefficient of meaning."

As participators we do not think of the work of art with reference to categories applicable to objects—such as what kind of thing it is. We grasp the work of art directly. When, for example, we participate with Cézanne's "Mont Sainte Victoire," we are not making geographical or geological observations. We are not thinking of the mountain as an object. For if we did, "Mont Sainte Victoire" would pale into a mere instance of the appropriate scientific categories. We might judge that the mountain is a certain type. But in that process the vivid impact of Cézanne's mountain would dim down as the focus of our attention shifted beyond, in the direction of generality. This is the natural thing to do with mountains if you are a geologist. It is also the natural thing to do with this particular photograph of the mountain. The photograph lends itself to the direction of generality because its form fails to hold us to the photograph in all its specificity. But on the other hand, to be only a spectator of the Cézanne is unnatural in the sense that we block off much of the satisfaction we might have. Also, we screen

[1] Mark Twain, "Life on the Mississippi," in *The Family Mark Twain*, Harper, New York and London, 1935, p. 46.

FIGURE 2-5 Mont Sainte
Victoire. Photograph courtesy
of John Rewald.

FIGURE 2-6 Paul Cézanne,
"Mont Sainte Victoire." 1886–
1887. Oil on canvas, 23½ by
28½ inches, unsigned. The
Phillips Collection,
Washington.

ourselves from insights that could make our lives more meaningful. We sell ourselves short.

When we participate, we *think from*. The artistic form initiates and controls every thought and feeling. When we are spectators, we *think at*. We set the object into our framework. We see the Cézanne—name it, identify its maker, classify its style, recall its background information—in order, let us say, to do a term paper. We may succeed in getting a passing grade, but this approach will never get us into the Cézanne as a work of art. Such knowledge, of course, can be very helpful. But that knowledge is most helpful when it is under the control of the work of art working in our experience. This happens when the artistic form not only triggers that knowledge but draws it back within the boundaries of the painting. Otherwise the painting will fade away. Its specificity will be sacrificed for some generality. Its content will be missed.

The participator is thrust out of his ordinary, everyday, business-as-usual attitude. He is thrust out of himself. The content of the work of art makes contact. And then the "concrete suchness" of the work of art penetrates and completely permeates his consciousness. Even if, which is unlikely, he forgets such an experience, a significant change has taken place in his perceptive organs. A new set of lenses, so to speak, has been more or less permanently built into his vision. After participating with Cézanne's "Mont Saint Victoire," the participator will automatically see mountains differently.

These are strong claims, and they may not be convincing. In any case, before concluding our search for what a work of art is, let us seek further clarification of our other basic distinctions—artistic form, content, and subject matter. This is worth our trouble. Clarification, even if we disagree with the conclusions, helps understanding. And understanding helps appreciation. Anything that can help us appreciate art is exceptionally important, because art is one of the most important things man makes. This has a platitudinous ring. But listen to what Alfred North Whitehead, one of the greatest philosophers of the twentieth century, has to say:

> Great art is the arrangement of the environment so as to provide for the soul vivid . . . values. Human beings require something which absorbs them for a time, something out of the routine which they can stare at. But you cannot subdivide life, except in the abstract analysis of thought. Accordingly, the great art is more than a transient refreshment. It is something which adds to the permanent richness of the soul's self-attainment. It justifies itself both by its immediate enjoyment, and also by its discipline of the inmost being. Its discipline is not distinct from enjoyment, but by reason of it. It transforms the soul into the permanent realization of values extending beyond its former self.[2]

[2] Alfred North Whitehead, *Science and The Modern World*, Macmillan, New York, 1925, pp. 209f.

ARTISTIC FORM: EXAMPLES

Let us examine artistic form in a series of examples taken from the work of Roy Lichtenstein, a contemporary American painter, in which the subject matter, compared with "May 3, 1808," is not so obviously important. With such examples, a purely formal analysis should seem less artificial. In the late fifties and early sixties, Lichtenstein became interested in comic strips as subject matter. The story goes that his two young boys asked him to paint a Donald Duck "straight," without the encumbrances of art. But much more was involved. Born in 1923, Lichtenstein grew up before television. By the thirties the comic strip had become one of the most important of the mass media. Sex, sentimentality, sadism, terror, adventure, and romance found expression in the stories of Tarzan, Flash Gordon, Superman, Steve Roper, Winnie Winkle, Mickey Mouse, Donald Duck, Batman and Robin, etc. Even today, despite the competition of the "soap operas" of television, the comic strip remains an important mass medium.

The purpose of the comic strip for its producers is strictly commercial. And because of the comics' very large market, a premium has always been put on making the processes of production as inexpensive as possible. Thus generations of mostly unknown commercial artists, going well back into the nineteenth century, developed ways of cheap, quick color printing. They had to develop a technique that could turn out their cartoons like the products of mass-production of an assembly line. Since, moreover, their market included a large number of children, they developed ways of producing images that were immediately understandable and of striking impact. They evolved a tradition that became a common vocabulary. Both the technique and its product became increasingly standardized. The printed images became increasingly impersonal. Donald Duck, Bugs Bunny, and Batman all seem to come from the same hand, or, rather, the same machine.

Lichtenstein reports that he was attracted to the comic strip by its stark simplicity—the blatant primary colors, the ungainly black lines that encircle the shapes, the "balloons" that isolate the spoken words or the thoughts of the characters. He was struck by the apparent inconsistency between the strong emotions of the stories and the highly impersonal, mechanical style in which they were expressed. Despite the crudity of the comic strip, Lichtenstein saw power in the strong directness of the medium. Somehow something very much about ourselves was mirrored in those cartoons. Lichtenstein set out to clarify what that "something" was. At first people laughed, as was to be expected. He was called "the worst artist in America." Today he is considered to be one of our major artists.

The accompanying examples (Figures 2-7 through 2-16) pair the original cartoon with Lichtenstein's transformation.[3] Both the comic strips

[3] These examples were suggested to us by a very interesting article on Lichtenstein's "balloons" by Albert Boime, "Roy Lichtenstein and the Comic Strip," *Art Journal*, vol. 28, no. 2, pp. 155–159, Winter 1968–1969.

and the transformations originally were in color, and Lichtenstein's paintings were very much larger than the comic strip. For the purposes of analysis, however, our reproductions are presented in black and white, and the sizes more or less equalized. The absence of color and the reduction of size all but destroy the power of Lichtenstein's work, but these changes will help us compare the structures. They will also help us to concentrate upon what is usually the most obvious element of visual structure—line. The five pairs of examples have been scrambled so that either the comic strip or Lichtenstein's painting of it may be on the left or right.

PERCEPTION KEY COMIC STRIPS AND LICHTENSTEIN'S TRANSFORMATIONS

Decide which are the comic strips and which are Lichtenstein's transformations. Defend your decisions with reference to the strength of organization. Presumably Lichtenstein's works will possess much stronger structures than those of the commercial artists. Be as specific and detailed as possible. For example, compare the lines and shapes as they more or less work together in each example. Take plenty of time, for the perception of artistic form is something that must "work" in you. Such perception never comes instantaneously. Compare your judgments with others.

Compare your analysis with ours in the case of pair 1 (Figures 2-7 and 2-8). Example *a* of pair 1, we think, has a much stronger structure than *b*. The organization of the parts of *a* is much more tightly unified. The circles

FIGURE 2-7   Pair 1, example *a*.

FIGURE 2-8   Pair 1, example *b*.

formed by the peephole and its cover in *a* have a graceful rhythmic unity lacking in *b*. Note how in *a* the contour, formed by the overlapping of the cover just below and to the right of the extended finger, has a long sweeping effect. These lines look as if they had been drawn by a human hand. In *b*, the analogous contour as well as the circles to which the contour belongs look as if they had been drawn with the aid of a compass. In *a*, the circular border of the cover is broken at the right edge and by the balloon above. These devices help soften the hard definiteness not only of this circle but also of the contours it forms with the circle of the peephole. In *a* also, most of the man's face and his entire hand are shadowed. These contrasts help give variety and irregularity to the peephole circle, which blends in smoothly with its surroundings compared to the abrupt insularity of the peephole in *b*. Notice too, that in b a white outline goes around the cover, whereas in *a* this is avoided. Thus in *a* the uniformity of the cover is not so sharply accented. Moreover, the balloon in *a* overlies a significant portion of the cover. In *b*, the balloon is isolated and leaves the cover alone.

In *a*, the line outlining the balloon as it overlies the cover repeats the contours of the overlapping cover and its peephole. Rhythm depends upon repetition, and repetition unifies. But repetition that is absolutely regular is monotonous. Try tapping a pencil with a strong beat followed by a weak beat, and continue to repeat this rhythm as exactly as you can. Against your will and unconsciously you will desire some variations in stress. You will do this because absolute repetition becomes boring. In *a*, the repetitions of the contour formed by the peephole and its cover, as well as other repetitions, have variations. The repetitions unify, while the variations excite interest. In *b*, there are fewer repetitions. And lacking variations except of the most obvious kind, these repetitions are monotonous. For example, the size of the peephole and cover appear exactly the same. In *a*, on the other hand, sometimes the peephole appears larger and sometimes the cover. The variation very subtly depends on the area your eyes focus upon. And this, in turn, is controlled by the lines and shapes in dynamic interrelationship. In *b*, this kind of moving control is missing.

In *a*, no part remains isolated. Thus the balloon as it extends over the breadth of the painting helps bind the lower parts together. And at the same time, the shape and contours of the balloon help accent the shape and contours of the other details. Even the shape of the man's mouth is duplicated partially by the shape of the balloon. Conversely, the balloon in *b* is much more isolated from the other details. It just hangs there. Notice, on the other hand, how the tail of the balloon in *a*, just below the exclamation point, repeats the curve of the cover's latch, and also how the curve of the tail is caught up in the sweep of the curves of the peephole and cover. In *a*, the latch of the cover unobtrusively helps to orbit the cover around the peephole. In *b*, the latch of the cover is awkwardly large, and this helps to block any sense of dynamic interrelationship between the peephole and its cover. In *a*, the cover seems light and graceful, and only the top of a finger is needed to turn it back. In *b*, however, a much heavier finger is necessary. Similarly, the lines of face and hand in *a* lightly integrate, whereas in *b* they are heavy and fail to work together. Compare, for example, the eye in *a* with the eye in *b*. Finally, there are meaningless details in *b*—the bright knob on the cover, for instance, and the white square with the name of the illustrator. In *a*, these details are eliminated. Even the shape of the lettering in *a* belongs to the whole in a way completely lacking in *b*.

Now turn to pair 2 (Figures 2-9 and 2-10).

PERCEPTION KEY COMIC STRIP AND LICHTENSTEIN'S
TRANSFORMATION, PAIR 2.

Limit your analysis to the design functioning of the lettering in the balloons of pair 2.

1. Does the shape of the lettering in *a* play an important part in the formal organization? Articulate your reasons.

2. Does the shape of the lettering in *b* play an important part in the formal organization? Articulate your reasons.

Compare your analyses with ours. It is only in *b* that the shape of the lettering, we think, plays an important part in the formal organization. In *a*, conversely, the shape of the lettering is distracting. In *b*, the bulky balloons are eliminated and only two words are kept—"torpedo . . . LOS!" The three alphabetic characters of which "LOS" is composed stand out very

FIGURE 2-9 Pair 2, example *a*.   FIGURE 2-10 Pair 2, example *b*.

vividly. The balloon's simple shape helps, a regular shape among so many irregular shapes. Also, "LOS" is larger, darker, and more centrally located than "torpedo." Notice, on the other hand, how in *a* no word or lettering stands out. Moreover, as Boime points out, the shapes of "LOS" are clues to the panel's structure.

> The "L" is mirrored in the angle formed by the captain's hand and the vertical contour of his head and in that of the periscope. The "O" is repeated in the tubing of the periscope handle and in smaller details throughout the work. The oblique "S" recurs in the highlight of the captain's hat just left of the balloon, in the contours of the hat itself, in the shadow that falls along the left side of the captain's face, in the lines around his nose and in the curvilinear tubing of the periscope. Thus the dialogue enclosed within the balloon is visually exploited in the interests of compositional structure.

Now consider pair 3 (Figures 2-11 and 2-12), pair 4 (Figures 2-13 and 2-14), and pair 5 (Figures 2-15 and 2-16). Then turn to the perception key on page 46.

FIGURE 2-12   Pair 3, example *b*.

FIGURE 2-11   Pair 3, example *a*.

FIGURE 2-14   Pair 4, example *b*.

FIGURE 2-13   Pair 4, example *a*.

FIGURE 2-15   Pair 5, example *a*.

FIGURE 2-16   Pair 5, example *b*.

1. Decide once again which are the comic strips and which the transformations.

2. If you have changed any of your decisions or your reasoning, how do you account for these changes?

It should not be surprising to you if you have changed some of your decisions, and it may be that your reasoning has been expanded. The analyses of other people, even when you disagree with them, will usually suggest new ways of perceiving things. In the case of good criticism, this is almost always the case. The correct identifications follow, and they should help you test your perceptive abilities.

Pair 1a   Lichtenstein, "I Can See the Whole Room . . . and There's Nobody in It!" 1961. Oil on Canvas. Collection, Mr. and Mrs. Burton Tremaine, New York.

Pair 1b   Panel from William Overgrad's comic strip "Steve Roper."

Pair 2a   Anonymous comic book panel.

Pair 2b   Lichtenstein, "Torpedo . . . Los!" 1963. Magna on Canvas. Courtesy of the Leo Castelli Gallery, New York.

Pair 3a   Anonymous comic book panel.

Pair 3b   Lichtenstein, "Image Duplicator." 1963. Magna on Canvas. Courtesy of the Leo Castelli Gallery, New York.

Pair 4a   Lichtenstein, "The Engagement Ring." 1961. Courtesy of the Leo Castelli Gallery, New York.

Pair 4b   Panel from Martin Branner's comic strip "Winnie Winkle."

Pair 5a   Anonymous comic book panel.

Pair 5b   Lichtenstein, "Hopeless." 1963. Magna on Canvas. Courtesy of the Leo Castelli Gallery, New York.

If you have been mistaken, do not be discouraged. Learning how to see takes time. Furthermore, it is not possible to decide beyond all doubt, as with the proof that $2 + 2 = 4$, whether Lichtenstein is a creator of artistic form and comic-strip makers are not. We think it is highly probable that this is the case, but absolute certainty here is not possible. And it should be noted that the comic-strip makers, as Boime points out, generally look upon Lichtenstein's work as "strongly 'decorative' and backward looking."

The examination of these examples makes it fairly evident, we believe, that Lichtenstein is a master at composing forms. But are these paintings works of art? Do these forms inform? Do they have a content? If so, what are their subject matters? What is the subject matter of "Torpedo . . . Los!"? The aggressiveness of submarine commanders? Or, rather, the energy, passion, directness, and mechanicality of comic strips? Or could the subject matter be made up of both these things? Perhaps there is no interpreted subject matter—perhaps the event in the submarine is just an excuse for composing a form. Perhaps this form is best understood and appreciated not as informing but rather as simply attractive and pleasing. This kind of form we shall call "decorative form."

DECORATIVE FORM OR DECORATION

Decorative form, unlike artistic form, lacks content. The function of decoration is to be suitable. Wallpaper, for example, is usually chosen because it is pleasing and fitting for an interior wall area. Usually we do not expect wallpaper to have a form that presents a subject matter, as Adams's photograph does. Nor do we expect wallpaper to have a form that interprets a subject matter, as Goya's painting does. If we found wallpaper with artistic form, we would—if we were wise—buy it and frame it as art. The chances of such a discovery, of course, are highly remote. However, if we were that lucky, then the paper would no longer be wallpaper. What we expect from wallpaper is a form that neither presents subject matter nor informs about it but rather just pleases. If, as sometimes is the case, wallpaper includes subject matter, it is there primarily to add to the pleasure. Then the wallpaper is full of "pretty things," like idyllic country scenes. We do not expect to find in wallpaper powerful images, as in Adams's photograph, that stir up our thoughts and feelings. Maybe, therefore, we should classify Lichtenstein's comic-strip paintings as works of decoration. Admittedly their forms are far stronger than those in things that are usually called "decorative," like wallpaper and linoleum. Yet are Lichtenstein's forms informing? Do we gain insight from them? Obviously we are into a very complex set of questions. And in the case of Lichtenstein's paintings, these questions are posed in a very difficult way. We need a further analysis of subject matter and content in examples that are less complex. The female nude is such an example and is, perhaps, more interesting.

SUBJECT MATTER AND CONTENT

The female nude of the *Playboy* type juts out from almost every commercial magazine rack. The subject matter—the female nude—is almost invariably presented without any significant transformation. There is some form, of course, but only enough to display—not interpret—the subject matter. In this respect, this kind of photograph is like Adams's photograph. The nude's position, the lighting, the angle and distance of the shot, etc., have been selected. But this forming or organizing has been

FIGURE 2-17 "Nude under Piano." 1973. Photograph by Ralph Gibson.

FIGURE 2-18 Giorgione, "Sleeping Venus." 1508–1510. Oil on canvas, 43 by 69 inches. Alinari.

so minimal or uninspired that it fails to inform. Thus these nudes all look pretty much alike. We get clichés of the female body. In other words, we are presented with a subject matter, not a content. Or, if you disagree, what are your arguments?

Compare any photograph of the *Playboy* type—call it photograph *a*—with Figure 2-17—call it photograph *b*. Has *b* a stronger form? Are there meaningless details? Do the details interrelate tightly? If so, how is this accomplished? If you agree with us that *b* has a strong form, would you maintain that this form not only presents but informs? That is, does the form of *b* interpret the female body, reveal it in such a way that you have an increased understanding of and sensitivity to the female body? In other words, does *b* have content?

Before deciding, consider the six paintings of the female nude shown in Figures 2-18, 2-19, 2-20, 2-21, 2-22, and 2-23.

Most of these paintings are very highly valued—some as masterpieces. Why? Surely not because they present the female nude as subject matter. In this respect, *Playboy* does a much better job. These paintings are highly valued as works of art because they are powerful interpretations of their subject matter. *Think from* rather than *at* these paintings. Then notice how different the interpretations are. Any important subject matter has many different facets. That is why shovels and soup cans have limited utility as subject matters. They have very few facets to offer for interpretation. The female nude, on the other hand, is almost limitless. The next artist interprets something about the female nude that had never been interpreted before, because the female nude seems to be inexhaustible as a subject matter.

FIGURE 2-19 Pierre-August Renoir, "Reclining Nude." 1902. Oil on canvas, 26½ by 60⅝ inches. Collection, The Museum of Modern Art, New York. Gift of Mr. and Mrs. Paul Rosenberg.

FIGURE 2-20   Amadeo Modigliani, "Reclining Nude" *(Le Grand Nu)*. 1919. Collection, the Museum of Modern Art. Mrs. Simon Guggenheim Fund.

FIGURE 2-21   Pablo Picasso, "Nude on a Black Couch." 1932. Photograph courtesy of Galerie Louise Leiris. Permission, 1974 French Reproduction Rights, Inc./SPADEM.

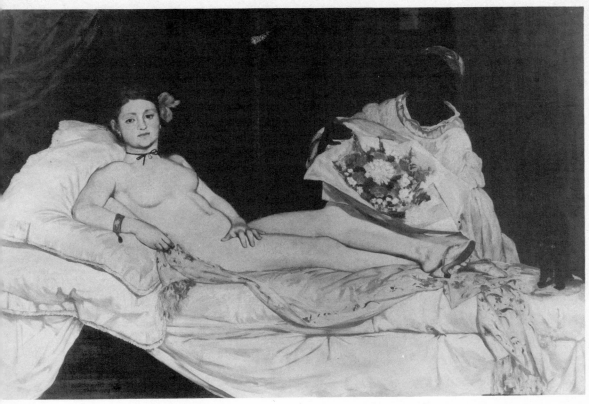

FIGURE 2-22   Edouard Manet, "Olympia." 1863. Oil on canvas, 51¼ by 74¾ inches. Musee de l'Impressionnisme, Paris.

FIGURE 2-23   Tom Wesselmann, "Nude #1." 1970. Oil on canvas, 25 by 45 inches. Private collection. Photograph by Sidney Janis Gallery, New York.

More precisely, the six paintings all have somewhat different subject matters. All are about the nude. But the painting by Giorgione is about the nude as idealized, as a goddess, as Venus. Now there is a great deal that all of us could say in trying to describe Giorgione's interpretation. But notice how language inevitably fails us. Giorgione has said it in his own language, the language of painting, and any translation into words falls far short. This is always the case with works of art, including poems and novels. They are their own statement. Their meaning or content is inextricably interwoven in their forms. Thus, every time we try to speak about the content of a work of art, we are always at an unbridgeable distance from the fullness of that content. Hence it is usually better to try to describe the subject matter rather than the content. The description of the subject matter can help us see, if we have missed it, the content. In understanding what the form worked on—i.e., the subject matter—our perceptive apparatus is better prepared to perceive the "form-content."

The subject matter of Renoir's painting is the nude as earth mother. In the Modigliani, the subject matter is the sensual nude. In the Picasso, it is the nude as abandoned, enfleshed in her sex. In the Manet, it is the nude as prostitute. In the Wesselmann, it is the nude as exploited. In all six paintings the subject matter is the female nude—but qualified. The subject matter is qualified in relation to what the artistic form focuses upon and makes lucid. This qualification, we believe, is lacking in most *Playboy*-type photographs because an artistic form is also lacking.

PERCEPTION KEY "NUDE UNDER PIANO"

Return to Figure 2-17.

1. Does this photograph have artistic form?
2. If so, how is this accomplished?
3. What is the subject matter of the photograph? Be precise.
4. What is the content of the photograph?
5. Or if you think content is lacking, why?

FORM-CONTENT

To recapitulate, a work of art is a form-content. An artistic form is a form-content. An artistic form is more than just an organization of the elements of an artistic medium, such as the lines and colors of painting. The artistic form interprets or clarifies some subject matter. The subject matter, strictly speaking, is not *in* a work of art. Thus the subject matter is only imaginable, not perceptible. It is only suggested by the work of art.

The interpretation of the subject matter is the content or meaning of the work of art. Content is enmeshed in the form. The content, unlike the subject matter, is *in* the work of art, fused with the form. We can separate content from form only by analysis. The ultimate justification of any analysis is whether it enriches our participation with that work, whether it helps that work "work" in us. Good analysis or criticism does just that. But conversely, any analysis not based on participation is unlikely to be very helpful. Participation is the way—the only way—of getting into direct contact with the form-content. Thus any analysis that is not based upon a participative experience inevitably misses the work of art. Good analysis and participation, although necessarily occurring at different times, always end up hand in hand.

When we get down to specific cases, it is by no means always easy to decide whether something is a work of art. Goya's "May 3, 1808," it seems to us, is an easy case in the affirmative. But there are hard cases, borderline examples. What about Dine's "Shovel" (Figure 2-1), Lichtenstein's transformations (Figures 2-7 through 2-16), and "Nude under Piano" (Figure 2-17)? The basic distinctions that we have discussed—participation, subject matter, form, and content—provide us with guidelines that help in posing and answering these questions. But how to apply this set of guidelines or other sets of guidelines precisely is not obvious. That job, when done with precision, requires an expertise that only a few highly sensitive and highly trained people—called "critics"—have achieved.

In this chapter, we have elaborated one set of guidelines. Other sets, of course, are possible. We have discussed one other set very briefly: that a work of art is significant form. If you can conceive of other sets of guidelines, make them explicit and try them out. The ultimate test is clear: Which set helps you most in appreciating works of art? We think the set we have proposed meets that test better than other proposals. But this is a very large question indeed, and your decision should be delayed. In any event, we will now investigate the principles of criticism. These principles should help show us how to apply our set of guidelines to specific examples. Then we will be properly prepared to examine the uniqueness of the various arts.

3 BEING A CRITIC OF THE ARTS

All too often we think of a critic as someone who does little more than find fault with things. Or we sometimes think of him as a person who enjoys taking something apart more than he enjoys the thing itself. We must recognize that critics have frequently earned such reputations. But we should also recognize that these are bad critics and this is bad criticism. The good critic, by sharpening our perception and revealing what we had missed, deepens our participation and enhances our delight in works of art.

YOU ARE ALREADY AN ART CRITIC

Whether we know it or not, we all operate as critics of art much of the time. When we look for a while at a film on television and decide to change the channel to look for something better, we act as critics. This is a particularly broad critical function if someone else is in the room with us. The question to ask is not a simple one: On what basis do we change the channel? When we turn a radio dial looking for music we like, we are being critics of music. If we stop to admire a building or a painting, we are being, in a minor way, critics. If we stop to think about it, we realize that we are critics of art in more ways than we usually realize. Take a moment and fill out the following perception key, listing the ways in which you yourself have actually been an art critic in the last two days.

The Art Form	The Circumstances

The next question is touchy: What qualifies you to make the critical judgments you make all the time? What is the training that underlies your constant criticism of such arts as film, music, and architecture? Of course that is an embarrassing question for many people, but it should not be. If you have no special training in any of these fields, you do have—just by virtue of being "around" and of having grown up in a culture saturated with arts of all kinds—considerable background and experience. You probably have listened to music on the radio, watched television, and gone to the movies since before you can remember. The least experienced among us at age twenty can count on fifteen years of seeing architecture, of responding to the industrial design of automobiles and other objects, of seeing public sculpture or any of a host of other works of art and design. Perhaps it is more fair and realistic to say that at age twenty we can count on having had almost twenty years of experience to draw from. This is no inconsiderable background and it makes us all, at almost any age, formidable critics who make critical judgments without hesitation.

But even though all this is true, we realize something further. We have limitations as critics. When we are left to our own devices and grow up with little specific critical training, even in a society rich in art, we find ourselves capable of going only so far. We all know people who have, at age forty, remained the same kinds of critics they were at age twenty. Even if such people were very good critics at age twenty, they must be thought of as emotionally or culturally retarded if they still make the same choices in art twenty years later. This should be obvious if only on the basis that art—not to mention the rest of the society—changes enormously in twenty years. A decade in art in the twentieth century produces the changes a century would have produced in the days of Leonardo. A person who stands still with respect to the arts is a person left behind. He is a critic whose development stops prematurely, leaving him somewhat unable to see what it is other people like about the "new" art.

Each of us is a practicing critic, but if we do nothing to increase our critical skills, it is likely that our skills, twenty years from now, will not have significantly advanced. And when you hear people rebelling against becoming more refined critics because they feel they have no credentials that qualify them to examine Shakespeare or Mozart or Velasquez, you will see that what they are often rebelling against is the effort it takes to look closely at something and participate with it. As it is, many people stop reading Shakespeare in the middle of a play because they do not feel it is good enough to keep them involved. Similarly some people turn off Mozart and turn on a popular song. No one can be excused on the "Who am I to judge Mozart?" disclaimer. We are all capable of judging Mozart. Some of us are more capable, of course; and that is the point. By learning some essentials about criticism and how to put them to work more thoughtfully than we do, we will help develop our own capacities as critics.

PARTICIPATION AND THE CRITIC

One of the reasons many of us resist our roles as critics is that we value very highly the participative experience we get from the works of art that excite us. Criticism interferes with that participative delight. For example, most of us lose ourselves in a good film and never think about the film in any objective or "distant" way. It "ruins" the experience to stop and be critical, for the act of criticism is quite different from the act of participative enjoyment. And if we were to choose which act is the more important, then, of course, we would have to stand firm behind enjoyment. Art is, above all, enjoyable. Yet the kinds of enjoyment it affords are sometimes very complex and subtle. The critic is the person who can begin to make the complexities and subtleties a bit more available to others and, if he is a really good critic, even to himself. In other words, taking a moment to reflect upon the participative experience we have had might help any of us deepen our next participation. Thus the critical act is—at its very best—an act which is very much related to the act of participatory enjoyment. Criticism, when performed sensitively and knowingly, aids enjoyment. A fine critical sense helps us develop our participatory capacities. The reason is simple: a fine critical sense helps us develop the perceptions which are essential to knowing what's "going on" in a work of art.

Criticism involves description, interpretation, and evaluation. All are essential for a thorough understanding of any work of art. And the critic who is participating with a work of art is doing all of these things, though he is by no means explicitly conscious of doing so. What he *is* conscious of is the work itself, not the act of describing, interpreting, and judging. As critic, however, he must, once the participative experience is past, reconsider what it was he was aware of. He must reflect on his responses and make them as explicit as he can. Unfortunately, there are many people who feel that reflecting on their responses to a work of art is being too analytical, too remote from the act of responding. But we should realize that the act of reflection does not lessen the delights of involvement with a work of art. That delight has already been achieved. Moreover, reflection can intensify the delight of our next experience with that work if that reflection reveals anything significantly relevant to us that we were unaware of during our earlier experience.

Seeing a film twice, for instance, is often interesting. At first our personalities may melt away and we become involved and "lost" in the experience. If the film maker is competent and clever, he can cause us to do this quickly and efficiently—the first time. But if he is *only* competent and clever, as opposed to being creative, then the second time we see the film its flaws are likely to be obvious and we are likely to have a less complete participatory experience. When, however, a really great film is involved, then the second experience is likely to be more exciting than the first. If we have become good critics and if we have reflected wisely on our first experience, then we will find that the second experience of any great work of art will be more intense and our sense of participation deeper. For one thing, our understanding of the artistic form and content will be considerably more refined in our second experience and in all subsequent experiences.

It is obvious that only those works of art which are successful on most or all levels can possibly be as interesting the second time we experience them as they were the first. This presumes, however, a reliable and full perception of the work. For example, the first experience of most works of art will not be very satisfying—it will perhaps not produce the participative experience at all—if we do not perceive that work fully. Consequently it is possible that the first experience of a difficult poem, for instance, will be less than enjoyable. If, however, we have gained helpful information from the first experience and thus made ourselves more capable of perceiving the poem, the second experience will be more satisfying.

When we criticize, one of the first questions we should ask concerns whether or not we actually have had a participative experience. Has the work of art taken us out of ourselves? If it is a good work of art, we should find ourselves "lost" in the delight of experiencing it. However, as we have been suggesting all along, if we are not so carried away by a given work, the reason may not be because it is not successful. It may be because we do not see all there is to see. We may not "get it" well enough for it to transport us into participation. Consequently we have to be critical of ourselves, some of the time, in order to be sure we have laid the basic groundwork that is essential to participation. When we are sure that we have done as much as we can to prepare ourselves, then we are in a better position to decide whether the deficiency is in the work or in us. In the final analysis, the participative experience can be said to be something that we not only *can* but also *must* have if we are to fully apprehend a work of art.

KINDS OF CRITICISM

Now, with our basic critical purpose clearly in mind—i.e., to learn, by reflecting on works of art, how to participate with these works more intensely and enjoyably—let us now analyze the practice of criticism more closely. If, as we have argued in Chapter 2, a work of art is essentially a form-content, then good criticism will sharpen our perception of the form of a work of art and increase our understanding of its content. Take some considerable time now with the following perception key.

PERCEPTION KEY KINDS OF CRITICISM

Seek out at least five examples of criticism from any available place, including, if you like, Chapters 1 and 2 of this book. Film or book reviews in newspapers or magazines may be used. Analyze these examples with reference to the following questions:

1. Does this criticism focus mainly on the form or the content?
2. Can you find any examples in which the criticism is entirely about the form?
3. Can you find any examples in which the criticism is entirely about the content?
4. Can you find any examples in which the focus is upon neither the form nor the content but on evaluating the work as good or bad or better or worse than some other work?
5. Can you find any examples in which there is not some evaluation?
6. Which kind of criticism do you find most helpful—that bearing on the form, the content, or the evaluation? Why?
7. Do you find any examples in which it is not clear whether the emphasis is upon form, content, or evaluation?

This perception key suggests, of course, that there are at least three basic kinds of criticism: (1) *descriptive*—focusing on the form, (2) *interpretive*—focusing on the content, and (3) *evaluative*—focusing on the relative merits of a work of art. In the chapter on painting, we will also present examples of criticism that are historically oriented. However, historical criticism is, we believe, most usefully classified as a supplemental kind of criticism that enriches the three basic kinds of criticism.

DESCRIPTIVE CRITICISM

Descriptive criticism concentrates on the form of a work of art, describing, sometimes exhaustively, the important characteristics of that form in order to improve our understanding of the entire work. At first glance this kind of criticism may seem unnecessary. After all, the form is all there, completely given—all we have to do is observe. Anybody can do that. But it is not that simple, for the forms of works of art are usually complex and subtle. Even when they are simple, they are usually deceptively simple. Most of us know all too well that we can spend time attending to a work we are very much interested in and yet not perceive all there is to perceive. We miss things, and oftentimes we miss things that are right there for us to observe. For example, did you notice the visual form of E. E. Cummings's "l(a"—the spiraling downward curve (Figure 1-6)—before it was called to your attention? Or did you really see in Goya's painting (Figure 2-3) the way the line of the long dark shadow at the bottom right underlines the line of the firing squad?

The descriptive critic calls our attention to what we otherwise might miss in an artistic form we are concerned about. And even more important, he helps us do his work when he is not around. We can, if we carefully attend to his descriptive criticism, develop and enhance our own descriptive powers. That is worth thinking about. None of us can afford to have a professional critic with us all the time in order to observe everything that we should. And there are not enough published critical studies of works of art easily available so that we can always consult one if we have questions about something or if we feel that there is something missing in our responsiveness to a work of art. The critic can really help us if we need help, but he is not always available. Consequently we must ourselves learn to become descriptive critics. No other learning is as likely to improve our participation with a work of art, for such criticism turns us directly to the work itself.

PERCEPTION KEY   DESCRIPTIVE CRITICISM AND MODIGLIANI NUDE

1. Descriptively criticize Modigliani's nude (Figure 2-20). Point out every facet of the form that seems important. Discuss this painting in class or with others if possible.

2. After this criticism, return to the painting and participate with it. Do you now have a sharper perception of the painting and, in turn, a more intense feeling of participation?

Texture and Structure

As you worked through question 1 of this perception key you may have found it difficult to organize your descriptions. After all, we have defined form as the interrelationship of part to part and part to whole in a work of art, and connections like this may seem endless. Two distinctions about form may be of help here—texture and structure.

A connection of one part of form to another part we shall call a "textural relation." In poetry, for instance, it would be the relationship of one word to another, one phrase to another, one image to another, or any of these to any other. In the dance, it is the relationship of a given figure's motion at one moment to his motion at another moment, of one dancer's hand as related to another dancer's hand. Texture in music has to do with the relationships of simultaneously sounded tones or of the relationships of tones sounded one after another. Texture has to do with the connections among details within a limited region in the composition. Even if you do not read music, you can see that there is a considerable difference in the texture of the following examples of music:

1. An American Indian song (Figure 3-1)
2. Two bars from Mendelssohn's Violin Concerto (Figure 3-2)
3. A passage from Berlioz (Figure 3-3)

FIGURE 3-1   Line from an American Indian song.

FIGURE 3-2   Two bars from Mendelssohn's Violin Concerto.

FIGURE 3-3   A passage from Berlioz.

PERCEPTION KEY   TEXTURE AND MUSIC

1. Which example has the thinnest texture?
2. Which example has the thickest texture?
3. Does it make sense to characterize the texture in these examples as possessing qualities similar to those of feeling states—such as nervous or secure or sad or joyful?

A connection of one part of form to the whole form we shall call a "structural relation." As texture concerns itself with the details within a

FIGURE 3-4 African mask. Liberia, Cape Palmas region: Grebo. Wood, paint; 27½ inches high. Museum of Primitive Art, New York. Photograph by Charles Uht.

FIGURE 3-5 "Smiling Head," fragment. Vera Cruz, Mexico: Remojadas. Clay, 8⅜ inches high. Museum of Primitive Art, New York. Photograph by Charles Uht.

limited region, structure concerns itself with the totality of the work of art and the relationship of any details or regions to that totality. In some works of art the structure is not immediately perceptible. For example, in all forms which take time to unfold because the percepta come to us successively—in literature, music, dance, and film, for example—we are not aware of the totality of structural qualities until the unfolding is over or nearly over. Only then can we begin to grasp the complete structural characteristics. Plot is sometimes the key to the structure of a narrative or a film. The statement, development, and repetition of musical themes or motifs is part of the structural form of a symphony or of a popular song. And in forms such as these we often need some guidance to discover what the structural qualities are. This is basic to all of us in developing an educated sensibility.

The chapters on individual arts which follow will treat the problems of texture and structure more directly. Right now, however, you will see that you are already rather well equipped to observe textural details and structural characteristics in such an art as sculpture. Examine closely Figures 3-4 and 3-5: one is an example of African mask art (Figure 3-4), the other an example of early Mexican sculpture (Figure 3-5).

A wide variety of observations can be made about these two works with respect to their textures and structures, particularly as they differ from or compare with one another. Essentially they have the same subject matter: the human face. But they interpret that subject matter quite differently. For the moment, consider the textural and structural qualities of these two works. If the interpretation of the subject matter differs from one work to the other, then the form, with its texture and structure—which is, in fact, responsible for the difference in interpretation—will differ from one to the other. The perception key will help you focus on some of the differences:

PERCEPTION KEY   AFRICAN MASK AND EARLY MEXICAN SCULPTURE

1. What are the structural shapes of each of the works? Draw them on a separate sheet of paper.
2. Compare the smaller textures or details of these two works.
3. Compare the larger textures (for example, mouth, nose, eyes) of these two works.
4. Do the textures of these works reinforce their structures? How?

You will note that it is not the fact that these forms represent the human face that gives them their particular power. Rather, it is the *way* they represent. If you are sensitive to these ways, then you are likely to be sensitive to the power of these forms and their content.

INTERPRETIVE CRITICISM

Interpretive criticism concentrates on the content of a work of art. This kind of criticism explains the meaning of the work, tells us what the form reveals about its subject matter. For example, the forms of the African mask and the Mexican sculpture both have the same subject matter—the human face. They do not present us with the human face; they interpret the human face. The forms inform us about the human face.

PERCEPTION KEY: AFRICAN MASK AND EARLY MEXICAN SCULPTURE

Explain how these two interpretations (Figures 3-4 and 3-5) of the human face differ.

What you have done in this perception key is interpretive criticism.

These two examples probably have been quite easy for you to interpret. The human face is easy to comment on. Just make a funny face, and you have a comment. The subject matter is so familiar none of us have trouble identifying it. In the two examples from modern architecture (Figures 3-6 and 3-7), however, we have a different problem. Here the subject matter, or at least an important component of it, is a practical function. These buildings, furthermore, were designed for different functions. One is a

FIGURE 3-6 Louis Henry Sullivan, Guaranty (Prudential) Building, Buffalo, New York. 1894. Buffalo Historical Society.

FIGURE 3-7 Le Corbusier, Notre-Dame-du-Haut, Ronchamps, France. 1950–1955. Ezra Stoller © ESTO.

bank and one a church. Have you any doubt which is which, even before you take note of the captions?

In the perception key, consider why it is so easy to tell which building is which, even though neither is a "typical" example of its kind of architecture.

PERCEPTION KEY   SULLIVAN'S BANK AND LE CORBUSIER'S CHURCH

1. Which of these forms suggests solidity? Which suggests flight and motion? What have these things got to do with practical function?

2. How does the texture of each building reinforce the structure?

3. Explain the content of each building.

Form-Content

The interpretive critic's job is to find out as much about an artistic form as possible in order to explain its meaning. This is a particularly useful task for the amateur critic—which is to say for us in particular—since there are numerous works of art whose form seems important but not immediately understandable. When we look at the examples of the bank and the church, we ought to realize that the artistic power of these buildings is expressed by means of the form-content. It is true that without knowing the functions of these buildings we could appreciate them as abstract structures, but knowing about their functions deepens our appreciation. Thus the lofty arc of Le Corbusier's roof soars heavenward more mightily when we recognize the building as a church. The form takes us up toward heaven, at least in the sense that it moves our eyes upward. For a Christian church such a reference is perfect. The bank, on the other hand, looks like a pile, almost like a pile of square coins or banknotes. Certainly the form "amasses" something, and the sense of this is just what is appropriate for a bank. We won't belabor these examples, since it should be fun for you to do this kind of critical job yourself. Observe how much more you "get out of" these examples of architecture when you consider each form in relation to its meaning, i.e., the form as form-content. Such analyses, furthermore, should convince you that interpretive criticism operates in a vacuum unless it is based on descriptive criticism. Unless we perceive the form with sensitivity—and this means that we have the basis for good descriptive criticism—we simply cannot understand the content. In turn, any interpretive criticism will be useless.

Consider now Donald Justice's love poem and give some thought to the job an interpretive critic might have in explaining the poem to someone who does not understand or like it. What are the kinds of questions such a critic might ask about the work as a poem (not, in other words, about himself or the poet or the woman addressed in the poem)?

LOVE'S MAP

Your face more than others' faces
Maps the half-remembered places
I have come to while I slept—
Continents a dream had kept
Secret from all waking folk
Till to your face I awoke,
And remembered then the shore,
And the dark interior.

This is the kind of poem which one needs to think about for quite a while, for its content is not obvious. And while thinking about it one could be asking some questions which might help the poem come into sharper focus. In the accompanying perception key, provide some questions of your own. What three questions could you ask which could help put the poem into better perspective, the kind of perspective we think of as "depth" when we talk about a poem as having a "deep" meaning? If you have difficulty doing this, try some questions which deal with the idea of using a map and references to geography in a love poem, or the use of sleep in the poem, or about the poem's rhyme and its effect.

PERCEPTION KEY "LOVE'S MAP"

Questions:

1.

2.

3.

In a way, everyone's serious questions about this poem are relevant, no matter how strange they may seem at first. This is particularly true if a person has the opportunity to talk about his questions with others. A discussion of a variety of questions about this poem can help us gain insight into its content which we could probably get in no other way. Listening to the questions of others should give us some useful ideas about the ways in which works of art are understood by other people, providing us also with ideas about new ways in which we can understand works of art for ourselves. When you see it from this point of view you realize that an open discussion, far from being vague and irrelevant to the sharpening of our understanding, ought to be one of the most valuable kinds of instruction we can get about the arts.

The relativity of explanations about the content of works of art is important for us to grasp. Even the descriptive critic, who tries to tell us about what is "really there," will see things in a way that is relative to his own perspective. As N. J. Berrill points out in *Man's Emerging Mind*, "The statement you often hear that 'seeing is believing' is one of the most misleading ones a man has ever made, for you are more likely to see what you believe than believe what you see. To see anything as it really exists is about as hard an exercise of mind and eyes as it is possible to perform. . . ."[1]

Two descriptive critics can often "see" quite different things in an artistic form. This is not only to be expected but desirable; it is one of the reasons great works of art keep us intrigued for centuries. But even though they may see quite different aspects when they look independently at a work of art, they will usually, when they get together and talk it over, come to some kind of agreement about the aspects each of them sees. The thing being described, after all, has qualities each of us can perceive and talk about, and these are the things described. A work of art possesses objective qualities in the sense that they belong to the work and can be verified by a number of different observers. But they are subjective as well, in the sense that they are observed only by "subjects."

In the case of interpretive criticism, the subjectivity and, in turn, the relativity of explanations are more obvious than in the case of descriptive criticism. The content is "there" in the form, and yet, unlike the form, it is not there in such a directly perceivable way. Thus, if someone were to read "Love's Map" and think that the only "map" in the poem was the face of the beloved woman, he might well be surprised to learn that there are other references to maps and to kinds of geography—"the interior" usually refers to the unmapped and "dark" places beyond the coasts of continents as yet not totally explored. Then, even if he did sense that maps were being used in a very large and meaningful sense, he might not be fully aware that the woman in the poem was being loved the way an explorer loves the country he explores, with all the surprises, terror, uncertainty, and excitement of dis-

[1] N. J. Berrill, *Man's Emerging Mind*, Dodd, Mead, New York, 1955, p. 147.

covery which famous explorers have written about. He might not be fully aware that the act of love can be a way of getting new knowledge, of being in an unfamiliar relationship with someone, and of being in an unfamiliar relationship with oneself. Few people will deny that the concept of the map is present in the poem, but many may disagree that it implies the other ideas we have suggested. For you it may imply something else. But before we can begin to decide what is implied by the poem, we must know what is there that we can agree upon as equally perceivable and conceivable by most readers of the poem. This is descriptive criticism, preliminary to interpretive criticism—to the coming to terms with the content of the poem.

Interpretive criticism, then, at its best, is perhaps more demandingly creative than descriptive criticism: the interpretive critic, more than the descriptive critic, must be familiar with the subject matter that the content reveals. Someone innocent of the complexity of the love of some women will be unable to explain very helpfully Donald Justice's love poem. The interpretive critic explores and discovers meanings, as initiated and controlled by the artistic form, which he had not at first understood.

EVALUATIVE CRITICISM

To evaluate a work of art is to judge its artistic merits. This seems, at first glance, to suggest that evaluative criticism is prescriptive criticism, which prescribes what is good as if it were a medicine and tells us that this work is superior to that work.

PERCEPTION KEY EVALUATIVE CRITICISM

1. Suppose you are a judge of an exhibition of painting and the six nude paintings discussed in Chapter 2 (Figures 2-18 through 2-23) have been placed into competition. First, second, and third prizes are to be awarded by you. What would be your decisions? Why?

2. Suppose, further, that you are asked to judge which is the best work of art from the following selection: Cummings's "l(a," Cézanne's "Mont Sainte Victoire" (Figure 2-6), the African mask (Figure 3-4), and Le Corbusier's church (Figure 3-7). What would be your decision? Why?

It may be that this kind of evaluative criticism—sometimes called "judgmental criticism"—makes you a little uncomfortable. If so, we think your reaction is based on good instincts. In the first place, each work of art is such an individual thing that a relative merit ranking of several of them seems arbitrary. This is especially the case when the works are in different media and have different subject matter as in the second question of the perception key. In the second place, it is not very clear how such judging helps us in our basic critical purpose—to learn from our reflections about works of art how to participate with these works more intensely and enjoyably. It is true, of course, that judgmental criticism of some kind is necessary. We have been making such judgments continually in this book—in the selections for illustrations, for example. You are making such judgments when, as you enter a museum of art, you decide to spend your time with this painting rather than that. Obviously, also, the director of the museum must make judgmental criticisms, for not everything can be left in. Someone might argue, for example, that his old pair of shoes that have been cemented to a pedestal belong in The Museum of Modern Art. Someone has to decide. If a Velasquez is on sale, and recently one of his paintings was bought by the Metropolitan Art Museum of New York City for over $5 million, someone has to decide its relative worth. Evaluative criticism, then, is always functioning, at least implicitly. Even when we are participating with a work, we are implicitly evaluating its worth. Our participation implies its worth. If it were worthless, we would more or less explicitly judge it so and not even attempt participation.

The problem, then, is how to use evaluative criticism as constructively as possible. How can we use such criticism to help our participation with works of art? Whether Giorgione's painting (Figure 2-18) deserves first prize over Modigliani's (Figure 2-20) seems trivial. Who really cares about that? But if almost all critics agree that Shakespeare's poetry is far superior to Edward Guest's and we have been thinking Guest's poetry is great, we would probably be wise to do some reevaluating. Or if we hear a music critic we respect state that John Cage's music is worth listening to—and up to this time we have dismissed this music as worthless—then we should indeed make an effort to listen. Perhaps the greatest value of evaluative criticism lies in its commendation of works that we might otherwise dismiss. This may lead us to delightful experiences. Such criticism may also make us more skeptical in our judgments. If we think that the poetry of Edward Guest and the paintings of Grandma Moses are among the very best, it may be very helpful for us to know that other informed people think otherwise.

Furthermore, evaluative criticism when it is done well aids descriptive and interpretive criticism. All three kinds of criticism are interdependent. As we have already suggested, it is impossible to describe an artistic form adequately without understanding its content. For example, the line of the shadow in the bottom right of Goya's "May 3, 1808" (Figure 2-3) reinforces the line of the firing squad even if we fail to note what the firing squad is doing. But if we do notice—that is, if we are aware of the form's informing—then the textural relations of these lines become far stronger. Similarly, any adequate attempt to interpret the content necessarily demands attention to the form that is informing. To talk about the executions that Goya portrayed without relating them to such things as those ominous, dreadful lines is to reduce our talk to clichés. Moreover, every effort to describe or interpret implies value judgments that the description or interpretation is worth doing, and such value judgments have the power to evoke more adequate descriptions and interpretations. One of the authors recalls an example of this. One morning in Florence a historian of architecture and he were conducting a class in the Laurentian Library, designed by Michelangelo. The historian and the author were in disagreement about the architectural merits of the library in general and the stairwell in particular. In order to defend his value judgments, the author began to restate both his descriptions and interpretations. In that process he began to see things he had not seen before. His value judgments not only acted as catalysts to the discussion but also provided precise contexts that centered the issues involved, especially the interpretations. By making explicit our appreciation, evaluation may sharpen our perception and deepen our understanding. Furthermore, a truly creative evaluative critic, like the creative scientist, asks new questions based on his new way of judging things; in doing so, he helps us see anew. He shows us how our prejudgments of what is valuable in art may have limited our perception.

Evaluative criticism generally works with three fundamental standards —perfection, insight, and inexhaustibility. When the evaluation centers on the form, it usually values a form highly only if the texture and structure are tightly organized. If a textural detail fails to cohere with the structure, this usually will be condemned as distracting and thus inhibiting participation. An artistic form in which everything works together may be called perfect. A work may have perfect organization, however, and still be evaluated as poor unless it satisfies the standard of insight. If the form fails to inform us about some subject matter—if it just pleases us but doesn't make some significant difference in the way we live our lives—then that form may be called decorative rather than artistic. And decorative form is valued below artistic form because the participation it evokes, if it evokes any at all, is not as intense, delightful, or as lastingly significant. Finally, works of art may differ greatly in the breadth and depth of their content. The subject matter of Mondrian's "Composition in White, Black and Red" (Figure 1-4) —colors, lines, and space—is not as broad as Cézanne's "Mont Sainte Victoire" (Figure 2-6). And the depth of penetration into the subject matter is far deeper in the Cézanne, we believe, than in the photograph of the mountain (Figure 2-5). The stronger the content—i.e., the richer the interpretation of the subject matter—the more intense our participation, for we have more to keep us involved in the work. Such works resist monotony, no matter how often we return to them. Such works apparently are inexhaustible, and evaluative critics usually will rate only those kinds of works as masterpieces.

PERCEPTION KEY EVALUATIVE CRITICISM

1. Evaluate the seven nudes (Figures 2-17 through 2-23) with reference to the perfection of their forms.

FIGURE 3-8 Sculpture of Caesar Augustus. Marble, 6 feet 8 inches high. Vatican Museums, Rome. Alinari.

2. Evaluate these works with reference to their insight.
3. Evaluate these works with reference to their inexhaustibility.

Notice how unimportant it is how you ultimately rank these works. But notice, also, how these evaluative questions provide precise contexts for your attention. Thus your evaluations can sharpen your perceptions and broaden and deepen your interpretations.

PERCEPTION KEY EVALUATIVE CRITICISM

1. Evaluate the relative artistic merits of Justice's "Love's Map" and Mondrian's painting (Figure 1-4).
2. Evaluate the relative artistic merits of Mondrian's painting and Rothko's "Earth Greens" (Figure 4-2 and Color Plate 5).
3. What is the point of the above two questions?

SOME EXAMPLES FOR CRITICISM

The following are some examples to study as a critic. You can decide whether or not you have any sense of participation with the works here— though remember that a photograph of a sculpture is not a sculpture, any more than a photograph of a building is a building. No one can hope to have a very intense participative experience except in the presence of the genuine work of art itself. Still, we can sometimes get something of a participative experience even from a photograph.

FIGURE 3-9 Sculpture of a seated man with a harp. Antiquities—classical Cycladic sculpture. Marble, 11½ inches high. The Metropolitan Museum of Art. Rogers Fund, 1947.

The following plates are set up in pairs because useful criticisms are more likely to occur when we criticize works of the same artistic medium and at least roughly the same subject matter. (That is why we doubt that question 1 of the preceding perception key, taken by itself, is of much value.) All criticisms are at least implicitly comparative, though there are some that seem entirely individual. But the important point for us is the fact that when we are beginning to develop our critical sense, we find that comparative judgments are easier and much more valuable than judgments about individual works without reference to any other.

Consider the following perception keys as mere starting points for your criticisms. Go as far beyond them as you feel is useful.

PERCEPTION KEY CAESAR AUGUSTUS (FIGURE 3-8) AND CYCLADIC IDOL (FIGURE 3-9)

1. Evaluate the effect of textural simplicity or complexity in these two works. How does the simplicity or complexity of textural detail affect your grasp of the structural whole of each of these works?

2. Analyze the posture of the two figures. Does either reveal much about the figure's relationship to military, legal, or other worldly pursuits?

3. Is it possible to adequately evaluate the structure of either of these figures without considering posture? What does this imply for the work?

4. Do the forms of these works reveal anything about the concerns of the societies that produced them for the natural world (as opposed to a supernatural world)? Which figure reveals a greater concern for the natural world? This question becomes more complex once you have observed that the figure of Caesar Augustus represents a Caesar as a deity.

5. If possible, find two persons who hold differing views on the artistic value of these figures and ask them to present their arguments to a group or class. Then discuss.

PERCEPTION KEY THREE NUDES: INGRES, "THE TURKISH BATH" (FIGURE 3-10); CÉZANNE, "LES BAIGNEURS" (FIGURE 3-11); ANONYMOUS, "ODALISQUE" (FIGURE 3-12)

1. One of these works seems predominantly structural, the other two are predominantly textural in emphasis. How different is the emphasis on structure versus texture in its effect on the overall treatment of the nude? What do the two paintings with textural emphasis have in common in their treatment of the nude that the painting with structural emphasis does not share?

2. Which of these paintings would *Playboy* magazine be most likely to reproduce? Why? Which painting would be the least likely to be reproduced in *Playboy*? Why? Consider these questions in an open forum. First, see if there is unanimity within your group about which of these paintings does or does not fit *Playboy* taste. Then discuss what kind of critical judgment such imputed behavior on the part of *Playboy* represents.

FIGURE 3-10 Jean-Auguste-Dominique Ingres, "The Turkish Bath" *(Le Bain Turque).* 1863. Oil on canvas, 42½ inches in diameter. Louvre. Musées Nationaux.

FIGURE 3-11   Paul Cézanne,
"The Bathers" *(Les Baigneurs).*
1883–1887. Lithograph printed
in colors. The Cleveland
Museum of Art, in memory of
John H. McBride II.

FIGURE 3-12   Anonymous,
"Odalisque." 1850. Oil on
canvas, 28¼ by 36¼ inches.
The Cleveland Museum of
Art, Leonard C. Hanna, Jr.,
Collection.

3. Evaluate what is revealed by each of these paintings about the nude. Do any of them tend to devalue the nude? In what ways? Do any of them show the nude in a socially harmful way? Do any show the nude in an artistically unsuccessful way? Is it possible to have a socially harmful work that is artistically successful? Discuss.

4. What is the function of distortion or the lack of it in these paintings? How does distortion make possible revelation of a subject matter such as the nude? Does the absence of distortion imply that no interpretation of the subject matter is being made, and that—therefore—there is no content to the painting? Consider this carefully in light of the discussion made of the Adams photograph and the Goya painting in Chapter 2.

5. Which kind of criticism—descriptive, interpretive, or evaluative—do these paintings seem most to demand? Compare your judgment with the judgments of a group of friends. Back up your judgment by carefully criticizing one or more of these paintings.

FIGURE 3-14 Nataraja, Lord of the Dance. South India, eleventh century, Chola period. Copper, 43⅞ by 40 inches. The Cleveland Museum of Art, J. H. Wade Collection.

FIGURE 3-13 The Bodhisattva Kuan-yin. China, late Northern Ch'i or early Sui, c. 575–600. Sandstone with polychrome, 54⅝ inches high. The Cleveland Museum of Art, John L. Severance Fund.

1. These figures represent Oriental deities. Which reveals more fully the nature of godliness to you? Compare your judgments with those of others. Is there extensive agreement or disagreement? Could your judgment of what is revealed be conditioned by your cultural experiences? How?

2. Do these figures pertain to the same religion or to different religions? On what grounds do you base your judgment? Is such a judgment evaluative criticism, or is it one of the other varieties of criticism we have suggested?

3. What would it mean to say that neither of these figures has perceptible religious qualities? Is it possible to decide which of these figures possesses a greater religious quality? In a discussion group, explore the question of whether it is reasonable to suggest that such figures could or could not reveal religious values. Explore, as well, the question of whether they could reveal religious values to a Westerner unacquainted with Oriental religious beliefs.

4. The basic structure of one of these figures is the circle; the basic structure of the other is the vertical line or upright. Choose one of these works and find a fellow student to choose the other. Then both present your views to a group in such a way as to offer an exploration of the effect of the basic structural emphasis on your descriptions, interpretations, and evaluations of the figure.

FIGURE 3-15 Sagrada Familia, Barcelona, Spain. Photograph by Frederic Lewis, Inc., New York.

FIGURE 3-16 Siena Cathedral. Alinari.

1. Set up a debate between two groups on the question of whether these buildings are appropriate in appearance for churches. As the debate goes on,
   keep a record of the basic points each team raises in defense of its position
   and identify them with reference to their critical usefulness. Are some of the
   points not specifically critical at all? If not, what are they? What kinds of
   points seem to have had the most profound effect on the opinions of those
   listening? What kinds of points had the most profound effect on your
   opinions?

2. Both churches have extremely rich textures. What do you feel is revealed by
   this amazing attention to detail in such colossal buildings? Does the attention to detail imply any attitude toward religion on the part of the community that built these churches? Are there any nonreligious values revealed
   by these buildings?

3. These churches share many of the same structural qualities. By means of
   descriptive criticism, establish what the structural similarities are. Are there
   significant structural differences?

4. Almost six hundred years separate the building of these churches—and they
   were built in different countries—yet both churches serve the same (Catholic) religion. In view of these facts, what religious values do you feel these
   churches reveal? What attitudes on the part of worshipers do the churches
   reveal? Are these revelations limited by the cultural experience of the critic?
   Consider this last question as thoroughly as possible and suggest the limitations of the critic as well as reasons why the perceptible qualities of the
   churches might overcome these limitations to some extent.

5. If you had to choose one of these buildings as artistically superior to the
   other, which building would you choose? What would be the basis of your
   judgment? Consider all the kinds of criticism at your disposal and, in de-
   fending your view, use as many of them as possible. Are any of your arguments outside the scope of the kinds of criticism we have described? Are
   they still critical arguments?

Good critics can help us understand specific works of art while also
giving us the means or techniques which will help us become good critics
ourselves. By watching the critic perform, we can learn something about
what the critical function is and how to adapt it to our purposes. Principally,
we can learn a good deal about what kinds of questions to ask about given
works of art. Each of the following chapters on the individual arts is designed to do just that—to give some help about what kinds of questions a
serious viewer should ask in order to come to a clearer perception and
deeper understanding of any specific work. In the arts, unlike many other
areas of human concern, the questions are often more important than the
answers. The real lover of the arts will often not be the person with all the
answers but rather the one who has the best questions. And the reason for

this is not that the answers are worthless but that the questions, when properly applied, lead us to a new awareness, a more exalted consciousness of what works of art have to offer us. Then, when we get to the last chapter, we will be better prepared to understand something of how each of the arts is related to the other branches of the humanities.

4 PAINTING

INTRODUCTION

Painting is the art that has most to do with revealing the visual appearance of things. The eye is the chief sense organ involved in our participation with painting and one of the chief sense organs involved in our dealings with our everyday world. But our ordinary vision of our everyday world is usually very fragmentary. We usually see scenes with their objects and events only to the degree necessary for our practical purposes. The full visual appearance of things is missed. For example, imagine yourself walking along Broadway at Wall Street (Figure 6-5) rather than just looking at the photograph. Is it very likely that you would "see" the patterns formed by the vertical and horizontal lines of the scene? Even in such a simple act as walking safely on a sidewalk, we either ignore or abstract from the full qualitativeness of colors, lines, etc. Otherwise we would be late for our appointment or get run down by a car. And anyway, the qualities of things in most sidewalk scenes are hardly worth the trouble. We hurry on. Usually, when things cannot be ignored, we quantify them. In order to survive, we reduce things to data. In that way we exert our control over things, manage them for our purposes. Behind the wheel of a car, our lives depend on our judgment of how far away and how fast-moving that oncoming car really is. We just do not have time to enjoy its splendor of color and speed. Of course, someone else may be driving, and then the qualities of the visually perceptible may be enjoyed for their own sake rather than being mastered by some manner of quantification. Or we may be walking leisurely in the mountains on a safe path, and then the fullness of the scene has a chance to unfold itself.

But this shift to enjoying things as they show themselves rather than passing them by or reducing them to data is not, for most of us, automatic. The habits of practical life tend to harden the lenses of our eyes, like cataracts, so that we become blind both to the qualities of things and the things themselves. Thus, even on the safe path on the mountain, we may miss both the blueness as well as the solidity of that mountain.

Although the habits of practical vision are often necessary for survival, we may make the grand mistake of assuming that we know the thing if we can place a label on it or fit it into a formula. Thus we learn to notice only the most prominent features of a thing—those features that enable us to place it conveniently into a particular mental slot or category (e.g., mineral, vegetable, animal). Perhaps there is a terrible danger in allowing such a process to dominate our mental activities. Then we regard each two-legged creature with head and arms not as an individual having a particular name and an unusual combination of needs and talents but merely as a *man*, or—perhaps a bit more specifically—as a Christian, Jewish, American, Chinese, Democratic, Republican, Communist, Socialist, black, white, red, or yellow man, etc. The particular individual becomes lost in these abstract classificational shuffles. Maybe this kind of mental process, if it is not checked by strong qualifications, is the seed bed for racial or religious or political prejudices, hates, and rivalries. In its extreme form, maybe it creates the conditions that permit an Adolph Hitler to practice genocide. Maybe it results in mutually exclusive suspicions and hates between "majority" and "minority" groups whose values permit them to think of themselves first as Catholics or Protestants, second as Christians, and third as members of a universal brotherhood of man bound together by the common recognition of the fatherhood of God. Maybe this kind of inverted value system permits groups to think of themselves first as Democrats, second as Southerners or Northerners or Westerners or Easterners, third as Americans, and last as citizens of a worldwide society. If there is some truth in these points, then sharpening our visual and other perceptual powers to be aware of the qualities of things and the things themselves may have something to do with the moral dimensions of our lives.

Test your visual powers for yourself.

PERCEPTION KEY   YOUR VISUAL POWERS

---

1. What color are the eyes of members of your family and those of your best friends?

2. Have you ever followed closely the swirl of a falling leaf?

3. Are you aware of the spatial locations of the buildings on the main street of your home town? Are they pleasing or distressing?

4. Are you aware very often of the qualities of things—such as the fluidity of water, the roughness of rocks, or the greenness of grass?

5. Take some green paint and some red paint, a brush, and paper. Or, if these are not readily available, take any materials at hand, such as marbles and chips that are green and red. Now place the green and red side by side in such a way that, as far as possible, you make the greenness of the green shine forth. Maybe this will require a different tone of green or red or a different placement. Or maybe you need to remove the red altogether and substitute another color. Notice how, as you go about this, you must really see the green. This is not like looking at the green of a stop light. Then we see right through the green because it is a signal that directs our safe driving. To hold our sight on the green could be dangerous. Thus we give the green no more than a glance and move on. But if we are trying to see the greenness of a green, we must hold on the green itself. We must let the green dominate and control our seeing. The qualities of the green must be allowed to show themselves for what they are.

6. Are you aware very often of things as things, their "thingliness"—such as the mountainness of mountains, the marbleness of marble, the glassiness of glass? Do you care about things in this sense?

7. Go into the fields if this is possible and seek a rock that will enhance the appearance of an area of the yard or building or room where you live. Select both the rock and the area so that the rockiness of the rock—its hardness, roughness or smoothness, shape, and especially its solidity—will be visible.

8. John Ruskin, the great nineteenth-century critic, noted in his *Modern Painters* "that there is hardly a roadside pond or pool which has not as much landscape *in* it as above it. It is not the brown, muddy, dull thing we suppose it to be; it has a heart like ourselves, and in the bottom of that there are the boughs of the tall trees and the blades of the shaking grass, and all manner of hues, of variable pleasant light out of the sky; nay the ugly gutter that stagnates over the drain bars in the heart of the foul city is not altogether base; down in that, if you will look deep enough, you may see the dark, serious blue of the far-off sky, and the passing of pure clouds. It is at your own will that you see in that despised stream either the refuse of the street or the image of the sky—so it is with almost all other things that we kindly despise." Do you agree with Ruskin? If not, why not?

If you have found yourself tending to answer the questions of this perception key negatively or if you see the assignments about the green and the rock as being difficult and perhaps pointless, you should not be surprised or discouraged. Like the great majority of us, you probably have been educated away from sensitivity to the qualities of things and things as things. You have been taught how to manage and control things by thinking *at* them, as in the scientific method. This does not mean that such education is bad in itself. Without this education the business of the world would grind to a halt. But if not supplemented, this training may blind you like some terrible disease of the eye. You must go to the artists, especially the painters—those who are most sensitive to the visual appearances of things. With their help, our vision can be made whole again, as when we were children. Their paintings accomplish this, in the first place, by making things and their qualities much clearer than they are in nature. "If the world were clear," as Camus says, "art would not exist." The artist purges from our sight the films of familiarity. Secondly, painting, with its "all-at-onceness," more than any other art, gives us the time to allow our vision to participate.

THE CLARITY OF PAINTING

Examine again the photograph of Mont Sainte Victoire and Cézanne's painting (Figures 2-5, 2-6, 4-1, and Color Plate 4). The photograph was taken many years after Cézanne was there but, aside from a few more buildings and older trees, the scene of the photograph shows us essentially what Cézanne saw. Although much of the power of Cézanne's painting depends on his color, let us initially compare the photograph of the mountain with the black-and-white reproduction of the painting. At first glance, you might conclude that the photograph is clearer than the painting, for there is a kind of blurry effect about the painting. But look again. Rather, let the painting control your seeing—see from it.

PERCEPTION KEY "MONT SAINTE VICTOIRE"

1. Why did Cézanne put the two trees in the foreground at the left and right edges? Why are they cut off by the frame? Why are the trees trembling as if they had been hit by a bolt of lightning?

2. In the photograph, there is an abrupt gap between the foreground and the middle distance. In the painting, this gap is filled in. Why?

3. Why, in the painting, has the viaduct been moved over to the left?

4. In the painting, the lines of the viaduct appear to move toward the left. Why?

5. The viaduct lines, furthermore, lead to a meeting point with the long road that runs toward the left side of the mountain. The fields and buildings within that triangle all seem drawn toward that apex. Why did Cézanne organize this middle ground more geometrically than the foreground or the mountain? And why is the apex of the triangle the unifying area for that region?

6. Why is the peak of the mountain in the painting given a slightly concave shape?

7. In the painting, the ridge of the mountain above the viaduct is brought into much closer proximity to the peak of the mountain. Why?

8. In the painting, the lines, ridges, and shapes of the mountain are much more tightly organized than in the photograph. How is this accomplished?

The subject matter of Cézanne's painting is surely the mountain. Suppose the title of the painting were "Trees." This would strike us as strange because when we look at a title we usually expect it to tell us what the painting is about, i.e., its subject matter. And although the trees in Cézanne's painting are important, they obviously are not as important as the mountain. A title such as "Viaduct" would also be misleading.

The basic content of the painting is, then, the interpretation of the mountain, the insight Cézanne's form gives us about the mountainness of the mountain—especially its solid rhythm and massive power. The form accomplishes this in so many ways that a complete description is very difficult. Some of the ways have already been suggested by the questions of the accompanying perception key. Every way helps bring forth the energy of Mont Sainte Victoire, which seems to roll down through the valley and even up into the foreground trees. Everything is dominated by and unified around the mountain. The roll of its ridges are like waves of the sea—but far more durable, as we sense the impenetrable solidity of the masses underneath.

The firm compositional strength of the structure of this painting is readily apparent even from a black-and-white reproduction. But now turn to the color reproduction (Color Plate 4). Is the compositional strength even firmer? And if so, why? Yet no reproduction, even the best in color, can tell you very much about the subtler textures, the relationships of the smaller details, of this work. If possible, study this painting in the Phillips Gallery in Washington. Or if this is impossible, study almost any of Cézanne's landscapes after 1885—he did, incidentally, a great many sketches and paintings of Mont Sainte Victoire—in some nearby museum or gallery.

You will notice that the brushstrokes themselves are usually perceptible, angular, and organized in units that function something like pieces in a mosaic. These units move toward each other in receding space, and yet their intersections are rigid, as if their impact froze their movement. Almost all the colors reflect light, like the facets of a crystal, so that a solid color or one-piece effect rarely appears. Generally, you will find within each unit a series of color tones of the same basic tint. The colors, moreover, are laid on in small overlapping patches, often crossed with delicate parallel lines to indicate shading. These hatchings also model the depth dimension of objects, so we perceive the solidity of their volumes more directly, strangely enough, than we perceive them in nature. Compare again the photograph of Mont Sainte Victoire with the painting. Lines are not drawn around objects like outlines; rather, the lines emerge from the buildup of color, light, shadow, and volume much as, although this also may seem strange, lines emerge from the objects of nature. And the color tones, variously modulated, are repeated endlessly throughout the planes of space. The color tones of the mountain are repeated in the viaduct and the fields and buildings of the middle ground and the trees of the foreground. Color animates everything, mainly because the color seems to be always moving out of the depth of everything rather than being laid on flat like house paint. The vibrating colors, in turn, rhythmically charge into one another and then settle down, reaching an equilibrium in which everything except the limbs of the foreground trees seems to come to rest.

Cézanne's form distorts reality in order to reveal reality. He makes Mont Sainte Victoire far clearer in his painting than you will ever see it in nature or in the best of photographs. Once you have participated with this and similar paintings, you will find that you will begin to see mountains like Mont Sainte Victoire with something like Cézanne's vision. A new set of lenses begins to grow in your eyes, and with it a way of seeing such things as mountains with extraordinary clarity and satisfaction.

THE "ALL-AT-ONCENESS" OF PAINTING

All paintings, in addition to revealing the visually perceptible more clearly, give us time for our vision to focus, hold, and participate. Of course, there are times when we can hold on a scene in nature. We are resting with no pressing worries and with time on our hands, and the sunset is so striking that our attention fixes on its redness. But then darkness descends and the mosquitoes begin to bite. In front of a painting, however, we find that things can "stand still," like the red in Mondrian's "Composition in White, Black and Red" (Figure 1-4). Here the red is peculiarly impervious and reliable, infallibly fixed and settled in its place. It can be surveyed and brought out again and again; it can be visualized with closed eyes and checked with open eyes. There is no hurry, for all of the painting is present and, under normal conditions, it is going to stay present; it is not changing in any significant perceptual sense. The same is true of Cézanne's "Mont Sainte Victoire."

Painting, more than any other art, presents itself as an entirety. Every part of a painting is all there at once and everything stays put within the frame. The elements of a painting are not presented successively, as with the sound after sound of music or the word after word of literature. This "all-at-onceness" frees our perception from any sense of compulsion. Even our memories are rested. By simply a turn of our eye, the forgotten can be taken in again. Moreover, we can "hold on" any part or region or the totality as long as we like and follow any order of regions at our own pace. No region of a painting strictly presupposes another region temporally. The sequence is subject to no absolute constraint. Whereas there is only one route in listening to music, for example, there is a freedom of routes in seeing paintings.

With "Mont Sainte Victoire" I may focus on the foreground trees, then on the middle ground, and finally on the mountain. The next time around I may reverse the order. "Paths are made," as the painter Paul Klee perceived, "for the eye of the beholder which moves along from patch to patch like an animal grazing." There is a "rapt resting" on any part, an unhurried series of one-after-the-other of "nows," each of which has its own temporal spread. "Mont Sainte Victoire," like most paintings, has a feudal constitution. Although certain regions—especially the mountain in this case—have hierarchical rights over others, each region maintains its personal rights and particularity, its intrinsic value. Each region has its own center of gravity and thus is a place of rest—of arrest. Each region is a calculated trap for sensuous meditation and consummation. Each region fills our eyes so completely that there is no desire to move to the next region, at least for awhile. Thus we are filled with a sense of the intensified immediate.

Paintings make it possible for us to stop in the present and enjoy at our leisure the sensations provided by the show of the visible. That is the second reason why paintings can help make our vision whole. They not only clarify our world but also free us from worrying about the future and the past, because paintings are a framed context in which everything stands still. There is the "here-now" and nothing but the "here-now." Our vision, for once, has time to let the qualities of things and the things themselves unfold.

REPRESENTATIONAL AND ABSTRACT PAINTING

The artistic medium of painting is made up of qualities such as colors, lines, and light. These qualities are elements or aspects of the visible which lend themselves to being organized. They are the "stuff" that the painter forms in order to reveal some subject matter, i.e., to transform that subject matter into a content. These qualities we shall call *sensa*.

SENSA

Sensa are the stimulators of our sense organs—the causes of sensations, whether visual, tactile, aural, or olfactory. In the case of visual sensations, the sensa are usually a part of such things as white paper, black pencils, or red erasers. But on the painter's palette the white, red, and black are just blobs of different-colored paints ready to be brushed on a canvas. Sensa, in other words, may or may not be associated with specific objects and events. In the case of paper, pencils, and erasers, the sensa appear to us as associated with specific objects. In the case of that student erasing, the sensa are not only associated with specific objects but with a specific event: the act of erasing. In the case of the red, white, and black on the painter's palette, these sensa are disassociated or abstracted from specific objects and events.

PERCEPTION KEY   CÉZANNE, GOYA, AND MONDRIAN

Compare Cézanne's "Mont Sainte Victoire" (Figure 4-1), Goya's "May 3, 1808" (Figure 2-3) and Mondrian's "Composition in White, Black and Red" (Figure 1-4).

1. In which painting are the sensa basically associated with only specific objects?

2. In which painting are the sensa associated with both specific objects and events?

3. In which painting are the sensa abstracted from specific objects and events?

4. What is the subject matter, respectively, of each of these paintings?

Representational painting has as its subject matter specific objects and events. Thus Cézanne's "Mont Sainte Victoire" basically is about a specific object—that mountain. Its form reveals something about that mountain and similar mountains. Thus Goya's "May 3, 1808" basically is about a specific event—that execution. Its form reveals something about that execution and similar executions. Representational paintings also reveal something about sensa. "Mont Sainte Victoire," among other things, reveals something about colors, lines, and light. And so does Goya's painting. But sensa are not the primary subject matter—not what these paintings are most basically about.

Abstract painting, on the other hand, has sensa or the sensuous as its primary subject matter. Such painting abstracts from specific objects and events and reveals sensa for their own sake. Thus Mondrian's "Composition in White, Black and Red" is basically about the sensa of unvaried white, black, and red in a pattern of rigid lines. Thus Mark Rothko's "Earth Greens" (Figure 4-2 and Color Plate 5) is basically about the sensa of varied reds, greens, and blues in a pattern of soft lines. The sensa *in* both paintings are specific, of course, but they do not refer to any specific object or event *outside* the painting. The basic subject matter of both paintings is sensa or the sensuous. The basic content of both paintings is the insight they give about these sensa or the sensuous.

ABSTRACT PAINTING

Abstract painting might seem to have nothing to do with reality because it contains no reference to things. Some theorists, as we indicated in Chapter 2, even go so far as to proclaim that artistic form is significant not because it informs about our world but because the form is its own significance. And they point to abstract painting along with pure music (as opposed to program music and opera) as prime examples to prove their case. We shall consider this issue in more detail later on in the chapter on music, where the problem is more complex, but with abstract painting we think the "significant form" theory is plainly inadequate. Abstract painting, after all, obviously contains and refers to the qualities of things, and these qualities are with us all the time. There are many times when we are without an awareness of things, for example, when we are waking from a deep sleep. But there is never a time, except when we are totally unconscious, when we are without an awareness of qualities. Of course it is true, because we are necessarily practical beings, that we see qualities or sensa most of the time mainly as signs that point to the things of which they presumably are a part. We see, for example, the white shape of the paper only as an indication of a piece of paper we want to use. Thus our sense of sensa is usually not very vivid. That is one of the reasons why, at first, abstract painting may seem so strange as well as why it is sometimes argued that such painting is totally disconnected from reality.

FIGURE 4-2 Mark Rothko, "Earth Greens." 1955. Oil on canvas, 90¼ by 73½ inches. Courtesy of Galerie Beyeler Basel. *(See also Color Plate 5.)*

We see some colored sensa in a certain shape and we conclude, "There is a chair." Alfred North Whitehead remarks:

> But what we have is the mere coloured shape. Perhaps an artist might not have jumped to the notion of a chair. He might have stopped at the mere contemplation of a beautiful colour and a beautiful shape. . . . I am very sceptical as to the high-grade character of the mentality required to get from the coloured shape to the chair. One reason for this scepticism is that my friend the artist, who kept himself to the contemplation of colour, shape and

COLOR PLATE 1 (FIGURE 1-2) Peter Blume, "Eternal City." 1937. Oil on composition board, 34 by 47⅞ inches. Collection, The Museum of Modern Art, New York. Mrs. Simon Guggenheim Fund.

COLOR PLATE 2 (FIGURE 1-4)   Piet Mondrian, "Composition in White, Black and Red." 1936. Oil on canvas, 40½ by 41 inches. Collection, The Museum of Modern Art, New York. Gift of the Advisory Committee.

COLOR PLATE 3 (FIGURE 2-3)   Francisco Goya, "May 3, 1808." 1814–1815. Canvas, 8 feet 9 inches by 13 feet 4 inches. The Prado, Madrid.

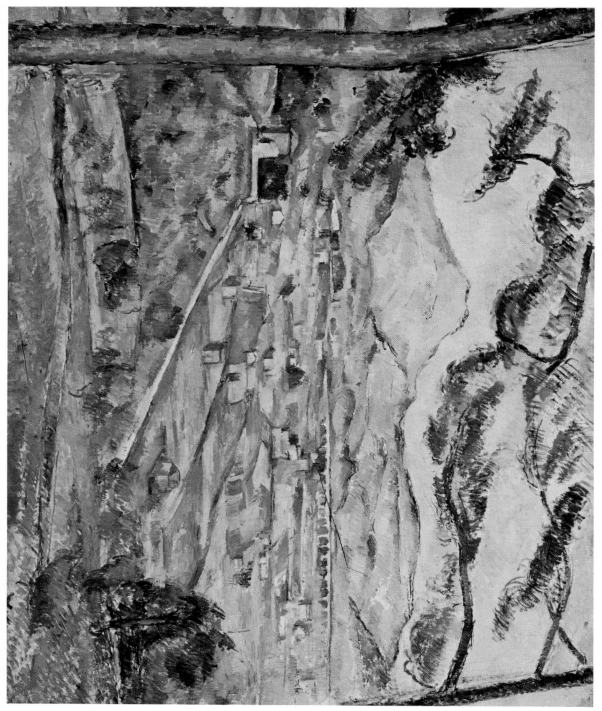

COLOR PLATE 4 (FIGURE 4-1) Paul Cézanne, "Mont Sainte Victorie." 1886–1887. Oil on canvas, 23½ by 28½ inches. The Phillips Collection, Washington, D.C.

COLOR PLATE 5 (FIGURE 4-2)   Mark Rothko, "Earth Greens." 1955. Oil on canvas, 90¼ by 73½ inches. Courtesy of Galerie Beyeler Basel.

COLOR PLATE 6 (FIGURE 4-3) Henri Matisse, "Pineapple and Anemones." 1940. Oil on canvas, 29 by 36 inches. Private collection.

COLOR PLATE 7 (FIGURE 4-9) Parmigianino, "The Madonna with the Long Neck." c. 1535. Panel painting, 36⅝ by 53¾ inches. Uffizi, Florence.

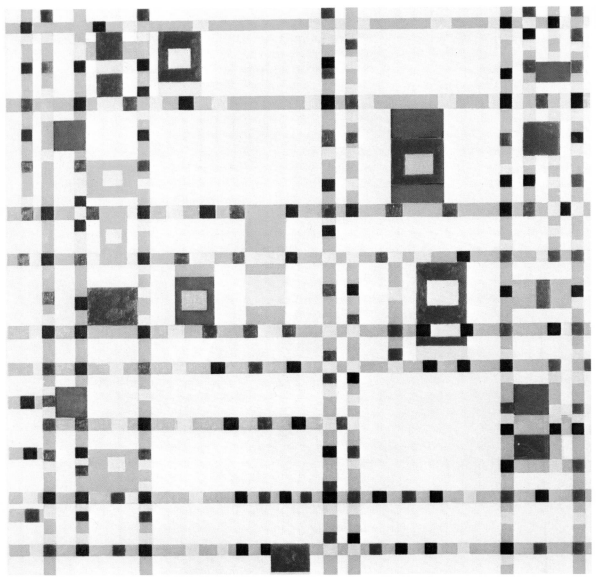

COLOR PLATE 8 (FIGURE 5-10)   Piet Mondrian, "Broadway Boogie Woogie." 1942–1943. Oil on canvas, 50 by 50 inches. Collection, The Museum of Modern Art, New York. Given anonymously.

position, was a very highly trained man, and had acquired this facility of ignoring the chair at the cost of great labour.[1]

Ignoring the chair is an abstraction from the chair. But it is not a total abstraction from reality, just an abstraction from the things of reality—its specific objects and events. Thus the Mondrian (Figure 1-4) and the Rothko (Figure 4-2) are not pure forms, as the proponents of significant form claim. They inform about sensa or qualities in various relationships.

PRESENTATIONAL IMMEDIACY

An abstract painter, by eliminating reference to everything but sensa from his work, liberates us from the habits of referring sensa to specific objects and events. He makes it easy for us, even though we are not artists ourselves, to focus on the sensa themselves. Then the radiant and vivid values of the sensuous are enjoyed for their own sake, satisfying a primal fundamental need. Abstractions can help fulfill this need if we dare, despite our habits of practice and Puritan heritage, to behold and treasure the images of the sensuous. Then, instead of our controlling the sensa, transforming them into data or signs, the sensa control us, transforming us into participators. Moreover, because references to specific objects and things are eliminated, there is a peculiar abstraction from the future and the past. Abstract painting, more than any other art, gives us an intensified sense of "here-now" or *presentational immediacy*. When we look at representational paintings such as "Mont Sainte Victoire" (Figure 4-1), we may think about our chances of getting to southern France some time in the future. Or when we see "May 3, 1808" (Figure 2-3), we may think about similar executions. These suggestions bring the future and past into our participation, causing the "here-now" to be somewhat compromised. The "here-now" still dominates because of painting's "all-at-onceness." But with abstract painting—because there is no portrayal of specific objects or events that suggest the past or the future—the sense of presentational immediacy is more intense.

Although sensa appear everywhere, in paintings sensa shine forth. This is especially true with abstract paintings, because there is nothing to attend to but sensa. In nature the light usually appears as external to the colors and surface of sensa. The light plays *on* the colors and surface. In paintings the light usually appears immanent *in* the colors and surface, seems to come—in part at least—through them, even in the flat polished colors of a Mondrian. When a light source is represented—the candles in paintings of La Tour, for example, or the sunlight coming through windows in the paintings of Rembrandt or Vermeer—the light seems to be absorbed

[1] Alfred North Whitehead, *Symbolism, Its Meaning and Effect*, Macmillan, New York, 1927, pp. 2f.

into the colors and surfaces. There is a depth of luminosity about the sensa of paintings that even nature at its glorious best seldom surpasses. Generally the colors of nature are more brilliant than the colors of painting; but usually in nature sensa are either so glittering that our squints miss their inner luminosity or the sensa are so changing that we lack the time to participate and penetrate. The swift currents of sensa in nature tend to stupefy our sensitiveness. In paintings—except in some Op Art where the sensa of the painting either actually are moved by some device or seem to move because of our movement—glittering change is absent. There is a fixation of the flux. Thus the depth of sensa is unveiled primarily by simply allowing them "to be." This is the pious respect for sensa that all painters possess. To ignore the allure of the sensa in a painting, and, in turn, in nature, is to miss one of the chief glories life provides. It is especially the abstract painter—the caretaker or shepherd of sensa—who is most likely to call us back to our senses.

Participate with the Mondrian (Figure 1-4) or the Rothko (Figure 4-2). After your participation, reflect on how you experienced a series of durations, vivid solipsisms of present moments—"spots of time" (Wordsworth)—that are ordered by the relationships between the regions of sensa. Compare your experience with listening to music.

PERCEPTION KEY MONDRIAN, ROTHKO, AND MUSIC

1. The sensa of music come to us successively. Do the sounds interpenetrate more than the sensa of the Mondrian or the Rothko?
2. Is the rhythm of listening to music different from the rhythm in seeing abstractions?

The sensa and regions of abstractions (and the same is largely true of representational paintings) are divided from one another, we think, in a different way from the more fluid progressions felt in listening to music. Whereas when we listen to music the sensa interpenetrate, when we see an abstraction the sensa are more juxtaposed. Whereas the rhythm of perceiving music is continuous, the rhythm of perceiving abstract painting is discontinuous. Whereas music is perceived as motion, abstract painting is perceived as motionless. We are fascinated by the vibrant novelty and the primeval power of the red of an abstraction for its own sake, cut off from explicit consciousness of past and future. But then, sooner or later, we notice the connection of the red to the blue, and then we are fascinated by the blue. Or then, sooner or later, we are fascinated by the interaction or contrast between the red and blue. Our eye travels over the canvas step by step, free to pause at any step as long as it desires. With music this pausing is impossible. If we "hold on" a tone or passage, the oncoming tones sweep by us and are lost. Music is always in part elsewhere—gone or coming—and we are swept up in the flow of process. The rhythms of hearing music and seeing abstractions are at opposite poles.

PERCEPTION KEY   BLUME, MATISSE, AND ROTHKO

Analyze your experience of Blume's "Eternal City" (Figure 1-2), Matisse's "Still Life" (Figure 4-3 and Color Plate 6), and Rothko's "Earth Greens" (Figure 4-2). Do you find that the Rothko locks you into the "now" more than the Matisse, and the Matisse more than the Blume? If so, why?

The sensa of representational paintings, like those of abstract painting, are not presented successively as in music. Yet since in representational painting the sensa refer to definite objects and events, we inevitably feel process—an awareness of past and future as involved with the present— more than with abstract painting. In the case of a painting that refers primarily to events, such as "May 3, 1808," (Figure 2-3), there is an aware-

FIGURE 4-3   Henri Matisse, "Pineapple and Anemones." 1940. Oil on canvas, 29 by 36 inches. Private Collection. *(See also Color Plate 6.)*

ness of the time of the event. But even in a still life where the primary reference is to objects, as in Matisse's "Still Life," the sense of "here-now" is somewhat compromised. Although there may be no definite dating, there is, as in the experience of an eventful painting, a definite placing. Thus our attention is directed from the sensuous surface of the design to the objects designated, such as fruit, flowers, and a table. For the participator there will be a fusion of sensa and objects. He will see the fruit and the table *in* the lines, colors, and shapes of the painting. Nevertheless, the awareness of definite objects breaks up the sheer "here-nowness" of the participation. In ordinary, nonparticipative experience, we see, for example, the front side of a table over there. We cannot see the back side simultaneously with the front side. Yet in seeing the front we usually remember, more or less vaguely, the image of the back if we have already seen that table. Or if we have not seen that particular table, we still imagine what its back looks like because we have seen similar tables. Then, too, we are likely to anticipate the possibility of seeing the back simply by moving around the table. Past and future images of the back side synthesize with our present image of the front side. This synthesis introduces an awareness of process, of past and future as immanent in the present experience. The sheer immediacy of the present is fused with past and future; that is to say, there is no longer sheer immediacy. Now when we participate with Matisse's picture and see his table, we know, of course, that we cannot actually see the back side, for this is a painted table rather than an actual table. Yet we carry over from ordinary experience, in most cases completely automatically, the habit of synthesizing images of the absent aspects of an object (like the back side of a table) with the directly given aspect (the front side). Thus, even with a representational painting that is noneventful, such as Matisse's "Still Life," the sense of "here-now" is not as strong as with abstract paintings.

Just as a still life is likely to stimulate a sense of "here-now" more than a historical painting, so abstractions differ in their ability to stimulate the sense of "here-now." The vast canvas of Pollock's "Autumn Rhythm" (Figure 4-4), full of the chaos of chance, is so forceful, rhythmic, and seemingly spontaneous in the presentation of its sensa that our eye tends to get caught up in the violent rush in a way that inhibits resting on a part. With work such as this—some of the abstractions of Willem de Kooning and Hans Hofmann, for example, and much of Op Art with its flashing, iridescent colors and shapes—abstract painting comes closest to music in the way it propels perception. Even in our perception of such works, however, there is no more than a sense of the "saddle-back present"—as William James called it—of riding the present with a piece of the past and a piece of the future. There is no long stretch into the past and future as in the perception of most music. And, furthermore, the persistent presence of the whole of such abstractions inhibits any feeling of process from becoming compulsive. Malevich's chilly "Supremacist Composition: White on White" (Figure 4-5)

FIGURE 4-4   Jackson Pollock, "Autumn Rhythm." Oil on canvas, 105 by 207 inches. The Metropolitan Museum of Art, Gerald A. Hearn Fund, 1957.

FIGURE 4-5   Kasimir Malevich, "Supremacist Composition: White on White." 1918. Oil on canvas, 31¼ by 31¼ inches. Collection, The Museum of Modern Art, New York.

illustrates the opposite extreme. The dimensions are so small, the parts and regions so simply and sharply profiled, and the regions so economically interrelated that there tends to be simply one rather than a series of time-less moments. The shades of white sit so quietly and subtly side by side that "Supremacist Composition," like many of the abstractions of Mondrian, is viewed within such a chaste and unified field of vision that it appears to have no parts or regions. And no matter how long we participate with this painting, it seems as if a single glance has sufficed. The vast majority of abstractions fall between these extremes of restlessness and stillness—for example, Rothko's "Earth Greens" (Figure 4-2)—and at the present time there seems to be no prevailing tendency toward either extreme.

INTENSITY AND RESTFULNESS

Abstract painting presents sensa in their primitive but powerful state of innocence. Thus the persistent presence of abstract painting arouses our senses from their sleep by attracting our vision so that it holds clearly and distinctly on the bits and pieces and structures of sensa that get lost in theoretical and technical work and get blurred in the crowded confusion of everyday experience. In turn, this intensity of vision renews the spontaneity of our perception and enhances the tone of our physical existence. We clothe our visual sensations in positive feelings, living in these sensations instead of using them as means to ends. And such sensuous activity—sight, for once, minus anxiety and eyestrain—is sheer delight. Abstract painting offers us a complete rest from practical concerns. Abstract painting is, as Matisse in 1908 was beginning to see,

> an art of balance, of purity and serenity devoid of troubling or depressing subject matter, an art which might be for every mental worker, be he business-man or writer, like an appeasing influence, like a mental soother, something like a good armchair in which to rest from physical fatigue.[2]

Or as Hilla Rebay remarks:

> The contemplation of a Non-objective picture offers a complete rest to the mind. It is particularly beneficial to business men, as it carries them away from the tiresome rush of earth, and strengthens their nerves, once they are familiar with this real art. If they lift their eyes to these pictures in a tired moment, their attention will be absorbed in a joyful way, thus resting their minds from earthly troubles and thoughts.[3]

[2] *La grande revue*, Dec. 25, 1908.
[3] Hilla Rebay, "Value of Non-Objectivity," *Third Enlarged Catalogue of the Solomon R. Guggenheim Collection of Non-Objective Paintings*, Solomon R. Guggenheim Collection, New York, 1938, p. 7.

Abstract painting frees us from the grip of the past and future by holding us in relatively isolated durations of "here-nows." The intrinsic values of the sensuous entrance our sight because the "all-at-onceness" of an abstraction and the absence of references to definite objects and events entice us to be one with the sensa. There is a stillness about those areas of red, green, and blue in Rothko's "Earth Greens" (Figure 4–2) that is about as unchanging as anything in this world can be. The only reference of the red, green, and blue are to the reds, greens, and blues of the external world in general. The designations are not, as in representational painting, to the sensuous as situated in definite objects and events. Thus specific place and time are irrelevant. Furthermore, even the connections of the regions of sensa to one another within an abstraction have a static character. Thus the duration of the experience of the red in the Rothko may terminate with the awareness of the red as a stimulus that refers to the green. The duration of the experience of the green, in turn, may terminate with the awareness of green as a stimulus that refers to the blue. The next duration may include the blue and green locked together as crossing vectors in a plane which, in turn, may refer to the red. These reversing and interlocking references of regions further freeze our sense of temporality. Goethe described architecture as frozen music, but abstract painting is a much better example of the metaphor. Abstract painting frees us from explicit awareness of past and future. Once we focus in on the present for its own sake, there results an intensity and exhilaration of experience that is unique.

When we participate with an abstraction, we suspend the habits of ordinary experience. The very framing of an abstraction sets it apart from the tyranny of time and space and the fury of functions. The habit of using sensa as signs to objects and events is abolished. Michel Seuphor claims:

> Every man awaits the revelation. It takes place today through abstract art in particular, in the clearest and simplest language that was ever found. . . . I believe that religious sentiment, in all religions, resides first of all in an immobilization before life, a prolonged attention, a questioning and expectant attitude that suspends all corporeal activity and that is a prelude to an activity of a quite different nature that we call inner life, spiritual life. Now art—and abstract art above all—is the expression of the attentive life, of the free life of the spirit, of this contemplation.[4]

Abstract painting holds sensa still without impoverishing them. Thus abstractions rest our restless eyes. Abstractions anchor us from transit sickness. If anything is likely to calm our nervous souls, it is an abstraction. Then, as we stand in front of Ad Reinhardt's "Abstract Painting" in The Museum of Modern Art, the guard rails disappear. We forget where we are. Instead of staring from a standpoint at a vast black glob of alien meaning-

[4] Michel Seuphor, *The Spiritual Mission of Art*, Galerie Chalette, New York, 1960, p. 26.

lessness that in saying nothing seems to be conspiring against us, the painting comes to us and we begin to see with insight nine very subtly related squares of luminous blacks. We become what we behold. Our awareness becomes black. And in the inner intimacy of that participative experience there is a silence that rings, as in the darkness of the night. "Give her a silence, that the soul may softly turn home into the flooding and the fullness in which she lived" (Rilke).

TIMELESSNESS

Abstract painters seize sensa with tender care. They take the most transient aspects of reality and make them stand still in their paintings. They purge from our sight the films of familiarity that confuse sensa, let them be as they are, just as the pop artist clears away the covers of mundane objects disguised by repetition. In the structure of an abstraction, sensa take on a powerful and pervasive static quality, timeless within time. The transience of the sensuous gives way to a steadily standing "now" that suggests everlastingness. No other art is as unchangeable—the light changes on the cathedral and the sculpture, music and the dance are always rendered differently, representational painting or literature or drama or the film acquire new connotations more rapidly because they refer to definite objects and events. An abstraction "is." No other thing in art or nature, unless it be the geological patterns in certain rocks, matches its unchangeability. Nothing is as likely to save us from the slavery of functions as abstractions.

PERCEPTION KEY "EARTH GREENS"

Rothko's "Earth Greens" (Figure 4-2) is, we think, an exceptional example of timelessness. Analyze why this is or is not so. Then compare our analysis which follows.

The underlying blue rectangle of "Earth Greens" is cool and recessive with a pronounced vertical emphasis (91 inches by 74 inches), accented by the way the bands of blue gradually expand upward. However, the green and rusty-red rectangles, smaller but much more prominent because they "stretch over" most of the blue, have a horizontal "lying down" emphasis that quiets the upward thrust. The vertical and the horizontal—the simplest, most universal, and potentially the most tightly "relatable" of all axes, but which in everyday experience usually are cut by diagonals and oblique curves or are strewn about chaotically—are brought together in perfect peace. This fulfilling harmony is enhanced by the way the lines, with one exception, of all these rectangles are soft and slightly irregular, avoiding the stiffness of straight lines that isolate. Only the outside boundary line of the blue rectangle is strictly straight, and this serves to separate the three rectangles from the outside world. Within the firm frontal symmetry of this painting's world, the green rectangle is the most secure and weighty. This rectangle comes the closest to the stability of a square; the upper part occupies the actual center of the picture which, along with the lower blue border, provides an anchorage; and the location of the rectangle in the lower section of the painting suggests weight because in our world heavy objects seek and possess low places. But even more importantly, this green, like so many earth colors, is a peculiarly quiet and immobile color. Wassily Kandinsky, one of the best abstract painters, finds green generally an "earthly, self-satisfied repose." It is "the most restful color in existence, moves in no direction, has no corresponding appeal, such as joy, sorrow, or passion, demands nothing." Rothko's green, furthermore, has the texture of earth thickening its appearance. Although in the green there are slight variations in hue, brightness, and saturation, their movement is congealed in a stable pattern. The green rectangle does not look as though it wanted to move to a more suitable place.

The rusty red rectangle, on the other hand, is much less secure and weighty. Whereas the blue rectangle recedes and the green rectangle stays put, the rusty red rectangle moves toward us, locking the green in depth between itself and the blue. Similarly, whereas the blue is cold and the rusty red warm, the "temperature" of the green mediates between them. Unlike the blue and green rectangles, the rusty red seems light and floating, radiating vital energy. Not only is the rusty red rectangle the smallest but its winding, swelling shadows and the dynamism of its blurred, obliquely oriented brushstrokes produce an impression of self-contained movement that sustains this lovely shape like a cloud above the green below. This effect is enhanced by the blue, which serves as a kind of firmament for this sensuous world; for blue is the closest to darkness, and this blue, especially the middle band, seems lit up as if by starlight. Yet despite its amorphous inner activity, the rusty red rectangle keeps its place, also serenely harmonizing with its neighbors. Delicately, a pervasive violet tinge touches everything. And everything seems locked together forever, an image of eternity.

REPRESENTATIONAL PAINTING

In the participative experience with representational paintings, the sense of "here-now," so overwhelming in the participative experience with abstractions, is somewhat weakened. Representational paintings situate the sensuous in specific objects and events. These references—unless we arbitrarily ignore them, as the proponents of significant form such as Clive Bell propose—make place and time relevant associations. A representational painting, just like an abstraction, is "all there" and "holds still." But past and future are more relevant than in our experience of abstractions because we are seeing representations of definite objects and events. Inevitably we are aware of place and date, and, in turn, a sense of past and future is a part of that awareness. Our experience is a little more ordinary than it is when we feel the extraordinary isolation from specific objects and events that occurs in the perception of abstractions. Representational paintings always bring in some suggestion of "once upon a time." Hence we are not held quite so tightly as with abstractions in the immediacy of the present. We are kept a little closer to the experience of everyday, moreover, because images that refer to specific objects and events usually lack something of the strangeness of images that refer only to sensa. Consequently representational paintings, other things being equal, are not quite so seductive as abstractions in charming us beyond our everyday habits.

Representational paintings, nevertheless, entice. Like abstractions, representational paintings have a framed "all-at-onceness." A scene or action that—in ordinary experience—would become lost in another scene or action is isolated. Moreover, the sensa of a representational painting, as of an abstraction, have an inner luminosity that lures our vision, while the form holds everything still for our leisurely contemplation. Thus the references to definite places and times are fused with the sensa. Only abstractions seduce us more securely into durations dominated by the "here-now."

Representational painting furnishes the world of abstractions with definite objects and events. The horizon is sketched out more closely and clearly and the spaces of the sensuous are filled, more or less, with things. But even when these furnishings (subject matter) are the same, the interpretation (content) of every painting is always different. This point is clarified any time paintings of basically the same subject matter are compared, as, for example, the Madonna holding her Child, a subject matter that fascinated Florentine painters from the twelfth through the sixteenth centuries.

COMPARISONS OF PAINTINGS WITH SIMILAR SUBJECT MATTER

Compare two great Florentine works that helped lead the way into the Italian Renaissance: a "Madonna and Child" (Figure 4-6) by Cimabue, completed around 1285, and a "Madonna Enthroned" (Figure 4-7) by Giotto, completed around 1306.

Cimabue and Giotto

PERCEPTION KEY CIMABUE AND GIOTTO

These paintings have basically the same subject matter, as their titles indicate. Yet their forms inform about their subject matter very differently. Describe

FIGURE 4-6   Cimabue, "Madonna and Child Enthroned with Angels." c. 1285–1290. Panel painting, 151¾ by 78⅞ inches. Uffizi, Florence. Alinari.

FIGURE 4-7　Giotto, "Madonna Enthroned." c. 1310. Panel painting, 128¾₁₆ by 80⅜ inches. Uffizi, Florence. Alinari.

the differences between the forms and contents of these two pictures. Be as specific and detailed as possible. Then compare our attempt at the same analysis. Do not, of course, take our analysis as definitive. There simply is no such thing as a criticism that cannot be improved.

The figures in Cimabue's panel at first sight seem utterly lacking in human liveliness. The fine hands of the Madonna, for example, are extremely stylized. Moreover, the geometricized facial features of the Madonna, very similar to those of the angels, and the stiff, unnaturally regular features of the Child seem almost as unnatural as masks. But Cimabue's "Madonna and Child" begins to grow and glow in liveliness when Cimabue's panel is juxtaposed with contemporary paintings, such as the Magdalen Master's "Madonna Enthroned" (Figure 4-8), c. 1270, and only in the context of its tradition can a work of art be fully understood and in turn fully appreciated. Thus historical criticism—which attempts to illuminate the tradition of works of art—provides the often indispensable background information for descriptive, interpretive, and evaluative criticism.

Magdalen Master

Everything in this slightly earlier work by the Magdalen Master is subordinated to the portrayal of theoretical, practical, and sociological expressions of the medieval Catholic conception of the sacred. For example, the Child is portrayed as divine (mainly a theoretical expression), as the mediator between us and God (mainly a practical expression), and as a king or prince (mainly a sociological expression). Everything secular in the picture is interpreted as completely dependent on the sacred as its source of existence. Conventional Christian symbols, such as halos, crowns, and the blessing gesture of the Child, dominate everything. The sacred, moreover, comes very close to being represented as totally separate from the secular, for the Madonna and Child are barely incarnated in this world. It is impossible, of course, to interpret the sacred "absolutely," as totally "ab-solved" from our world, for this would negate the possibility of any portrayal of the sacred whatsoever. But the Magdalen Master's panel is typical of the way the artists of the thirteenth and the immediately preceding centuries came as close as possible to representing the sacred absolutely. Thus, the Madonna and Child are bilaterally immobile, symmetrically and compactly enclosed, and their fantastic sizes relative to the bitlike donor at the bottom left of the throne resist references to the sacred as incarnate in this world. The Madonna and Child are interpreted more as emblems rather than as living embodiments of the divine. "Love not the world, neither the things that are in the world. . . . For all that is in the world . . . passeth away" (John 2:15–17). And so the human qualities of the Madonna and Child are barely recognizable. Note, for example, how the fish-shaped, long-

FIGURE 4-8 Magdalen Master, "Madonna Enthroned." c. 1270. Panel painting, 36⅝ by 53¾ inches. Musée des Arts Decoratifs. Alinari.

tailed eyes of the Madonna cannot blink, and how the popping pupils stare out and slightly up in a Sphinxlike glance that seems fixed forever. Her features are written large and seem added to rather than molded with the head. Only in the careful tender way she holds the Child is there any hint of human sorrow and affection. The spirits of this Madonna and Child belong to a supernatural world; and their bodies are hardly bodies at all but, in the words of St. Thomas Aquinas, "corporeal metaphors of spiritual things." The secular is mainly appearance, a secondary reality. The sacred is the primary reality.

Nevertheless the secular, even if it is interpreted as appearance, appears very powerfully indeed, for this panel is a very fine work of art. The sensa shine forth, especially the glimmering gold, the crystal cabochons set in the crowns of the Madonna and Child, and the rhythmic, sharply edged lines. We are lured by the sensa and their designs beyond mere illustrations of doctrine by images. We are caught up in durations of the "here-now." But, unlike our experience of abstractions, these durations include, because of the conventional symbols, doctrinal interpretations of the sacred. And if we participate, we "understand"—even if we disagree—rather than having mere "knowledge of" these doctrines. The expressions of ultimate concern, reverence, and peace in the saints and donor provide a context in which the intent of the Christian conventional symbols are unlikely to be mistaken by the sensitive recipient, even if he does not know the conventions of the symbols.

Cimabue

When Cimabue's panel is compared with the Magdalen Master's, we can readily see that something of the rigid separation between the sacred and the secular has been relaxed. Cimabue was one of the first to portray, however haltingly, the change in Florentine society toward a more secular orientation. Florence in the twelfth and thirteenth centuries was making great strides in bending nature, for the first time since the Roman Empire, to man's needs. A resurgence in confidence in the powers of man began to clash with the medieval view that man was nothing without God, that nature was valuable only as a stepping-stone to heaven, that—as St. Peter Damiani in the first half of the eleventh century asserted—"The world is so filthy with vices that any holy mind is befouled by even thinking of it." The emerging view was not yet "man is the measure of all things," but the honor of being a man began to be taken seriously, an idea that "was to traverse all later Italian art like the muffled, persistent sound of a subterranean river" (Malraux).

Cimabue had assimilated from the Byzantine tradition its conventions, hierography, technical perfection, and richness of detail. He enriched that inheritance, and in turn helped break ground for the Renaissance, by endowing the old style with more liveliness and mixing the divine into the human, as in this panel, which reveals human emotions in the Madonna. The inert passivity of the Byzantine and the hard dogmatic grimness of the Tuscan style, both so evident in the Magdalen Master's work, are revitalized with a spiritual subtlety and psychic awareness, a warmth and tenderness, that make unforgettable the Madonna's benevolently inclined face, to which one returns with unwearying delight. With this face begins the scaling down of the divine into this world. The anthropocentric view—man at the center of things—is beginning to focus. A human face has awakened! And it leans forward to come more closely into spiritual contact with us. Its liveliness fell like a refreshing shower on a parched and long-neglected soil, and from that soil a new world began to rise.

Brown-gold tones play softly across the Madonna's features, merging them organically despite the incisive lines, setting the background for the sweeping eyebrows and large, deep eye sockets that form a stage on which the pathetic eyes play their drama of tragic foreknowledge. These eyes seem to pulsate with the beat of the soul because they are more flexible than the eyes in contemporary paintings—the irises rest comfortably and dreamily within their whites; the delicately curved lids, now shortened, detach themselves gracefully to meet neatly at the inner pockets; and the doubling line of the lower lid is replaced by fragile shadows that flow into the cheeks and nose. Although the Greek or bridgeless nose is still high and marked, furthermore, by a conspicuous triangle, the sensitive modeling of the nose, its dainty shape, and the tucking in of the pinched tip help blend it into the general perspective of the face. Light shadows fall under the shapely chin to the slender neck and around the cheeks to merge indistinctly with the surrounding veil, whose heavy shadows add to the contemplative atmosphere. But the full lips, depressed at the corners and tightly drawn far to the left, add a contrasting touch of intensity, even grimness, to what otherwise would be pure poignancy. The immense, exquisitely decorated throne, with the bristling and curiously vehement prophets below, enhances by its contrasting monumentality the feminine gentleness of the Madonna. Her large size relative to the angels and prophets is minimized by her robe, which, with its close-meshed lines of gold feathering over the cascading folds, is one of the loveliest in western art. In a skillfully worked counterpoint, the angel heads and the rainbow-colored wings form an angular rhythm that tenses towards and then quietly pauses at the Madonna's face. This pause is sustained by the simple dotted edge of the centered halo and by the shape of the pedimental top of the rectangular frame. The facial features of the angels resemble the Madonna's, especially the almond-shaped eyes, separated by the stencillike triangles, and the heavy mouths squared at the corners. Nevertheless they lack the refined qualities and liveliness that betray so feelingly the soulful sadness of the Madonna. Now in the city of Florence

> . . . Mercy has a human heart,
> Pity a human face,
> And Love, the human form divine,
> And Peace, the human dress.
> William Blake

But into this peaceful hush that spreads around her sound with anguished apprehension the tragic tones of the Pietà, like the melody of a requiem continued by our imaginations into the pregnant pause.

In Cimabue's panel, unlike the Magdalen Master's, there is no longer the sure suggestion of the sacred as almost completely separate from the secular. The sacred and the secular are only narrowly joined, but the juncture seems much more secure. The sacred is portrayed as clearly immanent in at least some things of our world—the Madonna, Child, and saints having some earthly aspects—but the emphasis, of course, is upon the transcendency of the sacred. There is not the slightest hint of the secular taking precedence over the sacred.

Cimabue and Giotto

Cimabue, according to the legend reported by Ghiberti and embellished by Vasari,

> going one day on some business of his own from Florence to Vespignano, found Giotto, while his sheep were browsing, portraying a sheep from nature on a flat and polished slab, with a stone slightly pointed, without having learnt any method of doing this from others, but only from nature; whence Cimabue, standing fast all in a marvel, asked him if he wished to go live with him. The child answered that, his father consenting, he would go willingly. Cimabue then asking this from Bondone, the latter lovingly granted it to him, and was content that he should take the boy with him to Florence; whither having come, in a short time, assisted by nature and taught by Cimabue, the child not only equalled the manner of his master, but became so good an imitator of nature that he banished completely that rude Greek manner and revived the modern and good art of painting, introducing the portraying well from nature of living people.[5]

Giotto's "Madonna Enthroned" and Cimabue's "Madonna and Child," both originally placed in churches, now hang side by side in the first room of the Uffizi Gallery in Florence. The contrast between the panels is striking. Cimabue's Madonna, who seems to float into our world, is abruptly brought to earth by Giotto; or, as Ruskin puts it, now we have Mama. She sits solidly, bell-shaped, without evasion, in three-dimensional space subject to gravitational forces, her frank, focused gaze alerted to her surroundings; whereas Cimabue's Madonna, oblivious of space, is steeped in moodiness. The forms of Giotto's Madonna seem to have been abstracted, however radically, from nature, whereas Cimabue seems to have started from Byzantine forms. In subject matter Giotto seems to have begun more from "here," whereas Cimabue seems to have begun more from "hereafter."

The eyes of Giotto's Madonna, surrounded by her high forehead and the immense cheeks, have a fascinating asymmetry that gives her face a

[5] Giorgio Vasari, *Lives of the Most Eminent Painters*, Gaston Duc Devere (trans.), Macmillan, London, 1912, vol. 1, p. 72.

mark of idiosyncrasy and adds to its liveliness. The fish-shaped left eye with its half-covered pupil is twisted to the left, so that it appears to be looking in a different direction than the more realistic right eye. Yet since this is not quite obvious, the resulting tension fixes our attention and heightens our feeling of being caught in her level gaze, which gains further intensity by being the focus of the gazes of the saints and angels. Since the open space below the Madonna provides us with a figurative path of access, we are directly engaged with her in a way that Cimabue carefully avoids by, among other devices, putting the throne of his Madonna on a high-arched platform and then placing the little prophets within the arches. The smallness of the sensual mouth of Giotto's Madonna, barely wider than the breadth of her long and snouty nose, accentuates its expressiveness. Also, for the first time, the lips of a Madonna open—however slightly, shyly revealing two teeth—as if she were about to gasp or speak. It does not matter, for the mobility of inner responsiveness is conveyed. Everything else expresses her stoicism, a rocklike kind of endurance—the untooled, centered halo, the steady gaze, the calm, impersonal expression, the cool and silvery skin color with green underpainting that suggests bone structures beneath, the heavy jaw and towerlike neck, the long unbroken verticals and broad sweeping curves of the simply colored robe and tunic, the firm hand that no longer points but holds, and above all her upright monumental massiveness, as solid as if hewn in granite. The saints and angels are compactly arranged in depth and stand on the same ground as the earthly throne. Although the saints express peace and the angels awe, they are natural beings, not imaginary supporters of a heavenly throne as in Cimabue's picture.

The Child shares with his mother the monumentality of Giotto's style —the square, forthright head, the powerful body, the physical density and solidity that make Giotto's figures so statuesque. Giotto's Child, compared with Cimabue's, seems almost coarse, especially in the shaping of the hands and feet, and the incorrect indication of his position from a naturalistic standpoint is physically much more uncomfortable, primarily because such a standpoint is almost irrelevant in Cimabue's picture. The hair and ears are not so stylized as in Cimabue's Child, light and shadow sink more organically into the flesh, the eyes and nose are given the most realistic rendition since Roman times, and the expression is dynamically alert. Yet the lack of irregularity and flexibility in these less conventional features, combined with the effect of maturity in miniature, keep the Child from being an ordinary baby. The content of Giotto's painting is clearly Christian, but not quite so obviously as in the paintings of the Magdalen Master and Cimabue. The portrayal of religious feeling is not quite so strong, and for the first time in Florence there is the suggestion, however muted, of the secular challenging the sacred. If Mama gets much more earthly and independent, then the sacred no longer will be so obviously in control.

Giotto and Parmigianino

Compare now Giotto's painting with "The Madonna with the Long Neck" (Figure 4-9 and Color Plate 7), painted by Francesco Parmigianino in the waning years of the Italian Renaissance, c. 1535.

PERCEPTION KEY GIOTTO AND PARMIGIANINO

1. "The Madonna with the Long Neck" was never quite finished, and so far as we know Parmigianino did not provide a title. Vasari, later in the sixteenth century, baptized it "The Virgin and Sleeping Child." Do you believe Parmigianino would have accepted this naming as appropriate? What about the appropriateness of its present title—"The Madonna with the Long Neck"?

2. How does the content of this picture differ from Giotto's?

3. How does Parmigianino's form accomplish a different interpretation of what apparently is the same subject matter?

4. Jacob Burckhardt, a very knowledgeable and famous critic and historian of the nineteenth century, complained of this work's "unsupportable affectation," and, somewhat more tolerantly, of "the bringing of the manners of the great world divertingly into the holy scenes." Generally, until very recent times, this work has been an object of derision. Do you agree with these negative judgments? Explain.

Although natural structures in Parmigianino's painting are suggested, they are not interpreted as natural. The light is neither quite indoors nor outdoors, the perspectives are inconsistent, gravity is defied, the bodies are artificially proportioned and drained of mass and physical power, the protagonists are psychologically detached from one another, and above all the poreless, porcelain facial features allow no hint of liveliness. Thus the head of the Madonna is shaped like a well-wrought urn, while the ears, set out abnormally in order to emphasize their serpentine calligraphy, look like its handles. The nerveless skin is unnaturally cold and pale, glazed like ceramic, and beneath that polished surface the urn seems hollow. Hence the pure geometrical design of the fastidious lines of the eyebrows, eyes, nose, and mouth are assembled on a surface without organic foundation— no pulsating blood coursing through arteries and veins integrates these features and no muscular structure can move them. And so the gaze down upon the Child—the most lifeless Child of the Renaissance—is too stylized and superficial to be expressive of any psychic meaning, let alone sacramental intensity. Like an Attic amphora, the head of the Madonna rises from its swanlike neck, while the hair decorates the lid with the preciosity of fine goldwork. The features of the angels are similarly constructed, ex-

FIGURE 4-9 Parmigianino, "The Madonna with the Long Neck." c. 1535. Panel painting, 84⅜ by 52⅜ inches. Uffizi, Florence. (*See also Color Plate 7.*)

changeable like coins. They are made even more masklike by the repetition, a device that almost always increases rigidity.

If the subject matter of "The Madonna with the Long Neck" is a sacred scene, then Burckhardt's denunciation of "unsupportable affectation" is certainly justified. If, however, the Christian symbols are no more than a support or an excuse for an interpretation of line, color, and volume, then Burckhardt's denunciation is irrelevant. To meet this painting halfway—and surely this is the responsibility of every serious viewer—the religious symbols can be dismissed, and then the subject matter can be experienced as secular. The design of this delicate work, this "splendor of form shining on the proportionate parts of matter," ought to bring one to a better understanding and appreciation of the rhythmic qualities of line, the sinuous sensuousness of spiraling shapes, the fluidity of bulkless volumes, and the cooling, calming powers of certain surfaces and colors. But this heretical design, despite its lifting flow, will never waft you to a Christian heaven on the wings of faith.

"The Madonna with the Long Neck" is such a magnificently secular work of art that the excommunication of the Christian symbols is rather easily accomplished, at least in our day. That is why the present title seems more appropriate to most of us than Vasari's title. Abstract painting has opened our eyes to the intrinsic values of sensa, and a strong case can be made that "The Madonna with the Long Neck" is a kind of abstract painting. An even more appropriate title today, perhaps, might be "Sinuous Spiraling of Sensuous Volumes."

Bronzino

PERCEPTION KEY "CHRIST IN LIMBO"

In 1552, a few years after Parmigianino's work, Angelo Bronzino completed "Christ in Limbo" (Figure 4-10). This work also possesses Christian symbols.

1. Is the content of this work religious, as in the case of the works of the Magdalen Master, Cimabue, and Giotto?
2. Is this work a kind of abstract painting, as is the case, perhaps, of "The Madonna with the Long Neck"?

The quality of Bronzino's painting is so much poorer, we think, that the use of Christian symbols is a parody rather than an excuse. Christ advances with an affected dancing step, his curled and perfumed face almost indistinguishable from the man in profile immediately to the right and the man whose figure is cut by the frame. The aphrodisiac figure of Mary,

FIGURE 4-10 A. Bronzino, "Christ in Limbo." 1552. Panel painting, 174⅜ by 114½ inches. Museum of Santa Croce, Florence. Alinari.

posing between these two men, would better grace a poster of a Pigalle nightclub. All the bodies are overmuscular but unexercised and listless, a cold, contorted, claustrophobic display of striptease sensuality. Despite the inclusion of Christian symbols, it is difficult to discover a work of art that is so clearly nonreligious. And whereas in Parmigianino's painting the sensa shine forth and are revealed, in Bronzino's painting the sensa are as dull as in a typical advertising poster.

A work such as "The Madonna with the Long Neck" makes plain that the subject matter of a painting is not always easily ascertained, and in answering such questions historical information can be of great help. Nevertheless, historical information is not necessarily decisive. Thus there can be little doubt that in Parmigianino's time its subject matter was understood as Christian—the work, for example, was commissioned for a church by the clergy. Yet today the subject matter is likely to be understood, and properly so we believe, as the sensuous. The decisive test is what we perceive as the content.

DETERMINING THE SUBJECT MATTER

Consider a contemporary example by Arshile Gorky (Figure 4-11).

PERCEPTION KEY   A PAINTING BY ARSHILE GORKY

1. Is this painting abstract or representational? Take plenty of time before you decide, but disregard the title.
2. The title is "Waterfall." Do you see a waterfall when you ignore the title? Do you see a waterfall when you take the title into consideration?
3. If you do, in fact, see a waterfall when taking notice of the title, does this make the painting representational?

The last question of the perception key is tricky. We suggest the following principle as a basis for answering such questions. If a work only "shows" (presents) but does not interpret (reveal) the objects and events that the title indicates, this is not enough to make it representational. These objects and events must be interpreted if the work is to be usefully classified as representational. "The Madonna with the Long Neck" shows a Madonna and Child, but they are not interpreted as a Madonna and Child. Thus to call this work representational is misleading, because the Madonna and Child are not part of the content. Our view is that the waterfall in Gorky's painting is interpreted, that our perception of the bounce and rhythm of colors of waterfalls is intensified by Gorky's work. If this judgment is correct, then the work is representational. On the other hand, your view may be that recognition of a waterfall in the painting only helps intensify your perception of sensa—the bounce and rhythm of colors. If this judgment is correct, then the work is abstract.

Study Jean Arp's "Mountain, Table, Anchors, Navel" (Figure 4-12).

FIGURE 4-11 Arshile Gorky,
"Waterfall." c. 1943. Oil on
canvas, 60½ by 44½ inches.
The Tate Gallery, London.

PERCEPTION KEY "MOUNTAIN, TABLE, ANCHORS, NAVEL"

1. What is the subject matter of this work?
2. Does Arp succeed in revealing mountains, tables, anchors, and navels so that you have a heightened awareness of such objects?

If your answer to question 2 in the perception key is negative, then you should deny that the objects listed in the title are the subject matter of this painting.

It is true, of course, that the references of the title are supported by the painting, for we can see a mountain, etc., in the painting once we have noted the title. But these references are misleading, if taken as anything more than identification tags, because the recognition of the objects designated is of

FIGURE 4-12 Jean Arp, "Mountain, Table, Anchors, Navel." 1925. Oil on cardboard with cutouts, 29⅝ by 33½ inches. Collection, The Museum of Modern Art, New York.

little significant importance in our perception. "Colors and Positions"—for they seem to us to be the subject matter of Arp's painting—perhaps would be a much more appropriate title.

Sometimes, as we have seen with Gorky's "Waterfall," it is extremely difficult to distinguish between abstract and representational painting. Whether the recognition of definite objects and events in a painting intensifies perception may differ with the differences in temperament and background of the recipients. Nevertheless, the distinction between abstract and representational painting is very useful because it points up this important fact: whereas in abstract painting definite objects and events are not designated as part of the content, in representational paintings they are. And by being clear about this, we can better focus upon what is most important in any particular painting.

RECENT PAINTING

Painting, whether abstract or representational, sets forth the visually perceptible in such a way that it works in our experience with heightened intensity. Every style of painting finds facets of the visually perceptible that had previously been missed. The painting of the last hundred years has, for example, given us Impressionism, a style that reveals the play of sunlight on color, as in the work of Renoir (Figure 2-19); Post-Impressionism, using the surface techniques of Impressionism but drawing out the solidity of things, as in Cézanne (Figure 4-1); Expressionism, scenes portraying strong emotion, as in Munch; Cubism, showing the permanent properties of things and their three-dimensional qualities in closed space—without perspective or cast light—through a geometrical crystallization, as in Picasso; Dada, poking fun at the absurdity of everything including painting, as in Duchamp; Surrealism, the expression of the subconscious, as in Dali; Futurism, the portrayal of sensa and things in motion, as in Severini; Suprematism or Constructivism, the portrayal of sensa in sharp geometrical patterns, as in Mondrian and Malevich (Figures 1-4 and 1-5); Abstract Expressionism, the portrayal of sensa in movement with—as in Expressionism—the expression of powerful emotion or energy, as in Pollock (Figure 4-4); Pop Art, the revelation of mass-produced products, as in Dine and Lichtenstein (Figures 2-1 and 2-7); Op Art, the glittering show of sensa in motion or in different aspects as the participator changes his perspective, as in Larry Poons; etc. And today and tomorrow new dimensions are and will be portrayed. Never in the history of painting has there been such rapid change and vitality. Never in history has there been so much help available for those of us who, in varying degrees, are blind to the fullness of the visually perceptible. If we take advantage of this help, the rewards will be priceless:

> For don't you mark, we're made so that we love
> First when we see them painted, things we have passed
> Perhaps a hundred times nor cared to see.
> Robert Browning, "Fra Lippo Lippi"

5 SCULPTURE

SCULPTURE AND TOUCH

Painting and sculpture, along with architecture, are sometimes but not very usefully classified as visual arts. Such classification suggests that the eye is the chief sense organ involved in our participation with sculpture, as it is with painting. Yet observe participants at an exhibition of both paintings and sculptures. Usually at least a few will touch—despite the "Do Not Touch" signs—some of the sculptures, whereas the paintings usually are left alone. Some kinds of sculpture invite us to explore and caress them with our hands, and even, if they are not too large or heavy, to pick them up. Marcel Duchamp noticed this and experimented with a kind of sculpture not to be seen but only to be touched. Within a box with an opening at the top large enough to allow passage of the hand, he placed forms with varying shapes and textures. And Brancusi created a "Sculpture for the Blind."

PERCEPTION KEY EXPERIMENT WITH TOUCH

Using scissors or some similar tool, cut out four approximately 6-inch cardboard squares. Shape them with curves or angles into abstract patterns (structures that do not represent actual things), and put one into a bag. Ask a friend to feel that sample in the bag without looking at the sample. Then ask him or her to (1) draw with pencil on paper the pattern felt. Then ask your friend to (2) model the pattern in putty. Continue the same procedure with the other three samples. Have your friend make four samples for you, and follow the same procedures yourself. Analyze both your results. Were the drawings or the modelings more closely imitative of the samples? What is the significance, if any, of this experiment?

SCULPTURE AND DENSITY

Somehow, it seems, sculpture engages our senses differently from painting. And somehow this seems to have something to do with the fact that sculpture occupies space as a three-dimensional mass, whereas painting is essentially a two-dimensional surface that can only represent ("re-present") three dimensionality. Painting, of course, can *suggest* density—for example, "Mont Saint Victoire" (Figure 4-1 and Color Plate 4)—but sculpture *is* dense. Henry Moore, one of the best of contemporary sculptors, states that the sculptor "gets the solid shape, as it were, inside his head—he thinks of it, whatever its size, as if he were holding it completely enclosed in the hollow of his hand. He mentally visualizes a complex form *from all round itself*; he knows while he looks at one side what the other side is like; he identifies himself with its center of gravity, its mass, its weight; he realizes its volume, as the space that the shape displaces in the air."[1] Apparently we can only fully apprehend sculpture by senses that are alive not only to visual and tactile (touchable) surfaces but also to the weight and volume lying behind those surfaces.

SENSORY INTERCONNECTIONS

It is surely an oversimplification to distinguish the various arts on the basis of any one sensation or sense organ; for example, to claim that painting is experienced solely by sight and sculpture solely by touch. Our nervous systems are far more complicated than that. Generally no clear separation is made in experience between the faculties of sight and touch. The sensa of touch, for instance, are normally joined with other sensa— visual, aural, and olfactory. Even if only one kind of sensum initiates a perception, a chain reaction triggers off other sensations, either by sensory motor connections or by memory associations. We are constantly grasping and handling things as well as seeing, hearing, and smelling them. And so when we see a thing, we have a pretty good idea of what its surface would

[1] Henry Moore, "Notes on Sculpture," in David Sylvester (ed.), *Sculpture and Drawings 1921–48*, 4th rev. ed., George Wittenborn, Inc., New York, 1957, pp. xxxiii f.

feel like, how it would sound if struck, and how it would smell as we approach. And if we grasp or handle a thing in the dark, we have some idea of what its shape looks like.

We see someone sitting on a bench. But do we? Only if our vision includes information gathered from other sources. "Sitting on" is not the same as "situated above." "Sitting on" is possible because of gravity, and we do not see gravity but rather sense it in our bodies. When we stand, we feel gravity bearing down. And we feel the ground as support against that force. Memories of such feelings are touched off when we see someone "situated above" the bench. And so we say "sitting on." As we approach a stone wall, we see various shapes. And these shapes recall certain information. We know something about how the surface of those stones would feel and that it would hurt if we walked into them. We do not know about the surface, volume, and mass of these stones by sight alone but by sight associated with manual experience. Both painting and sculpture involve especially sight and touch. But touch apparently is much more involved in our participation with sculpture. If we can clarify such differences as these, our understanding of sculpture will be deeper and, in turn, our participation more rewarding.

SCULPTURE AND PAINTING COMPARED

Compare Rothko's "Earth Greens" (Figure 4-2 and Color Plate 5) with Arp's "Growth" (Frontispiece).

PERCEPTION KEY   "EARTH GREENS" AND "GROWTH"

1.   Would you like to touch either of these works?
2.   Would you expect either the Rothko or the Arp to feel hot or cold to your touch?
3.   Which work seems to require the more careful placement of lighting?
4.   Is space perceived differently in and around these two works? How?
5.   Which of the two works appears to be the more unchangeable in your perception?
6.   Which of the two works is more abstract?

Both works are abstract, we suggest, for neither has as its primary subject matter specific objects or events (see above, pages 84ff.). Arp's sculpture has something to do with growth, of course, as confirmed by the title. But is it human, animal, or vegetative growth? Male or female? Clear-cut answers do not seem possible. Specificity of reference, just as in the Rothko, is missing. And yet, if you agree that the subject matter of the

Rothko is sensa, would you say the same for the Arp? To affirm this may bother you, for Arp's marble is dense material. This substantiality of the marble is very much a part of its appearing as sculpture. Conversely, "Earth Greens" as painting—i.e., as a work of art rather than as a physical canvas of such and such a weight—does not appear as a material thing. The weight of the canvas is irrelevant to our participation with "Earth Greens" as a work of art. Indeed, if that weight becomes relevant, we are no longer participating with the painting. That weight becomes relevant if we are hanging "Earth Greens" on a wall, of course, but that is a procedure antecedent to our participation with it as a painting.

Rothko has abstracted sensa, especially colors, from things, whereas Arp has brought out the substantiality of a thing—the marbleness of the marble. Rothko has left behind things such as earth and grass and sky. Arp, conversely, has kept his marble as a thing relevant to his sculpture. This kind of difference, incidentally, is perhaps the underlying reason why the term "abstract painting" is used more frequently than the term "abstract sculpture." There is an awkwardness about describing something as material as most sculpture as abstract. Picasso once remarked: "There is no abstract art. You must always start with something. There is no danger then anyway because the idea of the object will have left an indelible mark." This may be an overstatement with respect to painting, but his point rings true with sculpture. Still, the distinction between abstract and representational sculpture is worth making, just as with painting, for being clear about the subject matter of a work of art is the sine qua non of all sensitive participation. It is the key to understanding the content, for the content is the subject matter interpreted by means of the form. We should remember, however, that abstract sculpture, like abstract painting, abstracts from specific objects and events. On the other hand, abstract sculpture generally does not, unlike abstract painting, abstract from the materiality of things. Arp brings out rather than abstracts from his marble.

Most sculpture, whether abstract or representational, returns us to the voluminosity (bulk), density (mass), and tactile quality of things. Thus sculpture has tactile appeal. Sculpture brings us back into touch with things by allowing the thickness of things to permeate its surface. Most sculptures make us feel them as resistant, as substantial. Thus the primary subject matter of most abstract sculpture is the density of sensa. Sculpture is more than skin deep. Abstract painting can only *represent* the density of sensa, whereas sculpture, whether abstract or representational, *presents* that density. The abstract painter generally emphasizes the surfaces of sensa, as in "Earth Greens." Thus his interest is in the vast ranges of color qualities and the play of light to bring out their nuances. The abstract sculptor, on the other hand, generally restricts himself to a minimal range of color qualities and emphasizes light not only to play on these qualities but also to bring out the inherence of these qualities in things. Whereas the abstract painter is a shepherd of surface sensa, the abstract sculptor is a shepherd of depth sensa.

Sculpture has many species, and even within the species of abstract sculpture any general statement, such as the one that concludes the previous paragraph, should be understood as subject to qualification and exception. Any art is too creative, too expansive, to lend itself to significant unexceptional generalizations. And in our time, the art of sculpture is one of the most adventurous of all. It is even difficult sometimes to know how to distinguish sculpture from painting at one extreme and architecture at the other, and this difficulty began long before our time.

SUNKEN-RELIEF SCULPTURE

Compare, for example, Figure 5-1, a detail of an Egyptian work in limestone from about 2100 B.C., with a work of Pollock (Figure 4-4). We usually think of sculpture, with its emphasis on density, as projecting out into space. Yet sometimes some of the lines and patches of paint in Pollock's works, which are generally described as paintings, are laid on so thickly that they stand out as much as a half inch or so from the flat surface of the canvas. In the Egyptian work there is no projection whatsoever. Rather, the carving cuts grooves of various depths into the surface plane of the stone to outline each object, a technique called "sunken relief." The firmness, clarity, and brilliance of these linear grooves in the Egyptian work is brought out by the way their sharp outside edges catch the light. Did this technique in this instance produce sculpture rather than painting? Only if it brings out in some significant sense the voluminosity or density or surface feel of its materials: only then will the tactile appeal be significant as well as the visual. This work, we think, has significant tactile appeal. The density of the limestone is especially evident. In other words, we are suggesting that this work is more than a linear drawing—it is a *limestone* linear drawing. Pollock's work, on the other hand, lacks significant tactile appeal despite the projection of its heavy thick oils. It is conceivable that this work could have been made in some other medium—aluminum paint or paint with more white lead, for example—and still be essentially the same work. It is inconceivable that the Egyptian relief could have been carved out of different material and still be essentially the same work. The surface as seen is what counts in Pollock's art—the materials that make that surface possible are basically irrelevant. In the Egyptian relief, the surface as seen and felt as well as the depth count. Thus the materials that make the surface possible are basically relevant. And yet, the differences between Pollock's painting and this Egyptian work are hardly clear-cut. You may with good reasons disagree.

FIGURE 5-1   King Akhen-aten and Queen Nefertiti, Egyptian sunken relief from El-Amarra.
XVIII dynasty. Photograph, The Metropolitan Museum of Art.

FIGURE 5-2 Heuler, war memorial in Würzburg. Photograph by R. Kellner.

PERCEPTION KEY CEMETERY SCULPTURE, HEULER, AND NICHOLSON

1. Visit a cemetery. Make a rough statistical estimate of the sculpture that is low relief, i.e., sculpture which projects only slightly from its background plane, as in Figure 5-12. Then estimate roughly the percentage of relief that is sunken, as in Figure 5-1. In all probability, you will find a high percentage of sunken relief. If so, what is the explanation? Does the presence or absence of first-rate sculptors doing cemetery sculpture have any relevance to the question?

2. Pick out a couple of examples of the worst sculpture in the cemetery and a couple examples of the best. Can you find in the cemetery any sculpture that approaches the artistic quality of Heuler's war memorial (Figure 5-2)? Then analyze the presuppositions or assumptions that were the basis for your judgments.

3. The title of Ben Nicholson's "Painted Relief" (Figure 5-3)—made of painted synthetic board mounted on plywood—is ambiguous. Would you classify this work as painting or sculpture? Or do you think it would be more useful to classify this kind of work as a hybrid between painting and sculpture?

FLAT-RELIEF SCULPTURE

Consider, also, Ghiberti's bronze doors of the Baptistry of Florence (Figure 5-4), completed in 1452, and called by Michelangelo "The Gates of Para-

FIGURE 5-3 Ben Nicholson, "Painted Relief." 1939. Synthetic board mounted on plywood, painted, 32⅞ by 45 inches. Collection, The Museum of Modern Art, New York. Gift of H. S. Ede and the artist.

dise." How different are the panels of these doors from representational paintings? There are some clearly noticeable projections out into space, but almost every device available to the painter of the fifteenth century for creating the *illusion* rather than the actuality of spatial depth—foreshortening, landscape vistas, perspective effects, etc.—is used. These pictorial methods when used with sculptural materials produce what is called "flat relief." The surface planes of the panels are part of the composition, and there is no clear perceptual distinction between the relief that comes out into space and the surface planes. Behind the surface planes the backgrounds are nonplanar; thus no limits to the backgrounds are perceptible, suggesting an infinity of space. The perspective of such things as the lines of trees, the retreating undulations of the ground, the receding arches, the overlapping and diminishing sizes of people, the increase in delicacy of modeling as the size of objects decreases, and even a progression from clear to hazy atmosphere all suggest an unlimited background space in which the various biblical actions take place. In other words, there are no background starting points that function as the bases for the planar organizations. Rather, the surface planes of the panels function as the basic organizing planes: hence the expression "surface" or "flat relief." Does Ghiberti's "flat relief" produce sculpture? We think so (although some critics think otherwise), because the tactile qualities of the bronze significantly stimulate our tactile senses. Some desire, admittedly not very strong, to touch as well as look at these doors is aroused.

SCULPTURE AND ARCHITECTURE COMPARED

Architecture is the art of separating inner from outer space in such a way that the inner space can be used for practical purposes. There is much more

FIGURE 5-4 Lorenzo Ghiberti, Doors of the Baptistry of Florence. 1425–1452. Bronze, 16½ feet high. Alinari.

FIGURE 5-5 Mathias Goeritz, "The Five Towers of the Satellite City." 1957. Painted concrete pylons, 121 to 187 feet high, near Mexico City. Photograph from *Matrix of Man*, 1968, by Sibyl Moholy-Nagy, Praeger Publishers. Courtesy of Hattula Moholy-Nagy Hug.

to architecture than that, of course, as we shall discuss in the next chapter. But how can sculpture be distinguished from architecture? Despite the architectural monumentality of Mathias Goeritz's "Five Towers of the Satellite City" (Figure 5-5), this is clearly sculpture because there is no inner space. But what about the Sphinx and the Pyramid at Memphis (Figure 5-6)? Like "The Five Towers of the Satellite City," both the Sphinx and the Pyramid are among the densest and most substantial of all works. They attract us visually and tactually. Since there is no space within the Spinx, it is sculpture. But within the Pyramid, space was provided for the burial of the dead. There is a separation of inner from outer space for the functional use of the inner space. Yet the use of this inner space is so limited that the living often have a very difficult time finding it. The inner space is functional only in a very restricted sense—for the dead only. Is then this Pyramid sculpture or architecture? We shall delay our answer until the next chapter. The difficulty of the question, however, points up an important factor that we should keep in mind. The distinctions between the arts that we have and will be making are necessary in order to talk about them intelligibly, but the arts resist neat pigeonholing and any attempt at that would be futile.

Compare Arp's "Growth" (Frontispiece) with Chryssa's "Times Square Sky" (Figure 5-7), with Calder's "Ghost" (Figure 5-8), and with Calder's "Three Arches" (Figure 5-9).

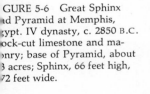

FIGURE 5-6   Great Sphinx and Pyramid at Memphis, Egypt. IV dynasty, c. 2850 B.C. Rock-cut limestone and masonry; base of Pyramid, about 13 acres; Sphinx, 66 feet high, 172 feet wide.

FIGURE 5-7 Chryssa, "Times Square Sky." 1962. Neon, aluminum, steel; 60 by 60 by 9½ inches. Collection, Walker Art Center, Minneapolis. Photograph by Eric Sutherland.

FIGURE 5-8 Alexander Calder, "Ghost." 1964. Mobile of sheet metal and metal rods, 288 by 414 inches. Philadelphia Museum of Art: purchased with the New Members' Fund.

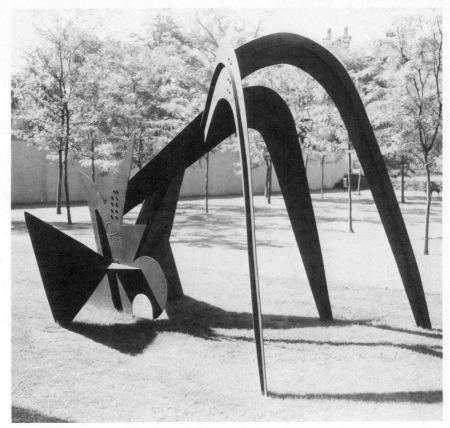

FIGURE 5-9 Alexander Calder, "Three Arches." 1963. Painted metal stabile; 9 feet high, 9 feet 4½ inches wide, 12 feet long. Munson-Williams-Proctor Institute, Utica, New York.

PERCEPTION KEY ARP, CHRYSSA, AND CALDER

1. Which of these four works is most obviously sculpture? Why?

2. In some of Pollock's paintings (Figure 4-4), as we have already indicated, the paint stands out from the canvas surface somewhat the way the aluminum and neon tubing in Chryssa's work stand out from the flat surface of the steel. These Pollocks are usually classified as paintings, the Chryssas as sculpture. Do you agree? Why or why not?

3. Both "The Ghost" and "Three Arches" are usually classified as sculpture. Do you agree? Why or why not?

4. How is space perceived differently around the Calders compared with the space around the Chryssa and that around the Arp? As you reflect about this, consider how your body is involved with these works.

5. Which of the four works are abstract and which representational?

LOW-RELIEF SCULPTURE

Relief sculpture, with the exception of sunken and flat relief, projects from a background plane such as a wall or column. Low-relief sculpture projects relatively slightly from its background plane, and so its depth dimension is diminished or condensed. Medium and, in turn, high-relief sculpture project further from their backgrounds, and so their depth dimensions are expanded. Sculpture in the round is freed from any background plane, and so its depth dimension is completely unrestricted. "Times Square Sky" is, we think, most usefully classified as sculpture of the low-relief species. The materiality of the steel, neon tubing, and especially the aluminum is brought out very powerfully by their juxtaposition. Unfortunately, this is somewhat difficult to perceive from a photograph. Sculpture, because of its three-dimensionality, generally suffers even more than painting from being seen only in a photograph. But if you cannot get to the Walker Art Center in Minneapolis, you can see works in a style similar to Chryssa's at almost any museum, gallery, or exhibition of contemporary sculpture. Note how in such works the sculptors—unlike painters—allow the substantiality of the materials that make up their work to come forth. Sculptors usually are possessed with care for the materiality of things. Chryssa in "Times Square Sky" is especially sensitive to aluminum, the neon light helping to bring out that metal's special sheen, which flashes forth in smooth and rough textures through subtle shadows.

Yet "Times Square Sky," as the title suggests, is representational. The subject matter is about a quite specific place, and the content of "Times Square Sky"—by means of its form—is an interpretation of that subject matter. Times Square is closed in almost entirely by manufactured products, such as aluminum and steel, animated especially at night by a chaos of flashing neon signs. Letters and words—often as free of syntax as in the sculpture—clutter that noisy space with its normally noxious air with a senselessness that almost overwhelms us. The feel of that fascinating square is Chryssa's subject matter, just as it is in Mondrian's "Broadway Boogie Woogie" (Figure 5-10 and Color Plate 8). Both reveal something of the rhythm, bounce, color, noise, and chaos of Times Square, but "Times Square Sky" interprets more physicality. Whereas Mondrian abstracts from the material physiognomy of Broadway, Chryssa gives you a heightened sense of the way Broadway feels as your body is bombarded by the street and its crowds. That bumping—tactile, visual, aural, and olfactory—can have a metallic, mechanical, impersonal, and threatening character, and something of this comes through in "Times Square Sky." The physicality of that effect is, we suggest, what distinguishes this work as sculpture rather than painting. And yet the line here cannot be too sharply drawn. For if the neon tubing and aluminum were flattened down on the steel somewhat or if Pollock had laid on his paints an inch or so thicker, would these works then be sculpture or painting?

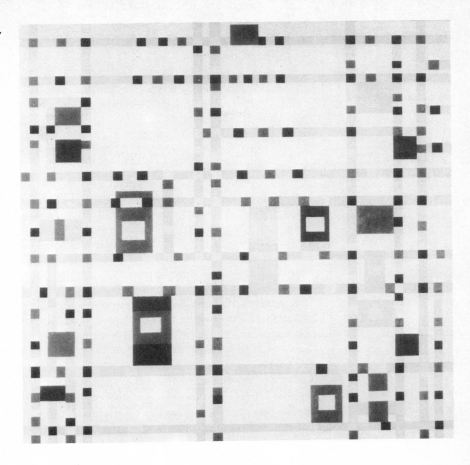

PERCEPTION KEY "THE CITY OF THE CIRCLE AND THE SQUARE" AND "TIMES SQUARE SKY"

Compare Paolozzi's "City of the Circle and the Square" (Figure 5-11), entirely in aluminum, with "Times Square Sky."

1. Do Paolozzi's shapes reveal anything about our urban world? Be specific.

2. Are these shapes as revelatory as Chryssa's of a large contemporary city? Or of Times Square?

3. In Paolozzi's sculpture much of the aluminum, unlike Chryssa's, is masked by paint. Is this not a kind of "untruth" to his materials? If so, is this artis-tically justifiable?

Relief sculpture—with a few exceptions like those previously discussed —allows its materials to stand out from a background plane, as in "Times Square Sky." Thus relief sculpture in at least one way reveals its materials

FIGURE 5-12 "Running Animals." Seal cylinder, Sumerian, Jamdet Nasr Period. Walters Art Gallery, Baltimore.

simply by showing us, directly, their surface and something of their depth. By moving to a side of "Times Square Sky," we can see that the steel, neon tubing, and aluminum are of such and such thickness. However, this three-dimensionality in relief sculpture, this movement out into space, is not allowed to lose its ties to its background plane. Thus relief sculpture, like painting, is usually best viewed from a basically frontal position. You cannot walk around a relief sculpture and see its back side as sculpture any more than you can walk around a painting and see its back side as painting. That is why both relief sculptures and paintings are usually best placed on walls or in niches.

Low-relief sculpture comes closest to painting when the movement out from the background plane is very slight, as in that very ancient and lovely Sumerian stone seal called "Running Animals" (Figure 5-12). Even here, however, we are aware of the stoniness of the stone as it takes on the configurations of graceful animal movement. And this awakens our sense of touch. Even if we were blind, we could get some feeling of this work's stoniness and what this work is about by passing our hands over its surface. Even the temperature of the stone would be a significant element in our perception. But would passing our hands over "Earth Greens" (Figure 4-2) enhance our perception of that work as a painting? Would our sensing its temperature? Or what about a canvas of Pollock's (Figure 4-4)? Our hands would feel the rhythmic textures, no doubt, but would the feel of the oil paints as oil be of any significance? Would we be aware of the concentration of white lead? And even if we were, would that awareness be significant in our experience of the canvas and its contents as a work of art? Would it make sense to talk about the oiliness of its oil paint? Would touching alone give us any significant understanding of what the work is about?

Charles Biederman's "Structurist Relief, Red Wing #6" (Figure 5-13), like "Times Square Sky," is in considerably higher relief than "Running Animals."

PERCEPTION KEY "STRUCTURIST RELIEF, RED WING #6"

Biederman's sculpture is made of sheet aluminum, machine-tooled and sprayed with several coats of paint in order to build up bright, lustrous surfaces. The placement of the squares and rectangles with their right-angled lines is reminiscent of Mondrian's style (Figures 1-4 and 5-10). And in fact Biederman was strongly influenced by Mondrian. Unlike "Times Square Sky," the metallic character of the aluminum of "Structurist Relief, Red Wing #6" is covered over rather than brought out. Despite the close relationship in style to Mondrian's paintings, would you be satisfied describing Biederman's work as a painting? Explain.

"Structurist Relief, Red Wing #6" differs from most sculpture in several respects. In the first place, Biederman—unlike Chryssa, for example—

FIGURE 5-13   Charles Biederman, "Structurist Relief, Red Wing #6." 1957–1963. Painted aluminum, 38⁷⁄₁₆ by 26¼ by 8⅝ inches. Walker Art Center, Minneapolis.

FIGURE 5-14 Dancing Asparas. XII to XIII century. Rajasthan, India. Relief, sandstone, 28 inches high. The Metropolitan Museum of Art. Gift of Mrs. John D. Rockefeller, Jr., 1942.

covers up his material, the aluminum. Secondly, he uses a wider color range than most sculptors and even painters such as Mondrian. Yet we think "Structurist Relief, Red Wing #6" is an example of sculpture. The squares and rectangles, unlike Mondrian's, possess some density. Moreover, they move strongly with a clean simplicity out into space, and their smooth surfaces lure our hands. In contrast to our participation with "Broadway Boogie Woogie," here our tactile senses are strongly aroused. If we were blindfolded and felt this work, we would be able to make some sense of it. Furthermore, these sharply edged planes with their high-luster skins reflect the play of light out into and through space in a way that suggests the luminosity of crystals. And perhaps this is the key to the content of this abstract sculpture—the interpretation of the molecular and crystal structures of nature. And perhaps also, there is the suggestion of how the kinetics of modern technology are derivative from these natural structures, for in the absolute precision of this work there is something very machinelike. Biederman covers up his aluminum, but in such a way that he uncovers something of the matter of nature and its relationship to the machine. This is a highly debatable interpretation, of course; as you debate, reconsider your answer to question 3 of the perception key on page 129.

HIGH-RELIEF SCULPTURE

The voluptuous Hindu "Nymph" (Figure 5-14), from a temple of the thirteenth century after Christ at Rajasthan in India, is an example of high-relief sculpture. Bursting with energy, the nymph almost escapes from her pillar. On the other hand, the small admiring handmaiden is in relatively low relief, closely integrated with the pillar. Partly because the nymph is almost completely in the round, we sense her bulk and mass with exceptional force. Rather than starting with the appearance of a naked woman, the sculptor must have started with the appearance of his stone and allowed that stone to suggest a naked woman capable of providing an eternity of sexual delight. He allowed woman to come forth as that kind of sandstone would say it, and rarely has such stone revealed such erotic qualities. Sensuality and sexuality are completely embodied in a shape that attracts our need to touch. Indeed it may even be, at least for older westerners with Puritan roots, that the erotic excitation reduces us to dwarfs like the handmaiden. In any case, there is a great deal of humor in this remarkable work.

SCULPTURE IN THE ROUND

Michelangelo's "Pietà" (Figure 5-15) of the Cathedral of Florence, one of his last sculptures, c. 1550–1555, was unfinished. Originally, according to

FIGURE 5-15 Michelangelo Buonarroti, "Pietà." c. 1550–1555. Marble, 7 feet 8 inches high; in Florence Cathedral. The Bettman Archive, Inc.

Vasari and Condivi, Michelangelo wanted to be buried at the foot of this sculpture, which was to be placed in Santa Maria Maggiore in Rome. Thus he portrayed his own features in the head of Nicodemus, the figure hovering above, and apparently was making good progress. But then a series of accidents occurred, some involuntary and some probably voluntary. While the legs of Christ were being carved, a vein in the marble broke. There are also breaks above the left elbow of Christ, his chest on the left, and on the fingers of the hand of the Virgin. The story goes that, in despair, Michelangelo did some of this damage himself. In any case, he gave it up as a monument for his tomb and sold it in 1561, deciding that he preferred burial in Florence.

PERCEPTION KEY "PIETÀ"

1. Of the four figures of this statue—Nicodemus, Christ, the Virgin to the right, and Mary Magdalene to the left—one seems to be not only somewhat stylistically out of harmony with the other three but of lesser artistic quality. Historians and critics generally agree that this figure was not done or at least not completed by Michelangelo but rather by a second-rate sculptor, presumably Tiberio Calcagni. Which figure is this? What are your reasons for choosing it?

2. Michelangelo, perhaps more than any other sculptor, was obsessed with marble. He spent months at a time searching the hills of Carrara near Pisa for those marble blocks from which he, like a midwife, could help sculptural shapes emerge. Something of his love for marble, perhaps, is revealed in this "Pietà." Do you see and feel this? And if so, how do you think it was achieved?

3. Is this sculpture in the round? The figures are freed from a base background, and one can walk around the work. But is this "Pietà" in the round in the same way as Arp's "Growth" (Frontispiece)?

The answer to the first question is the Magdalene. Her figure and pose, relative to the others, are artificial and stiff. Her robe—compare it with the Virgin's—fails to integrate with the body beneath. And, in turn, her figure fails to integrate with the others. For no accountable reason she is both very aloof and much smaller, and the rhythms of her figure fail to harmonize with the others. Finally, the marbleness of the marble fails to come out with the Magdalene.

In the other figures—and this is the key to the second question—Michelangelo barely allows his shapes, except for the polished surfaces of the body of Christ, to emerge from the marble blocks. The features of the Virgin's face, for example, are very roughly sketched. It is as if she were still partially a prisoner in her stone. The Virgin is a marble Virgin; the Magdalene is a Magdalene and marble. Or, to put it another way, Michelangelo saw the Virgin in the marble and helped her image out without allowing it to betray its origin. Calcagni, or whoever did the Magdalene, saw the image of Magdalene and then fitted the marble to the image. Thus the claim that the face of the Virgin was unfinished is mistaken. It is hard to conceive, for us at least, how more chiseling or any polishing could have avoided weakening the expression of tender sorrow. The face of the Magdalene is more finished in a realistic sense, of course, but the forms of art reveal rather than reproduce reality. In the case of the body of Christ—compared

FIGURE 5-16 Jean Arp, "Growth." 1938. Philadelphia Museum of Art. Photograph by A. J. Wyatt, Staff Photographer.

with the rest of the statue except the Magdalene—the much more "finished" chiseling and the high polish was appropriate because it helped reveal the bodily suffering that preceded death.

Since there is no background plane from which the figures emerge, the "Pietà" is usually described as sculpture in the round. Yet when compared with Arp's "Growth" (Frontispiece), it is obvious that the "Pietà" is not so clearly in the round. When we walk behind the "Pietà," we find the rough-hewn back side unintegrated with the sides and front and of little intrinsic interest. Michelangelo intended this essentially three-sided pyramid, as with practically all of his sculptures, to be placed in a niche so that it could be seen principally from the front. In this sense, the "Pietà" is a transition piece between high-relief sculpture, such as the "Nymph" (Figure 5-14), and unqualified sculpture in the round, such as "Growth."

There is no principal position from which to perceive "Growth." The smooth, rounded shapes, with their swelling shadows, gently move out into space and lure our bodies around the figure. Not only does each aspect possess equal rights, but each aspect is incomplete—enticing us to the next for fulfillment. As we slowly circle, we both remember the aspects that were and anticipate the aspects to come. The remembered and anticipatory images merge into the present aspect or image. And as we circle again, this synthesis becomes increasingly fulfilled. Arp did a bronze version of essentially the same figure (Figure 5-16), and as you compare the photographs of the bronze and marble (Frontispiece), you will notice that they are taken from slightly different angles. Notice how even this slight variation in point of view helps bring out different shapes.

The space around a sculpture in the round is sensory rather than empty. Despite its invisibility, sensory space—like the wind—is felt. Sculptures such as "Growth" are like magnets from which radiating vectors flow forth. As we focus on such sculptures, we find ourselves being drawn in and around by these invisible but perceptible radiating forces. With relief sculptures, except for very high relief such as the "Nymph" (Figure 5-14), our bodies tend to get stabilized in one favored position. The framework of front and sides meeting at sharp angles, as in "Running Animals" (Figure 5-12) and "Times Square Sky" (Figure 5-7), limits our movements to 180 degrees at most. Although we are likely to move around within this limited range for awhile, our movements gradually slow down, like finally getting settled in a comfortable chair. We are not Cyclops with just one eye, and so we see something of the three-dimensionality of things even when restricted to one position. But even low-relief sculpture encourages some movement of the body, because we sense that a different perspective, however slight, may bring out something we have not directly perceived, especially something more of the three-dimensionality of the materials. With paintings, since there is no significant three-dimensionality of materials, this tendency is much more restricted, and that is one of the reasons why paintings come at us with such "all-at-onceness." With paintings there is usually one principal position from which to participate, and it does not take long to find it. In short, the space in front of a painting is relatively free of forces; low-relief sculpture projects some force; high-relief more; and, finally, the space in front of a sculpture in the round is full of forces because the frontal space is dynamically integral with the spaces of the sides and back.

PERCEPTION KEY   "GROWTH"—TWO VERSIONS

1. Compare the two versions of "Growth" (Frontispiece and Figure 5-16). Do the planes and masses stretch out and pull back more strongly in the marble or the bronze? As you reflect about this, compare the way light acts on the two statues. On which one does the light reflect and contrast more sharply and rapidly? As a consequence, does the sensory character of the respective spaces surrounding the two statues differ? In what ways?

2. Suppose the marble "Growth" were backed into a corner in such a way that it would be difficult to walk around it. Would you feel that somehow the natural forces of the statue had been disturbed?

3. Imagine the bronze "Growth" in the same position. Would you feel that the space of the bronze was being violated more or less than the space of the marble? Why? In thinking about this, recall your answers to the first question.

4. If you agree that somehow our bodies are more involved with sculpture— especially sculpture in the round—than with paintings, how is this to be explained? Is it simply because with most sculpture we have to move our bodies around in order to see the whole sculpture as a succession of two-dimensional images? Or is there more to it than this? Reflect on the following statement by Naum Gabo, one of the most innovative and important sculptors of the twentieth century: "To think about sculpture as a succession of two-dimensional images would mean to think about something else, but not sculpture."[2] Consider also the fact that the subject matter of most sculpture—roughly estimated as close to 90 percent—is the human body. Even if this estimate is too high (and if restricted to contemporary sculpture it surely is), nevertheless it remains generally true that sculptors usually find the human body a far more interesting subject matter than most painters. How is this to be explained?

SCULPTURE AND THE HUMAN BODY

Sculptures generally are more or less a center—the place of most importance which organizes the places around it—of actual three-dimensional space: "more" in the case of sculpture in the round, "less" in the case of low relief. That is why sculpture in the round is more typically sculpture than the

[2] Quoted by Herbert Read and Leslie Martin in *Gabo: Constructions, Sculpture, Drawings, Engravings*, Harvard University Press, Cambridge, Mass., 1957, p. 156.

other species. Other things being equal, sculpture in the round, because of its three-dimensional centeredness, brings out the voluminosity and density of things more certainly than any other kind of sculpture. First of all, we can see and touch all sides. But more importantly, our sense of density has something to do with our awareness of our bodies as three-dimensional centers thrusting out into our surrounding environment. Gaston Bachelard remarks that "immensity is within ourselves. It is attached to a sort of expansion of being which life curbs and caution arrests, but which starts again when we are alone. As soon as we become motionless, we are elsewhere; we are dreaming in a world that is immense. Indeed, immensity is the movement of a motionless man."[3] Lachaise's "Floating Figure" (Figure 5-17), emerging with lonely but powerful internal animation from a graceful ellipse, not only expresses this feeling but also something of the instinctual longing we have to become one with the world about us. Sculpture in the round, even when it does not portray the human body, often gives us something of an objective image of our internal bodily awareness as related to its surrounding space. When, furthermore, the human body is portrayed in the round, we may have the most vivid material counterpoint of our internal feelings and mental images of our bodily existence.

PERCEPTION KEY   EXERCISE IN DRAWING AND MODELING

1. Take a pencil and paper. Close your eyes. Now draw the shape of a human being but leave out the arms.

2. Take some clay or putty elastic enough to mold easily. Close your eyes. Now model your material into the shape of a human being, again leaving out the arms.

3. Analyze your two efforts. Which was easier to do? Which produced the better result? What do you mean by "better"? Was your drawing process guided by any other factor than your memory images of the human body? What about your modeling process? Did any significant factors other than your memory images come into play? Was the feel of the clay or putty important in your shaping? Did the awareness of your internal bodily sensations contribute to the shaping? Did you exaggerate any of the functional parts of the body where movement originates, such as the neck muscles, shoulder bones, knees, or ankles? Could these exaggerations, if they occurred, have been a consequence of your inner bodily sensations?

In Greek mythology, the young Narcissus fell in love with his image as reflected in a clear spring. Being unable, unfortunately, to endow that image with corporeality, he pined away and died. In this as in most myths, there is an element of profound truth. The Narcissus myth expresses the insatiable

[3] From *The Poetics of Space* by Gaston Bachelard. Translation © 1964 by The Orion Press, Inc. Reprinted by permission of Grossman Publishers.

desire most of us have to arrive at a satisfactory image of our bodily selves.
Mirror images help, of course, and so do paintings. But these are not quite
enough. They present or show directly the surface of our bodies, but they
can only represent or show indirectly the density of the interior. The sight
and especially the touch of other humans is of some help, because then we
have immediate experience of three-dimensionality. But even then such
experience is usually blurred with irrelevancies, such as concealing clothes.

Sculpture can strip away the irrelevancies. Thus it can bring out density directly and powerfully, presenting clarifying images of both the exterior and interior of our bodies.

TACTILITY: INWARD AND OUTWARD SENSATIONS

Tactile or touch sensations are both inward and outward. We feel our internal bodily sensations—such as muscular tension and relaxation, strength and lassitude, pleasure and pain, and desire—as three-dimensional forces filling out our bodily space and, in turn, being met by external forces or bodies. We feel gravity, for example, as a force limiting our bodily forces. Through our inward sensations we perceive ourselves constantly. Only in deep sleep do these sensations cease. Our outward sensations—i.e., sensations of the outside of our bodies, as when we scratch our skin—are less constant. Moreover, usually our outward sensations are directed toward external things rather than our bodies. Our visual sensations of ourselves are even more sporadic than the tactile, except for sensations like those of Narcissus. We can still perceive ourselves inwardly even if we are blind and paralyzed. Once we can no longer feel ourselves inwardly, we no longer are. Even the so-called "totally paralyzed" person feels something of his head.

Our first experiences are tactile rather than visual. The baby feels his hunger and thirst inwardly. And he touches his mother's breast before he sees it. Young children, some psychologists are convinced, are severely handicapped in their development if they are shut off from fondling. However that may be, all of us have learned something about the limits of our bodies the harder way—as toddlers trying to stand up and banging into things. Our bumps and bruises have told us more about our bodies than mirrors. Our body image is built primarily from our contacts with other bodies, our visual sensations of ourselves being supplemental. The boundaries of our bodies are based upon the obstruction of those objects which "object" to being incorporated. Our inward sensations thrust outward to meet and be bounded by our outward sensations of other bodies. Without outward sensations, we would be unaware of things beyond us. Without inward sensations, our outward sensations would have no center.

SCULPTURE IN THE ROUND AND THE HUMAN BODY

No object is more important to us than our body, and it is always "with" us. Yet when something is continually present to us, we find great difficulty in focusing our attention upon it. Thus we are usually only vaguely aware of air except when it is deficient in some way. Similarly, we are usually only vaguely aware of our bodies except when we are in pain. Nevertheless, our bodies are part of our most intimate selves—we are our bodies—and if we have any of Narcissus in us, we have a deep-down driving need to find a

FIGURE 5-18 Aphrodite (Venus Anadyomene). c. first century B.C. Marble, slightly under life-size. Found at Cyrene. Museo Nazionale delle Terme, Rome.

satisfactory material counterpoint for the mental images of our bodies. If that is the case, we are lovers of sculpture in the round. All sculpture always evokes our outward sensations and sometimes our inward sensations. Sculpture in the round often evokes our inward sensations, for such sculpture often is anthropomorphic in some respect. And sculpture in the round that has as its subject matter the human body—as in the "Aphrodite" (Figure 5-18), Michelangelo's "David" (Figure 5-19), or Rodin's "Danaïde" (Figure 5-20)—not only often evokes our inward sensations but interprets them. Rodin, one of the greatest sculptors of the human body, wrote that "instead of imagining the different parts of the body as surfaces more or less flat, I represented them as projectures of interior volumes. I forced myself to express in each swelling of the torso or of the limbs the efflorescence of a muscle or a bone which lay beneath the skin. And so the truth of my figures,

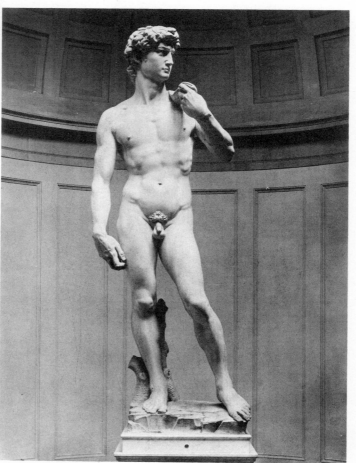

FIGURE 5-19 Michelangelo Buonarroti, "David." 1501–1504. Marble 16 feet high. Accademia, Florence.

FIGURE 5-20 Auguste Rodin, "Danaïde." 1885. Marble, 35 by 73 by 57 centimeters. Musee Rodin, Paris.

instead of being merely superficial, seems to blossom from within to the outside, like life itself."[4] Such sculpture presents an objective correlative—an image that is objective in the sense that it is "out there" and yet correlates or is similar to a subjective awareness—that clarifies our internal bodily sensations as well as our outward appearance.

These are large claims and highly speculative. You may disagree, of course, but we hope they will stimulate your thinking.

PERCEPTION KEY "APHRODITE" AND GIORGIONE'S "VENUS"

The marble "Aphrodite" (Figure 5-18), slightly under life size, found at Cyrene, is a Roman copy of a Greek original of the first century B.C. It is extraordinary both for the delicacy of its carving, for most Roman copies of Greek works crudely deaden their liveliness, and the translucency of its marble, which seems to reflect light from below its surface. Compare this work with Giorgione's "Venus" (Figure 2-18).

1. Which of the two would you rather touch?
2. Which of the two evokes more inward sensations?
3. In both these works, graceful lassitude and sexuality have something to do with their subject matter. Yet they are interpreted, we think, quite differently. What do you think?

[4] Auguste Rodin, *Art*, Romilly Fedden (trans.), Small, Boston, 1912, p. 65.

4. If the head and arms of the "Venus" were represented as broken off, would this injure the work as much as the "Aphrodite?" Some critics claim that the "Aphrodite" is not very seriously injured as an artistic object by the destruction of her head and arms. Yet how can this be? As you reflect about this, ask yourself why we excluded the arms in the drawing and modeling exercises of the previous perception key. Suppose the "Aphrodite" were to come off her pedestal and walk. Would you not find this monstrous? Yet many people treasure her as one of the most beautiful of all females. How is this to be explained? As you consider this question, review the discussion on inward sensations as a possible clue.

When we participate with sculpture such as the "Aphrodite," we find something of our bodily selves confronting us. If we demanded all of our bodily selves, we would be both disappointed and stupid. Art is always a transformation of reality, never a duplication. Thus the absence of head and arms in the "Aphrodite" does not shock us as it would if we were confronting a real woman. Nor does their absence ruin our perception of this statue's beauty. Even before the damage, the work was only a partial image of a female. Now the "Aphrodite" is even more partial. But even so, she is in that partiality exceptionally substantial. The "Aphrodite" is more substantial than a real woman because the female shape, texture, grace, sensuosity, sexuality, and beauty are interpreted by a form and thus clarified. And with all those feminine qualities, density is present in a more vivid way than in reality. Even the most perfect real woman—at least from a male chauvinist viewpoint—is always moving away, or covering up, or talking too much, or in bad light, or sick, or getting old. The sculptor can make her stand still, strip her, shut her up, give her good light, and keep her in good health and young. The painter can do this too, of course, except that, unlike the sculptor, he has to sacrifice the density.

Giorgione's "Venus" is perhaps even lovelier than the "Aphrodite." Yet the body of "Venus" is only represented; the body of "Aphrodite" is presented. And this difference makes our participations with the two works quite different. Thus we are bound to be drawn close to "Aphrodite" and to circle her. And if the guards are not looking—she is watched over in Rome's Museo Nazionale della Terme by some of Italy's most zealot puritans—to touch and caress her. Such does not seem to be the case with the "Venus." Paintings, even one so erotically attractive as this, tend to keep their distance. For one thing, if we get too close, we lose our best view. Although this also happens with sculpture, the visual loss is compensated by the tactile gain. Second, there is no thrust forward into the space in front of the picture plane. Thus there are no channeling forces—except the need to find the position of best sight—to draw us in. And so the picture plane remains a dividing plane that we have no desire to penetrate.

Considerations such as we have been discussing may account, perhaps, for some of the less conscious motivations that lead sculptors to the human body as subject matter. Are there other motivations? In thinking about this, imagine yourself a sculptor. Are there any three-dimensional shapes more subtle or complex than that of the human body?

The human body is supremely beautiful. To begin with, there is its sensuous charm. There may be other things in the world as sensuously attractive—for example, the full glory of autumnal leaves—but the human body also possesses a sexuality that greatly enhances its sensuousness. Moreover, in the human body, mind is incarnate. Feeling, thought, purposefulness—what in sum is loosely called "spirit"—have taken shape. Thus the absent head of the "Aphrodite" (Figure 5-18) is not really so absent after all. There is a dignity of spirit that permeates her body. It is abhorrent to conceive of her as having an idiotic or wrathful head. Better no head at all. It is the manifestation of Aphrodite's composed spirit in the shaping of her body that, in the final analysis, explains why we are not repulsed by the sight of the broken neck.

Compare Michelangelo's "David" (Figure 5-19) and "Pietà" (Figure 5-15) with the "Aphrodite."

PERCEPTION KEY   "DAVID," "APHRODITE," AND THE "PIETÀ".

1. Suppose the head of the "David" were broken off and, like the head of "Aphrodite," you had never seen it. Is it conceivable that a head something like that of the Christ of the "Pietà" could be satisfactorily substituted?

2. The "David," about 16 feet in height, is not portrayed as ready for battle with Goliath, for the sling is lying open and unprepared across his back. Yet the strong, bony face of David—with its distended nostrils, glaring eyes, and furrowed brow surmounted with hair like tangled flames—expresses something of a state of moral character, a fearless, defiant attitude full of strength and wrath. Now suppose only the head remained and we knew nothing about its body. Is it conceivable that a body something like that of the Christ of the "Pietà" could be satisfactorily substituted?

3. Both the "Aphrodite" and the "David" are in marble, although of very different kinds. Which statue is more evocative of your outward sensations? Your inward sensations? Henry Moore claims that "sculpture is more affected by actual size considerations than painting. A painting is isolated by a frame from its surroundings (unless it serves just a decorative purpose) and so retains more easily its own imaginary scale." He makes the further claim that the actual physical size of sculpture has an emotional meaning. "We relate everything to our own size, and our emotional response to size

FIGURE 5-21 "Venus of Willendorf." c. 15,000 to 10,000 B.C. Stone, 4⅜ inches high. Naturhistorisches Museum, Vienna.

is controlled by the fact that men on the average are between five and six feet high."[5] Does the fact that the "David" is much larger in size than the "Aphrodite" make any significant difference with respect to your tactile sensations?

4. Both statues respect the relative proportions of the human body. Yet one of the statues has one part of its anatomy greatly out of proportion to the other parts. Identify this part and explain why this is the case.

Both the "Aphrodite" and the "David" are exceptional examples of idealized sculpture, i.e., figures more beautiful than those found in nature. Compare the "Aphrodite" with one of the earliest known sculptures, also in the round—the compact "Venus of Willendorf" (Figure 5-21) from the Paleolithic period, in limestone and just over 4 inches in height. Apparently there was no attempt to idealize this "Venus," even granting the technical limitations of the sculptor.

PERCEPTION KEY "VENUS OF WILLENDORF" AND "APHRODITE"

1. Can you suggest a more appropriate title than the "Venus of Willendorf?" In reflecting about this, identify the subject matter. Perhaps the fact that the sculpture is small enough to be encompassed by your hands is a clue.

2. Does it follow, because of the lack of idealization, that the "Venus" is of lesser artistic quality than the "Aphrodite?" Explain your response.

3. Which of the two works arouses your outward sensations more? Inward sensations? Why? Be specific.

4. Is the limestone of the "Venus" an appropriate material for the forming of this figure? Consider how the figure would appear if carved in a marble like that of the "Aphrodite." Would its artistic quality have been enhanced? Suppose the material had been relatively light, like rubber. Would this change our perception of the figure greatly?

5. Is the head of the "Venus," with its very abstract treatment, suitable to the body?

6. The structure of the "Venus" is composed of parts that suggest geometrical shapes. Analyze these parts in relation to the whole. Do the same with the "Aphrodite." Which of the two works has the more complex textural-structural (part-to-whole) composition?

Return once again to the marble and bronze versions of Arp's "Growth" (Frontispiece and Figure 5-16).

[5] Moore, "Notes on Sculpture," op. cit., p. xxxiv.

FIGURE 5-22 Colonel Glenn
and John F. Kennedy in wax.
Madame Tussaud's Wax Mu-
seum, London. British Tourist
Authority, New York.

PERCEPTION KEY TWO VERSIONS OF "GROWTH" AND WAXWORKS

1. The Arp statues certainly do not look like any human beings in a realistic sense. If someone resembling these statues came walking down the street we would be horrified. Yet is there nothing revealingly human about these figures?

2. Compare these figures with the waxworks of Colonel Glenn and John F. Kennedy (Figure 5-22) in Madame Tussaud's collection. Are the waxworks more revealingly human?

3. Is one of the versions of "Growth" more feminine than the other? If so, how is this to be explained?

Relief sculpture tends to be horizontally oriented because generally it is placed on or against a wall or in a niche[6]—a vertical background serves as the basic "plane of departure" for the relief. Thus its basic three-dimensionality extends from a background plane toward a frontal plane. Sculpture in the round tends to be vertically oriented because generally it is placed on the earth (inclusive of floors and bases). Thus its basic three-dimensionality extends upward. There are three main possibilities for the relation of sculpture in the round to the earth: the sculpture is either rooted in the earth, resting on it, or rising above it.

[6] Recumbent tomb figures placed on the floors of churches and chapels, as commonly done in the medieval period, are a notable exception.

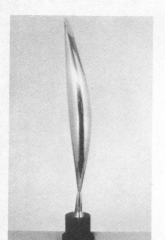

The "Aphrodite" (Figure 5-18), "David" (Figure 5-19), "Dananïde" (Figure 5-20), Brancusi's "Bird in Space" (Figure 5-23), Lachaise's "Floating Figure" (Figure 5-17), and Moore's "Reclining Figure" (Figure 5-24) are all sculptures in the round.

1. Which ones are rooted in the earth? Which rest on it? Which rise above it?

2. Return to Calder's "Ghost" (Figure 5-8) and "Three Arches" (Figure 5-9) and your answers to questions 3 and 4 of the perception key on page 127. "The Ghost" is based neither on a wall nor on a floor but hung from the ceiling so that you can walk under it. Most of its materials move with the air currents and have little significant density. "Three Arches" is based on the floor, but its materials also have little density and you can walk under it. Once again, are these sculptures?

FIGURE 5-23   Constantin Brancusi, "Bird in Space." 1925. Polished bronze, marble and oak base; 50¼ inches high. Philadelphia Museum of Art, The Louise and Walter Arensberg Collection. Photograph by A. J. Wyatt, Staff Photographer.

SPACE SCULPTURE

The history of sculpture shows something of an evolution from low to high relief to sculpture in the round. But this is an exceedingly rough generalization. For example, the "Venus of Willendorf" (Figure 5-21) is one of the earliest known sculptures, and she is very much in the round. What can be claimed with little qualification, however, is that work such as "The Ghost" and "Three Arches" has emerged in the last half-century. So new is this species that it has yet to be baptized with a universally accepted name. We shall call it "space sculpture." What distinguishes space sculpture from the earlier kinds is its emphasis upon spatial relationships, and, consequently, its tendency to deemphasize the density and materiality of its materials. As a further consequence, the appeal of space sculpture is more visual and less tactile than that of earlier sculpture. Nevertheless, the tactile appeal remains to some degree. Work that lacks significant tactile appeal completely, it seems to us, is not usefully described as sculpture. More precisely, space sculpture differs from sculpture in relief and in the round in technique, in density, and in its relationships with space. If we can be clear about these differences, we should have a better appreciation of the various species of sculpture.

TECHNIQUES OF SCULPTURE

Sculpture in relief and in the round generally is made either by modeling or carving. Space sculpture, on the other hand, generally is made by assembling preformed pieces of material.

FIGURE 5-24 Henry Moore, "Reclining Figure." 1959–1964. Elmwood, 90 inches. By permission of the artist.

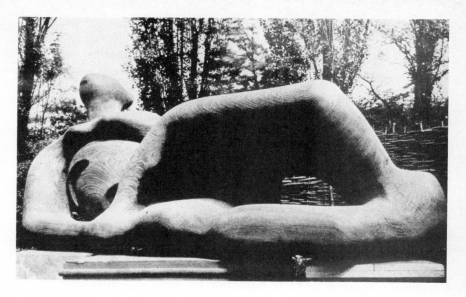

The modeler starts with some plastic or malleable material such as clay, wax, or plaster and builds up his sculpture piece by piece. If the design is complex or involves long or thin extensions, he probably will have to use an internal wooden or metal support (armature) that functions something like a skeleton. Whereas "Floating Figure" (Figure 5-17) and "Bird in Space" (Figure 5-23) required armatures, the "Venus of Willendorf" (Figure 5-21) did not. In either case, the modeler builds from the inside outward to his surface finish, which then may be scratched, polished, painted, etc. But when nonplastic materials such as bronze are used, the technical procedures are much more complicated. Bronze cannot be built up like clay. Nor—although it can be lined, scratched, etc.—can bronze be carved like stone. Thus the sculptor in bronze or any material that is cast must use further processes. We can present here only a grossly oversimplified account. For those who want to pursue the techniques of sculpture further—and this can be very helpful in sharpening your perceptual faculties—a large number of excellent technical handbooks are available.[7]

The sculptor in bronze begins with clay or some similar material and builds up a model to a more or less high degree of finish. This is a solid or *positive* shape. Then he makes a plaster mold—a hollow or *negative* shape—from the solid model. This negative shape is usually divisible into

[7] For example, William Zorach, *Zorach Explains Sculpture*, American Artists Group, New York, 1947. Learning the techniques of handling various artistic media is one of the best ways of improving our perception and understanding of the arts. We do not have the space to go into these techniques, but good technical handbooks in all the arts abound.

sections, so that the inside can easily be worked on to make changes or remove any defects that may have developed. Then the sculptor makes a positive or solid plaster cast from his negative plaster mold and perfects its surface. This cast is then given to a specialized foundry, unless the sculptor does this work for himself, and a negative mold is again made of such materials as plaster, rubber, or gelatin. Inside this mold—again usually divisible into sections to allow for work in the interior—a coating of liquid wax is brushed on, normally at least ⅛ inch in thickness but varying with the size of the sculpture. After the wax dries, a mixture of materials, such as sand and plaster, is poured into the hollow space within the mold. The wax now is completely surrounded.

Intense heat is now applied, causing the wax to melt out through channels drilled through the outside mold and the molds on both sides of the wax to be baked hard. Then the bronze is poured into the space the wax has vacated. After the bronze hardens, the surrounding molds are removed. Finally, the sculptor may file, chase, polish, or add patinas (by means of chemicals) to the surface. One of the most interesting and dramatic descriptions of casting, incidentally, can be found in the *Autobiography* of Benvenuto Cellini, the swashbuckling Renaissance sculptor. His "Perseus," probably his finest sculpture, was almost stillborn in the casting process.

The carver uses non-malleable material, such as marble, that cannot be built up. Thus he must start with a lump of material and work inward from the outside by removing surplus material until he arrives at his surface finish. Thus for his "David" (Figure 5-19), Michelangelo was given a huge marble block that Agostino di Duccio had failed to finally shape into either a David or, more likely, a prophet for one of the buttresses of the Cathedral of Florence. Agostino's carving had reduced the original block considerably, putting severe restrictions upon what Michelangelo could do. This kind of restriction is foreign to the modeler, for there is no frame of reference such as the limits of a marble block to prevent the expansion of his sculpture into space. And when a model is cast in materials of great tensile strength, such as bronze, this spatial freedom becomes relatively unlimited.

It should be noted that many carvers, including Michelangelo, sometimes modeled before they carved. A sketch model often can help the carver find his way around in such materials as marble. It is not easy to visualize before the fact the whereabouts of complicated shapes in blocks of material. And once a mistake is made in nonplastic materials, it is not so easily remedied as with plastic materials.

The shapes of the "David" had to be ordered from the outside inward, the smaller shapes being contained within the larger shapes. Whereas the modeler works up the most simplified and primary shapes which *underlie* all the secondary shapes and details, the carver roughs out the simplified and primary shapes *within* which all the secondary shapes and details are contained. Michelangelo, for example, roughed out the head of the "David" as a solid sphere, working down in the front from the outermost planes of the forehead and nose to the outline of the eyes and then to the details of the eyes, etc. Thus the primary shape of the head, the solid sphere, is not only preserved to some extent but points to its original containment within the largest containing shape, the block itself. Consequently, we can sense in the "David" something of the block from which Michelangelo started. This original shape is suggested by the limits of the projecting parts and the high points of the surfaces. Thus we are aware of the thinness of the "David" as a consequence of the block Michelangelo inherited. There remains the huge imprint of that vertical block that had been sliced into. This accounts, perhaps, for the feeling we may have with some carved works of their being contained within a private space, introverted and to some extent separate. Modeled sculpture generally is more extroverted.

PERCEPTION KEY   "GROWTH"—TWO VERSIONS

1. Compare again the marble and bronze versions of "Growth" (Frontispiece and Figure 5-16). If the bronze was made first, then the modeling technique was basic to both versions. If the marble was made first—assuming that no sketch model played a dominant role—then the carving technique was basic to both versions. Which technique do you think was basic?

2. Which statue is the more private and introverted?

3. Do you believe that your answer to question 2 has something to do with your knowledge of the technical processes of how these statues were made? But if so, is this legitimate, since you were, presumably, judging the sculpture produced and not the producing process?

"The Ghost" (Figure 5-8) and "Three Arches" (Figure 5-9) obviously were neither modeled nor carved. Their wires and sheets of metal have little mass to be shaped and no interior to be structured. Although the materials of these works exist in three-dimensional space, as does everything else in this world, they are not themselves significantly three-dimensional. Calder preformed these pieces and then assembled them, attached, furthermore, at clearly discernible joints and intersections. These pieces relate across and frame space; in the case of "The Ghost," there is even movement through space. Thus the appeal of these works is more visual than that of earlier sculpture. Calder's materials fill space only slightly, and so their tactile appeal, while still present, is considerably reduced.

The assemblage technique does not rule out the presentation of density —Paolozzi's "The City of the Circle and the Square" (Figure 5-11), for example, was assembled and yet is quite dense—but assemblage lends itself to the lightening of materials. This, in turn, lends itself to the creating of

FIGURE 5-25 Alexander Calder, "Bougainvillea." 1947. Mobile of wire and sheet metal, 76 inches high. Collection of Mr. and Mrs. Burton Tremaine, Meriden, Connecticut. Photograph by Herbert Matter.

spatial relationships that become at least as interesting as the materials. Moore's "Reclining Figure" (Figure 5-24) is hollowed out with holes that open up space within the figure. Brancusi's "Bird in Space" (Figure 5-23) rises above the earth and opens up the space outside the figure. But in both these examples, the density of the materials, the wood and the bronze respectively, dominates space. With "The Ghost" and "Three Arches," however, space is opened up both within and without, and it is sliced up in such a way that the spatial relationships become more interesting than or at least as interesting as the materials.

Calder's "Bougainvillea" (Figure 5-25), made of wire and sheet metal, is an especially lovely example of spatial relationships. It is as if we were standing under a large vine, as the title suggests. The sinuous wires expand in all directions with the fibrous strength of wood branches, and the graceful disks, like blossoms, ride the breezes. Here our visual perception of spatial relationships is clearly more important than the tactile qualities of wire and metal. We have little desire to touch these pieces. Yet in their flowing movement to and from each other through space, they help bring out the tactile qualities of the open air. To cage "Bougainvillea" in a museum or any inside place would be as deadening to its natural forces as to back either version of Arp's "Growth" (Frontispiece and Figure 5-16) into a corner. "Bougainvillea," much more than "The Ghost," belongs to the wind and sky.

"Bougainvillea" and "The Ghost" are rather aptly described as "space drawings." Their primarily visual appeal, like very low-relief sculpture (Figure 5-12), has close affinities to painting. On the other hand, Calder's "Gates of Spoleto" (Figure 5-26) and, to a lesser extent, his "Three Arches" are examples of space sculpture with close affinities to architecture. As with many of the materials of architecture, Calder's materials sometimes are not only preformed and assembled but also massive. This makes it easily possible for inner space to be separated from outer space for practical purposes. If, for example, Calder had extended the upper steel sheets of "The Gates of Spoleto" horizontally, this work would serve as a functional shelter.

TACTILITY, MASS, AND SPACE

Space sculpture never loses completely its ties to the materiality of its materials. Otherwise tactile qualities would be largely missing also, and then it would be doubtful if such work could usefully be classified as sculpture. The materials of "The Ghost" and "Bougainvillea" carry with them the feel of the air. The sheets of steel of "Three Arches" and "The Gates of Spoleto," despite their thinness, appear heavy. Naum Gabo, one of the fathers of space sculpture along with his brother Antoine Pevsner, often uses translucent materials, as in "Spiral Theme" (Figure 5-27). Although the

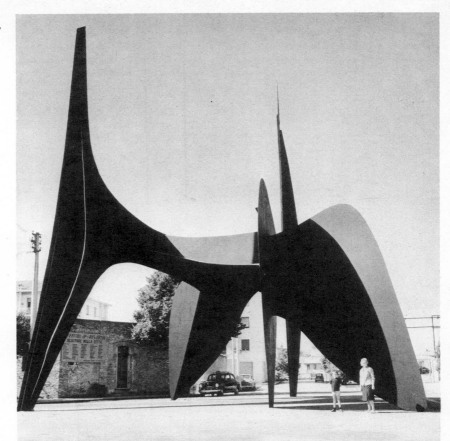

FIGURE 5-26 Alexander
Calder, "The Gates of Spoleto."
1962. Steel. Photograph by
Edvard Trier.

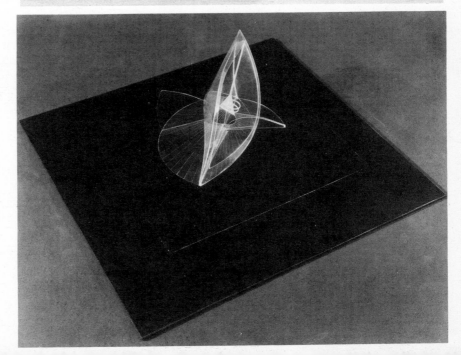

FIGURE 5-27 Naum Gabo,
"Spiral Theme." 1941.
Construction in plastic, 5½ by
13¼ by 9⅜ inches, on base 24
inches square. Collection, The
Museum of Modern Art, New
York. Advisory Committee
Fund.

FIGURE 5-28 Barbara
Hepworth, "Pelagos." 1946.
Wood with color and strings,
16 inches in diameter. The
Tate Gallery, London.

planes of plastic divide space with multidirectional movement, no visual
barriers develop. Each plane varies in translucency as our angle of vision
varies, and in seeing through each, we see them all—allowing for freely
flowing transitions between the space without and the space within. In turn,
the tactile attraction of plastic, especially its smooth surface and rapid fluidity, is enhanced. As Gabo has written: ". . . Volume still remains one of the
fundamental attributes of sculpture, and we still use it in our sculptures. . . .
We are not at all intending to dematerialize a sculptural work. . . . On the
contrary, adding Space perception to the perception of Masses, emphasizing
it and forming it, we enrich the expression of Mass, making it more essential
through the contact between them whereby Mass retains its solidity and
Space its extension."[8]

PERCEPTION KEY "RECLINING FIGURE," "PELAGOS," "BRUSSELS
CONSTRUCTION," AND "SPACE SCULPTURE"

1.   Compare Moore's "Reclining Figure" (Figure 5-24), Hepworth's "Pelagos"
     (Figure 5-28), Rivera's "Brussels Construction" (Figure 5-29), and Kricke's

[8] Quoted by Herbert Read and Leslie Martin in *Gabo: Constructions, Sculpture, Drawings,
Engravings*, Harvard University Press, Cambridge, Mass., 1957, p. 168.

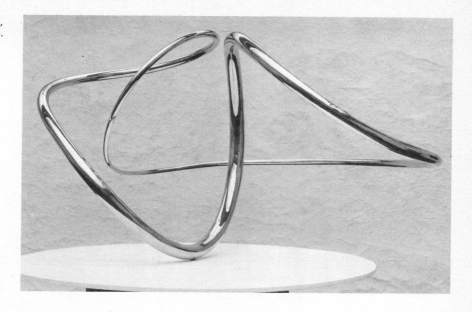

FIGURE 5-29 Jose de Rivera, "Brussels Construction." 1958. Stainless steel. The Art Institute of Chicago. Gift of Mr. and Mrs. R. Howard Goldsmith.

"Space Sculpture" (Figure 5-30). Is there in these four works, as Gabo claims for his, an equal emphasis on mass and space? If not, in which one does mass dominate space? Vice versa?

2. Moore has written that "The first hole made through a piece of stone [or most three-dimensional materials] is a revelation. The hole connects one side to the other, making it immediately more three-dimensional. A hole can itself have as much shape-meaning as a solid mass."[9] Is Moore's claim applicable to all four of these works?

3. Compare another "Reclining Figure" (Figure 5-31) by Moore with an earlier one (Figure 5-32). Both are in Hornton stone, although of different colors. Do the holes in Figure 5-31 help bring out the stoniness of the stone? Or in this respect is Figure 5-32 more revealing?

4. Compare Moore's sculptures in Figures 5-24 and 5-31 with those in Figure 5-32. Do you sense in the figures with holes any suggestion of the rhythm of breathing? What role do the holes play with reference to the content of the first two works? Do the holes increase or decrease the liveliness of the figures, for example? What is Moore saying differently about women in the first two works compared with the third?

5. In "Pelagos," how many holes are there? What is the function of the strings? Why did Hepworth use the color white in the inside?

6. "Brussels Construction" is mounted on a flat disk turned by a low-revolution motor. Is it useful to refer to holes in this sculpture? The three-dimensional curve of "Brussels Construction" proceeds in a long, smooth, con-

FIGURE 5-30 Norbert Kricke, "Space Sculpture." 1958. Stainless steel. Photograph by Edvard Trier.

[9] "Notes on Sculpture," op. cit., p. xxxlv.

FIGURE 5-31 Henry Moore, "Reclining Figure." 1938. Green Hornton stone, 54 inches long. By permission of the artist.

FIGURE 5-32 Henry Moore, "Reclining Figure." 1929. Solid elmwood, brown Hornton stone; 32 inches long. By permission of the artist.

tinuous flow. Does this have anything to do with the changing diameter of the chromium-plated stainless steel? Suppose the material absorbed rather than reflected light. Would this change the structure significantly? Do you think this sculpture should be displayed under diffused light, or in dim illumination with one or more spotlights? Is there any reference to human life in the simplicity and elegant vitality of this work? Or is the subject matter just about stainless steel and space? Or is the subject matter about something else? Do you agree that this work is an example of space sculpture? And what about "Pelagos"? Note that there is no assemblage of pieces in the case of "Brussels Construction," whereas, because of the addition of strings, there is some assemblage in "Pelagos." Would you classify Moore's works in Figures 5-24 and 5-31 as space sculptures?

7. "Space Sculpture" is an assemblage of welded metal strips. Does this work require, as does "Bougainvillea" (Figure 5-25), the open air? Could it be appropriately placed in Times Square? Suppose it were to be placed either at the entrance of Kennedy Airport or on the Hudson River pier of the Holland-America Line. Which would provide the more suitable space? Can you think of a specific place where this work could be best displayed? Is this work an example of space sculpture? Is the title an index to the subject matter or nothing more than an identification tag? Can you think of a more appropriate title?

It seems to us that "Pelagos" and the works by Moore in Figures 5-24 and 5-31 are not space sculptures because, although they open up space within, the density of their materials dominates space. "Brussels Construction," on the other hand, is space sculpture because the spatial relationships are at least as interesting as the stainless steel. The fact that "Pelagos" was assembled in part and "Brussels Construction" was not is not conclusive. Assemblage is the technique generally used in space sculpture, but what we are perceiving and should be judging is the product, not the producing process. Of course, the producing process affects what is produced, and that is why it can be helpful to know about the producing process. That is why we went into some detail about the differences between modeling, carving and assemblage. But the basis of a sound judgment about a work of art is that work as it is given to us in perception. Any kind of background information is relevant *provided* it aids that perception. But if we permit the producing process rather than the work of art itself to be the basis of our judgment—in the jargon of the critics this is called the "intentional fallacy"—we are led away from, rather than into, the work. This destroys the usefulness of criticism.

CONTEMPORARY SCULPTURE

Developments in sculpture are emerging and changing so quickly that no attempt can be made here even to begin to classify them. These developments fall into the species of low, medium, and high relief, sculpture in the round, space sculpture, and some hybrids of these. But beyond that not very helpful generalization, the innovations of contemporary sculptors escape pigeonholing.

TRUTH TO MATERIALS

There is, however, at least one tendency, more of a reaffirmation than an innovation, that is fairly pervasive—respect for the materials used in the sculpture. In the flamboyancy of much of late Baroque, in the early-nineteenth-century Neoclassicism of many of the followers of Canova such as Thorwaldsen, and in some of the Romanticism of the later nineteenth century, respect for materials was ignored. In the twentieth century the realistic waxworks (Figure 5-22) of Madame Tussaud are the ultimate conclusion of this ignorance. Thus Karl Knappe refers to "the crisis through which art [sculpture] is passing [as] one that concerns . . . the artistic media. An image cannot be created without regard for the laws of nature, and each kind of material has natural laws of its own. Every block of stone, every piece of wood is subject to its own rules. Every medium has, so to speak, its own tempo: the tempo of a pencil or a piece of charcoal is quite different from the tempo of a woodcut. But the habit of mind which creates, for instance, a pen drawing cannot simply be applied mechanically to the making of a woodcut; to do this would be to deny the validity of the spiritual as well as the technical tempo."[10] In contemporary sculpture, perhaps in part as a reaction, respect for materials has come back with a vengeance. It has even been given a name—"truth to materials."

PERCEPTION KEY   TRUTH TO MATERIALS

1. Review the examples of twentieth-century sculpture we have discussed. Assuming that these examples are fairly representative, do you find a pervasive tendency to truth to materials? Do you find exceptions, and, if so, how might these be explained?

2. Henry Moore has stated that "Every material has its own individual qualities. It is only when the sculptor works direct, when there is an active relationship with his material, that the material can take its part in the shaping of an idea. Stone, for example, is hard and concentrated and should not be falsified to look like soft flesh—it should not be forced beyond its constructive build to a point of weakness. It should keep its hard tense stoniness."[11] Figures 5-31 and 5-32 by Moore are both in stone. Do they illustrate Moore's point? If so, point out as specifically as possible how this is done.

3. Are the wax figures (Figure 5-22) true to their material?

---

[10] Karl Knappe, quoted in Kurt Herberts, *The Complete Book of Artists' Techniques*, Thames and Hudson, 1958, p. 16. Published in the United States by Frederick A. Praeger.
[11] Quoted by Herbert Read, *Henry Moore, Sculptor*, A. Zwemmer, London, 1934, p. 29.

FIGURE 5-33 "Mother and Child." From the Ivory Coast (Senufo). Wood, 26¾ by 7 inches. Private collection, Amsterdam.

In Moore's "Reclining Figure" (Figure 5-24), notice how the grains of wood flow over the shoulders and arms and down the body, and how these grains lead into the concavities and climax at the convexities, for example, the upper knee. The silhouette and contour lines were carved to conform to those grains, which, in turn, bring out the woodiness of the wood. This truth to materials can be found in the best of every sculptural tradition, even Canova's, but it is found almost everywhere in so-called "primitive" sculpture. Go to any such exhibition (North American Indian art is rather widely accessible) and you will invariably find this care for materials. African sculpture—the "Mother and Child" (Figure 5-33), for example, from the Ivory Coast—is especially notable in this respect. Societies in which technology has not been developed very far live much closer to nature than we do, and so their feeling for natural things usually is reverent. As technology has gained more and more ascendancy, this reverence toward natural things has receded. In highly industrialized societies, people tend to revere artificial things, and the pollution of our environment is one result. Another result is the flooding of the commercial market with imitations of primitive sculpture, which are easily identified because of the lack of truth to the materials (test this for yourself). Even the contemporary sculptors, as distinguished from the "hackers," have lost some of their innocence toward things simply because they live in a technological age. Most of them, however, are far more innocent than the rest of us. Many sculptors still possess something of the primitive way of feeling things, and so they find in primitive sculpture inspiration, even if to reach it requires repentance. Despite its abstract subject matter, Marta Pan's "Balance en deux" (Figure 5-34), with its reverence to walnut wood, has a close spiritual affinity to the "Mother and Child" (Figure 5-33).

Truth to material sculpture—such as Hepworth's (Figure 5-28), Moore's (Figures 5-24, 5-31, and 5-32) and Pan's (Figure 5-34)—is an implicit protest against technological ascendancy.

PROTEST AGAINST TECHNOLOGY

PERCEPTION KEY   TROVA, SEGAL, GIACOMETTI, AND TRŠAR

Is protest expressed against our technologically dominated culture in Trova's "Study: Falling Man (Wheelman)" (Figure 5-35)? Segal's "Bus Driver" (Figure 5-36)? Giacometti's "City Square" (Figure 5-37)? Tršar's "Demonstrators II" (Figure 5-38)? If so, is this protest implicit or explicit? If explicit, how is this accomplished in each of these four works?

Explicit protest is part of the subject matter of all these works, we think, although perhaps only in "Wheelman" is that protest unequivocally di-

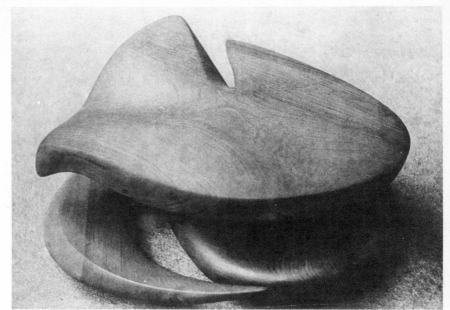

FIGURE 5-34 Marta Pan, *"Balance en deux."* Collection of the artist.

FIGURE 5-35 Ernest Trova, "Study: Falling Man (Wheelman)." 1965. Silicon bronze, one of six casts, 60 by 48 by 20 13/16 inches. Collection, Walker Art Center, Minneapolis. Photography by Eric Sutherland.

rected at technology. Flaccid, faceless, and sexless, this anonymous robot has "grown" spoked wheels instead of arms. Attached below the hips, this mechanism produces a sense of eerie instability—that this antiseptically cleansed automaton with the slack, protruding abdomen, who somehow is us, may tip over from the slightest push. No free will is left to resist. The value of man, as in Aldous Huxley's *Brave New World*, has been reduced to manpower, functions he performs in the world of goods and services. For since another individual can also perform these functions, the given man has no special worth. His value is that of a unit which can easily be replaced by another.

FIGURE 5-37 Alberto
Giacometti, "City Square"
(La Place). 1948. Bronze, 8½
by 25⅜ by 17¼ inches. Collection, The Museum of Modern Art, purchase.

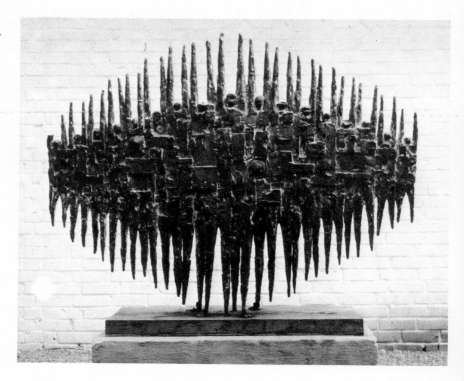

FIGURE 5-38 Drago Tršar,
"The Demonstrators II." 1957.
Bronze, 53⅞ by 66⅞ inches.
Photograph by Edvard Trier.

"The Bus Driver" is an example of "environmental sculpture." Grimly set behind a wheel and coin box taken from an old bus, the driver is a plaster cast made in sections over a living but well-greased model. Despite the "real" environment and model, the stark white figure with its rough and generalized features is both real and strangely unreal. In the empty air around him, we sense the hubbub of the streets, the smell of fumes, the ceaseless comings and goings of unknown customers. Yet despite all these suggestions of a crowded, nervous atmosphere, there is a heart-rending immobility and loneliness about this driver. Worn down day after day by the same grind, Segal's man, like Trova's, has been flattened into an X—an unknown quantity.

In Giacometti's emaciated figures, the huge, solidly implanted feet suggest nostalgia for the earth; the soaring upward of the elongated bodies suggests aspiration for the heavens. The surrounding environment has eaten away at the flesh, leaving lumpy, irregular surfaces with dark hollows that bore into the bone. Each figure is without contact with anyone, as despairingly isolated as "The Bus Driver." They stand in or walk through an utterly alienated space, but, unlike "Wheelman," they seem to know it. And whereas the habitat of "Wheelman" is the clean, air-conditioned factory or office of *Brave New World*, Giacometti's people, even when in neat galleries, always seem to be in the grubby streets of our decaying cities, as in T. S. Eliot's "Morning at the Window."

They are rattling breakfast plates in basement kitchens,
And along the trampled edges of the street
I am aware of the damp souls of housemaids
Sprouting despondently at area gates.

The brown waves of fog toss up to me
Twisted faces from the bottom of the street,
And tear from a passer-by with muddy skirts
An aimless smile that hovers in the air
And vanishes along the level of the roofs.

"The Demonstrators II" is a powerful tactile and visual image of the potential violence embedded in demonstrations generally. More specifically, although the work was completed in 1957, it is a prophecy of the sixties in the United States. To take just one example, "The Demonstrators II" may evoke images of the Kent State massacre: the anonymous mass of gas-masked guardsmen, their rifles, and the upraised arms of those in defiance packed together in a design that expresses blind, fanatical rigidity. No smiles lighten this rough dark mass. Irrationality reigns, as in a machine which has gotten beyond human control.

PERCEPTION KEY "THE DEMONSTRATORS II" AND KENT STATE

1. Do you believe it would be appropriate to place "The Demonstrators II" on the Kent State campus as a memorial?

2. Is it possible or likely that works of art can play a healing function in such highly explosive situations? Or can works of art make such a situation worse? Discuss with others.

To blame technology entirely for the dehumanization of man interpreted in these sculptures is a gross oversimplification, of course. But this kind of work does bring out something of the horror of technology when it is misused. Look around—there are people who have become scheduled by-products of the power plants. Technology can drive us into the dubious safety zones of isolation, as in Figure 5-37, or the herd, as in Figure 5-38. Works such as these vividly clarify what we are all up against.

ACCOMMODATION WITH TECHNOLOGY

Not all contemporary sculptors are concerned in their work with the misuses of technology. Many see in technology blessings for mankind. It is true that sculpture can be accomplished with the most primitive of tools (that, incidentally, is one of the basic reasons why sculpture in primitive cultures apparently not only precedes painting but also usually dominates both qualitatively and quantitatively). Nevertheless, sculpture in our day, far more than painting, can take advantage of some of the most sophisticated advances of technology, surpassed in this respect only by architecture. Many sculptors today interpret the positive rather than the negative aspects of technology. This respect for technology is expressed by (1) truth to its materials or (2) care for its products or (3) use of its methodology.

David Smith's "Cubi X" (Figure 5-39), like Chryssa's "Times Square Sky" (Figure 5-7), illustrates truth to technological materials. But Smith, unlike Chryssa, usually accomplishes this by wedding these materials to nature. The stainless steel cylinders of the "Cubi" support a juggling act of hollow rectangular and square cubes that barely touch one another as they cantilever out into space. Delicate buffing modulates the bright planes of steel so that they reflect, like rippling water, the colorings of their environment. Smith writes, "I like outdoor sculpture and the most practical thing for outdoor sculpture is stainless steel, and I make them and I polish them in such a way that on a dull day, they take on the dull blue, or the color of the sky in the late afternoon sun, the glow, golden like the

rays, the colors of nature. And in a particular sense, I have used atmosphere
in a reflective way on the surfaces. They are colored by the sky and the
surroundings, the green or blue of water. Some are down by the water and
some are by the mountains. They reflect the colors. They are designed for
outdoors."[12] But Smith's steel is not just a mirror, for in the reflections
the fluid surfaces and tensile strength of the steel emerge. There is a care
for this man-made material comparable to Pan's care for natural material
(Figure 5-34).

Kurt Schwitters's "Merz Konstruktion" (Figure 5-40) is—except for the
old wood—an assemblage of worn-out, discarded and despised manufactured materials such as cardboard, wire mesh, paper, and nails. But with
sensitive ordering with respect to shape, surface, color, and density, these
rejects are rehabilitated. We see and feel them, perhaps for the first·time,

[12] David Smith in Cleve Gray (ed.), *David Smith*, Holt, Rinehart and Winston, New York,
1968, p. 123.

FIGURE 5-40   Kurt Schwitters, "Merz Konstruktion." 1921. Painted wood, wire, and paper; 14½ by 8½ inches. Philadelphia Museum of Art. The A. E. Gallatin Collection. Photograph A. J. Wyatt, Staff Photographer.

FIGURE 5-41 John Chamberlain, "Velvet White." 1962. Welded automobile metals, 81½ inches high, 61 inches wide, 54½ inches deep. Collection of Whitney Museum of American Art, New York. Gift of the Albert A. List Fund. Photograph by Geoffrey Clements.

FIGURE 5-42 Marcel Duchamp, "Bottle Rack." 1914. Galvanized iron, 23¼ inches high. Photograph of lost original by Man Ray.

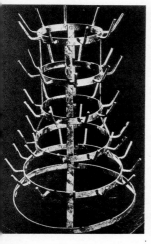

as things-in-themselves, like returning to an old abandoned house we once lived in but ignored except for practical purposes. We made and used these things, Schwitters seems to be saying, and despite their lowly status, they have a dignity that demands our respect.

John Chamberlain's "Velvet White" (Figure 5-41) is an example of "junk art." Whereas Schwitters delicately assembled small industrial debris, Chamberlain roughly assembled large sheets of twisted, torn metal from junkyards. Most of these macabre shapes carry with them the gashes of violence—accident and death. A walk through a junkyard can be a terrifying experience. And Chamberlain preserves and makes even more vivid this fury and horror in the discipline of his composition. But there is something more—the metallic character of these industrial materials is allowed to shine forth, powerfully and even monumentally, for its own sake.

Pop sculpture respects the products of technology as well as its materials. Duchamp's "Bottle Rack" (Figure 5-42) of 1914 was probably not so intended. Duchamp at that time was poking fun at overblown artistic pretensions. One of his more hilarious inventions, for example, is a urinal which he lined with fur, put on a pedestal, and exhibited. Nevertheless, "Bottle Rack" and works like it became prototypes for the Pop sculptor of the fifties and sixties. By separating an industrial product from its utilitarian context and isolating it for our contemplation, the opportunity to appreciate its intrinsic values is given. "Bottle Rack" is a "ready-made," for Duchamp had nothing to do with its making. But Duchamp was apparently the first to recognize the artistic qualities of what was then a very familiar object. The contrast of the diminishing rings with their spikey "branches" makes an interesting spatial pattern, especially if, as in Man Ray's photograph, light is played on the rough surfaces of galvanized iron. Duchamp saw this possibility, for rarely are bottle racks—or any other industrial products, for that matter—so effectively displayed.

Most Pop sculpture in recent years is not "ready-made." By using other material than the original, attention often can be drawn more strongly to the product itself. Thus Oldenburg's "Giant Soft Fan" (Figure 5-43) is made in the functionally impossible materials of vinyl, wood, and foam rubber. Someone might be tempted to use "Bottle Rack" for practical purposes, but "Giant Soft Fan" completely frustrates such temptation. The scale and character of the fans of the marketplace, the ones we usually see only dimly, are completely changed. Thus this 10-foot shining giant opens our eyes to the existence of all those everyday fans. Or as Oldenburg says: "I want people to get accustomed to recognize the power of objects. . . . I alter to unfold the object and to add to it other object qualities. . . ."[13] This kind of sculpture is concerned not so much with the materials of our consumer world but with its products.

[13] Quoted by Robert Goldwater in *What Is Modern Sculpture?* The Museum of Modern Art, New York, n.d., p. 113.

FIGURE 5-43 Claes Oldenburg, "Giant Soft Fan." 1966–1967. Construction of vinyl with wood, foam rubber, metal, and plastic tubing; 10 feet by 10 feet 4 inches by 6 feet 4 inches. The Museum of Modern Art, New York. The Sidney and Harriet Janis Collection.

MACHINE SCULPTURE

Some avant garde sculptors are interested not so much in the materials and products of technology but rather in the display or use of machine or technical methodology: their works are known as "machine sculpture." As in Calder's "Ghost" (Figure 5-8) and "Bougainvillea" (Figure 5-25), machine sculpture usually is "kinetic" or moving sculpture; but the motion of machine sculpture, unlike Calder's works, is primarily a result of mechanical rather than natural forces. Sculptors in this tradition, going back to the ideas and work of László Moholy-Nagy before World War II, welcome the machine and its sculptural possibilities. Rivera hides his machine under "Brussels Construction" (Figure 5-29), but many machine sculptors expose their machines. They are interested not only in the instrumental but also in the intrinsic values of the machine and its power. George Rickey,

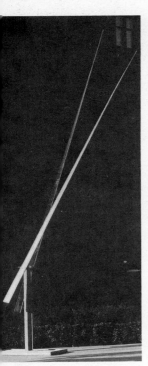

FIGURE 5-44 George Rickey, "Two Lines—Temporal I." 1964. Two stainless steel mobile blades on a painted steel base, 35 feet 2⅜ inches high. Collection, The Museum of Modern Art, New York. Mrs. Simon Guggenheim Fund.

the literary prophet of machine sculpture, writes that "A machine is not a projection of anything. The crank-shaft exists in its own right; it *is* the image. . . . The concreteness of machines is heartening."[14]

PERCEPTION KEY "TWO LINES – TEMPORAL I" AND "HOMAGE TO NEW YORK"

1. Rickey's "Two Lines—Temporal I" (Figure 5-44), although it depends upon air currents for its motion, is basically a machine—two 35-foot stainless steel "needles" balanced on knife-edge fulcrums. Is this work just an image of itself as a machine? Or does it suggest other images? Does its subject matter include more than just machinery? As you reflect about this, can you imagine perhaps more appropriate places than the garden of The Museum of Modern Art for the display of this work?

2. Is Jean Tinguely's "Homage to New York" (Figure 5-45) an image of itself as a machine? Does its subject matter include more than just machinery?

A good case can be made, we believe, for placing "Two Lines—Temporal I" in a grove of tall trees. Despite its mechanical character, this work belongs, like Calder's "Bougainvillea" (Figure 5-25) and Smith's "Cubi X" (Figure 5-39), in nature. Otherwise the lyrical poetry of its gentle swaying is reduced to a metronome. But even in its location in New York, it is much more than just an image of itself. "Two Lines—Temporal I" suggests something of the skeletal structure and vertical stretch of New York's buildings as well as something of the sway of the skyscrapers as we see them against the sky.

Tinguely's "Homage to New York," exhibited at the Museum of Modern Art (New York) in 1960, is probably a better example than "Two Lines—Temporal I" of the image of the machine in its own right. The mechanical parts, collected from junk heaps and dismembered from their original machines, stand out sharply in the photograph, and yet they are linked together by their spatial locations, shapes, and textures, and sometimes by nerve-like wires. Only the old player piano is intact. As the piano played, it was accompanied by howls and other weird sounds in irregular patterns that seemed to be issuing from the wheels, gears, and rods, as if they were painfully communicating with each other in some form of mechanical speech. Some of the machinery that runs New York City was exposed as vulnerable, pathetic, and comic, but Tinguely humanized this machinery as he exposed it. Even death was suggested, for "Homage to New York" was self-destructing: the piano burned and the structure collapsed. Thus the subject matter of this work seems to include not just machinery as such but the corrosive power it exerts both on itself and on man.

Rather than exposing the machine, sculptors such as Len Lye are more interested in using the machine's powers. Works of this type are usually highly expensive and, up to the present time, rarely exhibited. Unfortu-

[14] George Rickey, *Art and Artist*, University of California Press, Berkeley and Los Angeles, 1956, p. 172.

FIGURE 5-45   Jean Tinguely, "Homage to New York." 1960. Exhibited at the Museum of Modern Art, New York. Photograph by David Gahr.

nately also, it is very difficult to appreciate their effectiveness except by direct participation. One hopes, however, that more of this kind of sculpture will be made available. Lye's sculpture "The Loop" (Figure 5-46) was first exhibited in Buffalo in 1965, and Lye provided the following description in the exhibition catalogue:

"The Loop," a twenty-two foot strip of polished steel, is formed into a band, which rests on its back on a magnetized bed. The action starts when the

FIGURE 5-46 Len Lye, "The Loop." 1963. Stainless steel, ? by 6 inches. The Art Institute of Chicago.

charged magnets pull the loop of steel downwards, and then release it suddenly. As it struggles to resume its natural shape, the steel band bounds upwards and lurches from end to end with simultaneous leaping and rocking motions, orbiting powerful reflections at the viewer and emitting fanciful musical tones which pulsate in rhythm with "The Loop." Occasionally, as the boundless Loop reaches its greatest height, it strikes a suspended ball, causing it to emit a different yet harmonious musical note, and so it dances to a weird quavering composition of its own making.[15]

In work such as "The Loop," the machine is programmed independently of the environment. In "cyborg [cybernetic organism] sculpture," the machine, by means of feedback, is integrated with its environment, often including the participant. Thus the sixteen pivoting polychromed plates of Nicolas Shöffer's aluminum and steel frame "CYSP I" (Figure 5-47)—a name composed of the first letters of "cybernetics" and "spatio-

[15] *Len Lye's Bounding Steel Sculptures*, Howard Wise Gallery, New York, 1965.

FIGURE 5-47 Nicolas Shöffer, CYSP I." 1956. Aluminum and steel. Courtesy of Nicolas Shöffer.

FIGURE 5-48 Harold Lehr,
Ecological sculptures. 1971.
Courtesy of Harold Lehr.

dynamics"—are operated by small motors located under their axes. Built into the structure are photoelectric cells and microphones sensitive to a wide range of variations in the fields of color, light, and sound. These changes feed into an electronic brain (housed in the base of the sculpture), which, in turn, activates four sets of motor-powered wheels. Depending on the stimuli, the sculpture will move more or less rapidly about the floor, turning more or less sharp angles. Blue, for example, excites rapid movement and makes the plates turn quickly. Darkness and silence are also exciting, whereas intense light and noise are calming. Complex stimuli produce, as in human beings, unpredictable behavior. Moreover, the participant takes part in making the sculpture "come alive." In such work, technical methodology is extended not only to the sculpture but, in a sense, to ourselves.

PERCEPTION KEY: "CYSP I"

Does it strike you as surprising that with "CYSP I" darkness and silence are activating stimuli, whereas intense light and sound are nonactivating? Can you explain why Schöffer did this?

Harold Lehr has created machine sculptures with an ecological function. Looking like buoys or markers (Figure 5-48), they are placed in waters such as New York's East River, where they were first exhibited in 1971. Inside the sculptures are pumps and filters, powered by the sun and wind, which constantly clean the surrounding water. Lehr sees his sculptures as

a visual connection between two primordial forms of nature—water and air. The sculpture's interaction takes many forms. It is seen on two levels. One when tides, winds, waves and currents affect movement and they skim across the water as a group or divide and scatter randomly. Weather, light and the water's surface also affect this visual appearance. Secondly, interaction is visible over a period of time. It involves the sculpture's response to the animating variety of nature. As it responds to the wind and ocean, it moves and changes. Some of this energy is converted into electricity, which is stored and used to purify water. As a result, positive change is created. Cleaner water is a better environment. Sea life is attracted to the man-made structures, and the area is improved."[16]

PERCEPTION KEY MACHINE SCULPTURE

Can you conceive of any other kind of machine sculpture that would have an ecological function? Try your hand at some designs.

[16] *The New York Times*, January 23, 1972. © 1972 by The New York Times Company. Reprinted by permission.

Machine sculptures are being developed in many forms. For example, there are water-driven sculptures, works suspended in midair by magnets or by jets of air or water, synthetic membranes stretched like sails by mechanical forces, color and motion produced by polarized light, and mechanically powered environmental sculpture (although such power is absent in "The Bus Driver," Figure 5-36). Many of these developments are more experimental than artistic—the engineer often seems to dominate the artist. But the story is just beginning, and it will be fascinating to watch its unfolding. At the very least, machine sculpture has had considerable stimulating effect upon the more conventional species of sculpture. No machinery, for instance is involved in Marta Pan's "Floating Sculpture" (Figure 5-49). The structure was based on carved wood and then cast in polyester. But like much of the work of Rickey (Figure 5-44) and Schöffer (Figure 5-47), Pan calls on the environment—the movement of water and wind—for assistance. And, of course, the right kind of landscape is all-important for the full realization of this graceful structure.

EARTH SCULPTURE

Finally, another *avant garde* sculpture—"earth sculpture"—even goes so far as to make the earth itself the medium, the site, and the subject matter. The proper spatial selection becomes all-important, for the earth usually must be taken where it is found. Forms are traced in plains, meadows, sand, snow, etc., in order to help make us stop and see and enjoy the "form site"—

the earth transformed to be more meaningful. Usually nature rapidly breaks up the form and returns the site to its less ordered state. Thus many earth sculptors have a special need for the photographer to preserve their art.

PERCEPTION KEY: EARTH SCULPTURE

Study Michael Heizer's "Circumflex" (Figure 5-50), a 120-foot-long design "carved" out of the bed of a dry lake in Nevada.

1. Does the fact that probably the circumflex will be silted up in a short time disqualify this work as art? As you reflect about this, does the fact that the work has been elegantly photographed become relevant? Discuss with others.

2. Does the circumflex help bring out and make you notice the "earthiness" of the earth? The line of the mountain in the distance? The relation of the plain to the mountain?

FIGURE 5-50 Michael Heizer, "Circumflex." 1968. Massacre Creek Dry Lake, 120 feet long.

FIGURE 5-52   Naum Gabo, "Rotterdam Construction." Netherlands National Tourist Office, New York.

6 ARCHITECTURE

Buildings constantly assault us. Our only temporary escape is to the rarely accessible wilderness. We can close the novel, shut off the music, refuse to go to a play or dance, sleep through a movie, shut our eyes to a painting or a sculpture. But we cannot escape from buildings for very long, even in the wilderness. Fortunately, however, sometimes buildings possess artistic quality—i.e., they are architecture—drawing us to them rather than pushing us away. They make our living space more livable.

SPACE IN GENERAL

Space is the power of the positioned interrelationships of things. Space is not a mere collection of given things. Nor is space a mere imagined framework added to the sum of such given things, although since Newton—and despite Einstein—space is usually so conceived. Space is not a thing, and yet, because of the positioned interrelationships of things, space "spaces." Space has vitality. But in ordinary experience we pass by this power because we see the position of things only in order to use them. We abstract from the full reality of space and see space only as a means. We *know* space, but because of the anaesthesia of practicality, we fail to *feel* space.

1. How often in the last few days have you felt space as the positioned
   interrelationships of things? For example, did the furniture of some room
   bother you because it cramped your movement? Did the ceiling of some
   room give you a feeling of claustrophobia because it was too low in
   relation to the width and length of the room? Did the space around and
   between some buildings make you feel comfortable or uncomfortable?

2. Is there any space that seems to give your community a center, something
   like the hub of a wheel? Do the positioned interrelationships of buildings
   in your nearest shopping center invite you gracefully into the center?
   Are there any spaces in your community that draw you to them? That stand
   out? That you are blind to? That are repulsive? Are there any buildings
   in your community that seem to draw the sky and earth together harmoniously? Explain your judgments.

CENTERED SPACE

The painter does not command space; he only feigns it. The sculptor
molds out into space, but generally he does not enfold an enclosed or
inner space for our movement. The "holes" in the sculpture of Henry Moore
(Figures 5-24 and 5-31) are to be walked around, not into, whereas our
passage through inner space is one of the conditions under which the
solids and voids of architecture have their effect. Space is the material
of the architect, the primeval cutter,[1] who carves apart an inner space
from an outer space in such a way that both spaces become more fully
visible and, in turn, more intrinsically valuable. Invisible air seems to
be rendered visible. Inside his building, space is filled with emergent
forces. Outside his building, space becomes organized and focused. The
enfolded inner space is anchored to the earth. The convergent outer space
is oriented around the inner space. Thus sunlight, rain, snow, mist, and
night fall gracefully upon the cover protecting the inner space as if drawn
by a channeled and purposeful gravity, as if these events of the outside
belonged to the inside as much as the earth from which the building rises.

Inner and outer space come together to the earth to form a centered and
illuminated clearing. Centered space is the positioned interrelationships
of things organized around some paramount thing as the place to which
the other things seem to converge. Sometimes this center is a natural thing,
such as a great mountain or river or canyon or forest. Sometimes the center
is a natural site enhanced by a work of architecture. If we are near such
a building, we tend to be drawn into this clearing, for—unless practical

---

[1] This meaning is suggested by the Greek *architectón*.

FIGURE 6-1 Piazza before
St. Peter's. Alinari.

urgencies have completely desensitized us—centered space has an over-powering dynamism that captures both our attention and our bodies. Centered space is vital and insists upon drawing us to it. Centered space propels us out of the ordinary modes of experience in which space is used as a means. There is a pulling power from the center that is difficult to escape, that overwhelms and makes us acquiescent. We see and feel space not as a receptacle containing things but rather as a context empowered by the positioned interrelationships of things. Centered space intrudes as a force that is both "other" and imposing, as, even in our most harassed moments, we can hardly help feeling in such places as the piazza before St. Peter's (Figure 6-1). We find ourselves in the presence of a power that seems beyond our control. We feel the sublimity of space, but, at the same time, the centeredness beckons and welcomes us.

No special training is required to feel the sublimity of space, its over-whelming power. Space is breathing space, a part of the stuff of life, and space exerts its constant power by pushing in upon us. Gravitational force is only one, but the most obvious, manifestation of this power, for gravity works continuously on every aspect of everything. Without some sen-sitivity to space we cannot survive. But because of life's exigencies, we learn to push things around in space. Insofar as this pushing succeeds easily and efficiently, and in a technological age such success becomes increasingly possible, space tends to become no more than a framework —a vacuous place—within which we manipulate the positions of things. We become insensitive to the intrinsic value of the positioned interrelation-ships of things. We become explicitly conscious of space only when space frustrates us, and then only as an area within which we have to work. Space becomes a part of a problem. In our aggressiveness we enslave space to the point that we pass by the power of space. Then it takes either the embracing thrust of the great spaces of nature (and these spaces, such as in and around the Grand Canyon, are always centered to some significant extent) or the centered spaces of architecture to return us to an explicit awareness of the power and the embrace of the positioned interrelationships of things.

SPACE AND ARCHITECTURE

Architecture is the creative conservation of space. The architect sees the centers of space in nature and builds to preserve what he has seen. The architect is confronted by a centered space which desires to be made, through him, into a work. This space of nature is no offspring of his soul but an appearance which steps up to him, so to speak, and demands protection. If the architect succeeds in carrying through this request, the power of the natural space streams forth through him and the work arises. The architect is the shepherd of space. In turn, the paths around his shelter lead us away from those of our ordinary preoccupations that demand the utilization of space. We come to rest. Instead of our using up space, space takes possession of us with a ten-fingered grasp.

CHARTRES

On a hot summer's day some years ago, following the path of Henry Adams, one of the authors was attempting to drive from Mont Saint Michel to Chartres in time to catch the setting sun through the western

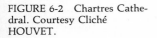

FIGURE 6-2 Chartres Cathedral. Courtesy Cliché HOUVET.

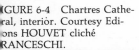

rose window of Chartres Cathedral. The following is his account of this experience:

In my rushing anxiety—I had to be in Paris the following day and I had never been to Chartres before—I became oblivious of space except as providing landmarks for my time-clocked progress. Thus I have no significant memories of the towns and countrysides I hurried through. Late that afternoon the two spires of Chartres (Figures 6-2 and 6-3), like two strangely woven strands of rope let down from the heavens, gradually came into focus. The blue dome of the sky also became visible for the first time, centering as I approached more and more firmly around the axis of those spires. The surrounding fields and then the town, coming out now in all their specificity, grew into tighter unity with the church and sky. I recalled a passage from Aeschylus: "The pure sky desires to penetrate the earth, and the earth is filled with love so that she longs for blissful unity with the sky. The rain falling from the sky impregnates the earth, so that she gives birth to plants and grain for beasts and men." No one rushed in or out or around the church. The space around seemed alive and dense with slow currents all ultimately being pulled to and through the central portal.[2] Inside, the space (Figure 6-4), although spacious far beyond the scale of practical human needs, seemed strangely compressed, full of forces thrusting and counterthrusting in dynamic interrelations. Slowly, in the cool silence inlaid with stone, I was drawn down the long nave, following the stately rhythms of the columns. But my eyes also followed the vast vertical stretches far up into the shifting shadows of the vaultings. It was as if I were being borne aloft. Yet I continued down the narrowing tunnel of the nave, but more and more slowly as the pull of the space above held back the pull of the space below. At the crossing of the transept, the flaming reds of the northern and southern roses transfixed my slowing pace, and then I turned back at last to the western rose and the three lancets beneath: a delirium of color, dominantly blue, was pouring through. Earthbound in the crossing, the blaze of the Without was merging with the Within. Radiant space took complete possession of my senses. In the protective grace of this sheltering space, even the outer space which I had dismissed in the traffic of my driving seemed to converge around the center of this crossing. Instead of being "out-side" things—my body, the church, the town, the fields, the sky, the sun—I was "inside" them, at one with them. This housing of holiness in this strange land made me feel at home in the homeland.

[2] Chartres, like most Gothic churches, is shaped roughly like a recumbent Latin cross:

The front (Figure 6-3)—with its large circular window shaped like a rose and the three vertical windows or lancets beneath—faces the west. The apse or eastern end of the building contains the high altar. The nave (Figure 6-4) is the central and largest aisle leading from the central portal to the high altar. But before the altar is reached, the transept cuts across the nave. The crossing is the meeting point of the nave and the transept. Both the north and south facades of the transept of Chartres contain, like the western facade, glorious rose windows.

LIVING SPACE

Living space is liberty of movement constrained by our feeling of the positioning of things in the environment within which we move or imagine that we can move. Taking possession of space is our first gesture, and sensitivity to the position of other things is a prerequisite of life. Space infiltrates through all our senses. A breeze accentuates a feeling of spaciousness in a room that opens out to a garden. A sound tells us something about the depth and shape of that room. A cozy temperature brings the furniture and walls into more intimate relationships. The smell of books gives that space a personality. Each of our senses records the positioning of things, expressed in such terms as "up–down," "left–right," and "near–far." This requires a reference system with a center. In the case of abstract perceptual space, as when we estimate distances visually, there is one center—the zero point located between the eyes. But with living space, since all the senses are involved, the whole body is a center. Furthermore, the body in relation to a place or places of most value, such as the home, form a configurational center. If we oversimplify, we can say that for the peasant his body and his farm, that place to which he most naturally belongs, constitute his configurational center—with the Roman it was Rome, with medieval man the church and castle, with a Babbitt the office, with a Sartre the café, and with a De Gaulle the nation. But for most men at almost any time, although probably more so in contemporary times, there are more than a couple of centers and often these are more or less confused and changing. In living space, in any case, places, principal directions, and distances arrange themselves around a configurational center.

The configurational center forms our personal space, to some extent private and protected. Outside the configurational center, space is more public and dangerous. The security of the home gradually lessens as we step out through the door into the yard, into the immediate neighborhood, and then into more remote places. As we move onto the typical modern highway in the northeastern United States, for example, the concrete cuts abusively into the earth and through the landscape as straight as possible, with speed the only aim. The arteries of commerce pump efficiency, and there is no time for reverence toward space. Everyone is aloof and passes hurriedly. There is no place for pedestrians or peace; even the roadside rests, if any, for the fatigued driver are drowned in the whine of tires. The necessities such as gas stations, restaurants, and motels are usually repetitious vulgarities that excite us to move on. Everyone from the hitchhiker to the other motorist is a threat. Only a police car or a severe accident is likely to slow us down. The machine takes over, and when we have reached our destination *on time*, the machine mentality is likely to maintain its clutch.

This desecration of space may even lead us to forget our configurational center, which gives orientation and meaning to other spaces. Then orientation with reference to intrinsic values is lacking. We become displaced persons, refugees from ourselves. Then living space, private as well as public, becomes used space. And then used space tends to become geometrical space, for the efficient use of used space requires precise placements. Space becomes a static schematic vacuum. The geometricians measure out coordinate systems whereby everything is related quantitatively. The centers now are entirely impersonal, for the basic characteristic of geometrical space is its homogeneity. No center and no direction in this democracy of places is preferred to another. When we, in turn, want to move through space most efficiently, geometrical space provides the map. To the degree that efficiency of movement dominates our concerns, living space becomes abstract space. Like the lumber barons of California ripping out the redwoods, we see straight through space. We still see things and the "between" of things, but only as means. Space itself—the power and hospitality of the positioned interrelationships of things—is ignored. Space becomes a wasteland.

FIGURE 6-5   Richard Upjohn, Trinity Church. 1839–1846. Broadway at Wall Street, New York City. Photograph by Eric Hass.

PERCEPTION KEY   NONARCHITECTURAL BUILDINGS

1.   Select a house that strikes you as the ugliest or one of the ugliest in your community. Now analyze why you make this judgment.
2.   Do the same for an apartment house, a school building, an office building, a gas station, a supermarket, a bridge, a city street.

A building that is not architecture, even if it encloses a convenient void, encourages us to ignore it. And normally we will be blind to the building and its space as long as it serves its practical purposes. However, if the roof leaks or a wall breaks down, then we will see the building, but only as a damaged instrument. A building that is architecture—by being a place around which other things appear to converge—brings us back to living space by centering space. Such a building raises to clarity preceding impressions that were obscure, confused, and inarticulate. The potentialities of power in the positioned interrelationships of things are captured and channeled. Our feeling for space is reawakened, and we become aware of the power and embrace of space.

PERCEPTION KEY   CHARTRES AND TRINITY CHURCH

Compare the facade and spires of Chartres Cathedral (Figure 6-3) with the facade and spire of Trinity Church (Figure 6-5) in New York City.

1. The spire of Trinity Church is higher than the spires of Chartres. Is this surprising? Why?

2. Do you believe that a church ought to strongly dominate the space that surrounds it? Would you expect a building that houses a dental clinic, for example, to dominate its surrounding space as strongly as a church does? Does Trinity Church dominate its surrounding space as strongly as does Chartres?

3. Which church seems best able to perform its function as a place of worship?

4. Which church seems to reveal religious values more profoundly?

When it was built in the nineteenth century, the spire of Trinity Church must have brought the sky of Manhattan into intimate relationship with the earth, somewhat the way Chartres still does for its region. But now the thrust of Trinity's spire is impotent, because the outer space it once centered is swamped by skyscrapers. Now the office buildings of Wall Street dominate that space. Commercial values look down upon religious values. If the church were a dental clinic, this would not seem odd. Or maybe this does not seem odd to you—but imagine how Richard Upjohn, the architect, now dead, would feel at the sight of his church if by some miracle he were able to return to Wall Street.

THE ARCHITECT

The architect's professional life is perhaps more difficult than that of any other artist. Architecture is a peculiarly public art because buildings generally have a social function, and many buildings require public funds. More than any other artist, the architect must consider his public. If he does not, very few of his plans are likely to materialize. Thus the architect must be a psychologist, sociologist, economist, businessman, politician, and courtier. He must also be an engineer, for he must be able to construct structurally stable buildings. And even then he will need luck. Upjohn could hardly have foreseen the fate of his church. And even as famous an architect as Frank Lloyd Wright could not prevent the destruction, for economic reasons, of one of his masterpieces—the Imperial Hotel in Tokyo.

The architect has to take into account four basic and closely interrelated necessities: technical or structural requirements, functioning or use, spatial relationships, and content. To succeed, his form must adjust itself to these necessities. As for what time will do to his creation, he can only prepare with foresight and hope. Wright's hotel withstood all the earthquakes, but ultimately every building is peculiarly susceptible to the whims of future taste.

TECHNICAL REQUIREMENTS OF ARCHITECTURE

The structural requirements of a building are the most obvious of the
architect's necessities. His building must stand (and withstand). Thus the
architect must know his materials and their potentialities; he must know
how to put them together; and he must know how they will work on a
particular site. Stilt construction, for instance, will not withstand earthquakes—and so the architect is also an engineer. But he is something more
as well—an artist. In solving his technical problems he must also make his
form revelatory, a form-content. His building must illuminate something
significant which we would otherwise fail to perceive.

Consider, for example, the relationship between the engineering
requirements and artistic qualities of the Parthenon, 447–432 B.C. (Figures
6-6 and 6-7). The engineering was superb, but unfortunately the building
was destroyed in 1687, when it was being used as an ammunition dump
by the Turks and was hit by a shell from Venetian guns. Basically the
technique used was post-and-lintel (or beam) construction. Set on a base
or stylobate, columns (verticals) support the architrave (horizontals) which,
in turn, composes, along with the frieze, the entablature that supports the
pediment or roof.

FIGURE 6-7 The Parthenon. 447–432 B.C. Photograph by Greek National Tourist Office, New York.

PERCEPTION KEY PARTHENON AND CHARTRES

Study the schematic drawing of the Doric order (Figure 6-8), the order followed in the Parthenon.

1. Why were the narrow vertical grooves or flutes carved into the marble columns?

2. Why do the columns bulge or swell slightly? (This curvature is called "entasis.")

3. Why are the columns wider at the base than at the top of the shaft?

4. Why is there a capital between the top of the shaft and the architrave (the plain lintels that span the voids from column to column and compose the lowest member of the entablature)?

5. The capital is made up of three parts: the circular grooves at the bottom (called the necking); the bulging cushionlike molding (called the echinus); and the square block (called the abacus). Why these parts at all?

6. The columns at the corners are a couple of inches thicker than the other columns. Why?

7. The corner and adjacent columns are slightly closer together than the other columns. Why?

8. All the columns slant slightly inward. Why?

9. Subtle refinements such as those mentioned above abound throughout the Parthenon. Few if any of them are necessary from a technical standpoint,

nor were these irregularities accidental. They are found repeatedly in other Greek temples of the time. Presumably, then, they are a result of a need to make the temple's form mean something, to be a form-content. Presumably then the Parthenon can still reveal something of the values of the ancient Greeks. What? Compare those values with the values revealed by Chartres. For example, which building seems to reveal a society that places more trust in God? And what kind of God? And in what way are those subtle refinements we have cited above relevant to these questions?

FUNCTIONAL REQUIREMENTS OF ARCHITECTURE

The architect must make his building not only stand but stand it in such a way that it reveals its function or use. One contemporary school of architects even goes so far as to claim that form must follow function. If the form succeeds in this, that is all the form should do. In any case, a form that disguises a building's function seems to irritate almost everyone.

FIGURE 6-8 Elements of the Doric order. Adapted from John Ives Sewell, *A History of Western Art*, rev. ed., Holt, Rinehart and Winston, New York, 1961.

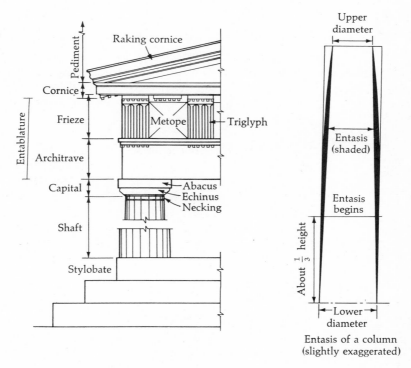

FIGURE 6-9 High school in Edinburgh.

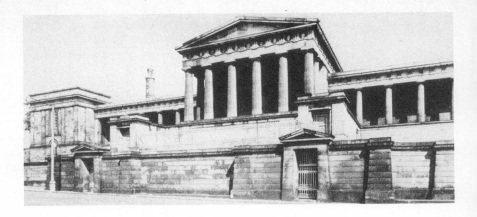

PERCEPTION KEY FUNCTION AND ARCHITECTURE

1. If the interior of Trinity Church (Figure 6-5) were remodeled into a dental clinic, would you feel dissatisfied with the relationship between the new interior and the old exterior?

2. Study Figure 6-9. What would you suppose the function of such a building to be?

3. Were you surprised to learn that this is a high school?

4. Is this building architecture?

5. Would you like to have such a building as a high school in your community? Does this involve you in the question of what architecture is?

6. In your opinion, what must a building be to be a work of architecture?

If form follows function in the sense that the form "stands for" the function of its building, then conventional forms or structures are often sufficient. No one is likely to mistake Trinity Church for an office building. We have seen the conventional structures of too many churches and office buildings to be mistaken about this. Nor are we likely to mistake the surrounding office buildings for churches. We recognize the functions of these buildings because they are in the conventional shapes that such buildings so often possess.

PERCEPTION KEY FORM, FUNCTION, CONTENT, AND SPACE

Study Figures 6-10 and 6-11.

1. What is the basic function of each of these buildings?

2. Notice that neither building has the commonplace conventional shapes that are seen in Figure 6-5. Then how do you know what the functions

FIGURE 6-10 Union Carbide Building, New York City. Photograph by Public Relations Department, Union Carbide Corporation.

are? How have the respective forms revealed the functions of their buildings? And does it seem more appropriate to use the term "reveal" for Figures 6-10 and 6-11, suggesting that these buildings have content, that their forms are revelatory, whereas the forms in Figure 6-5 are not? In other words, that in Figure 6-5 the forms are basically clichés and less than artistic because they fail to interpret the functions of their buildings? On

FIGURE 6-11   Le Corbusier,
Notre-Dame-du-Haut, Ron-
champs, France. 1950–1955.
Ezra Stoller © ESTO.

the other hand, is it true that in Figures 6-10 and 6-11 the forms are artistic because they do interpret? Would you agree that the buildings in Figure 6-5 are less than architecture, whereas the buildings in Figures 6-10 and 6-11 *are* architecture? And that they are architecture because the form of the building in Figure 6-11 is revelatory of the subject matter—of the tension, anguish, striving, and ultimate concern of religious faith; whereas in Figure 6-10 the form of the building is revelatory of the stripped-down, uniform efficiency of an American business corporation? Consider every possible relevant argument.

3.   In Figures 6-10 and 6-11, do the buildings center and organize their surrounding spaces? If so, how is this accomplished?

Study one of Frank Lloyd Wright's last and most famous works, the Solomon R. Guggenheim Museum in New York City (Figures 6-12 and 6-13), constructed in 1957–1959 but designed in 1943. Wright wrote:

Here for the first time architecture appears plastic, one floor flowing into another (more like sculpture) instead of the usual superimposition of stratified layers cutting and butting into each other by way of post and beam construction. The whole building, cast in concrete, is more like an egg shell—in form a great simplicity—rather than like a crisscross structure. The light concrete flesh is rendered strong enough everywhere to do its work by embedded filaments of steel either separate or in mesh. The structural calculations are those of cantilever and continuity rather than the post and beam. The net result of such construction is a greater repose, the atmosphere of the quiet unbroken wave: no meeting of the eye with abrupt changes of form.[3]

[3]Reprinted from *The Solomon R. Guggenheim Museum*, copyright 1960, by permission of the publishers The Solomon R. Guggenheim Foundation and Horizon Press, New York; pp. 16f.

FIGURE 6-12 Frank Lloyd Wright, The Solomon R. Guggenheim Museum, New York City. 1957–1959. Photograph, The Solomon R. Guggenheim Museum.

FIGURE 6-13 Frank Lloyd Wright, The Solomon R. Guggenheim Museum, interior. Courtesy of The Solomon R. Guggenheim Museum.

1. Does the exterior of this building harmonize with the interior?

2. Does the form reveal the building as an art museum?

3. Elevators take us to the top of the building, and then we participate with the exhibited works of art by walking down the spiraling ramp. This enables us to see each work from many perspectives. Does this seem to you to be an interesting, efficient, and comfortable way of exhibiting works of art?

4. The front of the museum faces Fifth Avenue. The surrounding buildings are tall rectangular solids evenly lined up along the sidewalks. Did Wright succeed in bringing his museum into a harmonious spatial relationship with these other buildings? Or was his purpose perhaps to make his museum stand out in sharp contrast, like a plant form among huge inorganic shapes? But if so, does the museum fit successfully into the spatial context—"the power and embrace of the positioned interrelationships of things"?

5. Originally the museum was to have been situated in Central Park. Do you think that a park site would have been better than its present site?

SPATIAL REQUIREMENTS OF ARCHITECTURE

Wright solved his technical problems (cantilevering, etc.[4]) and his functional problems (efficient and commodious exhibition of works of art) with considerable success. Moreover, the building functions well as a museum and reveals itself as a museum. But, if you can, check the site for yourself and see if you are satisfied with the spatial relationships between the museum and the surrounding buildings. It seems to us that Wright was not completely successful in this respect, and this, in turn, detracts from some of the "rightness" of the building. In any case, the technical, functional, and spatial necessities are obviously interdependent. If a building is going to be artistically meaningful—that is to say, if it is to be architecture—it must satisfy all of those necessities to some degree at least or its form will fail to be a form-content. A building that is technically awry with poor lighting or awkward passageways or cramped rooms will distract us from its form, and so will a form that fails to reveal the function of its building, and so will a form that fails to fit into its spatial context. We will go about our business and ignore those kinds of forms as much as possible.

[4] A *cantilever* is a projecting beam or structure anchored at one end to a pier and extending over a space to be bridged. Manuals that describe the technical problems of architecture and explain possible solutions are readily available. They can deepen our appreciation of architecture.

REVELATORY REQUIREMENTS OF ARCHITECTURE

The function or use of a building is an essential part of the subject matter of that building, what the architect interprets or gives insight into by means of his form. The function of the Union Carbide Building (Figure 6-10) is to house offices. The form of that building reveals that function. But does this function exhaust the subject matter of this building? Is only function revealed? Would we, perhaps, be closer to the truth by claiming that involved with this office function are values closely associated with but nevertheless distinguishable from this function? That somehow other values, beside functional ones, are interpreted in architecture? That somehow values from the architect's society impose themselves and he must be sensitive to them? We think that even if the architect criticizes or reacts against the values of his time, he must take account of them, that directly or indirectly they become involved with the functional values of his subject matter. Otherwise his buildings would stand for little more than clichés or his personal idiosyncracies.

We are claiming that the essential values of contemporary society are a part of any artist's subject matter, part of what he must interpret in his work, and this—because of the public character of architecture—is especially so with the architect. The way the architect (and the artist generally) is influenced by the values of his society has been given many explanations. According to the art historian Walter Abell, the state of mind of a society influences the architect directly. The historical and social circumstances generate psychosocial tensions and latent imagery in the minds of the members of a culture. The architect, one of the most sensitive members of a society, releases this tension and condenses this imagery in his art. The psyche of the artist, explained by Abell by means of psychoanalytic theory and social psychology, creates the basic forms of art; but this psyche is controlled by the state of mind of the artist's society, which, in turn, is controlled by the historical and social circumstances of which it is a part.

> Art is a symbolical projection of collective psychic tensions . . . . Within the organism of a culture, the artist functions as a kind of preconsciousness, providing a zone of infiltration through which the obscure stirrings of collective intuition can emerge into collective consciousness. The artist is the personal transformer within whose sensitivity a collective psychic charge, latent in society, condenses into a cultural image. He is in short the dreamer . . . of the collective dream.[5]

[5] Walter Abell, *The Collective Dream in Art*, Harvard University Press, Cambridge, Mass., 1957, p. 328.

Whereas Abell stresses the unconscious tensions of the social state of mind that influence the architect's creative process, Erwin Panofsky, another art historian, stresses the artist's mental habits, conscious as well as unconscious, that act as principles to guide the architect. For example:

> We can observe [between about 1130 and 1270] . . . a connection between Gothic art and Scholasticism which is more concrete than a mere "parallelism" and yet more general than those individual (and very important) "influences" which are inevitably exerted on painters, sculptors, or architects by erudite advisors. In contrast to a mere parallelism, the connection which I have in mind is a genuine cause-and-effect relation; but in contrast to an individual influence, this cause-and-effect relation comes about by diffusion rather than by direct impact. It comes about by the spreading of what may be called, for want of a better term, a mental habit—reducing this overworked cliché to its precise Scholastic sense as a "principle that regulates the act." Such mental habits are at work in all and every civilization.[6]

Whatever the explanation of the architect's relationship to his society, and Abell's and Panofsky's are two of the best,[7] the forms of architecture reflect and interpret some of the fundamental values of the society of the architect. Yet even as these forms are settling, society changes. Thus architecture, while keeping the past immanent in the present, takes on more and more the aura of the past, especially if the originating values are no longer viable or easily understandable. The Tomb of the Pulcella (young girl) in Tarquinia was built about the same time as the Parthenon, but because we have much more rapport with Greek than with Etruscan values, the tomb seems far older.

Anything that now exists but has a past may refer to or function as a sign of the past, but the forms of architecture interpret the past. The structures of architecture not only preserve the past more carefully than most things, for most architects build buildings to last, but these structures enlighten that past. They inform us about that society's values. The architect did the forming, of course, but from beginning to end that forming, insofar as it succeeded artistically, brought forth something of his society's values. Thus architectural structures are weighted with the past—a past, furthermore, that is more public than private. The past is preserved in the structures as part of the content of architecture.

Every stone of the Parthenon, in the way it is cut and fitted, reveals something about the values of the Age of Pericles—for example, the em-

[6] Erwin Panofsky, Gothic Architecture and Scholasticism, Archabbey Press, Latrobe, Pa.; 1951 (St. Vincent College Wimmer Lecture, 1948), pp. 20ff. Meridian Books, New York, 1957.
[7] For an evaluation of these and other explanations, see F. David Martin, "The Sociological Imperative of Stylistic Development," Bucknell Review, vol. XI, no. 4, pp. 54–80, December, 1963.

phasis upon moderation and harmony, the importance of mathematical measurement and yet its subordination to man's aesthetic needs, the respect for the "thingliness" of things, the eminence of man and his rationality, the immanence rather than the transcendence of the sacred.

Chartres is an exceptional example of the preservation of the past. The structure reveals three principal value areas of that medieval region: the special importance of Mary, to whom the cathedral is dedicated; the cathedral school, one of the most important centers of learning in Europe in the twelfth and thirteenth centuries; and the value preferences of the main patrons—the royal family, the lesser nobility, and the local guilds. The windows of the 175 surviving panels and the sculpture, including over two thousand carved figures, were a Bible in glass and stone for the illiterate, but they were also a visual encyclopedia for the literate. From these structures the iconographer—the decipherer of the meaning of icons or symbols—can trace almost every fundamental value of the society out of which Chartres Cathedral was built: the conception of the history of mankind from Adam and Eve to the Last Judgment; the story of Christ from his ancestors to his Ascension; church history; ancient lore and contemporary history; the latest scientific knowledge; the curriculum of the cathedral school as divided into the trivium and the quadrivium; the hierarchy of the nobility and the guilds; the code of chivalry and manners; and the hopes and fears of the time. Furthermore, the participator also becomes aware of a society that believed God to be transcendent but the Virgin to be both transcendent and immanent, not just a heavenly queen but also a mother. Chartres is Mary's home. For, as Henry Adams insisted: "You had better stop here, once for all, unless you are willing to feel that Chartres was made what it was, not by the artist, but by the Virgin." Even if we disagree with Adams, we understand, at least to some extent, Mary's special position within the context of awe aroused by God as "wholly other." The architecture of Chartres does many things, but, above all, its structures preserve that awe. Something of the society of the Chartres that was comes into our present awareness with overwhelming impact. And then we can understand something about the feelings of such medieval men as Abbot Haimon of Normandy who, after visiting Chartres, wrote to his brother monks in Tutbury, England:

> Who has ever heard tell, in times past, that powerful princes of the world, that men brought up in honor and wealth, that nobles, men and women, have bent their proud and haughty necks to the harness of carts, and that, like beasts of burden, they have dragged to the abode of Christ these waggons, loaded with wines, grains, oil, stone, wood, and all that is necessary for the wants of life, or for the construction of the church . . .? When they have reached the church, they arrange the waggons about it like a spiritual camp, and during the whole night they celebrate the watch by hymns and canticles. On each waggon they light tapers and lamps; they place there the infirm and sick, and bring them the precious relics of the Saints for their relief.

1. Describe other values in addition to the functional that are interpreted in the Union Carbide Building (Figure 6-10).

2. Do the same for Upjohn's Trinity Church (Figure 6-5) and Le Corbusier's Notre Dame du Haut (Figure 6-11). Is it easier to describe the values related to Le Corbusier's church? If so, how can this be explained?

3. Compare the Palazzo Vendramin-Calergi in Venice, completed in 1534 (Figure 6-14), with the building at 23 Havengade, in Copenhagen, completed in 1865 (Figure 6-15). Which one seems to you better architecturally? Explain. Ask yourself the same question about Chartres and the Trinity Church, but try to imagine the latter before it was submerged by skyscrapers.

To participate with a work of architecture fully, we must have as complete an understanding as possible of its subject matter—the building's function and the relevant values of the society from which that building emerged. The more we know about the region of Chartres in medieval times, the more we will appreciate its cathedral. The more we understand our own time, the more we will appreciate the Union Carbide Building. Similarly, the more we understand about the engineering problems involved in a work of architecture, including especially the potentialities of its materials, the better our appreciation. And, of course, the more we know about the stylistic history of architectural elements and structures and their possibilities, the deeper will be our appreciation. That tradition is a long and complex one, but you can learn its essentials in any good book on the history of architecture.

Let us return again to architecture and space, for what most clearly distinguishes architecture from painting and sculpture is the way it works in space. Works of architecture separate an inside space from an outside space. They make that inside space available for human functions.[8] And in interpreting their subject matter (functions and their society's values), architects make space "space." They bring out the power and embrace of the positioned interrelationships of things. Architecture in this respect can be divided into three main types—the earth-rooted, the sky-oriented, and the earth-resting.

EARTH-ROOTED ARCHITECTURE

The earth is the securing agency that grounds the place of our existence, our center. In most primitive cultures it is believed that man is born from the earth. And in many languages man is the "Earth-born." In countless myths, Mother Earth is the bearer of man from birth to death. Of all things the

[8] Since the inside space of the Memphis Pyramid (Figure 5-6) is useful only for the dead, the pyramid is not clearly classifiable as either architecture or sculpture.

FIGURE 6-14   Palazzo Vendramin-Calergi, Venice. 1534. Photograph by P. Lombardo, Anderson, Rome.

FIGURE 6-15   23 Havengade, Copenhagen. Completed 1865. Architect, F. Meldahl.

expansive earth, with its germinal riches and vegetative fecundity, most suggests or is symbolic of security. Moreover, since the solidity of the earth encloses its depth in darkness, the earth is also suggestive of mystery.

No other thing exposes its surface more pervasively and yet hides its depth dimension more completely. The earth is always closure in the midst of disclosure. If we dig below the surface, there is always a further depth in darkness that continues to escape our penetration. Thus the Earth Mother has a mysterious, nocturnal, even funerary aspect—she is also often a goddess of death. But, as the theologian Mircea Eliade points out, "even in respect of these negative aspects, one thing that must never be lost sight of, is that when the Earth becomes a goddess of Death, it is simply because she is felt to be the universal womb, the inexhaustible source of all creation."[9] Nothing in nature is more suggestive or symbolic of security and mystery than the earth. Earth-rooted architecture accentuates this natural symbolism more than any other art.

SITE

Architecture that is earth-rooted discloses the earth by drawing our attention to the building's site, or to its submission to gravity, or to its raw materials, or to its centrality in outer and inner space. Sites whose surrounding environment can be seen from great distances are especially favorable for helping a building bring out the earth. The site of the Parthenon (Figures 6-6 and 6-7), for example, is superior in this respect to the site of Chartres (Figures 6-2 and 6-3), because the Acropolis is a natural center that stands out prominently within a widespread concaved space. Thus the Parthenon is able to emphasize by continuity both the sheer heavy stoniness of the cliffs of the Acropolis and the gleaming whites of Athens. By contrast, it sets off the deep blue of the Mediterranean sky and sea and the grayish greens of the encompassing mountains that open out toward the weaving blue of the sea like the bent rims of a colossal flower. All these elements of the earth would be present without the Parthenon, of course, but the Parthenon, whose columns from a distance push up like stamens, centers these elements more tightly so that their interrelationships add to the vividness of each. Together they form the ground from which the Parthenon slowly and majestically rises.

GRAVITY

The Parthenon is also exceptional in the way it manifests a gentle surrender to gravity. The horizontal rectangularity of the entablature follows evenly along the plain of the Acropolis with the steady beat of its supporting columns and quiets their upward thrust. Gravity is accepted and accentuated in this serene stability; the hold of the earth is secure.

The site of Mont Saint Michel (Figure 6-16) can also be seen from great distances, especially from the sea, and the church, straining far up

[9] Mircea Eliade, *Myths, Dreams and Mysteries*, Philip Mairet (trans.), Harper, New York, 1961, p. 188.

from the great rock cliffs, organizes a vast scene of sea, sand, shallow
hills, and sky. But the spiny, lonely verticality of the church overwhelms
the pull of the earth. We are lured to the sky, to the world of light, whereas
the Parthenon draws us back into the womb of the earth. Mont Saint Michel
discloses the earth, for both the earth and a world to be opened up require
centering and thus each other, but the defiance of gravity weakens the
securing sense of place. Mont Saint Michel rapidly moves us around its
walls, when the tides permit, with a dizzying effect, whereas the Parthenon
moves us around slowly and securely so that our orientation is never in
doubt. The significance of the earth is felt much more deeply at the Parthenon than at Mont Saint Michel.

The complex of skyscrapers that composes Rockefeller Center (Figure
6-17) in New York City is an exceptional example of an architecture that
allows for only a minimal submission to gravity. The surrounding buildings,
unless we are high up in one nearby, block out the lower sections of the
Center. If we are able to see the lower sections by getting in close, we are
blocked from a clear and comprehensive view of the upper sections. Thus
the relationships between the lower and upper sections are somewhat
disintegrated, and there is a sense of these tapering towers, especially the
R. C. A. Building, not only scraping but being suspended from the sky.
The Union Carbide Building (Figure 6-10), not far away, carries this feeling
even further by the placement of the shaftlike box on stilts. This apparently
weightless building mitigates but does not annihilate our feeling of the
earth, for despite its arrowlike soaring, we are aware of its base. Even at
night, when the sides of this structure become dark curtains pierced by

FIGURE 6-17 Rockefeller Center, New York City. 1931–1940. Courtesy of Rockefeller Center, Inc. Photograph by Wendell MacRae.

hundreds of square lights, we feel these lights, as opposed to the light of the stars, as somehow grounded. Architecture in setting up a world always sets forth the earth, and vice versa.

RAW MATERIALS

When the medium of architecture is made up totally or in large part of unfinished materials furnished by nature, especially when they are from the site, these materials stand forth and also help to reveal the earthiness of the earth. In this respect stone, wood, and clay in a raw or relatively raw state are much more effective than steel, concrete, and glass. If the Parthenon had been made in concrete rather than in native Pentelic marble —the quarries can still be seen in the background—it would not grow out of the soil so organically and some of the feeling of the earth would be dissipated. On the other hand, if the paint that originally covered much of the Parthenon had remained, the effect would be considerably less earthy than at present. Frank Lloyd Wright's Kaufman house (Figure 6-18) is an excellent example of the combined use of manufactured and raw materials that helps set forth the earth. The concrete and glass bring out by contrast the textures of stone and wood taken from the site, while the lacelike flow of the falling water is made even more graceful by its reflection in the smooth clear flow of concrete and glass. Like a wide-spreading plant, drawing the sunlight and rain to its good earth, this home seems to breathe within its homeland.

CENTRALITY

Finally, a building that is strongly centered, both in relation to its outer space and within its inner space, helps disclose the earth. Perhaps no

FIGURE 6-18 Frank Lloyd Wright, Kaufman house ("Falling Water"), Bear Run, Pennsylvania. 1937–1939. Photograph by Bill Hedrich, Hedrich-Blessing, Chicago.

building is more centered in its site than the Parthenon, but the weak
centering of its inner space slackens somewhat the significance of the
earth. Unlike Chartres, there is no strong pull into the Parthenon, and
when we get inside, the inner space, as we reconstruct it, is divided in such
a way that no certain center can be felt. There is no place to come to an
unequivocal standstill as at Chartres. Even Versailles (Figure 6-19), despite
its seemingly never-ending partitions of inner space, brings us eventually
to something of a center in the bed of the bedroom of Louis XIV. Yet this
centering is made possible primarily by the view from the room that focuses
both the pivotal position of the room in the building and the room's placement in a straight line to Paris in the far distance. Conversely, the inner
space of Chartres, most of which from the crossing can be taken in with one
sweep of the eye, achieves centrality without this kind of dependence upon
outside orientation. Buildings such as the Parthenon and Versailles, which
divide the inner space with solid partitions, invariably are weaker in inner
centrality than buildings without such divisions. The endless boxes within
boxes of the Union Carbide Building (Figure 6-10) negate any possibility
of significant inner centering, adding to the unearthiness of this cage of
steel.

Buildings whose inner space not only draws us to a privileged position
but whose inner space or most of it can be seen from that privileged position evoke a feeling of powerful inner centeredness. This feeling is further
enhanced when the expanses of inner space are more or less equidistant

from the privileged position. Thus Greek-cross buildings,[10] such as Giuliano da Sangallo's Santa Maria delle Carceri (Figures 6-20 and 6-21) in Prato, are likely to center us in inner space more strongly than Latin-cross buildings, such as Chartres (Figure 6-4). If Bramante's and Michelangelo's Greek-cross plan for St. Peter's had been carried out, the centrality of the inner space would have been greatly enhanced. It does not follow, however, that all centrally planned buildings that open up all or almost all of the inner space will be strongly centered internally. San Vitale (Figures 6-22 and 6-23) in Ravenna, for example, is basically an octagon, but the enfolded interior spaces are not clearly outlined and differentiated as in Santa Maria delle Carceri. There is a floating and welling of space working out and up through the arcaded niches into the outer layers of the ambulatory and gallery that fade into semidarkness. The dazzling colors of the varied marble slabs and the mosaics lining the piers and walls, unlike the somber static grays and whites of Sangallo's inner church, add to our sense of spatial uncertainty. We can easily discover the center of San Vitale if we so desire, but there is no directed movement to it because the indeterminacy of the surrounding spaces makes the feeling of the center insecure and insignificant. The unanchored restlessness of the interior of San Vitale belies its solid weighty exterior.

Buildings in the round, other things being equal, are the most internally centered of all. In the Pantheon (Figure 6-24), all inner space can be seen

[10] The arms of a Greek cross, unlike those of a Latin cross, are equal in length. Thus the ground dimensions of a building in the shape of a Greek cross can be encompassed, more or less, within a circle.

FIGURE 6-22   San Vitale, Ravenna, Italy. 526–547. Alinari.

FIGURE 6-23 San Vitale, interior. Alinari.

with a turn of the head, and the grand and clear symmetry of the enclosing shell draws us to the center of the circle, the privileged position, beneath the "eye" of the dome opening to a bit of the sky. Few buildings root us more firmly in the earth. The massive dome with its stony bluntness seems to be drawn down by the funneled and dimly spreading light falling through the "eye." This is a dome of destiny pressed tightly down on men. We are driven earthward in this crushing ambience. Even on the outside the Pantheon seems to be forcing down. In the circular interior of Wright's Guggenheim Museum (Figure 6-13) not all of the inner space can be seen from the privileged position, but the smoothly curving ramp that comes down like a whirlpool makes us feel the earth beneath as our only support. The chapel of M. I. T. by Saarinen, also circular, accents the earth somewhat differently. No natural light is allowed to come inside directly; but natural light falls upon pools of water that lie below the floor and around the perimeter of the drum, the light flickering up the undulating interior walls. Thus in a strange way it appears as if the light, like the water, were coming up from the earth. This helps draw the drum down into the gound. In buildings such as these, especially in their centers, we are made to feel the presence of the earth with exceptional force. Whereas in buildings such as Mont Saint Michel and Chartres mass is overcome, the weight lightened, and the downward motion thwarted, in buildings such as the Pantheon, the Guggenheim Museum, and the chapel of M. I. T. mass comes out heavily and pushing down.

The importance of a center, usually within a circle, as a privileged and even sacred position in relation to the earth, is common among the spatial arrangements of ancient cultures, for example, Stonehenge, on the Salisbury

FIGURE 6-24 Giovanni Paolo Panini, "Interior of the Pantheon, Rome." 1691–1692. Canvas, 50½ by 39 inches. National Gallery of Art, Washington, D.C. Samuel H. Kress Collection. The Pantheon itself dates from the second century after Christ.

Plain of England. And the first city of Rome, according to Plutarch,[11] was laid out by the Etruscans around a circular trench or *mundus*, over which was placed a great capstone. Around the *mundus*, the Etruscans outlined a large circle for the walls which would enclose the city. Following a carefully prescribed ritual, a deep furrow was plowed along the circle and the plow was lifted from the ground wherever a gate was to appear. This circular plan was subdivided by two main cross streets: the *cardo*, running north and south in imitation of the axis of the earth, and the *decumanus*, running east and west. These divided the city into four equal

[11] John Dryden (trans.), *Plutarch's Lives*, Random House, Modern Library, New York, 1932, p. 31.

parts. These streets crossed at the site of the *mundus*, believed to be an entrance to the underworld, and the capstone was removed three times each year to allow the spirits passage between the world of the living and the world of the dead. Although such beliefs and customs have long been dead in Western civilization, we still can feel the power of the earth in circular city plans and buildings.

SKY-ORIENTED ARCHITECTURE

Architecture that is sky-oriented suggests or is symbolic of a world as the generating agency that enables us to project our possibilities and realize some of them. A horizon, always a necessary part of a world, is symbolic of the limitations placed upon our possibilities and realizations. The light and heat of the sun are more symbolic than anything else in nature of generative power. Dante declared that "there is no visible thing in the world more worthy to serve as symbol of God than the Sun; which illuminates with visible life itself first and then all the celestial and mundane bodies." The energy of the moving sun brightens the sky which, in turn, opens up for us a spacious context within which we attempt to realize our possibilities. In total darkness we may be able to orient ourselves to the earth, but in order to move with direction, as do the blind, we must imagine space as open in some way, as a world enlightened with light even if our imaginations must provide that light. Total darkness, at least until we can envision a world, is terrifying. That is why, as the Preacher of Ecclesiastes proclaims, "the light is sweet, and a pleasant thing it is for the eyes to behold the sun." The "light of the living" is a common Hebrew phrase, and in Greek "to behold light" is synonymous with "to live." The light of the sky reveals the positioned interrelationships of things. The semispherical space of the sky, with its limits provided by the horizon, embraces a world within which we find ourselves. But a world is above all the context for activity. Thus a world stirs our imaginations to possibilities. A world, with its suggestion of expectation, turns our faces to the future, just as the smile of the sun lures our eyes. Architecture organizes a world, usually far more tightly than nature, by centering that world on the earth by means of a building. By accentuating the natural symbolism of sunlight, sky, and horizon, sky-oriented architecture opens up a world that is symbolic of our projections into the future.

Such architecture discloses a world by drawing our attention to the sky bounded by a horizon. It accomplishes this by means of making a building appear high and centered within the sky, or defying gravity, or tightly integrating the light of outer with inner space. Negatively, architecture that accents a world deemphasizes the features that accent the earth. Thus the manufactured materials, such as the steel and glass, of the Union Carbide Building (Figure 6-10) help separate this building from the earth. Positively, the most effective means at the architect's disposal for accenting a world is turning his structure toward the sky in such a way that the sky's horizon forms a spacious context. Architecture is an art of bounding as well as opening.

AXIS MUNDI

Even before buildings become architecture, primitive man often expresses this need for a world by centering himself in relation to the sky by means of an *axis mundi*. Eliade presents many instances, for example, among the nomadic Australians, whose economy is still at the stage of gathering food and hunting small game:

> According to the traditions of an Arunta tribe, the Achipla, in mythical times the divine being Numbakula cosmicized their future territory, created their Ancestor, and established their institutions. From the trunk of a gum tree Numbakula fashioned the sacred pole *(kauwa-auwa)* and, after anointing it with blood, climbed it and disappeared into the sky. This pole (the *axis mundi*) represents a cosmic axis, for it is around the sacred pole that terrritory becomes habitable, hence is transformed into a world. The sacred pole consequently plays an important role ritually. During their wanderings the Achipla always carry it with them and choose the direction they are to take by the direction toward which it bends. This allows them, while being continually on the move, to be always in "their world" and, at the same time, in communication with the sky into which Numbakula vanished. For the pole to be broken denotes catastrophe; it is like "the end of the world," reversion to chaos. Spencer and Gillen report that once, when the pole was broken, "the entire clan were in consternation; they wandered about aimlessly for a time, and finally lay down on the ground together and waited for death to overtake them."[12]

When buildings accent a world, their turning to the sky invariably suggests a kind of *axis mundi*. The perpendicularity and centering of the Acropolis (Figure 6-6), for example, make it a kind of natural *axis mundi* that would open up the sky to some extent even if the Parthenon had never been built. But the flat plains around Chartres (Figure 6-2) would rarely turn us to the sky without the spires of the cathedral. At one time the spire of Trinity Church (Figure 6-5), beautifully proportioned despite its lack of originality, must have organized the sky. Buildings that stretch up far above the land and nearby structures, such as Mont Saint Michel (Figure 6-16), Durham Cathedral, Chartres (Figures 6-2 and 6-3), and Rockefeller Center (Figure 6-17), not only direct our eye to the sky but act as a center that orders the sunlight in such a way that a world with a horizon comes into view. The sky both opens up and takes on limits. Such buildings reach up like an *axis mundi*, and the sky reaches down to meet them in mutual

[12] Mircea Eliade, *The Sacred and the Profane*, Willard R. Trask (trans.), Harcourt Brace Jovanovich, Inc., 1959, pp. 32f.

FIGURE 6-25 Cass Gilbert,
Woolworth Building, New
York City. 1913. Photograph
from Ely-Cruikshank Com-
pany, Inc.

embrace. And we are blessed with an orienting center, our motion being
given direction and boundaries.

DEFIANCE OF GRAVITY

The more a building appears to defy gravity, the more it is likely to disclose the sky, for this defiance draws our eyes upward. The thrust against
gravity is not simply a question of how high the building goes. Most of the
skyscrapers of New York City, like the Woolworth Building (Figure 6-25)
and unlike the Union Carbide Building (Figure 6-10), seem to finally stop

FIGURE 6-26 Filippo Brunelleschi, dome of the Cathedral of Florence. 1420–1436. Italian Government Travel Office.

not because they have reached a more or less perfect union with the sky but because the space used up had exhausted them. They hang lifelessly despite their great height. They seem to have just enough strength to stand upright but no power to transcend the rudimentary laws of statics. Gravity wins out after all. The up and the down frustrate each other, and their conflict dims the world that might have been. Chartres is not nearly so tall as the Woolworth Building, and yet it appears far taller. The stony logic of the press of Chartres's flying buttresses and the arched roof, towers, and spires that carry on their upward thrust seem to overcome the binding of the earth, just as the stone birds on Chartres's walls seem about to break their bonds and fly out into the world. The reach up is full of vital force and finally comes to rest comfortably and securely in the bosom of the heavens. Mont Saint Michel and Durham Cathedral, mainly because of the advantages of their sites, are even more impressive in this respect. But perhaps Brunelleschi's dome of the Cathedral of Florence (Figure 6-26) is the most powerful structure ever built in seeming to defy gravity and achieving height in relation to its site. The eight outside ribs spring up to the cupola with tremendous energy, in part because they repeat the spring of the mountains that encircle Florence. The dome, visible from almost everywhere in and around Florence, appears to be precisely centered in the Arno Valley, precisely as high as it should be in order to organize its sky. The world of Florence begins and ends at the still point of this dome of aspiration. On the other hand, Michelangelo's dome of St. Peter's (Figure 6-1), although grander in proportions and over 50 feet higher, fails to organize the sky of Rome nearly so firmly, mainly because the hills of Rome do not lend themselves to centralized organization.

INTEGRATION OF LIGHT

When the light of outer space suffuses the light of inner space, especially when the light from the outside seems to dominate or draw the light from the inside, this also helps accent a world. Inside Chartres the light is so majestic that we cannot fail to imagine the light outside that is generating the transfiguration inside. For a medieval man like Abbot Suger the effect was mystical, separating the earth from the world of heaven:

> When the house of God, many colored as the radiance of precious jewels, called me from the cares of the world, then holy meditation led my mind to thoughts of piety, exalting my soul from the material to the immaterial, and I seemed to find myself, as it were, in some strange part of the universe which was neither wholly of the baseness of the earth, nor wholly of the serenity of heaven, but by the grace of God I seemed lifted in a mystic manner from this lower toward the upper sphere.

On the other hand, for a contemporary man the stained glass is likely to be felt more as integrating us with rather than separating us from a world. We sense the unity of inner with outer space by means of the light, the effect that Saarinen avoids in the chapel at M. I. T. The upper chapel of

FIGURE 6-27 Hagia Sophia, Istanbul, Turkey, interior. A.D. 532–537; restored 558, 975. From Turkish Tourism and Information Office, New York.

the Sainte-Chapelle in Paris, built by order of St. Louis, is an extraordinary example of how even a small building can accent a world by means of its stained glass. The inner space is so full of moving color energized by the sun, whose power changes with the hours and the seasons, that we image a great world outside even though we cannot see it directly and even though the structure of the building has little centralizing effect upon the sky. Unlike the Sainte-Chapelle, Hagia Sophia in Istanbul (Figure 6-27) has no stained glass and its glass areas are completely dominated by the walls and dome. Yet the subtle placement of the little windows, especially around the perimeter of the dome, seems to draw the light of the inner space up and out. Thus, unlike the Pantheon (Figure 6-24), the great masses of Hagia Sophia seem to rise. The dome floats gently, despite its diameter of 107 feet, and the great enfolded space beneath is absorbed into the even greater open space outside. We image a world.

Sky-oriented architecture suggests the generative activity of a world. The sun's energy is the ultimate source of all life. The sun's light enables us to see the physical environment and guides our steps accordingly. "Arise, shine, for thy light is come" (Isaiah 60:1). The sky with its horizon provides a spacious context for our progress. The world of nature vaguely suggests the potentialities of the future. Architecture, however, tightly centers a world on the earth by means of its structures. This unification gives us a sense of security.

EARTH-RESTING ARCHITECTURE

Most architecture accents neither earth nor sky but rests on the earth, using the earth like a platform and the sky as background. Earth-resting buildings may either dominate the earth, as in the case of the Palazzo Farnese (Figures 6-28 and 6-29) in Rome, or relate harmoniously to the earth, as in the case of Mies van der Rohe's residence of Dr. Edith Farnsworth (Figure 6-30), Plano, Illinois. Generally earth-resting buildings are not very tall, have flat roofs, and avoid strong vertical extensions such as spires and chimneys. Thus—unlike sky-oriented architecture—the earth-resting type does not strongly organize the sky around itself, as with Chartres (Figure 6-2) or the Cathedral of Florence (Figure 6-26). The sky is involved with earth-resting architecture, of course, but more as a setting.

With earth-resting architecture, unlike earth-rooted architecture, the earth does not appear as an organic part of the building as in Wright's Kaufman house (Figure 6-18) or as an integral part as in Saarinen's chapel at M. I. T. Rather, the earth appears as a stage. Earth-resting buildings, moreover, are usually cubes that avoid cantilevering structures, as in the Kaufman house, as well as curving lines, as in the chapel at M. I. T. Earth-rooted architecture seems to "hug to" the earth, as in the M. I. T. chapel and the Pantheon (Figure 6-24), or to grow out of the earth, as with the Kaufman house. Earth-resting architecture, on the other hand, seems to

FIGURE 6-28 Antonio da Sangallo and Michelangelo Buonarrotti, Palazzo Farnese, Rome. 1534. Alinari.

FIGURE 6-29 Palazzo Farnese, courtyard. Alinari.

"sit on" the earth. Thus this kind of architecture, because it does not relate to its environment quite as strongly as earth-rooted and sky-oriented architecture, usually tends to draw to itself more isolated attention with reference to its shape, articulation of the elements of its walls, lighting, etc.

Earth-resting architecture is usually more appropriate than earth-rooted architecture when the site is severely bounded by other buildings. Perhaps this is a basic deficiency of Wright's Guggenheim Museum (Figure 6-12). In any case, it is obvious that if buildings were constructed close to the Kaufman house—especially earth-resting or sky-oriented types—they would destroy much of the glory of Wright's creation.

PERCEPTION KEY: PALAZZO FARNESE

Study the Palazzo Farnese (Figures 6-28 and 6-29), c. 1534, by Antonio da Sangallo and Michelangelo.

1. The facade of this building is 185 feet by 96 1/2 feet. Is there any particular significance to the large size and proportion of these dimensions? Suppose, for example, that the construction had stopped with the second floor. Would the relationship between width and height be as "right" as it now appears?

2. Does the relationship between the sizes of the three floors have a "right-ness"? If so, how is this to be explained?

3. The window pediments of the first floor are all alike. On the second floor, however, there is an a/b rhythm, the windows at the ends of the facade being topped by triangles. Then, as we move toward the center of the facade, semicircular pediments interrupt the triangular pediments. Why this rhythm? Why not have the same rhythm on the first and third floors? Why do semicircular rather than triangular pediments lead to the central window, with its large family insignia and porch?

4. The cornice—the horizontal molding projecting along the top of the building—is very large, and the corners of the facade are accented by roughly cut stones. Why?

5. Does this palace require a large open space in front of its facade? If so, why?

6. Sangallo designed the first two floors and Michelangelo designed the third. The differences between their two styles are more evident in the courtyard (Figure 6-29). What are these differences? For example, which floor seems to have crowded elements, and which floor seems most restless? Did Michelangelo successfully unite his third floor with Sangallo's?

7. In answering the above questions are you inevitably led to consider the function of this building? If you were told that this building was a church, for example, would you be both surprised and distressed? Would your answers be different?

8. What function and what values are revealed in this building? In other words, what is the subject matter that the form informs about? And how does the form achieve its content?

The residence of Dr. Edith Farnsworth (Figure 6-30), designed by Mies van der Rohe, exemplifies his paradoxical doctrine that "less is more." On the Palazzo Farnese much ornament—for example, all the elements around the windows—could be removed and the building would still stand. But with Mies's work, it seems as if nothing is there that is not necessary for the technical solutions of making the building stand.

PERCEPTION KEY: FARNSWORTH RESIDENCE AND THE PALAZZO FARNESE

1. The simplicity of Mies's house may be misleading. Analyze the placement of the elements and their proportions, and see if you can discover why this work is considered to be a small masterpiece by one of the greatest of modern architects. For instance, why are the posts not out at the corners? Why do the posts meet a projecting line of the roof rather than coming up under the roof?

2. How are light and outer space related differently than with the Palazzo Farnese?

3. Why is absolute symmetry absent here, whereas in the Palazzo Farnese it is present?

4. What is the content of this home? And how does the form achieve it?

5. Mies' houses have sometimes been criticized as buildings made to be looked at rather than lived in. Do you agree?

6. Many of you someday will own your own home, perhaps build it. Try your hand at designing your ideal home. What form will reveal *your* home?

The Palazzo Farnese reveals the authority and power of a palace. It commands the earth and everything around it. Michelangelo's third floor, compared with Sangallo's floors, is even awesome, as if the power can no longer be contained and is ready to break through at any moment. Only the third floor in this mighty, sharply outlined, indestructible cube expresses movement. Mies's quiet house, conversely, rests on the earth and is a home. Its dignity is private rather than public, expressive of an efficiency that has learned much from the machine but has also learned how to control the machine. Light and air interpenetrate through the glass and post-and-lintel construction. This wedding of nature and the man-made is all the more impressive for its economy of means.

Study the Wiley House (Figure 6-31) by Philip Johnson, very much in the style of Mies van der Rohe. The functions of this house are explicitly separated—the ground floor contains the "private functions," and the open social functions are reserved for the modular glass pavilion above. Again, nothing seems to be there that does not work technically.

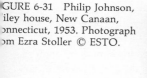

FIGURE 6-31 Philip Johnson, Wiley house, New Canaan, Connecticut, 1953. Photograph from Ezra Stoller © ESTO.

1. Do you think the ground floor and the pavilion relate to one another in a satisfactory way?

2. Are light and air integrated with the building's structure as gracefully as in Mies's building? Explain.

3. Some critics have remarked of this house that "less is a bore." Comment.

The problem of when to use earth-rooted or earth-resting or sky-oriented buildings is usually easily solved: the function of the building generally is the key. Churches and large office buildings, especially in crowded sites, lend themselves to sky orientation. Homes in rural areas lend themselves to earth orientation. Homes in crowded urban areas present special problems. Earth-rooted buildings, such as the Kaufman house (Figure 6-18), normally require relatively large open areas. Thus most urban dwellings are earth-resting. But as our populations have become increasingly dense, sky-oriented apartment buildings have become a common sight. In Reston, Virginia, for example, clusters of one-family houses of the earth-resting type are strewn over 7,400 acres of landscape. In the village plaza, however, one apartment tower rises (Figure 6-32), apparently to provide both more living space and a vertical accent that, like Chartres, would center the surrounding buildings.

PERCEPTION KEY: RESTON AND LAFAYETTE PARK

1. Does the Reston tower apartment spatially unify the one-family units around it?

2. Compare the one-story townhouses and the twenty-two-story high-rise apartment building (Figure 6-33) by Mies van der Rohe in Lafayette Park, Detroit. Does Mies succeed in integrating more harmoniously the earth-resting townhouses with the sky-oriented apartment building? If so, how?

We think Mies's solution is much more successful than the one in Reston. The windows of Mies's townhouses are broad horizontal rectangles that flow rhythmically along the earth, with just enough vertical lines to prepare for the sky orientation of the apartment building. The vertical lines of the apartment building dominate the horizontals because the height of the building somewhat exceeds its breadth. Nevertheless, the thickest lines are horizontals, and a delicate balance is achieved. Just as the horizontals slightly dominate the townhouses, the verticals slightly dominate the apartment building. The two sets of buildings require each other, and the power of their positioned relationships—their space—is brought out vividly and harmoniously.

FIGURE 6-32 Apartment complex in Reston, Virginia, 1965. Conklin and Rossant, architects. Photograph from *Matrix of Man*, 1968, by Sibyl Moholy-Nagy, Praeger Publishers. Courtesy of Hattula Moholy-Nagy Hug.

FIGURE 6-33 Ludwig Mies van der Rohe, Layfayette Park, Detroit, Michigan. Photograph from Hedrich-Blessing, Chicago.

FIGURE 6-34 National Gallery of Art, Washington, D.C., Mall entrance. Photograph from the National Gallery of Art.

In Reston, on the other hand, the vertical and horizontal lines of the one-family houses and the apartment tower fail to relate very effectively. The verticals of the tower, perhaps in part because of the isolation of the tower, seem to lack the restraint that would bring them into harmony with the family units. The latter, partly because we see them in relation to the tower, seem to be truncated towers, cut off before they had reached their proper height. Somehow both the family units and the tower fail to fit into the landscape, nor does the tower organize its surrounding buildings in a way that unifies them. Yet it seems obvious that unity was intended, and this failure is disturbing.

Consider another earth-resting building, one of the most expensive ever built in this country—the National Gallery of Art (Figure 6-34) in Washington, D. C.

PERCEPTION KEY: THE NATIONAL GALLERY OF ART

1. Would you know the function of this building just by observing it from the outside?

2. Do you find its entrance inviting? Compare St. Peter's (Figure 6-1) in this respect.

3. Does its form inform you about anything?

Combining the portico of the Temple of Diana and the dome of the Pantheon with vast wings that stretch out to a total length of 785 feet, this monstrous building, despite the very expensive materials and the great engineering skill that went into its making, reveals little except the imitative conservatism of its designers and the wealth and conservatism of its patrons. In the 1930s, when the National Gallery was planned, mainly by John Russell Pope, the United States had risen from its worst depression and was beginning to face, as potentially the most powerful nation in the world, the crisis of the coming Second World War. At the dedication of the gallery in March 1941, President Roosevelt concluded his address:

> Seventy-eight years ago, in the third year of the war between the States, men and women gathered here in the capitol of a divided nation, here in Washington, to see the bronze goddess of liberty set upon its top.
>
> It had been an expensive, a laborious business, diverting money and labor from the prosecution of the war and certain critics . . . found much to criticize. . . . But the President of the United States, whose name was Lincoln, when he heard those criticisms, answered: "If people see the Capitol going on it is a sign that we intend this Union shall go on."
>
> We may borrow the words for our own. We, too, intend the Union to go on. We intend it shall go on, carrying with it the great tradition of the human spirit which created it.
>
> The dedication of this gallery to a living past and to a greater and more richly living future is the measure of the earnestness of our intention that the freedom of the human spirit shall go on too.

Brave words by a brave President. But what living past does the architecture of this building disclose? And in what way does this building bring forth the freedom of the human spirit that shall go on? The gallery reveals rather the taste—derived from Jefferson's belief that the beautiful in architecture had been forever established in Roman masterpieces—that has bound the architecture of Washington to pale imitations of what had once been a living art. Nothing of the thrusting optimism of the United States, its ceaseless and ingenious ferment, its power and pragmatism comes out. Even the superb technology of our country is masked. Thus the engineering excellence of the steel structure is covered up, as if there were something shameful about the steel that helped make the United States prosperous. Even the immense dome gets lost in the mass of marble, and so the building spreads out without centering the outer space. Instead, the gallery awkwardly imposes its clumsy bulk into the graceful open ensemble of the Mall as planned by L'Enfant. Even the function of the building is hidden. The exterior tells us nothing about the use or even the structuring of the inner space. The building could have been constructed for just about any purpose that requires great inner dimensions. Even a "draw" by the inner into the outer space is lacking, surely an adjunct that a museum of art should provide. Indeed, the forty granite steps of mighty spread which mount up from the Mall to the main entrance, like the terror-inspiring stairways to the Mayan sacrificial platforms, tend to weaken the visitor or drive him away. The architecture, if it can be called that, goes un-

FIGURE 6-35   Paul Rudolph, Municipal Garage, New Haven, Connecticut. 1961. Photograph by Ezra Stoller Associates © ESTO.

noticed. Neither the earth nor the sky comes into focus. Unimaginatively conceived, the National Gallery of Art was stillborn.

CITY PLANNING

No use of space has become more critical in our time than in the city. In conclusion, therefore, the issues we have been discussing about space and architecture take on special relevance with respect to city planning. For example in New Haven, Connecticut, the home of Yale University, the largest and most grandiloquent building is the Municipal Garage (Figure 6-35). Wolf von Eckhardt, in an article in *Show*, December 1963, describes this building as "the most imposing shrine yet built to the automobile." With reference to the shopping center to be built next to it, Eckhardt declares that "its only virtue is that it will largely hide Mr. Rudolph's monstrous prehistoric garage." The nearby city hall, the three old churches on the lovely green, Yale University, and all other buildings of the central city tend to be dominated by this enormous storage facility.

1. Does it strike you that something is wrong about a garage having such dominance? What would you think of a house whose most predominant feature was its garage or its septic tank? Past cultures have built monuments to God and man. Does it worry you that our culture is building monuments to the automobile?

2. On the other hand, if you drive—as usually you must—into almost any city today, you find parking a tormenting, hazardous enterprise that is liable to reduce you to a nervous wreck. Then is not the New Haven garage, spacious and convenient, an excellent solution? Or, if not, what do you propose? Discuss with others.

Suppose spacious parking lots were located around the fringes of the city, rapid public transportation were readily available from those lots into the city, and in the city only public and emergency transportation—most of it undergound—were permitted. In place of poisonous fumes, screeching noises, and jammed streets, fresh air, fountains and sculpture, talk and music, and wide open spaces to walk in and to enjoy would be possible. Buildings could be participated with. All the diversified character of a city—its theaters, opera, concert halls, museums, shops, stores, offices, restaurants, markets, parks, lakes, squares, outdoor cafes—would take on some spatial unity again. If for no other reason, we could get to these various places without nervous prostration and the risk of life and limb. The city would be taken away from the automobile and given back to man.

One of the solutions proposed for the city is to decentralize. One area would be set aside for offices, another for factories, another for stores, another for residences, another for recreation, etc. Another solution is to move residences to the suburbs. But now suburbia is becoming as tyrannized by the automobile as the big city. Another solution is to develop outlying villages with a rural atmosphere, such as Reston (Fig. 6-32).

PERCEPTION KEY: CITY PLANNING

1. Do you think the city ought to be saved? What advantages does only the city possess? What still gives glamour to such cities as Florence, Rome, Paris, and London?

2. Suppose you agree that New York City is worth saving. Suppose further that you are a city planner for New York City, and assume that funds are available to implement your plans. What would you propose? For example, would you destroy all the old buildings? Joseph Hudnut has written that "There is in buildings that have withstood the seige of centuries a magic which is irrespective of form and technical excellence. . . . the wreckage of distant worlds are radioactive with a long-gathered energy. . . ."[13]

[13] Joseph Hudnut, *Architecture and the Spirit of Man*, Harvard University Press, Cambridge, Mass., 1949, pp. 15f.

FIGURE 6-36 High-rise apartments above the Bronx River, New York. Photograph from *Matrix of Man*, 1968, by Sibyl Moholy-Nagy, Praeger Publishers. Courtesy of Hattula Maholy-Nagy Hug.

Do you agree? Would you be satisfied with high-rise apartments such as those on a bluff above the Bronx River (Figure 6-36)? Or what do you think of the cluster of apartment buildings of Stuyvesant Town (Figure 6-37) in Manhattan? What would you do with such a Manhattan area as in Figure 6-38? Would you separate areas by function? The Wall Street area, for example, contains the financial interests. Is this a good idea? Would you allow factories within the city limits? Or do you think factories are cancers within the city? How would you handle transportation to and within the city? For instance, would you allow expressways to slice through the city, as in Detroit and Los Angeles? If you outlawed the private car from the city, what would you do with the streets? Could the streets become a unifier of the city?

3. Suppose one side of an old residential street is salvageable, as with these row houses (Figure 6-39) in Brooklyn Heights, and the other side is to be put to nonresidential use. Would you necessarily design your new buildings

FIGURE 6-37 Stuyvesant Town, New York. Photograph from *Matrix of Man*, 1968, by Sibyl Moholy-Nagy, Praeger Publishers. Courtesy of Hattula Moholy-Nagy Hug.

FIGURE 6-38 A section of Manhattan, New York. Photograph from *Matrix of Man*, 1968, by Sibyl Moholy-Nagy, Praeger Publishers. Courtesy of Hattula Moholy-Nagy Hug.

FIGURE 6-39 Row houses, Brooklyn Heights, New York. Photograph from *Matrix of Man*, 1968, by Sibyl Moholy-Nagy, Praeger Publishers. Courtesy of Hattula Moholy-Nagy Hug.

FIGURE 6-40 Osterleen Historical Museum, Hanover, Germany. 1964. Photograph by Hans Wagner, Hanover.

in the same style as the old? As you reflect about this, study Dieter Oster-leen's Historical Museum (Figure 6-40) in Hanover, Germany, built in 1964, in its relation to the old half-timbered houses across the street.

If we have been near the truth, then the architect is the shepherd of space. And to be sensitive to his building is to help, in our more humble way, to preserve his preservation. The architect makes space a gracious place. Such places, like a home, give us a center from which we can orient ourselves to other places. And then we can be at home in the homeland.

7 LITERATURE

INTRODUCTION

Language is the basic medium of literature. Drama involves, in addition, the spectacle of acting, while the lyric poem was originally sung or accompanied by a musical instrument. The marriage of lyric and music continues, although less frequently, even today. Drama, which we will not examine directly, involves spoken language, but—less obviously—this is true of all literature. Since we are living in an age in which the printed word is taken for granted and few people memorize literature, we forget that the invention of literature was oral. The bards who sang Homer's epics, *The Iliad* and *The Odyssey*, had them memorized entirely, and they spent hours chanting them—usually to the thrum of a one-stringed harplike instrument.

Geoffrey Chaucer wrote down his *Canterbury Tales* for convenience, more than a century before the invention of the printing press. But he read his tales out loud to an audience of courtly listeners who were much more attuned to hearing a good story than to reading it. Today, people interested in literature are usually described as readers, which underscores the dependence we have developed on the printed word for our literary experience. However, since words "sound" even when read silently, and since many writers and most poets actually read their work out loud when invited to do so, we will reemphasize the tradition: the medium of literature is spoken language. If possible, you should hear all the literature in this chapter in recitation. If this is not possible, read it out loud, or, if this disturbs your neighbors, let the sound of the words ring in your inner ear. Do not attempt speed reading literature. Let your eye follow the pace of the words as controlled by the way your mouth, tongue, and vocal chords form the words, even silently. Do not let sight overwhelm sound.

Interestingly enough, E. E. Cummings's poem, which we discussed on pages 13–15, might seem to be an exception. Built upon the arrangement of the *littera* (Latin for "letters"), the most basic elements of literature, the visual structure may seem more important than the sound structure. If Cummings's poem were to be recited aloud, it would take at least two people to recite it, since one word, "loneliness," has to be sustained while the other words, "a leaf falls," are spoken.

PERCEPTION KEY   RECITING CUMMINGS'S "l (a"

1. With a group of readers, try to stage a recitation of Cummings's "l (a" on page 13. Several groups could approach the problem from several directions—using individuals to be responsible for specific letters or syllables or a given word.

2. Comment at length on the recitations you have heard and evaluate them. Can this poem be effectively recited? If so, what conditions are necessary?

Treating literature as a phenomenon of spoken language points up its relationship to other serial arts like music, dance, and film. Literature happens in time and aural space. In order to perceive it we must be aware of what is happening now, remember what happened before, and anticipate what is to come. This is not so obvious to us in a short lyric poem or in Cummings's "l (a" because we are in the presence of something akin to a painting: it seems to be all there in front of us at once. But this is far from the truth. To prove this, simply read a short poem, either aloud or silently. One letter follows another; one word another; one sentence another; one line or one stanza another. There is no way for us to perceive the "all-at-onceness" of a literary work as we sometimes perceive a painting, although Cumming's poem comes close.

There is a sense in which a work of literature is a construction, like architecture, of separable elements. The textural details of a scene, a character or event, or a symbol pattern can be conceived as the bricks in the wall of a literary structure. If one of them is weakly conceived, it can weaken the entire structure. Likewise, if one of those details is imperfectly perceived, our understanding of the function of that detail—and, in turn, of the total structure—will be imperfect. The theme of a literary work is comparable to the architectural decision about the kind of space being enclosed: is it that of a house, church, shopping center, ballroom? The characters—principal and subordinate as well, the setting, the sound of the language, the uses of metaphor, symbol, and the mode of the narrative are all comparable to the decisions regarding the materials, size, shape, and landscaping of architecture. Here, perhaps, the analogy ends. But its usefulness will be seen as we proceed in our discussions about the texture and structure of literature. It is not just useful but essential to think of literature as works composed of elements which can be discussed individually in order to gain a more thorough perception of them. And it is equally important to realize that the discussion of these individual elements conduces to a fuller understanding of the whole structure.

Our structural emphasis in the following pages will be on the nature of the narrative, both the organic narrative, in which all or most of the individual textural details have a direct bearing on all other details, and the episodic narrative, in which the interdependence of the details is not so tightly organized. Once we have explored some of the basic structures of literature, we will examine some of the more important textural elements. Here our attention will be focused on linguistic details. If the medium of literature is language, we must be sensitive to the fact that literature explores the sounds and meanings of language. In everyday language situations, what we say is often what we mean. But in a work of literature things are rarely that simple. Language has denotation and connotation: a literal and obvious level and a more subtle and suggestive level. When we are being denotative, we say the rose is sick and mean nothing more than that. But if we are using language connotatively, we might mean any of several things by such a statement. When the poet William Blake says the rose is sick, he is describing a symbolic rose, something very different from a literal rose.

The literary symbol is only one kind of use of language which stretches language's capacity for meaning. Similes, metaphors, images (which make a more direct appeal to our sensory experience), and certain uses of language which have become conventionally acceptable, such as the sounds of the language of the psalms in the King James Bible, will concern us when we speak of textural elements in literature. All these qualities are possessed by poetry, fiction, drama, and even the essay.

Our emphasis in the following pages on narrative and lyric structures is not meant to imply that other structures—expository, argumentative, and other essayistic writings—are not worth close examination from a literary point of view. Nor is it meant to imply that the narrative and lyric structures are superior to others or totally independent of others. Some essays have narrative or story structure; some focus on a relatively isolated emotional situation which is the hallmark of lyric. The urge to tell a story and to explore an emotional situation seems basic to most literature. Moreover, some lyrics can be seen as narrative in that they tell a story which centers on an emotional situation. Likewise, some narratives can be regarded as lyric in some ways. It is important, therefore, to understand that we are not arguing for excluding the narrative from the lyric or vice versa.

We are separating, for the purpose of examination, structural approaches to the use of language which can intersect and which can help us understand all forms of literature.

What we are doing in the immediately following pages is examining the narrative resources of literature by identifying those approaches to narrative structure which we need most to understand. Much the same is true in our discussion of lyric. We are examining the resources of lyric structure which we need most to be sensitive to in developing our capacity to appreciate not only the lyric but all literary structures.

LITERARY STRUCTURES

We begin with the narrative—a basic structural principle that is often used to hold together the details of character, setting, theme, language, and action.

THE NARRATIVE AND THE NARRATOR

The narrative implies a story told by a teller who controls the order of events and the emphasis the events will receive. It also implies, of course, an audience to whom the story is told. Some kinds of narrative have very little action, but usually they reveal character through a careful examination of the details of response of the characters to their experiences. Sometimes the teller of the narrative is himself a character; sometimes he pretends an awareness of the audience to whom he speaks. Our understanding of the narrative will be qualified by the choice the writer makes in creating a narrator, imagining an audience, and deciding which events will give us an understanding of the characters, their situation, or whatever the writer's subject matter may be. By way of becoming acquainted with these concepts, consider the following narrative poem, which is presented in its entirety:

PIANO

Softly, in the dusk, a woman is singing to me;
Taking me back down the vista of years, till I see
A child sitting under the piano, in the boom of the tingling strings
And pressing the small, poised feet of a mother who smiles as she sings.

In spite of myself, the insidious mastery of song
Betrays me back, till the heart of me weeps to belong
To the old Sunday evenings at home, with winter outside
And hymns in the cozy parlor, the tinkling piano our guide.

So now it is vain for the singer to burst into clamor
With the great black piano appassionato. The glamor
Of childish days is upon me, my manhood is cast
Down in the flood of remembrance, I weep like a child for the past.

PERCEPTION KEY "PIANO"

1. What is narrated here—a story of events or a story of character? How do you decide? What are the events of the narrative?

2. What do we know about the narrator of the story? How does he reveal himself to us, and what do you think he wants us to feel about him?

3. Is the narrator aware of the audience to whom the narrative is addressed? How can you tell?

Lawrence's poem concentrates carefully on the narrator, but it also concentrates on the specific situation which has given rise to the narrative itself. It is what makes possible the double focus of the man as man and as child, with all the ambiguities which the narrator's memory evokes. Many narratives avoid such ambiguities in order to present a more directly focused view. Consider the beginning of the novel *Cane*, by Jean Toomer, a writer of the "Harlem renaissance" of the 1920s:

Men had always wanted her, this Karintha, even as a child, Karintha carrying beauty, perfect as dusk when the sun goes down. Old men rode her hobby-horse upon their knees. Young men danced with her at frolics when they should have been dancing with their grown-up girls. God grant us youth, secretly prayed the old men. The young fellows counted the time to pass before she would be old enough to mate with them. This interest of the male, who wishes to ripen a growing thing too soon, could mean no good to her.[1]

PERCEPTION KEY CANE

1. What do you know about the narrator of the passage? We know a great deal, but how is that knowledge revealed and what does it imply for the narrative?

2. What is actually narrated here? This is only part of a narrative, yet, even as a part, it tells a story.

3. Consider it as only a part—the beginning—of a narrative. Do you have any ideas about what is to come in the narrative?

[1] Copyright ® 1951 by Jean Toomer. Reprinted by permission of Liveright, Publishers, New York.

Clearly the technique of this opening passage is to establish the center of the narrative: it is Karintha. We could presume from this opening that it is Karintha and not the narrator who will engage most of our attention and perform most of the notable action of the narrative. But this may not be the case. What may be the case is that the narrator is keeping himself out of view so that we do not notice him. In other words, he may be protecting himself for reasons which will be revealed later.

One interesting feature of both these examples is that in order to be consistent we must treat the narrator as a character in the literary work. Thus we understand the "I" of "Piano" as a character in the poem just as much as the mother. But the problem with that is curious. Since each of us conceives of himself as "I," we also accept the "I" of a narrative with the same kind of lack of examination we apply to accepting ourselves. Lawrence is the "I," and that is all there is to it for some readers. Yet, there is no compelling reason for us to think this; it is merely a matter of psychological habit and convenience, leading, it may be, to misinterpretations that weaken the power of the poem.

A powerful example of the way in which a writer uses the first person but clearly creates a character apart from himself is the poem "Paralytic." It is told to us by someone in an iron lung:

PARALYTIC

It happens. Will it go on?—
My mind a rock,
No fingers to grip, no tongue,
My god the iron lung

That loves me, pumps
My two
Dust bags in and out,
Will not

Let me relapse
While the day outside glides by like ticker tape
The night brings violets,
Tapestries of eyes,

Lights,
The soft anonymous
Talkers: "You all right?"
The starched, inaccessible breast.

Dead egg, I lie
Whole
On a whole world I cannot touch,
At the white, tight

Drum of my sleeping couch
Photographs visit me—
My wife, dead and flat, in 1920 furs,
Mouth full of pearls,

Two girls
As flat as she, who whisper "We're your daughters."
The still waters
Wrap my lips,

Eyes, nose and ears,
A clear
Cellophane I cannot crack.
On my bare back

I smile, a buddha, all
Wants, desire
Falling from me like rings
Hugging their lights.

The claw
Of the magnolia,
Drunk on its own scents,
Asks nothing of life.

Once we know this poem is by a woman who did not live in an iron lung and could never have lived in one, or have had a wife in the 1920s, we begin to accept the person speaking as a character in the narrative rather than as a projection of a poet-narrator addressing us. Yet, without this outside information, the poem could never have revealed this "reality." Consequently, it has become a convention in literature to treat all narrators as part of the narrative, just as we would treat all words used in the piece as part of the narrative.

1. Analyze the narrative. What are the problems of telling a story from the point of view of a person who is paralyzed?

2. Explore some of the implications of the fact that the narrator of the poem is an imaginary character invented by the poet. Is this information crucial to a full understanding of the poem?

3. What is the role of the magnolia claw—a living but not a moving instrument, as with the hands of men—in the poem?

THE EPISODIC NARRATIVE

The term "episodic" implies significant disconnectedness in the parts of the structure. The episodic narrative is one of the oldest forms of literature —Homer's *Odyssey* is an example. We are aware of the overall structure of the story centering on the adventures of Odysseus, but each adventure is almost a complete structure in itself. We develop a clear sense of the character of Odysseus as we follow him in his adventures, but this does not always happen in episodic literature. Often the adventures are completely disconnected from one another, and the thread which is intended to connect everything—the character of the protagonist—is not strong enough to keep things together. Sometimes the character may even seem to be a different person from one episode to the next. This is often the case in oral literature, compositions which were "written" by tellers or singers of stories rather than by persons who wrote their narratives. In the former cases, the singers gathered adventures from many sources and joined them in one long narrative. The chances of disconnectedness, then, are naturally quite strong.

But disconnectedness is sometimes not undesirable. It is risked in the episodic narrative in order to gain several things: compression, speed of pacing, plenty of action, and variety which sustains attention. Some of the most important and famous episodic narratives are novels: Fielding's *Tom Jones*, Cervantes's *Don Quixote*, Defoe's *Moll Flanders*. These are older works, but Graham Greene's *Power and the Glory* and J. P. Donleavy's *Ginger Man* both give evidence that the mode is viable in contemporary literature.

PERCEPTION KEY THE EPISODIC NOVEL

If possible, read one of the novels cited above, or Homer's *Iliad* or *Odyssey*. In a group, discuss the question of how separate the major episodes are from the entirety of the work. Is the separateness objectionable? Does the separateness tend to characterize the entire work as a collection of occurrences? If so, does this fact weaken the work at all?

Novels and epics are not the only literary modes to use episodic structures, nor are all episodic structures long works. One very popular episodic structure is the ballad. It usually tells a story about a specific hero or heroine, and it has a peculiar quality of not respecting strict chronology or strict consistency of events. The ballad, since it was originally sung in the streets and along the byways of Europe, tends to be a casual genre. Heroes die in stanza four only to show up again hale and hearty in stanza eight. Such poems are usually the work of several wandering singers; each wishes to contribute something without undoing the work of his predecessor.

Wilfred Owen's "Disabled" is a literary ballad, that is, the product of one poet and not specifically composed orally. The time sequence is carefully controlled, with flashbacks to earlier periods in the soldier's life. Yet the very act of moving rapidly from present to earlier periods tends to give a balladic fragmentation to the poem. Jumps in time contribute to the episodic qualities of the poem, and each stanza has an independence which is typical of the ballad.

DISABLED

He sat in a wheeled chair, waiting for dark,
And shivered in his ghastly suit of gray,
Legless, sewn short at elbow. Through the park
Voices of boys rang saddening like a hymn,
Voices of play and pleasures after day,   5
Till gathering sleep had mothered them from him.

About this time Town used to swing so gay
When glow-lamps budded in the light blue trees,
And girls glanced lovelier as the air grew dim,—
In the old times, before he threw away his knees.   10
Now he will never feel again how slim
Girls' waists are, or how warm their subtle hands;
All of them touch him like some queer disease.

There was an artist silly for his face,
For it was younger than his youth, last year.   15
Now, he is old; his back will never brace;
He's lost his color very far from here,
Poured it down shell-holes till the veins ran dry,
And half his lifetime lapsed in the hot race,
And leap of purple spurted from his thigh.   20

One time he liked a blood-smear down his leg,
After the matches, carried shoulder-high.

It was after football, when he'd drunk a peg,
He thought he'd better join. —He wonders why.
Someone had said he'd look a god in kilts, 25
That's why; and may be, too, to please his Meg;
Aye, that was it, to please the giddy jilts
He asked to join. He didn't have to beg;

Smiling they wrote his lie; aged nineteen years.
Germans he scarcely thought of; all their guilt, 30
And Austria's, did not move him. And no fears
Of Fear came yet. He thought of jeweled hilts
For daggers in plaid socks; of smart salutes;
And care of arms; and leave; and pay arrears;
Esprit de corps, and hints for young recruits. 35
And soon he was drafted out with drums and cheers.
Some cheered him home, but not as crowds cheer Goal.
Only a solemn man who brought him fruits
Thanked him; and then inquired about his soul.

Now, he will spend a few sick years in Institutes, 40
And do what things the rules consider wise,
And take whatever pity they may dole.
Tonight he noticed how the women's eyes
Passed from him to the strong men that were whole.
How cold and late it is! Why don't they come 45
And put him into bed? Why don't they come?

Disabled by Wilfred Owen, taken from THE COLLECTED POEMS OF WILFRED OWEN, edited by C. Day Lewis, 1963. Chatto and Windus Ltd., London. By permission of the Executors of the Estate of Harold Owen and Chatto and Windus.

PERCEPTION KEY "DISABLED"

1. In what senses is this poem episodic? What are the episodes? Do they tend to be unrelated, or do they easily relate to one another? Discuss these points with others.

2. Consider the aspects of time and space in the narrative. What different places are focused on in the poem? How many different periods of time are mentioned?

3. How do shifts in space and time help the poem maintain an episodic quality?

4. How does the character of the disabled soldier hold the episodes together? What do the episodes reveal about him?

5. Owen was a British officer killed in the First World War. Is this information relevant to the poem? If so, in what way?

THE QUEST NARRATIVE

Any reader of mystery stories—such as those by Arthur Conan Doyle which feature Sherlock Holmes or the Miss Marple mysteries by Agatha Christie—will realize that one of the chief ingredients of many and perhaps most narratives is the quest. By quest is meant more—even in mystery stories—than just a quest for a murderer or a searching for clues and objects. Often, particularly in modern fiction, the quest is by the main character, or *protagonist*, for his own self. Since it is clear that most humans feel uncertain about their own nature—where they have come from, who they are, where they are going—it is natural that writers from all cultures should invent fictions which string adventures and character development and changes on the thread of the quest for self-identity. This quest is so attractive to our imaginations that we find it sustains our attention almost all the time. And while our attention is arrested by seemingly unimportant details, the author can broaden and deepen the meaning of the quest until it engages our conceptions of ourselves. When it becomes literature—i.e., takes on an artistic quality—the quest almost always becomes a search for self-identity.

One of the most important recent novels which employs this structure is Ralph Ellison's *Invisible Man*. The quest is so deeply rooted in the novel that the protagonist has no name. We know a great deal about him, though, because he narrates the story and tells us much about himself. He is black, Southern, and as a young college student, ambitious. His heroes are George Washington Carver and Booker T. Washington. He craves the dignity and the opportunity he associates with their lives. But things go wrong. He is dismissed unjustly from his college in the South and must, like Odysseus, leave his home to seek his fortune. He imagines himself destined for better things and eagerly pursues his fate, finding a place to live and work up North, beginning to find his identity as a black man. He discovers the sophisticated urban society of New York City, the political subtleties of communism, the pains of black nationalism, and the realities of his relationship to white people, to whom he is an invisible man. Yet he does not hate the whites, and in his own image of himself he remains an invisible man. The novel ends with the hero in an underground place he has found and which he has lighted, by tapping the electric company's lines, with almost two thousand electric light bulbs. Still, he cannot consider himself—despite this colossal illumination—visible. He ends his quest without finding out who he is beyond this fundamental fact: he is invisible.

The quest narrative is native to American culture. Mark Twain's *Huckleberry Finn*, a book we think of sometimes as a children's book, is one of the most important examples of the structure in American literature. But whereas *The Invisible Man* is an organic quest narrative, for the details of the novel are closely interwoven, *Huckleberry Finn* is an episodic quest narrative. Huck's travels along the great Mississippi River qualify as episodic in the same sense that *Don Quixote*, to which this novel is closely related, is episodic. Huck is questing for freedom for Jim, but also for freedom from his own father. Like Don Quixote, Huck comes back from his quest rich in the knowledge of who he is. But unlike Don Quixote, he does not come back to die—he comes back to live. In this sense one might say Don Quixote's quest is for the truth about who he is and was, since he is an old man when he begins. But Huck Finn is a child, so his quest must be for knowledge of who he is and can be.

PERCEPTION KEY: THE QUEST NARRATIVE

> Read a quest narrative. Some suggestions, in addition to those given above: Herman Melville, *Moby Dick*; T. S. Eliot, *The Waste Land*; William Faulkner, *Absalom, Absalom!*; Ernest Hemingway, *The Old Man and the Sea*; J. D. Salinger, *The Catcher in the Rye*; Graham Greene, *The Third Man.* You may get other suggestions from friends or teachers. What is the quest and what is actually found? How different are the various quests and their outcomes? How does the quest help the protagonist get to know himself better? Why does the quest structure help you get to know the character better?

The quest narrative is as common in poetry as in all other literary genres. Long poems, those we sometimes refer to as epic poems, seem natural for the quest motif, but they are not the only poems that use the structure. Lewis Carroll's famous nonsense poem "Jabberwocky" is fairly short, but it is the story of a boy's knightlike adventures in pursuit of the Jabberwock, whom he finds and slays. We can read the poem with understanding because it is held together by the orderliness of the quest, an order we already understand from our experiences with other literature. If there were not that kind of order operative in the poem, Carroll would not be able to ignore the usual logic of language, as he does when he begins the poem:

> Twas brillig and the slithy toves
> Did gyre and gimble in the wabe;
> All mimsy were the borogoves,
> And the mome raths outgrabe.

The poem which follows is not a nonsense poem, but it does rely on our experience with the quest pattern in literature. "Childe Roland to the Dark Tower Came" is said to have come like a dream that Robert Browning, the nineteenth-century English poet, remembered and wanted to explore. The poem retains the emotional aura of a dream, but it has other qualities we associate with dreams and with myths—which are themselves closely related to dreams. The quest pattern is a basic mythic pattern—a myth of discovery—which pervades all literatures. It seems to be basic to the psychology of humans no matter what their culture. Consequently, this particularly powerful marriage of dream and quest has significance for each of us in ways which are basic to our apprehension of life and literature. This is so much the case that Browning refused to give any clues as to the meaning of the quest—even to the point of admitting that the poem was one of his favorite compositions but not saying why. Apparently he once nodded agreement with a friend who suggested it was a poem in praise of endurance of the "you can do it if you try" variety. But many readers have seen it as a profoundly pessimistic poem mocking heroism. The "Childe" of the title indicates that Roland was in training to be a quester knight.

'CHILDE ROLAND TO THE DARK TOWER CAME'

(See Edgar's song in 'Lear')

I
My first thought was, he lied in every word,
   That hoary cripple, with malicious eye
   Askance to watch the working of his lie
On mine, and mouth scarce able to afford
Suppression of the glee that pursed and scored   5
   Its edge at one more victim gained thereby.

II
What else should he be set for, with his staff?
   What, save to waylay with his lies, ensnare
   All travellers that might find him posted there.
And ask the road? I guessed what skull-like laugh   10
Would break, what crutch 'gin write my epitaph
   For pastime in the dusty thoroughfare,

III
If at his counsel I should turn aside
   Into that ominous tract which, all agree,
   Hides the Dark Tower. Yet acquiescingly   15 ·
I did turn as he pointed; neither pride
Nor hope rekindling at the end descried,
   So much as gladness that some end might be.

IV
For, what with my whole world-wide wandering,
   What with my search drawn out thro' years, my hope   20
   Dwindled into a ghost not fit to cope

With that obstreperous joy success would bring,—
I hardly tried now to rebuke the spring
   My heart made, finding failure in its scope.

V

As when a sick man very near to death   25
   Seems dead indeed, and feels begin and end
   The tears, and takes the farewell of each friend,
And hears one bid the other go, draw breath
Freelier outside. ('since all is o'er,' he saith,
   'And the blow fallen no grieving can amend;')   30

VI

While some discuss if near the other graves
   Be room enough for this, and when a day
   Suits best for carrying the corpse away,
With care about the banners, scarves and staves,—
And still the man hears all, and only craves   35
   He may not shame such tender love and stay.

VII

Thus, I had so long suffered in this quest,
   Heard failure prophesied so oft, been writ
   So many times among 'The Band!'—to wit,
The knights who to the Dark Tower's search addressed   40
Their steps—that just to fail as they, seemed best.
   And all the doubt was now—should I be fit.

VIII

So, quiet as despair, I turned from him,
   That hateful cripple, out of his highway
   Into the path he pointed. All the day   45
Had been a dreary one at best, and dim
Was settling to its close, yet shot one grim
   Red leer to see the plain catch its estray.

IX

For mark! no sooner was I fairly found
   Pledged to the plain, after a pace or two,   50
   Than, pausing to throw backward a last view
To the safe road, 'twas gone; grey plain all round:
Nothing but plain to the horizon's bound.
   I might go on; nought else remained to do.

X

So, on I went. I think I never saw   55

Such starved ignoble nature; nothing throve:
For flowers—as well expect a cedar grove!
But cockle, spurge, according to their law
Might propagate their kind, with none to awe,
    You'd think; a burr had been a treasure-trove.   60

XI

No! penury, inertness and grimace,
    In some strange sort, were the land's portion. 'See
    Or shut your eyes.' said Nature peevishly,
'It nothing skills: I cannot help my case:
'Tis the Last Judgement's fire must cure this place,   65
    Calcine its clods and set my prisoners free.'

XII

If there pushed any ragged thistle-stalk
    Above its mates, the head was chopped—the bents
    Were jealous else. What made those holes and rents
In the dock's harsh swarth leaves—bruised as to baulk   70
All hope of greenness? 'tis a brute must walk
    Pashing their life out, with a brute's intents.

XIII

As for the grass, it grew as scant as hair
    In leprosy; thin dry blades pricked the mud
    Which underneath looked kneaded up with blood.   75
One stiff blind horse, his every bone a-stare,
Stood stupefied, however he came there:
    Thrust out past service from the devil's stud!

XIV

Alive? he might be dead for aught I know.
    With that red, gaunt and colloped neck a-strain,   80
    And shut eyes underneath the rusty mane;
Seldom went such grotesqueness with such woe;
I never saw a brute I hated so;
    He must be wicked to deserve such pain.

XV

I shut my eyes and turned them on my heart.   85
    As a man calls for wine before he fights,
    I asked one draught of earlier, happier sights.
Ere fitly I could hope to play my part.
Think first, fight afterwards—the soldier's art:
    One taste of the old time sets all to rights!   90

XVI

Not it! I fancied Cuthbert's reddening face
    Beneath its garniture of curly gold,
    Dear fellow, till I almost felt him fold
An arm in mine to fix me to the place,
That way he used, Alas! one night's disgrace!   95
    Out went my heart's new fire and left it cold.

XVII

Giles, then, the soul of honour—there he stands
    Frank as ten years ago when knighted first.
    What honest men should dare (he said) he durst.
Good—but the scene shifts—faugh! what hangman's
      hands   100
Pin to his breast a parchment? his own bands
    Read it. Poor traitor, spit upon and curst!

XVIII

Better this Present than a Past like that;
    Back therefore to my darkening path again.
    No sound, no sight as far as eye could strain.   105
Will the night send a howlet or a bat?
I asked: when something on the dismal flat
    Came to arrest my thoughts and change their train.

XIX

A sudden little river crossed my path
    As unexpected as a serpent comes.   110
    No sluggish tide congenial to the glooms—
This, as it frothed by, might have been a bath
For the fiend's glowing hoof—to see the wrath
    Of its black eddy bespate with flakes and spumes.

XX

So petty yet so spiteful! all along,   115
    Low scrubby alders kneeled down over it;
    Drenched willows flung them headlong in a fit
Of mute despair, a suicidal throng:
The river which had done them all the wrong,
    Whate'er that was, rolled by, deterred no whit.   120

XXI

Which, while I forded.—good saints, how I feared
    To set my foot upon a dead man's cheek,
    Each step, or feel the spear I thrust to seek
For hollows, tangled in his hair or beard!

—It may have been a water-rat I speared,   125
    But, ugh! it sounded like a baby's shriek.

XXII
Glad was I when I reached the other bank.
    Now for a better country. Vain presage!
    Who were the strugglers, what war did they wage,
Whose savage trample thus could pad the dank   130
Soil to a plash? toads in a poisoned tank,
    Or wild cats in a red-hot iron cage —

XXIII
The fight must so have seemed in that fell cirque.
    What penned them there, with all the plain to choose?
    No footprint leading to that horrid mews,   135
None of it. Mad brewage set to work
Their brains, no doubt, like galley-slaves the Turk
    Pits for his pastime, Christians against Jews.

XXIV
And more than that — a furlong on — why, there!
    What bad use was that engine for, that wheel,   140
    Or brake, not wheel — that harrow fit to reel
Men's bodies out like silk? with all the air
Of Tophet's tool, on earth left unaware,
    Or brought to sharpen its rusty teeth of steel.

XXV
Then came a bit of stubbed ground, once a wood,   145
    Next a marsh, it would seem, and now mere earth
    Desperate and done with; (so a fool finds mirth,
Makes a thing and then mars it, till his mood
Changes and off he goes!) within a rood —
    Bog, clay and rubble, sand and stark black dearth.   150

XXVI
Now blotches rankling, coloured gay and grim,
    Now patches where some leanness of the soil's
    Broke into moss or substances like boils;
Then came some palsied oak, a cleft in him
Like a distorted mouth that splits its rim   155
    Gaping at death, and dies while it recoils.

XXVII
And just as far as ever from the end!
    Nought in the distance but the evening, nought

To point my footsteps further! At the thought,
A great black bird. Apollyon's bosom-friend, 160
Sailed past, nor beat his wide wing dragon-penned
    That brushed my cap—perchance the guide I sought.

XXVIII

For, looking up, aware I somehow grew,
    'Spite of the dusk, the plain had given place
    All round to mountains—with such name to grace 165
Mere ugly heights and heaps now stolen in view.
How thus they had surprised me,—solve it, you!
    How to get from them was no clearer case.

XXIX

Yet half I seemed to recognize some trick
    Of mischief happened to me, God knows when— 170
    In a bad dream perhaps. Here ended, then,
Progress this way. When, in the very nick
Of giving up, one time more, came a click
    As when a trap shuts—you're inside the den!

XXX

Burningly it came on me all at once, 175
    This was the place! those two hills on the right,
    Crouched like two bulls locked horn in horn in fight:
While to the left, a tall scalped mountain . . . Dunce,
Fool, to be dozing at the very nonce,
    After a life spent training for the sight! 180

XXXI

What in the midst lay but the Tower itself?
    The round squat turret, blind as the fool's heart,
    Built of brown stone, without a counterpart
In the whole world. The tempest's mocking elf
Points to the shipman thus the unseen shelf 185
    He strikes on, only when the timbers start.

XXXII

Not see? because of night perhaps?—Why, day
    Came back again for that! before it left,
    The dying sunset kindled through a cleft:
The hills, like giants at a hunting, lay, 190
Chin upon hand, to see the game at bay,—
    'Now stab and end the creature—to the heft!'

XXXIII

Not here? when noise was everywhere! it tolled
   Increasing like a bell. Names in my ears,
   Of all the lost adventurers my peers.—   195
How such a one was strong, and such was bold,
And such was fortunate, yet each of old
   Lost. lost! one moment knelled the woe of years.

XXXIV

There they stood, ranged along the hillsides, met
   To view the last of me, a living frame   200
   For one more picture! in a sheet of flame
I saw them and I knew them all. And yet
Dauntless the slug-horn to my lips I set,
   And blew. *'Childe Roland to the Dark Tower came.'*

Robert Browning

PERCEPTION KEY   "CHILDE ROLAND TO THE DARK TOWER CAME"

---

1. What does Childe Roland seem to be seeking? Does he achieve his goal?

2. Explore the nature of the quest with some other readers of the poem. What does the quest seem to represent to them? What does it represent to you? Does your listening to others talk about the poem satisfy you that the poem is rich in meaning?

3. Do you get sufficient insight into the character of Childe Roland to feel that you "know" him fairly well? Does the nature of the quest help you get to know him?

4. Is it possible that the quest in this poem gives insight into your character—or into the character of those you have heard talk about the poem? How could the quest narrative do this?

"Childe Roland to the Dark Tower Came" is, we think, a fascinating poem, even for some of us who feel we do not understand very much of its meaning. Browning establishes a mysterious atmosphere throughout, evoked by descriptions such as, "Then came a bit of stubbed ground, once a wood,/Next a marsh, it would seem, and now mere earth/ Desperate and done with." Such lines not only describe the scene but reveal the emotional response of the quester, who is never certain that what he is looking at is real or imaginary. Was the ground really once a wood? And, how are we to understand the earth as desperate, much less done with? But the eeriness of this uncertainty about the most basic thing of all—the landscape of mother earth—powerfully establishes an atmosphere of fright and terror.

The setting, then, establishes a mood essential to the heart of the poem. If Roland were not sensitive and frightened, it is unlikely that we would respond with much interest to his situation. Here the narrator is himself the protagonist, and his narrative reveals something of his nature by giving us his perceptions about the situation and his feelings about his own predicament. Much of this can be appreciated by going through the poem looking for instances of perception through the five senses. For example, stanzas 32 and 33 begin with "Not see?" and "Not hear?"—calling our attention to those senses.

Time is also used very effectively throughout the poem. The pacing is careful, with long, descriptive, slow passages while Roland makes his way slowly over ground which startles and frightens him. The poem seems to take more time than it ordinarily should in reading aloud (time it at your own pace), which, in turn, gives a curious dimension to our experience. The dimension of time may not seem very significant in a short poem which is not a narrative, but in all narrative works time is a dimension which must be considered carefully. Novels encompass a time span which can be centuries long or a day or less. The novel, furthermore, usually will expand or compress that time span in order to emphasize or deemphasize the importance of given experiences as they are narrated to us. Sometimes these alterations will give us insight into the narrator by telling us what he thinks is important. We may not agree with him, and our feeling may ultimately be that his vision is incomplete or simply too limited. By such techniques, we can be given insight into the nature of the narrator.

One of the questions that "Childe Roland to the Dark Tower Came" surely raises is about the time at which this tale occurs in history. We are not able to answer that question easily, and this raises the further question of why Browning keeps the era so indefinite. It surely has something to do with the way in which we are to perceive and conceive the poem. The analysis of the use of time in this poem, as in all narratives, will get us closer to having a total experience of the work.

PERCEPTION KEY TIME AND "CHILDE ROLAND TO THE DARK TOWER CAME"

Explore the implications of the action for various time periods from biblical times to our own. How can the meaning of the poem be expanded by such exploration?

Another basic question must have to do with the nature of the quest. What is it that Childe Roland is searching for? What is the dark tower that looms so broodingly over the plain? Why is it watched over by so many failed predecessors? No answer will satisfy all readers, since the dreamlike character of the poem suggests that the answer must come from the psyche of each reader. Thus Browning refused to tell anyone what the tower had originally meant for him. If we think about the nature of the quest and the fact that most quests ultimately lead back to the quester, it will be clear that one strong possibility for the dark tower is that it is a symbol of the inmost self, the secret self—as Joseph Conrad would have described it—which all of us bear deep within our unconscious mind. When Browning wrote this poem, modern psychology was beginning, and soon the exploration of dreams ceased to be the exclusive province of fortune tellers. The dream was beginning to be understood as giving us insight into our inmost nature. The dreamlike qualities and mythic character of Browning's poem suggest that the quest is psychological, a quest that leads to our inmost soul. Childe Roland, against awful odds, faces his own dark tower—even at the risk of destroying himself.

THE LYRIC

The lyric is a structure, virtually always a poem, which is used primarily to reveal a relatively limited but deep feeling. The lyric is almost always associated with the feeling of a given poet, though we have already seen that it is not difficult for the poet to create a narrator distinct from himself for his lyric as well as for his narrative communications. Someone in the lyric poem, in any case, is speaking to us, and usually it is his or another's emotional situation which is explored in the lyric modes.

If we participate, we find ourselves caught up in the emotional situation of the lyric. It is usually revealed to us through a recounting of the circumstances the poet is reflecting on. T. S. Eliot has spoken of an objective correlative: an object which correlates with the feeling the poet has. Eliot has said that the poet must find the situation, event, or person which correlates with the poet's emotion in order for the poet to interpret that emotion and in order for a reader to comprehend that emotion for himself. Perhaps this is too narrow a view of the creative process of the poet, for it seems quite possible for the poet to understand and interpret emotions without necessarily undergoing them. Otherwise, it would seem that Shakespeare, for example, and even Eliot would have blown up like overcompressed boilers if they had had to directly experience all the emotions they interpreted in their poems. But in any case, it seems clear that the lyric has feeling—emotion and mood—as basic in its subject matter.

The word "lyric" implies a personal statement by an involved writer who feels deeply. Lyrics are, in one limited sense, poems to be sung to music. Most lyrics before the seventeenth century were set to music. Thus most medieval and renaissance lyrics were written to be sung with musical accompaniment, usually performed on a lute or other portable string instrument. And the writers who composed the words were usually the composers of the music—at least until the seventeenth century, when specialization began to separate those functions. Some of the examples which follow are meant to be sung to music; most of them could be sung if you wanted to find a tune which would suit them. No matter what, however, practically all lyric poems are meant to be heard and not simply read silently, even when the sounds ring in the inner ear. Thus, it is important to hear these samples — and all others in this chapter — recited aloud or sung with feeling.

The lyric which follows was written by John Keats (1795–1821), an English poet of the romantic period who died of tuberculosis. This sonnet, written in 1818, has a basis in biographical fact:

> When I have fears that I may cease to be
> Before my pen has glean'd my teeming brain,
> Before high-piled books, in charact'ry,
> Hold like rich garners the full-ripen'd grain;
> When I behold, upon the night's starr'd face,
> Huge cloudy symbols of a high romance,
> And think that I may never live to trace
> Their shadows, with the magic hand of chance;
> And when I feel, fair creature of an hour!
> That I shall never look upon thee more,
> Never have relish in the faery power
> Of unreflecting love! then on the shore
> Of the wide world I stand alone, and think
> Till love and fame to nothingness do sink.
>
> John Keats

PERCEPTION KEY "WHEN I HAVE FEARS . . ."

---

1. First establish what, for you, is the emotional situation in this lyric. Then, by asking others who have read the poem, find out how much of a range of understanding there is. Do most readers achieve approximately the same interpretation of the poem?

2. This poem has no setting, as "Childe Roland to the Dark Tower Came" has, yet it establishes an atmosphere of uncertainty and, possibly, of terror. How does Keats create this atmosphere?

A poem such as Keats's discusses a personal feeling about the nature of things. He realizes he may die before he can write his best poems. In fact, the epitaph Keats chose for his headstone just before he died is: "Here lies one whose name was writ on water." What he meant by that is simply that he felt his poems would not be read by posterity. He was wrong. Moreover, his work is so brilliant that we cannot help wondering what else he might have done. Had Chaucer, Shakespeare, Milton, or Joyce died at twenty-six, we might not know their names at all. All their most important work was yet to come.

It is not difficult to understand how Keats must have felt when he had fears that he might die before he had written what he wanted. But it is also important for us to see that the lyric mode makes it difficult for him to communicate his feelings to us. He has no story to tell, like Childe Roland's, and very little in the way of a setting to create an atmosphere which might give us a clue about his feelings. His interest in character is limited, even though he is himself the narrator of the poem. What, then, are his resources?

One is the fact that since we all will die, we can therefore sympathize with the thought of death's cutting a life work short. The tone Keats establishes in the poem, one of direct speech, honestly said, not overdone or melodramatic, is one of the most important resources he has. It gives the poem an immediacy: one human being telling something straight from the heart to another. Keats modulates the tone slightly, slowing things down enough at the end of the poem for us to sense and share the contemplative mood. If possible, listen to the poem read aloud by someone who reads well enough to establish a realistic tone of voice, as if someone were half speaking to himself, half speaking to an audience.

An entirely different mood established by quite different means characterizes the next poem. It was written in the second half of the nineteenth century by a poet who was also a Jesuit priest. It is very personal but also, like the psalms of the Bible, something of a prayer or hymn of praise.

PIED BEAUTY

Glory be to God for dappled things—
    For skies of couple-colour as a brinded cow;
      For rose-moles all in stiple upon trout that swim;
Fresh-firecoal chestnut-falls; finches' wings;
    Landscape plotted and pieced—fold, fallow, and plough;
      And all trades, their gear and tackle and trim.

All things counter, original, spare, strange;
    Whatever is fickle, freckled (who knows how?)
      With swift, slow; sweet, sour; adazzle, dim;
He fathers-forth whose beauty is past change:
              Praise him.[2]

                      Gerard Manley Hopkins

[2] *Pied:* spotted, like "dappled" and "couple-colour." *Brinded:* spots or streaks on a buff-colored background. *Chestnut-falls:* the skin of the hot chestnut, stripped off. *Plotted and pieced:* fields of different shaped rectangles. *Fold, fallow, and plough:* fields used for different purposes, and which thus look different to the eye.

1. Hopkins reveals joy in this poem. How is this accomplished? Are there elements inconsistent with joyousness?

2. How many senses does Hopkins make reference to in the poem? Is the awareness of the sensory important in our experience of the poem?

3. See what range of responses you can discover in those who read this poem. Query people who have read the poem under the same circumstances you have, then query people who come to it "cold." How different is their understanding of the poem's content?

4. God is referred to as him rather than Him in the last line. Is this simply a matter of being a printer's convention?

The range of the lyric is enormous. We have been talking about it as centering on a single powerful emotion, avoiding the narrative mode. But this is not quite accurate, for the lyric is often able to "narrate" the poet's range of interest in a subject matter; it is a structure which gives him free rein to explore a subject matter of almost any kind. One may wish to see in any such exploration the feelingful response of the poet, but such considerations ought not to delimit the lyric in any way.

The usefulness of the lyric for bringing out the significance of things as felt meditatively is so great that perhaps this is its most important purpose. It is a mode which, in its meditativeness, can explore any number of aspects of a subject matter. Without necessarily having a story to tell, the poet need not rush off into something which is not central to the meditation itself. One famous meditative poem is Walt Whitman's "A Noiseless Patient Spider," a poem which is perhaps as much a tribute to the patience of Walt Whitman as it is to the spider. But it goes beyond such tributes, because out of Whitman's contemplation of the spider comes insight into the human soul.

A NOISELESS PATIENT SPIDER

A noiseless patient spider,
I mark'd where on a little promontory it stood isolated,
Mark'd how to explore the vacant vast surrounding,
It launch'd forth filament, filament, filament, out of itself,
Ever unreeling them, ever tirelessly speeding them.

And you O my soul where you stand,
Surrounded, detached, in measureless oceans of space,
Ceaselessly musing, venturing, throwing, seeking the spheres to
    connect them,

Till the bridge you will need be form'd, till the ductile
   anchor hold,
Till the gossamer thread you fling catch somewhere, O my soul.

Walt Whitman

PERCEPTION KEY "A NOISELESS PATIENT SPIDER"

1. Whitman sees a connection between the spider and the human soul. What, exactly, is that connection? How reasonable does it seem to you?
2. Explore the meaning of this poem with other readers. Is there a consensus about the connection Whitman makes between the spider and the soul?

Examine closely the two poems that follow. Although these two poems illustrate aspects of the lyric we have already discussed, they may possess other qualities as well.

THE CLEARING

Trees & brown squares
of shadow. The green
washed out and drained into clumps of mist
that cloak more trees. And trees, outside
the window; or spreading heavy fronds   5
stepping away from the light. We come
to a forest, or we see it
from the window. We step into it,
spreading the heavy leaves, or drop the blind
& let it clatter in the damp breeze from the yard.   10

Where are the beasts? In a forest,
there are always wild beasts. And the sun, a woman,
goes there to sleep. Brown trunks
their shadows against the white wall, rain
spreading against the glass. Blue rain   15
outside, and shadows against the wall. A wet wind
moves them. The smells
come in. Leaves & darkness
wetting our faces. Breathing
through the leaves, and disappear.   20

Trees,
& shadows of trees (the wind
pushes them apart. I am

an animal watching
his forest. Listening   25
for your breathing, your merest
move in the dark. You wear
a gown of it. The dark
ness. And
we can move naked   30
through it, through
the forest
if it does not disappear. Who
will remember
the way back. When the blind   35
flings back
and more smells come in. As sound
or light moving against the wall. Where
are the beasts?
The eye is useless. Sound, Sound   40
& what you smell
or feel. I am someone else
who smells you. The lamp
at the corner is bleak
& leafless. Its light   45
does not even reach
the edge of the trees.

What bird
makes that noise? (If this
were a western place, a temperate hand   50
could shape it. A western mouth
could make it on this mist. Green mist
settling on our flesh. (If this
were a western place, a bank
of the Marne, Cezanne's greens   55
& yellows floating unreal
under a bridge. A blue bridge
for a temperate eye. We have
vines. (What bird
makes that noise?   60

Your voice down the hall. Are
you singing? A shadow song
we lock our movement
in. Were you singing?

down the hall. White plaster
on the walls, our fingers
leave their marks, on
the dust, or tearing
the wall away. Were you
singing? What song
was that?

65

70

I love you (& you be
quiet, & feel my wet mouth
on your fingers, I
love you
& bring you fish
& oranges. (Before the light fails
we should move to a dryer place,
but not too far from water.) I
Love you &
you are singing. What song
is that? (The blinds held up
by a wind, tearing
the shadows. I
Love you
& you hide yourself
in the shadows. The forest is huge
around us. The night
clings to our cries. (I hear
your voice
down the hall, through the window, above
all those trees, a light
it seems
& you are singing. What song
is that The words
are beautiful.

75

80

85

90

95

DIRGE

1-2-3 was the number he played but today the number came
   3-2-1;
Bought his Carbide at 30 and it went to 29; had the favorite at
   Bowie but the track was slow—

O executive type, would you like to drive a floating power,
knee-action, silk-upholstered six? Wed a Hollywood star?
Shoot the course in 58? Draw to the ace, king, jack?
O fellow with a will who won't take no, watch out for three
cigarettes on the same, single match; O democratic voter
born in August under Mars, beware of liquidated rails—

Denouement to denouement, he took a personal pride in the
certain, certain way he lived his own, private life,
But nevertheless, they shut off his gas; nevertheless, the bank
foreclosed; nevertheless, the landlord called; nevertheless,
the radio broke,

And twelve o'clock arrived just once too often,
Just the same he wore one gray tweed suit, bought one straw
hat, drank one straight Scotch, walked one short step, took
one long look, drew one deep breath,
Just one too many,

And wow he died as wow he lived,
Going whop to the office and blooie home to sleep and biff got
married and bam had children and oof got fired,
Zowie did he live and Zowie did he die,

With who the hell are you at the corner of his casket, and where
the hell're we going on the right-hand silver knob, and who
the hell cares walking second from the end with an American
Beauty wreath from why the hell not,

Very much missed by the circulation staff of the New York
Evening Post; deeply mourned by the B.M.T.[3]
Wham, Mr. Roosevelt; pow, Sears Roebuck;
awk, big dipper; bop, summer rain;
Bong, Mr., bong, Mr., bong, Mr., bong.

Reprinted from NEW AND SELECTED POEMS by Kenneth Fearing, © 1956
by Kenneth Fearing. Reprinted by permission of Indiana University Press.

Both these poems have a high degree of complexity which is achieved
partly by the use of symbols in Jones's case and the use of many specific
situations, such as horse-race betting and playing the stock market, in

[3] A New York subway line.

Fearing's case. Jones talks about being in a clearing in a forest, but his references to the one he loves and the songs of the bird and his lover suggest that the clearing is a symbolic one, perhaps an opening up of his emotional life. Yet, it seems that both he and his lover are still in the forest—which may be a symbol for confusion or cultural stress—and that the opening is temporary. Fearing's dirge is actually an epitaph for a man for whom everything seemed to go wrong: he lost his bets and his stocks, the gas was turned off and the mortgage foreclosed. He was an executive type, nevertheless, who had a personal pride in his certain, certain way of life. The ironies of the last stanza, suggesting that "he" will be missed by the newspaper, Sears Roebuck, and similar institutions, are a commentary on the American businessman's life-style.

PERCEPTION KEY VARIETIES OF LYRIC

1. In these poems by Jones (now known as Imamu Amiri Baraka) and Fearing, other resources of the lyric are used. What are they? How valuable are these poems as social commentary? Are these poems dominated, respectively, by a single emotion?

2. Try your hand at writing a lyric poem. Decide before or as you write what you are trying to achieve, then keep refining your lines in order to help achieve what you want. After you have written your lyric, give it to someone to read and find out what he thinks you have achieved.

LITERARY TEXTURES

So far we have been speaking of literature in terms of its structures, those principles of organization which give it an overall order and shape. But within every structure are textures—details or individual elements—which need close examination in many cases before structural principles can be fully understood. In the examples discussed so far, we have stressed the structural qualities. Now we turn to textural qualities.

Literature uses language in ways which are somewhat different from everyday uses. This is not to say literature is artificial and unrelated to the language we speak but rather that, as we speak, we sometimes do not see the fullest implications of our speech, and rarely take full advantage of the opportunities language affords us to say what we mean. Literature uses language to reveal meanings which are usually absent from our daily speech.

Our emphasis here in treating textural matters will be upon several special kinds of language usages: the image, the metaphor and simile, the symbol. There are other, often more subtle, usages of language which are also worthy of our attention, but those named are so central to literature of all genres that they will stand as introduction enough for our purposes.

To these particular usages of language we will add one further: diction. The term is ambiguous and so must be defined here: it is the choice of words for a given situation. The diction of a piece of literature will sometimes tend to make that piece seem "inevitable," as if there were no other way of saying the same thing. Oddly enough, sometimes the most artificial and stilted diction will produce results which will be perfect for the situation at hand. Other times, however, the most conversational diction will produce better results. Each situation must be examined independently, since no rules will serve for all.

THE IMAGE

Imagery involves any use of language which asks us to imagine what is being described. It may appeal to our sense of sight, sound, taste, odor, or touch—or any combination of these. The richness of the image partly depends on the capacity of the reader to fully reconstruct the image in his imagination. And much of this depends upon the care and creativity with which the writer has presented the images for our consideration. One of the most striking resources of any kind of literature is that of the capacity of language to help us reconstruct in our own minds the "reality" of perceptions which the author wishes to reveal. This resource is as important in prose as in poetry. Consider, for example, the following passage from Joseph Conrad's novel *Youth:*

> The boats, fast astern, lay in a deep shadow, and all around I could see the circle of the sea lighted by the fire. A gigantic flame arose forward straight and clear. It flared fierce, with noises like the whirr of wings, with fumbles as of thunder. There were cracks, detonations, and from the cone of flame the sparks flew upwards, as man is born to trouble, to leaky ships, and to ships that burn.

PERCEPTION KEY YOUTH

1. Which of our senses is most powerfully appealed to in this passage?
2. How would this passage differ from the average, "nonliterary" description of a burning boat? If possible, read a description of a burning boat (perhaps one written by yourself or one of your friends) which does not specifically try to involve the reader in the occurrence itself. What are the differences between it and Conrad's passage? Examine and compare the images in each.

In *Youth* this scene is fleeting, only an instant in the total structure of the book. But the entire book is composed of such textural moments, ensuring the reader's participation.

For some writers, like Ezra Pound in some of his poems, the image is almost all there is. Pound and several other writers of the early twentieth century bound together in a kind of league which then became known as the Imagist school of poets. One classic example of this school is Pound's famous poem:

IN A STATION OF THE METRO

The apparition of these faces in the crowd.
Petals on a wet, black bough.

The Metro is the Paris subway. The poem really does not make direct comment about the character of these faces—they are not good, not bad, not threatening, not loving. We really do not know much more about them in these respects than if we had been there ourselves to see them as Pound did. The poem asks us to "image" the scene; we must reconstruct it in our imagination. And in doing so we learn something about the appearance of these faces: they are like petals on a wet, black bough. This device is a metaphor (see the next section on this subject), and its function, in this case, is to clarify our imagining of the scene.

Pound was influenced in this poem and others by the achievement of Chinese and Japanese poets. Their use of image stimulated him to consider the possibilities in a language and in a culture which had not fully explored their techniques. The following poem is by the Chinese poet Tu Mu.

THE RETIRED OFFICIAL YÜAN'S HIGH PAVILION

The West River's watershed sounds beyond the sky.
Shadows of pines in front of the studio sweep the clouds
  flat.
Who shall coax me to blow the long flute
Leaning together on the spring wind with the moon-
  beams for our toys?

1. What are the most significant images in this poem?

2. How completely do you find yourself actively imaging scenes in response to the poem?

3. Do these images take you beyond themselves into meanings that in some sense are not perceivable? If so, how?

4. We think these images do go far beyond perception into concepts or ideas. In discussion with others, try to make explicit the concepts of the poem as evoked by the percepts.

THE METAPHOR

Metaphor helps the writer intensify language. Metaphor is a class of linguistic comparisons designed to change our conception of the things which are being compared. The poet or writer will usually let us know which of the two things compared is the main object of his attention. He will usually expect that the comparison will have a greater effect on that object than on the thing he uses to make the comparison. For example:

> Magnified one thousand times, the insect
> Looks farcically human; laugh if you will!
> Bald head, stage-fairy wings, blear eyes,
> A caved-in chest, hairy black mandibles,
>   Long spindly thighs.
>
>   From "Blue-Fly" by Robert Graves, in *Collected Poems*,
>   Collins–Knowlton–Wing, Inc., New York, 1961. Copyright © 1958, 1961
>   by Robert Graves. Reprinted by permission of Collins–Knowlton–Wing, Inc.

The blue-fly is being compared to a human being. Graves only alludes casually to the fact that he is making a comparison, then goes right ahead and describes the fly as if he were a somewhat comically shaped human.

Decide what kind of comment Graves is making in this metaphoric statement. Is he concerned more about the effect of the comparison for describing the fly or the human being? If possible, take a sampling of opinions from others who have read this stanza.

The standard definition for the metaphor is that it is a comparison made without any explicit words to tell us a comparison is being made. The simile is the kind of comparison which has explicit words: "like," "as," "than," "as if," and a few others. We have no trouble recognizing the simile, though we get so used to seeing similes in literature that we accept them usually with no special degree of awareness.

Some people make a fuss over the difference between a metaphor and a simile. We will not do so because basically both are forms of comparison for effect, and both are part of a general class of language uses called tropes (linguistic changes for effect). Our discussion, then, will use the general term "metaphor" and use the more special term "simile" only when necessary. On the other hand, the term "symbol," which is also metaphoric, will be treated separately, since its effect is usually much more specialized than either the nonsymbolic metaphor or simile.

Metaphoric language is not limited, of course, to the poetry and prose of Western culture. Non-Western writing finds the metaphor as congenial to its various languages as Western writing does. The use of metaphor seems to pervade all cultures. Daily conversation—usually none too literary in character—is full of metaphoric language used to emphasize our points and to give color and feeling to our speech (check this for yourself). The Chinese poet Li Ho shows us that the resources of metaphor and simile function for all of us:

THE GRAVE OF LITTLE SU

I ride a coach with lacquered sides,
My love rides a dark piebald horse.
Where shall we bind our hearts as one?
On West Mound, beneath the pines and cypresses.
      (Ballad ascribed to the singing girl Little Su, c. A.D. 500)

Dew on the secret orchid
Like crying eyes.
No thing to bind the heart to.
Misted flowers I cannot bear to cut.
Grass like a cushion,
The pine like a parasol:
The wind is a skirt,
The waters are tinkling pendants.
A coach with lacquered sides
Waits for someone in the evening.
Cold blue candle-flames

Strain to shine bright.
Beneath West Mound
The wind puffs the rain.

From *Poems of the Late T'ang*, A. C. Graham
(trans.), Penguin Books Ltd. (Penguin
Classics 1965), p. 113. © A. C. Graham,
1967.

Clearly, Little Su was important to the narrator. But the portrayal of his feeling for her is oblique—which is, perhaps, the reason for the use of so many metaphors in such a short poem. Instead of striking bluntly and immediately, the metaphoric language delicately resounds with nuances, so that we are aware of its cumulative impact only after the moment of reading.

PERCEPTION KEY "THE GRAVE OF LITTLE SU"

1. Enumerate the uses of metaphor in the poem. Compare what you find with the findings of other readers. Do you find disagreement on how many uses of metaphor there are? If so, what does that mean?

2. Along with two or three other readers, select for yourself the most impressive use of metaphor. The likelihood is that you and others will choose different examples. Explain to one another the reasons for the effectiveness of the metaphor you have chosen.

We often tend to accept the uses of metaphor in poetry, but we do not always realize how extensive the device is in other kinds of literature. Prose fiction, essays, drama or literature meant for the stage, and almost every form of writing we know uses the metaphoric mode to some extent or another. Poetry in general tends to have a higher metaphoric density than other forms of writing, partly because poetry is somewhat distilled and condensed to begin with. Rarely, however, is the density of metaphor quite as thick as in "The Grave of Little Su."

Since literature depends so heavily on metaphor, it is essential that we reflect on its use. One kind of metaphor tends to evoke an image and involves us mainly on a perceptual level—because we perceive in our imagination something of what we would perceive were we there. This kind we shall call a "perceptual metaphor." Another kind of the metaphor tends to evoke ideas, gives us information which is mainly conceptual. This kind of metaphor we shall call a "conceptual metaphor." To tell us the pine is like a parasol is basically perceptual: were we there, we would see that the cone shape of the pine resembles that of a parasol. But to tell us the wind is a skirt is to go far beyond perception and simple "likeness." The metaphor lures us to reflect upon the suggestion that the wind resembles a skirt, and we begin to think about the ways in which this might be true. Then, once we have understood the ways in which this is true, we are lured further—this is an enticing metaphor—to explore the implications of this truth. If the wind is like a skirt, what then is the significance of this in the poem? In what ways does this conceptual metaphor help us understand the poet's insights at the grave of Little Su? In what ways does the perceptual metaphor of the pine/parasol help us?

The answer to how the wind is a skirt is by no means simple. Its complexity is one of the most precious qualities of this poem. It is also one of the most precious possibilities of the conceptual metaphor, for then one can go beyond the relatively simple perceptual comparison into the more suggestive and significant acts of understanding. We might suggest, for instance, that if the wind is like a skirt it clothes a girl: Little Su. But Little Su is dead, so perhaps it clothes her spirit. The comparison is between the wind and the spirit. Both things are impossible to see, but their effects can be felt by writers and—when the idea is communicated—by their readers.

The same kind of complexity is present in Tu Mu's poem, "The Retired Official Yüan's High Pavilion." The last line suggests that the moonbeams are toys. The metaphor is quiet, restrained, but as direct as the wind/skirt metaphor. Moreover, the last line suggests that the wind is something that can be leaned against. It would be worth turning back to that poem to see just how these metaphors expand the mysterious quality of the poem.

THE SYMBOL

The symbol is a further use of metaphor. Being a metaphor, it is a comparison between two things; but unlike most perceptual and conceptual metaphors, only one of the things compared is clearly stated. The symbol is clearly stated, but what it is compared with (sometimes a very broad range of meaning) is only hinted at, more or less. For instance, the white whale in Herman Melville's novel, *Moby Dick*, is a symbol both in the novel and in the mind of Captain Ahab, the novel's main character. Ahab sees the whale as a symbol of all the malevolence and evil in a world committed to evil. But we may not necessarily share Ahab's views. We may believe that the whale is simply a beast and not a symbol at all. Or, we may believe that the whale is a symbol for nature, which is constantly being threatened by man's misunderstanding of it. Such a symbol can mean more than one thing. It is the peculiar quality of most symbols that they do not sit still; even their basic meanings keep changing or expanding. Symbols are usually vague, always ambiguous. It is said that many symbols are a product of the subconscious, which is always treating things symbolically and always searching for implicit meanings. If this is so, it accounts for the persistence of symbols in even the oldest literature.

Perhaps the most important thing to remember about the symbol is that it implies rather than explicitly states meaning. We sense that we are dealing with a symbol in those situations in which we feel there is more to what is said than meets the eye. Most writers are quite open about their symbols: they let us know that they are using symbols and that it is up to us to understand the meaning of their symbols in our own terms and in our way. William Blake's poetry is filled with symbols. He saw God's handiwork everywhere, but he also saw forces of destruction everywhere. Thus his poetry discovers implied meaning in almost every situation and thing, not just in those situations and things which are usually accepted as meaningful. The following poem is an example of his technique. At first the poem may seem needlessly confusing, because we do not know how to interpret the symbols. But the meanings of the symbols begin to come clear to some extent with some examination:

THE SICK ROSE

O rose, thou art sick!
    The invisible worm,
That flies in the night,
    In the howling storm,

Has found out thy bed
    Of crimson joy;
And his dark secret love
Does thy life destroy.
William Blake

PERCEPTION KEY   "THE SICK ROSE"

1. The rose and the worm stand as opposites in this poem, and as opposites they are symbolically antagonistic. In discussion with other readers, explore possible meanings for the rose and worm. What might they be symbols for? Begin with examining all that roses mean to most readers; then reflect on our reactions to worms.

2. The bed of crimson joy and the dark secret love are also symbols. What are their meanings? Consider them closely in relation to the rose and the worm.

Blake enjoyed working with such symbols because he saw a richness of implication in them that linked him to God. As a symbolist, he thus shared in a way the creative act with God and helped others understand the world in terms of symbolic meaningfulness. For most other writers the symbol is used more modestly as a means of expanding meaning, of including larger ranges of suggestion than a nonsymbolic statement can encompass. The symbol has been compared with the stone dropping into the still waters of a lake: the stone itself is very small, but the effects radiate from its center of action to all the edges of the lake. The symbol is dropped into our imagination, and it, too, radiates with meanings. But the curious thing with the symbol is that its meanings tend to be permanently expansive: who knows where the meaningfulness of Blake's rose ends?

Prose fiction has made extensive use of the symbol. In Melville's *Moby Dick*, the white whale is a symbol, but so too is Ahab, and so is the entire journey they undertake. The quest for Moby Dick is itself a symbolic quest. The albatross in Samuel Coleridge's *The Ancient Mariner* is a symbol, and so is the Ancient Mariner's stopping one of the wedding guests to make him hear the entire narrative. In these cases the symbols are operating both structurally, in terms of the entire narrative, and texturally, in terms of only a part of it. There is nothing incoherent about this; it shows, rather, the enormous resources of the symbol.

In Dostoevsky's *Crime and Punishment*, there is a symbolic dream which the murderer-to-be, Raskolnikov, has shortly before he is to kill the old woman, Alëna. In the dream Raskolnikov is a child again, walking through city streets with his father:

Suddenly there was a great explosion of laughter that drowned everything else: the old mare had rebelled against the hail of blows and was lashing out feebly with her hoofs. Even the old man could not help laughing. Indeed, it was ludicrous that such a decrepit old mare should still have a kick left in her.

Two men in the crowd got whips, ran to the horse, one on each side, and began to lash at her ribs.

"Hit her on the nose and across the eyes, beat her across the eyes!" yelled Mikolka.

"Let's have a song, lads!" someone called from the wagon, and the others joined in. Somebody struck up a coarse song, a tambourine rattled, somebody else whistled the chorus. The fat young woman went on cracking nuts and giggling.

. . . The boy ran towards the horse, then round in front, and saw them lashing her across the eyes, and actually striking her very eyeballs. He was weeping. His heart seemed to rise into his throat, and tears rained from his eyes. One of the whips stung his face, but he did not feel it; he was wringing his hands and crying aloud. He ran to a grey-haired, grey-bearded old man, who was shaking his head in reproof. A peasant-woman took him by the hand and tried to lead him away, but he tore himself loose and ran back to the mare. She was almost at her last gasp, but she began kicking again.

"The devil fly away with you!" shrieked Mikolka in a fury.

He flung away his whip, stooped down and dragged up from the floor of the cart a long thick wooden shaft, grasped one end with both hands, and swung it with an effort over the wretched animal.

Cries arose: "He'll crush her!" "He'll kill her!"

"She's my property," yelled Mikolka, and with a mighty swing let the shaft fall. There was a heavy thud.[4]

The symbolic value of this passage becomes clearer in the context of the entire novel. Raskolnikov is planning a brutal murder of an aged shopkeeper. Only a couple of pages later, Raskolnikov reflects on his dream:

"God!" he exclaimed, "is it possible, is it possible, that I really shall take an axe and strike her on the head, smash open her skull . . . that my feet will slip in warm, sticky blood, and that I shall break the lock, and steal, and tremble, and hide, all covered in blood . . . with the axe . . . ? God, is it possible?"[5]

PERCEPTION KEY CRIME AND PUNISHMENT

1. What is the old mare symbolic of in Raskolnikov's dream? What is the entire situation symbolic of?

2. Sample opinion from others and explore the effectiveness of having the beating of the horse revealed in a dream. Is this weaker or stronger for the symbolic value than if the scene had actually taken place on the streets in front of Raskolnikov? Why?

3. How much does this symbolic action reveal about Raskolnikov? Does he seem—considering what he is actually about to do—different as a boy than as an adult? How would you characterize his sensitivities and his compassion?

The problem most readers have with symbols centers either on the question of recognition—is this a symbol?—or on the question of what the symbol stands for. Usually an author will use something symbolically in situations which are pretty clearly identified. Blake does not tell us that his rose and worm are symbolic, but we readily realize that the poem says very little worth listening to if we do not begin to go beyond its literal meaning. The fact that worms will kill roses is more important to gardeners than it is to readers of poetry. But that there is a secret evil which travels mysteriously to kill beautiful things is not so important to gardeners as to readers of poetry.

Some readers tend to see everything as symbolic. This is as serious a problem as being unable to identify a symbol at all. The best rule of thumb is based on experience: symbols are very much alike from one kind of litera-

[4] From Dostoevsky's CRIME AND PUNISHMENT, translated by J. L. Coulson, published by Oxford University Press. Reprinted by permission of the publisher.
[5] Op cit.

ture to another. Once you begin to recognize symbols—the several presented here are various enough to offer a good beginning—other symbols and symbolic situations will be clearer and more unmistakeable. But the symbol should be compelling: the situation should be clearly symbolic before we begin to explore what the symbols mean. Not all black objects are symbolic of death; not all predators are symbolic of evil. Moreover, all symbols should be understood in the context in which they appear. Their context in the literature is what usually reveals their meaning, as we can see from the dream of Raskolnikov.

In those instances, as often in Blake's poems, in which there is no evident context to guide us to the meanings of the symbols, we need to interpret the symbols with extreme care and tentativeness. Symbolic objects usually have a fairly well-understood range of meaning which authors such as Blake are depending upon. For instance, the rose is often thought of in connection with beauty, romance, love. The worm is often thought of in connection with death, the grave, and if we include the serpent in the Garden of Eden (Blake, of course, had read Milton's *Paradise Lost*), the worm also suggests evil, sin, and perversion. Most of us know these things. Thus the act of interpreting the symbol is usually an act of getting this knowledge to the forefront of our minds so we can utilize it in our interpretations.

DICTION

"Diction" is a term which describes the language used in a piece of literature. Put more clumsily, it might be thought of as "choice of words." But the entire act of writing involves the choice of words, of course, so the term "diction" is usually reserved for literary acts (they can be speech as well as the written word) which use words chosen especially carefully for their impact. Perhaps the following example—in which one word carries the weight of the whole poem—will serve to show how diction can basically establish the effect of a poem:

UPON JULIA'S CLOTHES

Whenas in silks my Julia goes,
Then, then, methinks, how sweetly flows
That liquefaction of her clothes.

Next, when I cast mine eyes, and see
That brave vibration, each way free,
O, how that glittering taketh me!

Robert Herrick

1. What word receives most emphasis in the poem? Why is it so effective? Discuss this with others.

2. How much reliance is there on metaphor? What kind of metaphor?

But this example is isolated. A more interesting example is that of language used in a more even fashion, a fashion which produces a sense of inevitability: that what has been expressed is in the most perfect form the expression could possibly have. We have this sense probably most profoundly in the psalms of the King James Version of the Bible. The inevitability is partly a product of conditioning: most of us have heard the psalms in the King James Version many times, and thus all other versions sound "wrong" to our ears. But the fact is that the King James Version was only one of a good number of English translations. Because of the accuracy of its translation and the "rightfulness" of its diction, the King James Version, completed in 1611, was recognized even in its own time as a literary triumph.

Compare the following versions of the familiar Psalm 23:

My shepherd is the living Lord; nothing, therefore, I need.
In pastures fair, with waters calm, he set me for to feed.
He did convert and glad my soul, and brought my mind in frame
To walk in paths of righteousness for his most holy name.
Yea, though I walk in the vale of death, yet will I fear none ill;
Thy rod, thy staff doth comfort me, and thou art with me still.
And in the presence of my foes, my table thou has spread;
Thou shalt, O Lord, fill full my cup and eke anoint my head.
Through all my life thy favor is so frankly showed to me
That in thy house forevermore my dwelling place shall be.

Sternhold and Hopkins, 1567

The Lord is my shepherd; I shall not want.
He maketh me to lie down in green pastures: he leadeth me beside the
   still waters.
He restoreth my soul: he leadeth me in the paths of righteousness for
   his name's sake.
Yea, though I walk through the valley of the shadow of death,
I will fear no evil: for thou art with me; thy rod and thy staff they
   comfort me.

Thou preparest a table before me in the presence of mine enemies:
  thou anointest my head with oil; my cup runneth over.
Surely goodness and mercy shall follow me all the days of my life:
  and I will dwell in the house of the Lord forever.

King James Version, 1611

PERCEPTION KEY PSALM 23

1. Compare the Sternhold-Hopkins version with the King James Version. What word choices are particularly strong or weak in either version? Does the lack of rhyme in the King James Version weaken or strengthen the diction? Explain.

2. As an experiment, read the Sternhold-Hopkins version to a friend and ask him what the name of the piece of poetry is. Does it come as a surprise when he realizes which psalm it is?

3. With a group of other readers of this psalm, try your hand at revision. "Translate" it into contemporary English. Compare the best translation in your group with the King James Version. How does the diction in each contribute to the effectiveness of the translation?

The careful use of diction can sometimes conceal the immediate intention of a writer: making it difficult for us to ignore his words until they have, indeed, made their point. One classic example of this is Jonathan Swift's essay *A Modest Proposal*, in which he most decorously suggests that the solution to the poverty stricken Irish farmer's desperation was the sale of his infant children—for the purpose of serving them up as plump, tender roasts for Christmas dinners in England. The diction is so subtly ironic that it is with some difficulty that many readers finally realize Swift is writing satire. By the time one reaches the following passage in the essay, one hardly knows quite how to take it:

> I have been assured by a very knowing American of my acquaintance in London, that a young healthy child well nursed is at a year old a most delicious, nourishing, and wholesome food, whether stewed, roasted, baked, or boiled; and I make no doubt that it will equally serve in a fricasee or a ragout.

The matter-of-fact tone, with such careful choice of words and an apparently totally innocent approach, has fooled more than one reader into accepting the whole idea.

There are many kinds of diction available to the writer, from the casual and conversational to the archaic and the formal. Every piece of writing considers the problem of diction afresh, and every piece of writing solves the problem in its own way for its own purposes. Sometimes a literary work will suggest a prophetic quality through its diction; sometimes it will suggest a holy quality by borrowing biblical diction; sometimes a work can be frightening, arrogant, humble, or vindictive—all through the diction. There are times, too, when the choice of words seems so exact and right that any tampering destroys the value of the work for us almost entirely. No writer can tell you exactly how he achieves this "inevitability," but it seems to depend in part upon experimenting with word-sounds and rhythms. It is an act of finding the best combination of those elements which a choice of words will affect.

PERCEPTION KEY DICTION

1. Compare the following sets of lines:
   a. "Belching black disagreeable breath,
   They count the ways to love. . . ."
   b. "Belching black cacophonous breath,
   They count the ways to love. . . ."
   Which version seems better to you? Why?

2. In the following examples, all nineteenth-century works, the problems of diction are different from those discussed above. Describe for a friend exactly what seems to be achieved by the diction of these examples. Compare your findings with others.

3. Does there seem to be a significant difference between the prose and the poetry in terms of their ability to exploit the resources of diction?

But there can hardly be a doubt that we are descended from barbarians. The astonishment which I felt on first seeing a party of Fuegians [savages living on Tierra del Fuego in South America] on a wild and broken shore will never be forgotten by me, for the reflection at once rushed into my mind—such were our ancestors. These men were absolutely naked and bedaubed with paint, their long hair was tangled, their mouths frothed with excitement, and their expression was wild, startled, and distrustful. They possessed hardly any arts, and like wild animals lived on what they could catch; they had no government, and were merciless to everyone not of their own small tribe. He who has seen a savage in his native land will not feel much shame, if forced to acknowledge that the blood of some more humble creature flows in his veins. For my own part I would as soon be descended from that heroic little monkey, who braved his dreaded enemy in order to save the life of his keeper; or from that old baboon, who, descending from the mountains, carried away in triumph his young comrade from a crowd of astonished dogs—as from a savage who delights to torture his enemies, offers up wives like slaves, knows no decency, and is haunted by the grossest superstitions.[6]

[6] From Charles Darwin, *The Descent of Man.*

7

Come, fill the Cup, and in the fire of Spring
Your winter-garment of Repentance fling;
   The Bird of Time has but a little way
To flutter—and the Bird is on the Wing.

12

A Book of Verses underneath the Bough,
A jug of Wine, a Loaf of Bread—and Thou
   Beside me singing in the Wilderness—
Oh, Wilderness were Paradise enow!

13

Some for the Glories of This World; and some
Sigh for the Prophet's Paradise to come;
Ah, take the Cash, and let the Credit go,
Nor heed the rumble of a distant Drum!

From Edward Fitzgerald (trans.),
"The Rubaiyat of Omar Khayyam"

OZYMANDIAS

I met a traveler from an antique land
Who said: Two vast and trunkless legs of stone
Stand in the desert . . . Near them, on the sand,
Half sunk, a shattered visage lies, whose frown,
And wrinkled lip, and sneer of cold command,
Tell that its sculptor well those passions read
Which yet survive, stamped on these lifeless things,
The hand that mocked them, and the heart that fed:
And on the pedestal these words appear:
"My name is Ozymandias, king of kings:
Look on my works, ye Mighty, and despair!"
Nothing beside remains. Round the decay
Of that colossal wreck, boundless and bare,
The lone and level sands stretch far away.

Percy Bysshe Shelley

8 MUSIC

THE SUBJECT MATTER OF MUSIC

If music has a revelatory capacity, it has, like the other arts, a content which is achieved by the form's transformation of the subject matter. However, some commentators have denied that music has a subject matter, while others have suggested so many different possibilities as to create confusion. Our approach suggests two kinds of subject matter for music: human feeling (emotions or moods) and sound. The complexities implied in such an approach bear some discussion.

THE REFERENTIAL CAPACITY OF MUSIC

To begin with, it is difficult for music to refer to specific objects and events outside itself. Therefore it is difficult to think of music as having the same kind of subject matter as a representational painting, a figurative sculpture, or a realistic novel. Nonetheless, composers have tried to circumvent this limitation by a number of means. One is to use sounds that imitate the sounds we experience in life: birdsongs and clocks in Haydn's symphonies, a thunderstorm in Beethoven's Symphony No. 6, sirens in Charles Ives's works. Limited as this may be, it still represents one effort to overcome the abstract nature of music and to give it a recognizable subject matter.

Another means is a program—usually in the form of a descriptive title, a separate written description, or an accompanying narrative as in opera. *La Mer*, by Claude Debussy, has a program clearly indicated by its title—*The Sea*—and its subtitles: "From Dawn to Noon at Sea"; "Gambols of the Waves"; and "Dialogue Between the Wind and the Sea." Debussy tried to make *La Mer* refer to specific events which happen outside music. His success depends on our knowing the music's program and the relationship between the music and the events it is meant to interpret.

Yet, there is a problem involved with stating flatly that the sea is the subject matter of *La Mer*. The sea cannot be perceived in listening to *La Mer* in anything like the way it can be perceived imaginatively from a literary description or the way it can be perceived more directly in a painting. If *La Mer* were a work that used the actual sounds of the sea or closely imitated them—the crashing of waves, the roaring of winds, and similar sounds—the problem would be simplified. But *La Mer* uses much the same kinds of musical sounds we find in other symphonic compositions by Debussy which have nothing to do with the sea.

In light of this, it might be more reasonable to suggest that *La Mer* is an interpretation—using the medium of music—not of the sea but rather of our impressions of the sea. Since Debussy is often referred to as an Impressionist, many listeners seem to find this explanation plausible. In this sense the subject matter of *La Mer* can be said to be the feelings evoked by the sea. The music's content is the interpretation of those feelings. Given close attention to the program, this suggestion poses few difficulties. But most music has no program, and even *La Mer* can be enjoyed by those who are unaware of its program. Consequently, there may be some general emotional character to the music that can be appreciated apart from any recognition that the swelling of a theme implies the swelling of a sea wind, or that the crash of an orchestra suggests the crash of a wave, or that long, quiet passages suggest the stretches of the sea. Apparently those who do not know the program may still recognize general emotional qualities in these same passages despite the fact that they do not relate these qualities to their feelings about the sea. This suggests a general relationship between the structures of our feelings and the structures of music.

FEELING

Music seems to be able to interpret and thus clarify our feelings primarily because in some ways the structures of music parallel or are congruent with the structures of feelings. A rushing, busy passage can suggest unease or nervousness so powerfully that we sense that unease to be a quality of the music itself, even to the extent sometimes of feeling that unease within ourselves. A slow passage in a minor key—like a funeral march—can suggest gloom; a sprightly passage in a major key—like a dance—can suggest joy. These extremes, and others like them, are obvious and easy for most listeners to comprehend. But there are innumerable subtleties and variations of feelings between these extremes, none of which are as nameable or as discussible as those mentioned. How can music interpret such feelings?

To begin with, the power of sound to evoke feeling has been recognized by innumerable philosophers of art. John Dewey has said,

> Sounds *come* from outside the body, but sound itself is near, intimate; it is an excitation of the organism; we feel the clash of vibrations throughout the whole body. . . . A foot-fall, the breaking of a twig, the rustling of underbrush may signify attack or even death from hostile animal or man. . . . Vision arouses emotion in the form of interest—curiosity solicits further examination, but it attracts; or it institutes a balance between withdrawal and forward exploring action. It is sound that makes us jump.[1]

Secondly, emotion is an effect aroused when a tendency to respond is in some way arrested or inhibited. Suspense is fundamental to an emotional response. Musical stimuli activate tendencies that are frustrated by means of deviations from the expected, and then, usually, these frustrated tendencies are followed by meaningful resolutions. We hear a tone or tonal pattern and find it lacking in the sense that it demands other tones, for it seems to need or anticipate following tones that will presumably resolve its "needfulness." This is the basis of our later discussion on "Tonality: Scales and Keys." According to Leonard B. Meyer, the stronger and more cumulative the tensions of these tonal needs, and the more unexpected the resolutions, the more interesting the music. Furthermore:

> Musical experiences of suspense are very similar to those experienced in real life. Both in life and in music the emotions thus arising have essentially the same stimulus situation: the situation of ignorance, the awareness of the individual's impotence and inability to act where the future course of events is unknown. Because these musical experiences are so very similar to those existing in drama and in life itself, they are often felt to be particularly powerful.[2]

Thirdly, it may be that musical structures possess, at least at times, more than just a general resemblance to the structures of feelings. Susanne Langer maintains that

> the tonal structures we call "music" bear a close logical similarity to the forms of human feelings—forms of growth and attenuation, flowing and stowing, conflict and resolution, speed, arrest, terrific excitement, calm, or subtle activation and dreamy lapses—not joy and sorrow perhaps, but the poignancy of either and both—the greatness and brevity and eternal passing of everything vitally felt. Such is the pattern, or logical form, of sentience, and the pattern

[1] John Dewey, *Art as Experience*, Milton Balch and Co., New York, 1934, p. 237.
[2] Leonard B. Meyer, *Emotion and Meaning in Music*, The University of Chicago Press, Chicago, 1956, p. 20.

of music is that same form worked out in pure, measured sound and silence. Music is a tonal analogue of emotive life.[3]

Carroll C. Pratt, a psychologist, also maintains that the forms of music bear a close resemblance to certain characteristics of the forms of feelings. For example, the "staccato passages, trills, strong accents, quavers, rapid accelerandos and crescendos, shakes, wide jumps in pitch—all such devices conduce to the creation of an auditory structure which is appropriately described as restless."[4]

These points seem to indicate that musical structures may not only evoke emotion in the listener but also may reveal the structures of emotion. Presumably, then, the form of *La Mer* not only evokes feelings analogous to the feelings the sea arouses in us, but the musical form interprets those feelings and gives us insight into them. Now the Formalists of music, such as Eduard Hanslick and Edmund Gurney[5]—just like Clive Bell and Roger Fry, the Formalists of painting (see pages 28–29)—deny this connection of music with life situations. For them, the apprehension of the tonal structures of music is by a unique musical faculty that produces a unique aesthetic effect, and they refuse to call that effect emotion since this suggests alliance with everyday emotions. For them, the grasp of the form or tonal interrelationships of music is so intrinsically valuable that any attempt to relate music to anything else is spurious. As Igor Stravinsky, certainly one of the greatest composers of our century, insisted: "Music is by its very nature essentially powerless to *express* anything at all. . . ."[6] In other words, the Formalists deny that music has a subject matter and, in turn, this means that music has no content, that the form of music has no revelatory meaning. We think the Formalists' theory is plainly inadequate, but the theory is an important warning against thinking of music as a springboard for nonmusical conceptions and emotional debauchery. Moreover, much work remains—building on the work of philosophers of art such as Meyer, Langer, and Pratt—to make clearer the mechanism of how music's form may inform about feelings. We will return to these issues very briefly in the closing section of this chapter, for then we should have a clearer idea about the forms of music. This will make possible, in turn, a clearer idea of what the subject matter and content of music may be.

SOUND

Apart from feelings, sound might also be thought of as one of the subject matters of music. It seems that in some music the form gives us insight into sounds. This is somewhat similar to the claim that colors may be the subject

[3] Susanne Langer, *Feeling and Form*, Scribner's, New York, 1953, p. 27.
[4] Carroll C. Pratt, *The Meaning of Music*, McGraw-Hill, New York, 1931, p. 198.
[5] Eduard Hanslick, *The Beautiful in Music*, Gustav Cohen (trans.), Novello and Co., London, 1891, and Edmund Gurney, *The Power of Sound*, Smith, Elder and Co., London, 1880.
[6] Igor Stravinsky, *An Autobiography*, Simon and Schuster, New York, 1936, p. 83.

matter of some abstract painting (see pages 84–85). The difference is that the color red, for instance, has its analogue in nature, while the tone C is abstracted from nature. Tones and tonal structures are implied in nature in that all tones are present in white noise (see the definition for "noise" in the next section), though only some tones are present in birdsong, speech, and other natural sounds. Colors, like sounds, also exist in a continuous spectrum, though the individual "tones" of colors are more explicitly present in nature. Since we are aware of so many colors in nature, we do not necessarily think of painting as a source of insight into color—although we are aware of the capacity of color to suggest meanings in paintings, for example, the bilious green of Mussolini's head in "The Eternal City" (Figure 1-2) by Blume. Paintings can also reveal the interaction of colors which do not appear contiguous in nature, such as the "electric" clashing of bright red next to bright green. Yet even these have some analogues in nature, as collectors of moths and butterflies will attest. Because the mathematical relationships between tones have to be abstracted from nature, our insight into tonal relations in music is proportionately greater than our insight into color relations in painting. When Edna St. Vincent Millay said that only Euclid looked upon beauty bare, she meant that his grasp of mathematics gave him an insight into pure proportions that the rest of us could not have. Music—with tones that are, in themselves, mathematically exact in their relationship with one another—gives us a perceptual insight into tonal relationships that can be acquired in no other way.

Moreover, music which does not emphasize tonal relationships—such as that of John Cage—can give us insight of a different kind. Since we are surrounded by sounds of all kinds—humming machines, people talking, and banging garbage cans, to name a few—we usually "turn them off" in our conscious mind so as not to be distracted from more important things. This is such an effective "turn-off" that we are surprised and often delighted when a composer introduces ordinary sounds in a musical context which reveals their nature to use in a way we could not have done for ourselves.

PERCEPTION KEY   THE SUBJECT MATTER OF MUSIC

1. In a small group, present a piece of music that you think has feelings as its subject matter. Is it difficult for the others to perceive the subject matter as you do? How much agreement about the kinds of feelings revealed do you find among yourselves? How much disagreement? Can you make explicit the reasons for agreement or disagreement? What do you think about the possibility of feelings being one of the subject matters of music? Note: if you have no special favorites, try Tchaikovsky's *1812 Overture*; the "Tuba Mirum" from Berlioz's *Requiem*; Beethoven's *Grosse Fuge*, Op. 133; or "Der Erlkonig," a song by Schubert.

2. Try listening to an old Spike Jones record or to the recording called *Musique Concrete*, which explores everyday sounds by electronic means. With a

group, discuss the value of such recordings for making one more aware of the characteristics and qualities of sound we simply take for granted. John Cage's recordings would be useful for this purpose.

DEFINITIONS

Because of the technical nature of music it is essential that we pause for some basic definitions.

NOISE

Noise, like all sound, is a result of the movement of air in the form of waves. The more physical space between the crest of the waves, the lower the pitch of the sound; the closer the crest of the waves, the higher the pitch. Noise is a conglomerate of sounds with a variety of pitches—none distinguishable by the ear. For an example of "white noise"—noise with sounds of all pitches at once—listen to the noise between stations on an FM radio band.

TONE

A sound which has one definite frequency or which is dominated by one definite frequency is a tone. Music is usually made up of a succession of tones. Songs unfold by virtue of our ability to hear tones and remember them as they are played in succession. Tones on a musical instrument will have other related tones, or partials, sounding simultaneously, though not as loudly as the primary tone. Our ear is used to hearing a primary tone with fainter partials; therefore, when electronic instruments produce a pure tone of any frequency, it may sound very odd to us.

TIMBRE, OR TONE COLOR

All instruments produce a primary tone and a series of partials, such as— to name only two—tones of a fifth and an octave higher. But all instruments are different in the intensity or loudness of each of the partials. Consequently a trumpet or a piano playing C will each have its distinctive quality of sound. Each instrument and group of instruments has a distinctive timbre, or tone color, because of the variation in intensity of the simultaneously sounding partials which accompany the primary tone. (Figures 8-1 and 8-3.)

CONSONANCE

The sounding of partials implies that tones of different but related frequencies can have a tendency to sound soothing and pleasant together. When two or more tones are sounded simultaneously and the result is pleasing to

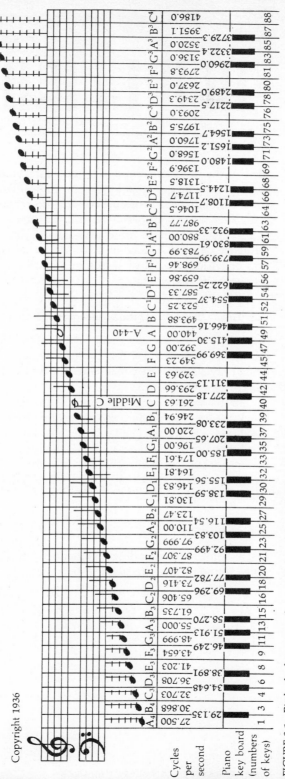

Copyright 1936

FIGURE 8-1 Pitch: the frequency of notes. (Adapted from Carl Seashore, *The Psychology of Music*, McGraw-Hill, 1938, p. 73.)

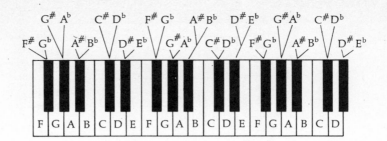

FIGURE 8-2 Notes of the piano keyboard.

the ear, the resultant sound is termed consonant. The phenomenon of consonance may be qualified by several things. For example, what sounds dissonant or unpleasant often becomes more consonant after repeated hearings. Thus the sounds of the music of a different culture may seem dissonant at first but consonant after some familiarity develops. Also, there is the influence of context: a combination of notes may seem dissonant in isolation or within one set of surrounding notes and consonant within another set. In the C major scale,

C	D	E	F	G	A	B	C'
First	Second	Third	Fourth	Fifth	Sixth	Seventh	Eighth (octave)

the strongest consonances will be the eighth (C + C') and the fifth (C + G), with the third (C + E,) the fourth (C + F), and the sixth (C + A) being only slightly less consonant. See the graph in Figure 8-3, based on research by Helmholtz.

In this experiment one violin held the note C' (the C above middle C— check Figure 8-2), while a second violin went up two octaves. The greater the distance of the curved line from the horizontal straight line, the greater the dissonance; the closer the lines, the greater the consonance. The degree of consonance is not directly related to the interest level of a given interval. An interval of a sixth may sound much more intriguing than the perfect consonance of the octave.

DISSONANCE

Just as some notes sounding together tend to be soothing and pleasant, other notes sounding together tend to be rough and unpleasant. This is a result

FIGURE 8-3 Graph of relative dissonance. (From Alexander Wood, *The Physics of Music*, 2d ed., Methuen, London, 1944, p. 157.)

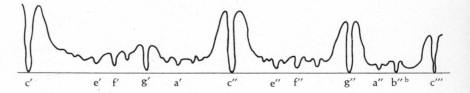

of wave interference and a phenomenon called "beating," which accounts for the roughness we perceive in dissonance. The most powerful dissonance is achieved when notes close to one another in pitch are sounded simultaneously. The second (C+D) and the seventh (C+B) are both strongly dissonant. Dissonance is important in building musical tension, since the desire to resolve dissonance with consonance is strong in most listeners. There is a story that Mozart's wife, for example, would retaliate against her husband after some quarrel by striking a dissonant chord on the piano: Wolfgang would be forced to come from wherever he was to play a resounding consonant chord to relieve the unbearable tension.

PERCEPTION KEY DEFINITIONS

1. Tone color: experiment by listening to a given note or series of notes played by different instruments, such as the piano, guitar (nylon and steel strings produce different tone colors), harmonica, kazoo, accordion, etc. Is it difficult to tell one instrument from another? Do any of the instruments tend to group into "families" by virtue of similarities of tone color? Do you find that people have developed preferences among tone colors?

2. Consonance and dissonance: using a piano or a guitar, strike the note C, then the note C' an octave higher. Use this combination as the standard for what is consonant. Then strike every combination of C plus another note and identify the consonant combinations. Also identify the most interesting combinations. What is their relationship to consonance or dissonance?

3. Dissonance: have someone with a good voice sing a note which he can hold for a few moments. Try to sing a note simultaneously with his that is definitely dissonant with his note. Is this difficult to do? If you cannot yourself sing, listen to two other people perform the experiment and decide how difficult it is to create dissonance. Does the ease or difficulty of producing dissonance surprise you in any way? What might it mean for our experiences in listening to music?

4. Experiment in listening: by paying close attention to tone color, begin trying to name the instruments you hear in the next piece of music you listen to. Listen with others until you are confident that, along with them, you can tell a trumpet from a trombone, a violin from a cello. If you have difficulties, Benjamin Britten's *Young Person's Guide to the Orchestra* is an especially interesting and helpful work.

5. Experiment in listening: listen closely to one of your favorite pieces of music. Where do the strongest consonances occur in the piece? Are they strong and well defined? Are they satisfying? Are they as interesting as the strongest dissonances? Do the consonances and dissonances seem to need each other? Why? Take a piece of music of a kind you do not usually listen to. How does it compare in terms of its level of consonance and dissonance with your favorite? Does this give you any insight into why you prefer your favorite?

THE PHYSICS OF MUSIC

Since we are suggesting that sound may be one subject matter of music, and since sound is governed by laws of physics, it is helpful to briefly consider the nature of these laws. The capacity of music to clarify sound is based on its ability to reveal the underlying orderliness of sound which we could understand—were we to go outside of music—only by a thorough study of the physics of sound. Music gives us knowledge *of* this orderliness, while a study of physics can only give us knowledge *about* it.

MATHEMATICS

Music is "governed" by the laws of physics to the extent that the relationships of the tones of a tonal structure can be predicted by mathematical analysis. Thus one can generally predict the consonance or the dissonance of two tones without having to hear those tones. Most composers can write consonant and dissonant tonal patterns without having to hear the harmonies played by the instruments for which they were invented.

The fact that mathematical theory enters into the creating of compositions makes it possible for composers to control certain kinds of effects, such as the building or releasing of tensions and the resolution of a tonal progression. Composers sometimes borrow not only rhythms, melodies, and harmonies from each other but also basic theory—which is often mathematical at root. At least one important method for composing, the Shillinger method, is based almost entirely on mathematics—very little actual playing of tones is necessary for the successful use of the method.

THE TUNED STRING

The mathematical basis of music was known from very early times. The ancient Greek mathematician Pythagoras is said to have understood the nature of the octave in mathematical terms and to have built a scale. Since this particular bit of mathematics is crucial to the existence of the scale and since scales are fundamental to tonal compositions, Pythagoras's discoveries have considerable significance for us. Let us assume he took a string and tuned it to C. By fretting or dividing it exactly in the center, he produced two strings whose frequencies are mathematically double that of the first string. That means he has produced C', the same note an octave higher. The mathematical relationship established is very simple—a ratio of 1:2. By further dividing his tuned string on the basis of simple whole numbers, Pythagoras produced a scale that resembles our modern diatonic scale in many particulars. A ratio of 2:3 produces G, a fifth; 3:4 produces F, a fourth; 4:5 produces E, a major third; 5:6 produces E^b, a minor third; 3:5 produces A, a major sixth; and so forth. Clearly, our scale is a profoundly orderly structure.

The most remarkable aspect of this is that our ear perceives the mathematical relationships directly, without the need of study or conscious knowledge of numbers and their relationships. Our awareness of the numbers and their relationships can help us build more sensitivity toward music, but it alone will never make us music lovers. Music can and does reveal the underlying order of sounds to us directly.

1. Experimenting with a tuned string will help demonstrate the principles discussed above. Fret a guitar string in the middle until you can sense the octave difference. Try fretting one-third, one-fourth, and one-fifth of the string to produce different notes. Can you produce an entire scale—a series of ordered notes from octave to octave—by using this method?

TONALITY: SCALES AND KEYS

Because of the technical complexities of scales and keys, we will limit ourselves at first to the scales of C major and F major, both diatonic scales. C major uses only the white notes of the piano. This scale is an ordering of notes which stand in a fixed mathematical relationship to one another: C–D–E–F–G–A–B–C. The fact that tones can be arranged in a fixed order is basic to the significance of keys and keyness. Western music did not always concern itself with keys, but when it did, it discovered a natural order for producing and releasing tension. Most simply put, the concept of key implies a given scale for use by a composer and it also implies a tonal center—the fundamental tone that gives the key its name.

TONAL CENTER

Another fairly simple scale is that of the key of F-major: F–G–A–B^b–C–D–E–F. In order to maintain the same fixed mathematical relationship between tones, B must be flatted or lowered a half tone in this scale. The tonic or basic tone is F. We will expect movements away from F to produce some uncertainty or tension in us, while movements back toward F should produce a sense of satisfaction and security. We almost certainly expect a composition in F to end with that tone. Referring constantly to F gives the listener's ear a point of reference, a point of stability: though he may not know the note is F, he feels its special importance. The melody of "Swing Low, Sweet Chariot" is a good case in point: after beginning with A, it moves toward F as a weighty rest point. The melody rises no higher than D' nor lower than middle C. See Figure 8-4; for convenience, the notes are labeled above the notation.

FIGURE 8-4

Swing Low, Sweet Chariot

Negro Spiritual

PERCEPTION KEY "SWING LOW, SWEET CHARIOT"

---

1. What is the proportion of tonic notes (F) to the rest of the notes in the composition? Can you make any judgments about the capacity of the piece to produce and release tension in the listener on the basis of the recurrence of F?

2. Are there any places in the composition where you think F ought to be the next note but is not? If F is always supplied when it seems necessary, what does that signify for the level of tension the piece creates?

3. The ending of a piece such as this produces a high degree of finality. Yet the middle portions are phrases that also seem to have a sense of finality—though not so complete. How does the composition handle the differences in demand? Compare measures 4, 6, and 10 with measures 8 and 16. Discuss the relative values of finality in these measures with others who have thought about this problem.

The notes in the scale of each key have special relationships to one another based upon their relative stability—which is to say their potential for consonance when sounded with the tonic note of the key. The most important of the eight tones in the key of C major are:

Tonic: C
Fifth (dominant): G

Third (mediant): E
Seventh (leading tone): B
Eighth (tonic): C

These five tones are not the only ones with names, though they are the tones which have the most basic and most perceptibly significant relationship to the tonic. They are especially important because they help establish the centrality of the tonic and guide our ear securely to recognize it when it is played. One useful procedure in tonal music is to establish the tonic solidly, veer away from it for a while, and then return to establish a secure "home base" feeling that constitutes much of the satisfaction listeners feel in such music. Consider the use of this procedure in a minuet written by Wolfgang Amadeus Mozart's father, Leopold (Figure 8-5).

FIGURE 8-5

Minuet

From Leopold Mozart's
"Notebook For Nannerl"
(1759)

1. How soon is the tonal center established in the G clef? In the bass clef?

2. In the G clef, how many tones are tonic, dominant, mediant, and leading? How many are none of these?

3. In the bass clef, what is the proportion of tonic, dominant, mediant, and leading tones to those which are none of these? What might it signify if there is a difference in proportion from one clef to another?

4. At the end of the piece, the pattern for completion is tonic (C), dominant (G), tonic (C). Does this pattern occur elsewhere in the composition? Could it occur without giving a sense of finality or completion?

5. The highest and lowest notes of the composition are the tonic (C). How might this fact contribute to our sense of completeness?

Note: if possible, have someone in your group play the piece so you may listen to it as well as look at it.

A piece such as Leopold Mozart's "Minuet" will probably sound pleasant and airy to most of us partly because there is such a preponderance of tonic, dominant, mediant, and leading tones in it. Such a large number of easy-to-grasp relationships of tones will help us relax and be at ease with the piece. It will not sound very dramatic or make us feel uneasy simply because there are few, if any, moments in the piece when we might feel uncertain about its tonal character. Measure 6 is the only measure without one of the four named tones. This produces some tension, which is enhanced by introducing a new rhythmic pattern of what sounds like a hesitation:

But this, too, is resolved by repetition in measures 8, 16, and 18, all ending on the security of the mediant and suggesting, also, that the dominant or the tonic are soon to follow. The movement toward or away from the tonic in any key produces expectations in us. As we move away from the tonic, we are likely to perceive a tense quality in the music and in ourselves. As we return to the tonic, we are likely to experience a relaxing quality in the music and ourselves. This is true in any key and it is true even if the listener knows nothing about keys or the function of the tonic.

ATONALITY

Atonal music abandons the key base and the tonal center. All twelve tones (including the sharps and flats—the black keys on the piano) are equal in value; thus, the other name for the music—twelve-tone music. No tone is returned to more frequently than any other, for if a system was not worked out to ensure that no tone was more frequently used than any other, the old phenomenon of the tonal center would take effect. Therefore Arnold Schoenberg devised a tone row: a sequence of twelve tones, usually arbitrarily chosen, which was the melodic line. This tone row then constituted the basic component of the music; it was arranged in a variety of sequences to form all melodic and harmonic material. Schoenberg's *Pierrot Lunaire* and his String Quartets Nos. 1 and 3 are good examples of atonality. It is still a technique contemporary composers use, and it is appearing in jazz and other popular music, though sparingly.

POLYTONALITY

Polytonal music has at least two different keys played simultaneously. The result is a curious kind of instability and, sometimes, mild confusion which the composer can resolve or not as he chooses. Sometimes polytonal music enables us to hear more distinctly two or more melodies being played simultaneously. The key separations help us hear the melodic separations. This technique has been used by composers as different as Maurice Ravel and Charles Ives. Igor Stravinsky's *History of a Soldier* is an exceptionally interesting example of the successful use of polytonality.

NONTONAL MUSIC

Some electronic composers, such as Milton Babbitt and Karl-Heinz Stockhausen, have been avoiding tonality most of the time. Their compositions depend on other techniques for developing structure. While tonal music can depend on our sense of the impending tonic to give "shape" to a musical composition, the electronic composers depend on repetition, loudness and softness, variations of speed and pitch, and sometimes silence. Often when they do produce tones—as they frequently do—the tones are pure; i.e., the familiar overtones, or partials, which identify tones for most of us, are absent. The novelty of hearing an absolutely pure tone is something that many listeners are not prepared to accept. Consequently, electronic music is sometimes shunned by listeners who prefer the traditional timbres of musical instruments.

John Cage has experimented in his music with breaking panes of glass, dropping objects, dripping water, turning on and off household appliances such as the radio, and even total silence. He is committed, at times, to an exploration of sounds of the everyday world. And he achieves some success by organizing them into structures which reveal the characteristics and qualities of these sounds. Have you, for instance, really listened to breaking glass? The fact that we are used to thinking of music only as organizations of tones makes it sometimes difficult for us to take Cage's work seriously. But if we think of music as organized sound rather than just as organized tones, the problem of acceptance is eased. Since it is the opinion of many young composers that nontonal music will be more and more the preference in composition for some time, it may be useful for us to broaden our personal conceptions of music.

THE BASIC ELEMENTS OF MUSIC

RHYTHM

"Rhythm" is a term referring to the temporal measurement of organized sounds. Rhythm measures the time it takes to play a given note (its duration) and the time when a given note is to be played. Our perception of rhythm in a composition is also affected by accent or stress on given notes. In the waltz, the accent is heavy on the first note (of three) in each musical measure. In most modern jazz, the stress falls on the second and fourth notes (of four) in each measure. Most marching music, which has six notes in each measure, emphasizes the first and fourth note.

TEMPO

The speed at which a composition is played is its tempo. We perceive tempo in terms of beats, just as we perceive the tempo of our heartbeat as seventy-two pulses per minute, approximately. Many tempos have descriptive names indicating the general time value for the basic note of a musical measure. *Presto* means "very fast"; *allegro* means "fast"; *andante* means "at a walking pace"; *moderato* means "at a moderate pace"; *lento* and *largo* mean "slow." Some metronomes are marked at these tempos, but musicians have not entirely agreed on any exact time figure in terms of beats per second for them. Tension, anticipation, and one's sense of musical security are strongly affected by tempo.

MELODY

"Melody" or "theme" is usually defined as a group of notes played one after another possessing a perceivable shape. The shape of a melody has, more or less, a beginning, middle, and end, and it is recognizable when replayed. Vague as this definition is, we rarely find ourselves in doubt about what is or is not a melody. We not only recognize melodies easily but can say a great deal about them. Some melodies are brief—only a few notes; while others seem extensive and are composed of a great many notes. Some melodies are slow, others fast; some are bouncy, others more somber; some are catchy, others less immediately interesting (though they may bear more relistening than catchy melodies); some seem very simple, others considerably more complex. Since melodies can be described in many ways, it is helpful to begin developing your own vocabulary for communicating what you perceive about melodies and comparing your perceptions with others.

1. With a small group of listeners, examine the rhythm and melody of a popular recording you feel has some musical interest. Have each listener describe the rhythm and the melody as carefully as possible and compare descriptions. How difficult is it to perceive rhythmic and melodic qualities? You might consider the following questions: Is the melody easy to remember? Is the tempo slower or faster than your heartbeat? Is the rhythm more noticeable than the melody? Is the rhythm more complex, more imaginative, or more interesting than the melody? Which is more important to you, the melody or the rhythm? Or are they equal in importance?

2. Perform this experiment with one or all of the following kinds of music:
   a. Indian music—Uday or Ravi Shankar
   b. Jazz, old or new
   c. Latin American music
   d. Country and western
   e. A movement of a symphony by Mozart or Beethoven
   f. A song by Strauss, Schubert, or Schumann
   g. Soul
   h. A hymn
   What are the similarities in terms of rhythmic and melodic qualities between these kinds of music? What are the differences? If you have preferences among these musics, are they based on your perception of their rhythmic and melodic qualities? Be as candid as possible about your preferences and discuss them with others who may hold different views.

COUNTERPOINT

In the Middle Ages the monks composing and performing church music began to realize that powerful musical effects could be obtained by singing or playing two or more melodic lines at the same time. They may be different melodies, or the same melody staggered like "Row, Row, Row, Your Boat." This is called "counterpoint"—a playing of two or more melodies against each other. It implies an independence of simultaneous melodic lines each of which can, at times, be the dominant melody. The opposition of melodic lines creates tension by virtue of their competition for our attention. Seventeenth- and eighteenth-century counterpoint became incredibly complex, though its origins were relatively simple. In the Middle Ages counterpoint began as organon bass—bass voices droning a sustained tone —above which the tenor voices sang or chanted the melodic line. Diagramed, it might look something like Figure 8-6.

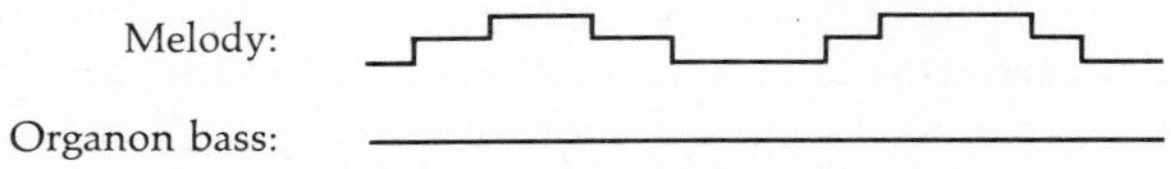

FIGURE 8-6 Organon bass.

Melody:

Organon bass:

The Scotch bagpipe and the organ are instruments especially adaptable for exploiting this kind of counterpoint. Even modern rock bands have picked up the idea—possibly influenced by the chanting of Tibetan monks—and have discovered its potential for building tension.

As the bass line grew more complex, it began to develop as a melody in its own right. Once this second melody was freed from its restrictions of pitch (being limited to the bass notes), the possibilities of interaction of the contrapuntal lines became enormous. Some typical situations are diagramed below. The higher the melodic line, the higher the pitch of the melody.

FIGURE 8-7   Counterpoint.

See Figure 8-7. In example A, melody 2 will probably remain subservient to melody 1 except at the moment when it rises in pitch above melody 1—assuming that the relative loudness of each melody remains the same. In example B, melody 1 will probably remain the dominant melody and receive most of our attention. In example C, melody 2 gradually wrests dominance from melody 1. This assumes not only that the loudness of each melody is relatively equal but also that the tone colors and rhythmic qualities are similar.

Fugue

One specialized form of counterpoint is called the fugue. It was developed in the seventeenth and eighteenth centuries and is closely connected with the name of J. S. Bach, whose monumental *Art of Fugue* ranks as one of the most exhaustive explorations of a melodic line in the history of music. Most fugues feature a melody—called the "statement"—which is given clearly in the beginning of the composition and usually begins with the tonic note of its key. Then that same melody—now called the "answer"—appears again, usually beginning with the dominant note (the fifth note) of that same key. The textural quality of the fugue—with the melodic lines of the statements and answers rising to command our attention, and then submerging into the background as episodes of somewhat contrasting material intervene to attract our notice—is complex but delightful. Consider the following diagram shown in Figure 8-8 as a suggestion of how the statements and answers of a fugue might interact; they compete for attention fiercely.

FIGURE 8-8   The fugue.

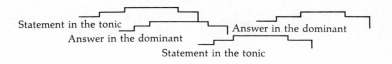

Statement in the tonic

Answer in the dominant

Answer in the dominant

Statement in the tonic

PERCEPTION KEY   COUNTERPOINT

1. Listen to a contrapuntal piece of music such as one of Bach's Brandenburg Concertos, a piece from his *Well-tempered Clavier*, or a concerto of Vivaldi. Identify as best you can each of the melodies you can hear distinctly and describe them carefully. Compare your descriptions with those of other listeners. Describe, too, the rhythmic character of the piece and the kinds of tone colors which are employed. Identify the instruments as they take turns playing the melodic lines.

2. Take a small section of a contrapuntal composition—a half minute or so— and see if you can diagram the melodic lines in the manner we have suggested above. Compare your diagram with those of others and listen again to those sections on which you may disagree. Do other listeners help you find melodies you did not know were there?

3. If you have access to one of Bach's organ fugues on a recording, listen closely to the first melodic statement. Trace it from the beginning of the composition to the end. Probably the simplest and best fugue for this would be Bach's Fugue in G Minor, the "Little Fugue." The first subject is shown in Figure 8-9.

FIGURE 8-9   First subject of Bach's "Little Fugue" in G minor.

4. In the event no contrapuntal music is available, you can sense the intricacy and pleasure of counterpoint by singing a round like "Frère Jacques" or "Row, Row, Row Your Boat" with a group of friends. In a round, one singer starts the melody, then at a selected point the next singer starts the same melody, etc.

HARMONY

Harmony is the sounding of tones simultaneously. The harmony that most of us hear is basically chordal. A chord is a group of notes sounded together which has a specific relationship to a given key: the chord C-E-G, for example, is a major triad in the key of C major. At the end of a composition in the key of C, it will emphasize the sense of arrival—or the sense of finality—more than almost any other technique we know.

Chords are particularly useful for establishing cadences: progressions to resting points that release tensions. Cadences move from relatively unstable chords to stable ones. You can test this on a piano by first playing the notes B-E-F together, then playing C-E-G (consult Figure 8-2 for the position of these notes on the keyboard). The result will be obvious: the first chord establishes tension and uncertainty making the chord unstable, while the second chord resolves the tension and uncertainty, bringing the sequence to a satisfying conclusion. You will probably recognize this progression at once as one you have heard in many compositions, for example, the "A-men" that closes most hymns. The progression exists in every key with the same sense of stability.

Every interval has a degree of stability or instability which composers rely upon when constructing harmonic passages. If they wish to emphasize instability, they will prefer intervals that are seconds (C+D) or sevenths (C+B). If they wish to emphasize stability, they will choose intervals of the octave (C+C') or the fifth (C+G). The thirds (C+E) and sixths (C+A) are fairly stable. The stability of these intervals is related to their approach toward consonance—and your earlier experiments should clarify the nature of stability in relation to consonance and dissonance. The more consonant an interval is, the more stable it is.

When we speak of harmony, we speak of the vertical element of music. Melody is the horizontal element, as can be seen at a glance from Figure 8-10. These are the opening notes of the chorus of "Battle Hymn of the

G or treble clef

F or bass clef

FIGURE 8-10 Harmony—the vertical element.

Republic": the octave C interval in the bass clef and the third plus the fifth interval in the treble clef.

Clearly these are the most stable intervals in the composition, with only the third, E, being even slightly less than optimum in stability. The piece then establishes a powerful stability through its harmony at the outset. Whatever may happen in the middle of the composition, we will expect the end to be just as stable. A glance at the last measure of the piece (Figure 8-11) will show this to be quite true. Whereas the opening included two C's, an E, and a G, the final harmony dispenses with the G and substitutes another C, adding even more stability to the ending.

FIGURE 8-11

Battle Hymn of the Republic

Attributed to William Steffe (Words by Julia Ward Howe)

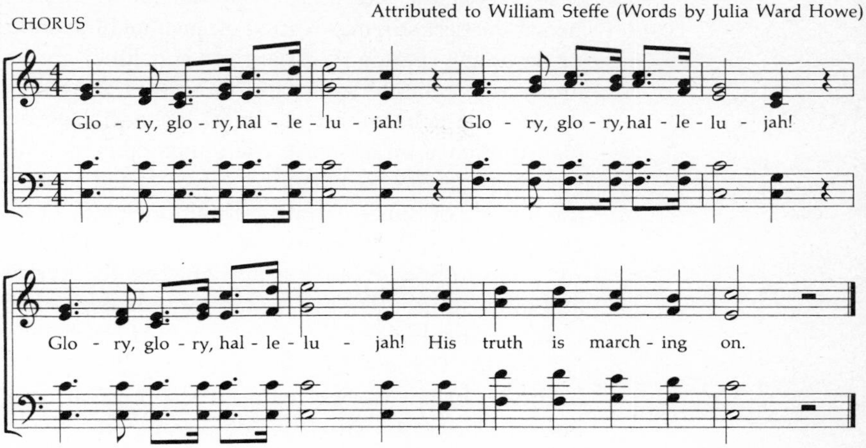

CHORUS

Glo - ry, glo - ry, hal - le - 'lu - jah!   Glo - ry, glo - ry, hal - le - lu - jah!

Glo - ry, glo - ry, hal - le - 'lu - jah!   His   truth   is   march - ing   on.

PERCEPTION KEY HARMONY

1. If possible, have someone play this piece on the piano so that you and others can hear it. Can you identify any points in which the harmony achieves more stability than in the opening notes? Are there any unstable harmonies in the piece?

2. Since this is just the chorus, have the entire piece played. Ask yourself the same questions as in question 1 above.

   Note: in lieu of the piano, the experiment may be conducted with voices or with other instruments.

The experiment with "Battle Hymn of the Republic" is important, but it reveals only some of the powers and significance of harmony. Harmonic techniques did not grow up overnight, nor are they common to music of all cultures. Rhythm and melody have enough power to sustain attention by themselves, so that what is supplied by harmony in western music is not missed by those who do not have it in their own music. However, once non-westerners absorb the techniques of harmony, they often incorporate it in their own music.

Harmony is based on apparently universal psychological reactions. The smoothness of consonance and the roughness of dissonance seem to be just as perceptible to the nonwestern as to the western ear. The effects will be somewhat different in each case due to cultural conditioning, but there is a generally predictable effect within a limited range. One anthropologist, when told about a Samoan ritual in which he was assured he could hear original Samoan music—as it had existed from early times—hauled his tape recorder to the site of the ceremonies, waited until dawn, and when he heard the first stirrings turned on his machine and captured the entire group of Samoans singing "You are my sunshine, my only sunshine." Their harmony was relatively simple, but it was clear they liked the song and responded to its harmonic qualities. The anthropologist was disappointed, but his experience underscores the universality of music.

Approaches to harmony have varied greatly in different periods of the history of music. Contrapuntal music of the seventeenth and eighteenth centuries does not usually emphasize harmony. From Bach, through Mozart, and to Beethoven, harmony begins to develop enormous complexities and interesting subleties. We cannot talk about them here, though you might wish to consult a history of western music, which will give you more technical details. We should note, however, that in the late eighteenth century harmony began to be "featured" in musical compositions. The harmony helped clarify the structure of the melodic lines as well as beginning to attract attention to its own qualities. By the middle of the nineteenth century —in the works of Wagner particularly—harmony began to be as obvious and important as melody and rhythm. Large expansive chords were developed and sustained. In extreme cases some critics felt the delights of melody were being sacrificed for what seemed a technical examination of harmonic effects.

PERCEPTION KEY HARMONY

Choose a musical composition from Haydn, Mozart, or Beethoven; choose another by Wagner, Richard Strauss, or Ralph Vaughan Williams. Compare them for their use of harmony. Ask yourself the following questions:

1. How important is the harmony in comparison with rhythm and melody?

2. What specific effects seem to be achieved by the harmony?

3. Which moments seem to be the most satisfying or dissatisfying in terms of harmony?

4. Are there moments which seem all harmony—when rhythm and melody seem to disappear? When? Can you discuss the importance of these moments to the overall success of the composition?

5. Is there agreement among others listeners and yourself about which harmonic moments are pleasing and which are not? Is there agreement about which are effective and which are not?

6. Can you detect any preference in yourself for the use of harmony? How does your preference compare with the preferences of other listeners? What does your preference seem to be based on?

DYNAMICS

One of the most easily perceived elements of music is dynamics: the music's loudness and softness. Composers vary their dynamics—as they vary keys, timbres, melodies, rhythms, and harmonies—to achieve variety, to establish a pattern against which they can play, to build tension and release it, to feature various moments of the composition, and to provide the surprise which can delight an audience. Two terms, *piano* ("soft") and *forte* ("loud"), with variations such as *pianissimo* ("very soft") and *fortissimo* ("very loud"), are used by composers to identify the desired dynamics at a given moment in the composition. A gradual building up of loudness is called a *crescendo*, while a gradual building down is called a *decrescendo*. Most compositions will have some of each, as well as passages which sustain a dynamic level.

The capacity of dynamics to emphasize segments of a composition and to clarify the relationship of one textural element to another—or to the total structure—is basic to the composer's means. Yet dynamics can be easily abused with too much shifting from loud to soft or simply too much loudness without relief or contrast. The subtlety of musical judgment almost always shows up in the subtle use of dynamics.

PERCEPTION KEY DYNAMICS

Listen closely to two different compositions. Choose one from a popular band like Chicago, Santana, Don Ellis, or Blood, Sweat, and Tears. Choose another from Charles Ives, Igor Stravinsky, Dmitri Shostakovich, or Pierre Boulez. Compare them for:

1. Variations in dynamics
2. Effective use of dynamics
3. Value of dynamics in relation to other musical elements, such as melody, rhythm, or harmony

CONTRAST

Clearly, one thing that helps us value dynamics in a given composition is the composer's use of contrast. But contrast is of value in other ways, too. When more than one instrument is involved, the composer can contrast timbres. The brasses, for example, may be used to offer tonal contrast to a passage which may have been played by the strings. The percussion section, in turn, can contrast with both those sections, with high-pitched bells and low-pitched kettledrums covering a wide tonal range. The woodwinds offer yet another range of tone color, and the composer writing for a large orchestra often will use all of these families of instruments in ways designed to exploit the differences in the way these instruments sound even when playing the same music.

Composers may approach rhythm and tempo with the same attention to contrast. Most symphonies begin with a fast movement (usually labeled *allegro*) in the major key, then a slow movement usually follows in a related or contrasting key, then a third movement with bright speed, and a final movement which resolves to some extent all that has gone before—again at a fast tempo, though sometimes with some contrasting sections within it. Such a symphony, and one worth examining in great detail, is Beethoven's favorite among his own: the *Eroica*, Symphony No. 3 in E flat major. The tempos of the four movements of that symphony are marked

1. *Allegro con brio* ("quickly, in a breezy fashion")
2. *Marcia funebre* ("funeral march"); *adagio assai* ("very slow")
3. *Scherzo* ("a joke"); *Allegro vivace* ("lively and fast")
4. *Allegro molto* ("very fast")

Beethoven begins the work with attention to contrasting timbres. For instance, the main theme of the first movement is stated in the opening passages by the cellos (Figure 8-12). Then it is restated by the horns, clarinets, and flutes. Later it is restated by the ensemble. This procedure of exploiting the tone colors of several families of instruments is used with several of the themes of the first movement.

FIGURE 8-12   First theme from Beethoven's Symphony No. 3, stated by cellos.

Another means of contrast is often apparent in the kinds of themes which are grouped together. Beethoven follows the opening theme above with a highly contrasting theme. It is basically a rapid punctuation which repeats the following chord (Figure 8-13).

FIGURE 8-13   Chord from the second theme of Beethoven's Symphony No. 3.

A variety of instruments play this theme, but its quality—since there is no melodic rise and fall, no movement toward or away from a tonic note—is radically different from the quality of the first theme. Therefore when the first theme is restated our ear responds to it gratefully, aware of its character in a new way. One of the values of contrast is that it gives us comparative grounds that make possible a better comprehension of such things as themes.

PERCEPTION KEY CONTRAST

1. Select a recording which you like and know well. Listen to it carefully for the presence of contrasting elements. Point out the kind of contrast you perceive to other listeners. Do they perceive the contrast as well as you do? Do they perceive some kinds of contrast you do not?

2. Can you tie in the nature of the contrasting elements with the overall success of the piece? How does contrast or the lack of it contribute to that success?

3. Can you identify all the kinds of contrast we mentioned above? Can you find other kinds of contrast?

MUSICAL STRUCTURES

The most familiar musical structures are based, in one sense or another, on repetition—of rhythm, melody, timbre, harmony, and dynamics. Even the refusal to repeat any of these will be effective mainly because repetition is usually anticipated by the listener. Repetition in music is of particular importance because of the serial nature of the medium. The ear cannot retain sound patterns for very long, and thus it needs repetition to help hear the musical elements and their relationships.

THEME AND VARIATIONS

Theme and variations of that theme constitute a favorite structure for composers from the seventeenth century to the present. We are usually presented with a clear statement of the theme which is to be varied. The theme is sometimes repeated so we have a full understanding of it; then modifications of the theme follow. We can identify the process schematically in this fashion, with A being the original theme: $A\text{-}A^1\text{-}A^2\text{-}A^3\text{-}A^4\text{-}A^5$ . . . and so on, to the end of the variations. Some marvelous examples of structures built on this principle are Bach's *Art of Fugue*, Beethoven's *Diabelli Variations*, Brahms's *Variations on a Theme by Joseph Haydn*, and Edward Elgar's *Enigma Variations*.

If the theme is not carefully perceived when it is originally stated, the listener will have little chance of hearing how the variations relate to the theme. Further, unless one knows the structure is theme and variations, much of the delight in the composer's ingenuity will be lost. Interestingly enough, theme and variations is a structure which many arts can employ, as in successive treatments of the same subject matter in successive paintings. Claude Monet, an Impressionist, painted Notre Dame Cathedral in Rouen at different hours of the day. He would paint on one canvas beginning at 10 A.M. Then, when the clock had moved ahead an hour, he removed that canvas and worked on the next, and so on. In architecture we might think of the churches of the world as theme and variations, though it is clear that in music we are not talking about a collection of structures but rather a collection of textural elements that add up to a structure.

RONDO

There are many rondo forms, but all have a similar approach to the question of repetition. The refrain or first section will include a theme or melody and may include a development of that theme. Then, after a contrasting section or episode with a different theme, the refrain is repeated. Occasionally, early episodes are also repeated, but usually not so often as the refrain. It can be described: A-B-A-C-A—either B or D—and so on, ending with the refrain, A. Sometimes composers will end on an episode instead of a refrain, though this is an unusual procedure. The rondo may be slow, as in Mozart's *Haffner Serenade*, or it may be played with blazing speed, as in Weber's *Rondo Brilliante*. The rondo may also suggest a question-answer pattern, as in the children's song, "Where is Thumbkin?" Sometimes the treatments reverse the A-B form, so the refrain comes second each time. The fast first and third movements of Vivaldi's *Seasons*, Haydn's *Gypsy Rondo*, Johann Pachelbel's popular *Dance Rondo*, and the slow second movement of Beethoven's Symphony No. 4 are all interesting examples of the rondo.

SONATA FORM

The eighteenth century brought the sonata form to full development, and contemporary composers still find it a useful structure. Its simplest version is described as A-B-A, with these letters representing the sections of the composition and not just themes, as the letters represent in the rondo. The first A is the exposition, with a statement of the main theme in the tonic key of the composition and usually a secondary theme or themes in the dominant key: the key of G if the tonic key is C. In the A section, the thematic material may be restated, but it is usually not developed. This occurs in the B or development section, with the themes in new but usually closely related keys. The development section usually explores contrasting dynamics, timbres, tempos, rhythms, and harmonic possibilities inherent in the material of the exposition. In the third section or recapitulation, the basic material of the first section or exposition is repeated, usually in the tonic key. After the contrasts of the development section, this repetition in the home key has a quality of return and finality.

The sonata form is ideal for revealing the resources of thematic material. For instance, the principal theme of the exposition when contrasted with a very different second theme, as in the opening movement of Beethoven's *Eroica* Symphony, takes on a new and surprising quality. We may even feel we did not fully hear the principal theme the first time. This is one of the major sources of satisfaction for the careful listener. Statement, contrasting development, and restatement is a useful pattern for revealing the resources of almost any basic musical material—not only thematic material —though its value for revealing thematic potentialities is perhaps the most useful.

The symphony usually is a four-movement structure often employing the sonata form for its opening and closing movements. The middle movement or movements usually are contrasted in dynamics, timbres, thematic materials, and most obviously in tempos with the first and last movements. The listener's ability to perceive how the sonata-form functions within most symphonies can be very important in helping him sense the unified quality of the total composition.

PERCEPTION KEY SONATA FORM

1. Examine closely the first movement of a symphony by Haydn, Mozart, Beethoven, or Brahms. Identify the exposition section—which will come first—and the beginning of the development section. When you can do this, examine the movement until you can identify the end of the development and the beginning of the recapitulation section. You should perceive some change in dynamics and tempo at each of these points, just as you will perceive changes in key, from home key or tonic to contrasting key and back to home key or tonic. You need not know the names of those keys in order to be aware of the changes. They are usually fairly perceptible.

2. Once you have developed the capacity to identify these sections of the sonata form, describe on paper the qualities of each of them so that you may make some useful comments on what makes each of these sections different. Be sure to describe the qualities of melody, harmony, timbres, dynamics, rhythm, tempo, and contrapuntal qualities if any. You may also wish to describe the sections in other terms, such as the qualities of feeling you might sense in them.

3. When you have confidence in your perception of the sonata form, do some comparative studies. Take the first movement of a Haydn symphony —Symphony No. 104 in D major, the *London*, would be useful—and compare each of the sections of the first movement with those of the first move-

ment of any of Brahms' four symphonies, the first movement of Symphony No. 7, *Antarctica*, by Ralph Vaughan Williams, or the first movement of Dmitri Shostakovich's Symphony No. 9. Is such a comparison useful for developing an understanding of the resources of the sonata form? Can you make any useful critical evaluations among these works by this means?

FANTASIA

Romantic composers (roughly, the period of 1830 to 1900) began working with looser structures than the demanding sonata form. We find compositions with terms to identify—presumably—their structures, such as rhapsodies, nocturnes, aubades, and fantasias. They are all somewhat impressionistic in nature, suggesting moods as their subject matter. The fantasia may be the most helpful of these to examine, since it is to the sonata form what free verse is to the sonnet. The word "fantasia" implies imagination, which suggests, in turn, the unexpected and the innovative. It is not a stable structure and its sections cannot be described in such conventional terms as A-B-A. The fantasia usually offers some stability by means of a recognizable melody of a singable quality, but then it shifts to material which is less identifiable thematically, less tonally certain, and less harmonically secure. The succession of musical motifs is presented without regard for any predetermined order. However, there are controls in terms of pacing, the quality of themes and their duration, the harmonic coloring, and the dynamics. Sometimes the fantasia will explore a wide range of feelings by contrasting fast and slow passages, loud and soft passages, richly harmonic and harmonically spare passages, and singable themes with themes that are less singable or appealing.

Many of Robert Schumann's best works are piano pieces he called fantasias. Mozart's Fantasia in C minor is an excellent example of the mode, but probably most of us are more familiar with Moussorgsky's Fantasia: "A Night on Bald Mountain," which was used as the basis for Walt Disney's *Fantasia*.

PROGRAM MUSIC

Another structure, and one related to the fantasia, is program music, in which the nature of the musical material is shaped according to the predetermined program for the composition. "A Night on Bald Mountain" is a good case in point because it interprets the program of a terrible storm and the calmness of the following morning, while also interpreting the terror and fright—in relation to the storm—and gratitude and calm as the sun rises and the birds sing. Often in program music, what is interpreted is not objects or events but the feelings evoked by objects or events. Were we present on Bald Mountain during the storm, we might indeed feel terror—as well as the gratitude that comes when the source of terror is removed. Moussorgsky's music interprets these feelings and reveals them to us partly because we are not distracted—as we would be if we were on the mountain—by having actually to be in terror or to be grateful. Thus we can examine, through the music, something of the structures and qualities of these feelings without being threatened by them.

Program music reveals feelings associated with specific objects and events which lie outside music. Some musicologists suggest that, by interpreting feelings, music—including program music—expands and develops the emotional life of the individual. This is thought to be the reason that people who know little about the technical aspects of music can respond excitedly to program music—since we already have some emotional awareness of objects and events outside of music and can relate meaningfully to references to that awareness. Responding to the more generalized interpretation of feelings in nonprogrammatic music—which does not interpret feelings related to specific objects and events—may be more difficult for most listeners. Without the specificity of a program, we may find the interpretation of feeling by such music less discernible and less comprehendible. To comprehend such interpretations, one must be more acutely aware of the character of the musical elements—rhythm, tempo, melody, timbre, harmony, and dynamics—and their structure. In short, program music reveals emotions associated with specific situations in life. Nonprogrammatic music reveals feelings of a more general character, such as moods, unrelated to specific objects or situations. In this respect, the distinction between program and nonprogrammatic music is analogous to the distinction between representational and abstract painting (see Chapter 4).

PERCEPTION KEY PROGRAM MUSIC

1. After reviewing the program of the music, listen to one of the following: Moussorgsky's *Pictures at an Exhibition* or Fantasia: "A Night on Bald Mountain"; Tchaikovsky's *1812 Overture* or Fantasia, "The Tempest" (particularly if you have recently read Shakespeare's *Tempest*); Debussy's *La Mer*; Ralph Vaughan Williams's Symphony No. 7, *Antarctica*; Charles Ives's *Three Places in New England* or Symphony. *Holidays*. Does the music evoke in you emotions similar to those which might be evoked by the situations referred to in the program? Does the music reveal these emotions—give you a better understanding of them? If so, how?

2. If you have friends who have also listened to the composition you chose, ask them if they were able to identify any emotions revealed or evoked by the music. Is there considerable variety of answers among you and your friends to the above question? What might this mean?

3. Examine the musical elements of your composition for the means by which emotion is revealed or evoked in you or in your friends. Refer to the section entitled "The Basic Elements of Music" to be sure you are considering as many of the basic elements as possible. Are the techniques you can isolate usable in nonprogrammatic music to reveal or evoke a generalized feeling —or do you think these techniques are strictly limited to program music? Explain your reasons.

A BRIEF GLOSSARY OF STYLES AND GENRES— WITH SUGGESTIONS FOR LISTENING

The following glossary treats music historically, from the Renaissance to contemporary times, then offers suggestions for listening to opera and contemporary popular music. All the compositions which are named are available on record and are in the *Schwann Record Guide*. No specific recording is suggested, since recordings come into and go out of print with such rapidity that such suggestions often become obsolete.

RENAISSANCE: 1300–1600

Guillaume Dufay (1400–1474), hymns and songs; Josquin Des Pres (c. 1440–1521), Missa Pange Lingua, Missa "L'Homme Arme," motets; Giovanni Palestrina (1525–1594), Magnificat, Missa Sine Nomine, motets; Roland de Lassus (1532–1594), *St. Matthew Passion*, motets, and madrigals; Giovanni Gabrieli (1551–1612), assorted canzoni for brass instruments, madrigals, and motets; Carlo Gesualdo (1560–1613), madrigals and motets.

Much of the instrumental music of the Renaissance was composed for dancers, though some was also composed for use in the church. The dance pieces of the Renaissance are still among the most delightful of any period. The slow pavanne, the more frenetic morris dance, and the speedy galiard are still being danced. The music composed for such dances naturally correlates with the needs—in terms of tempo and contrast—of the dances themselves. Some of the composers named above wrote music for the dance, and the best way to listen to it is to find an anthology record such as *Dance Music of the Renaissance* (Musical Heritage Society, Inc., New York).

The instrumental music composed for religious purposes seems designed for churches—such as Giovanni Gabrieli's antiphonal (meaning sounds opposite or answering one another) pieces for brass, in which one brass chorus in one cross section of a church would answer another chorus in the opposite section. The resounding echoes from the church stonework, with the persistence of partials as well as primary tones, produced unexpected timbres and unexpected consonant-dissonant combinations. This music is still played today and is still exciting to hear.

But the music written for the voice in the Renaissance probably seems more significant to us now than that written for instruments, brilliant as the instrumental writing is. The masses of Des Pres and Palestrina—as well as those by Dufay, whose Missa L'Homme Arme is almost as well known as Des Pres' on the same theme—are the most ambitious compositions of the period. Setting the words of the mass to music involves a careful attention to the meaning of those words and a careful interpretation in musical terms of that meaning. Consequently, it is always wise to read the words of the mass before listening to a mass of any period.

Madrigals—songs written in the native or vernacular language rather than in Latin—were immensely popular throughout the entire Renaissance. Roland de Lassus' madrigals are exceptionally influential and beautiful. Most important Renaissance composers wrote madrigals, and many contemporary singing societies include them in their repertory—consequently many may sound familiar. Motets were also words set to music, but usually Latin words. The form was contrapuntal, with an organon bass line and the words sung in the upper registers.

Listen For:

1. Smooth consonance and very little dissonance except for occasional accent.

2. Careful attention paid to the text, with the music, especially its rhythms, usually imitative to some extent of the words.

3. Relatively conservative and restricted use of dynamics except occasionally in some instrumental music.

4. A smooth, sonorous quality to the voices, with careful distinctions between soprano, alto, tenor, and bass, emphasizing the beauty of the voices, their contrasts, and their blending.

5. Relatively slight tension building, with very quick release in treatment of themes—theme one, usually a few measures, will come to a resting point just as theme two, often very similar in quality, will just begin. This pattern repeats throughout.

6. Slight use of contrasts; relatively restricted range of pitch.

PERCEPTION KEY   RENAISSANCE MUSIC

1. Listen to a Renaissance composition for instruments and one for voices. Compare them by means of descriptive analysis for their uses of musical elements. Which seems to you to be more imaginative or successful in the handling of timbres, tempos, contrasts, dynamics, and musical tension?

2. Listen to a song written by Byrd (1540–1623), Morley (1557–1602), or Dowland (1560–1626). How carefully integrated is the music with the text? What techniques were used by the composer to make the music congruent with the words? Was he successful? Be careful and detailed in your discussion.

BAROQUE: 1600–1750

Claudio Monteverdi (1567–1643), *Carnival Songs*, *Vespers for the Blessed Virgin*, madrigals and incidental songs; Henry Purcell (1659–1695), *Masque: The Faerie Queene*, *King Arthur*, songs; Antonio Vivaldi (1675–1741), *The Seasons*, concertos for lute, flute, and many combinations of instruments; J. S. Bach (1685–1750), the Brandenburg Concertos, Mass in B minor, *Art of Fugue*, *St. Matthew Passion*, *Well-tempered Clavier*, cantatas, fugues, and concertos for various instruments; G. F. Handel (1685–1759), *The Messiah*, *The Creation*, Concerto Grosso in D Major.

Madrigals and songs, as well as larger compositions for voice and instruments, continue to be important for the composers of this period. Most of these have a religious subject matter, but many do not. Purcell's writing is conspicuous for its treatment of secular English and Irish traditional material. Yet, masses and religious cantatas—as well as such church instrumental compositions as Bach's organ preludes—are consistently popular. The church's influence is all but imperceptible in the concertos of Vivaldi, Bach, and Handel, in which the subject matter is certainly not religious but much more the kind of subject matter we associate with pure music, that of a generalized feeling.

Purcell, Bach, and Handel are products of the Reformation, the splitting away of the Protestant churches from Catholicism. The Protestants needed religious music, though it was to be of a less gaudy nature than Catholic music—and, indeed, it seems very much the same to our ears even though much Protestant church music was based on religious hymns written by such men as Martin Luther. The rapid increase of wealthy families in this period made it possible to support a secular music designed not to uplift the listener in a religious sense but simply to entertain his sensibilities. The more purely instrumental music, as well as Monteverdi's songs and the vocal works of Purcell, were often designed to attend to the needs of a nonchurchly audience.

As a consequence, Baroque music tends to be more richly ornamented, brilliant, and vigorous than the simpler—relatively speaking—Renaissance compositions. It is also more ambitious and sometimes more superficial.

Listen For:

1. Considerable tension in the drive of tempos, though not necessarily much variety in tempos within a composition.

2. Virtuosity in melodic lines, with ingenious counterpoint and carefully sustained melodic tension developed by the constant playing of one melodic line against another.

3. Considerable contrast achieved through varieties of pitch in a composition—though most Baroque music emphasizes the upper registers—and through varieties in timbres.

4. Contrast achieved through the pitting of one instrument against the orchestra, the concerto; or contrast achieved by pitting a small group of instruments against the orchestra, the concerto grosso.

5. Attention to structures such as rondo and theme and variations, implying an attempt to explore the resources of thematic material.

6. Interesting uses of harmony, particularly in the passions and cantatas of Bach and in the oratorios of Handel (dramatic musical compositions closely related to opera, but without the addition of the spectacle of acting).

7. Greater tolerance of dissonances, particularly those which involve more than two dissonant tones.

PERCEPTION KEY BAROQUE MUSIC

1. Listen to two compositions, one religious, such as Bach's *St. Matthew Passion* or Monteverdi's Vespers for the Blessed Virgin, and one which is secular, such as Vivaldi's *Seasons*, or Purcell's *Masque: The Faerie Queene*. Begin by describing the general impressions they give you. Do you detect a religious subject matter in the religious composition? Do you detect the secular nature of the nonreligious composition? What uses of tempos, dynamics, timbres, and contrasts do the compositions share? What uses seem more peculiar to each? Can secular music be distinguished from religious music by reference to their use of musical elements?

2. Listen to at least one concerto or concerto grosso. Describe it as carefully as possible in terms of its use of melodic material, its concerns for counterpoint, its interest in harmony, and the means by which it achieves contrast and tension. Is tension relieved at the points of arrival—the endings of musical phrases or sections of the composition—by means of the cadences we described in discussing a sense of ending in question 3 of the perception key (page 282) on the subject of "Swing Low, Sweet Chariot"?

CLASSIC: 1750–1830

Franz Josef Haydn (1732–1809), Symphony in G major, No. 94, the *Surprise*; Symphony in D major, No. 101, the *Clock*; String Quartet No. 2 (Opus 76—which contains six fine quartets); *The Seven Last Words of Christ*. Wolfgang Amadeus Mozart (1756–1791), *Requiem*; *Symphony in C major*, the *Jupiter*; Concerto for Piano, No. 21 in C major; *Eine Kleine Nachtmusik* (or Serenade in G major). Ludwig van Beethoven (1770–1827), Symphony No. 3 in E♭ major, the *Eroica*; Symphony No. 6 in F major, the *Pastorale*; Symphony No. 9 in D minor, the *Chorale*; the Rasumovsky Quartets (Nos. 1, 2, 3).

Though most of the classic composers produced some religious music, it was not their principal activity. Haydn's Mass in D minor, for Lord Nelson, may be as political as it is religious. Yet, Mozart's *Requiem* may be the greatest ever written, and Beethoven's *Missa Solemnis* compares well with the masses of the great ages of religion. But these are limited examples. Haydn's 104 symphonies were written to amuse a small courtly audience that demanded new musical material for its weekly concerts. Mozart wrote for a broader musical audience which included the bourgeosie, not just the aristocrats. Their taste was not for religious music.

Classic composers built on the tonal experiments of the Baroque. They developed, for example, the sense of keyness and key interrelationship which Bach clearly valued. They also developed the vertical chordal texture which is usually lacking in most Baroque music, which emphasized counterpoint. Their harmony is basically triadic, as described in the section on tonal music, which builds on three-note chords and their variants—such as C-E-G in the key of C. The classic composers also developed the larger structures with predetermined repetitive structures, such as the sonata form, the rondo, and the minuet.

The melodic lines in classic compositions are often long and sustained, and they have a highly distinct quality to them which makes them more recognizable than most Baroque melodies. In Bach's Brandenburg Concerto No. 2 you will hear many melodies, but you will tend to be attracted to the texture of the sounds: the tone colors, dynamics, and contrapuntal effects. A classic composition calls attention to its structural qualities, since the textural elements of harmony and dynamics are controlled by the demands of strong key-based chords to "back up" the melodies as prescribed by the structure.

The texture of Beethoven's Symphony No. 5 does not closely resemble that of the Brandenburg Concerto No. 2. For one thing, our ear hears elements in the Beethoven which are clearly building blocks. The most famous motif in the symphony (see Figure 8-14) is stated first by all the strings and

FIGURE 8-14   Motif from Beethoven's Symphony No. 5.

the clarinets, then by second violins alone, then first violins, then violas, and on and on until another motif based on this first one appears, then the original motif finds its way into the background sounds which we have to strain to listen for until we begin to understand the motif is not there just to be listened to in isolation: it is there as a clearly identifiable unit that helps build the structure.

Listen For:

1. A dramatic variety in use of tempos, even within a small section of a composition.

2. Strong, well-highlighted melodies which are sometimes sustained for a relatively long time.

· · 3. Melodic material, such as the beginning motif in Beethoven's Symphony No. 5, which contributes as a building block to the structure of the work.

4. Contrast achieved by means of opposing timbres of different families of instruments: strings, brasses, woodwinds, and percussion all taking clearly identifiable roles in a piece for orchestra.

5. Great dynamic range, particularly in Beethoven and the music of the later part of the period; less of a dynamic range in Haydn, though his experiments—in the *Surprise* Symphony, for instance—are interesting.

6. Full development of forms such as the rondo, the sonata form, theme and variations.

7. Full triadic harmony, with emphasis on exploiting the keyness of the scale employed; dependence on a strong tonic center and the exploitation of the contrast of related keys.

8. Strong dissonant passages preparing for powerful resolutions of cadential consonance; dissonance for emphasis and dramatic purposes.

PERCEPTION KEY CLASSIC MUSIC

1. Listen closely to a symphony of Haydn. Describe each movement of the symphony in terms of its uses of basic musical elements. Can you determine the kinds of general feelings which might be revealed and evoked by each of the movements? Are they contrasted from movement to movement? What are the principal means of contrast used from movement to movement? Which movements seem to have the most in common in their uses of musical elements?

2. Listen to the last movement of Haydn's *Clock* Symphony, Mozart's *Jupiter* Symphony, and Beethoven's *Pastorale* Symphony. Which of these seems most clearly to have feeling as part of its subject matter? Which seems to have sound as the most prominent part of its subject matter? What kinds of insight, if any, are revealed to you by each? In answering this question, be as responsible as possible to the musical elements which influence your conclusions.

ROMANTIC: 1830–1900

Hector Berlioz (1803–1869), *Symphony Fantastique; Romeo and Juliet; Roman Carnival Overture; Requiem.* Felix Mendelssohn (1809–1847),

Concerto in E minor for Violin; *Incidental Music for A Midsummer Night's Dream*; Symphony No. 3, the *Scotch*. Frederick Chopin (1810–1849), preludes or etudes for piano. Johannes Brahms (1833–1897), Symphony No. 1 in C minor; *Variations on a Theme by Haydn*; Concerto for Violin and Orchestra; Double Concerto for Violin, Cello, and Orchestra; Hungarian Dances. Peter Tchaikovsky (1840–1893), *Swan Lake; The Nutcracker Suite:* Concerto No. 1 in B^b minor for Piano; *Romeo and Juliet.*

The careful work of the classic composers in establishing cadential patterns, leading to strong rest points and even stronger ending points at the conclusion of compositions, is modified in the romantic style—particularly the later music of Wagner (his works are suggested for listening in the section on opera). In some of Wagner's music, the horizontal line of the melody seems to have no rest points at all. The melodies seem almost interminable, though some are clearly shaped and recognizable as they return again and again. Wagner also often used building-unit motifs—somewhat similar to those used by Beethoven in his Symphony No 5—for example the "look motif" from *Tristan und Isolde*, and the "sword motif" from *The Ring of the Niebelungs*. Unlike Beethoven's, Wagner's motifs are associated with specific objects or events and are used to refer to or interpret them.

Reference to specific objects and events in romantic music is much greater, in general, than in classic music. Beethoven, in works such as the *Pastorale* Symphony, begins the trend toward such referential efforts. But romantic composers are vastly more ambitious in this regard than those who went before them. Berlioz and Tchaikovsky were not the only composers to dedicate a work to a Shakespeare play or to try to make their musical composition refer to and interpret a piece of literature. The occasional marriage of music, literature, and dance, as in Tchaikovsky's *Swan Lake* (see pages 327–331), seems entirely easy and natural in the romantic period.

Some of the classic structures—such as the sonata form and the larger structure built on it, the symphony—persist in the works of Mendelssohn, Brahms, and Tchaikovsky in particular. But the expansion of the orchestra, with sometimes more than a hundred pieces, helped the romantic composer build the classic structures into something enormously expansive, with huge waves of sound that were all but impossible for classic composers who rarely had or needed huge orchestras. The size of the orchestra seems also to have affected the character of the concerto, with the solo instrument concentrating on extraordinary virtuosity as a help in balancing the relationship between a piano or violin, say, and the entire orchestra.

Listen For:

1. Careful use of tempos, particularly those which are extreme in speed, or, more frequently, extreme in slowness.
2. Melodic lines which are lengthy, often growing into new melodic lines without clear transitions.

3. Greater contrasts of dynamics than found in classic music; occasional bombast as in certain works of Berlioz and Tchaikovsky.

4. Interest in varieties of timbres on a grand scale, with choruses of instruments of a different family.

5. Appearance of less predetermined structures such as the nocturne, the aubade, the serenade, the capriccio, etudes, and sonatas which are not sonata-form compositions.

6. Harmonic texture strong, noticeable, and sustained; harmonies generally much more significant than in classic music in the sense that they are more obvious, more in competition with the melodic line for attention.

7. Greater emphasis and reliance on dissonances and a lesser interest in consonance as a means of relieving tension.

8. Growing interest in exploring the capacities of music to refer to specific objects and events, and thus emphasis on program music and opera.

PERCEPTION KEY   ROMANTIC MUSIC

1. After having read Shakespeare's *Romeo and Juliet*, listen to Berlioz's and Tchaikovsky's compositions of the same title. Is there a perceptible connection between the musical compositions and the play? Can you conclude that the compositions are interpretations of the play? Is it possible to decide which of the musical compositions is more faithful to the play, or which is more successful in its effort at interpretation?

2. Analyze the use of musical elements in a nonprogrammatic piece of music such as a concerto or a symphony. Describe carefully the use of tempos, melodic lines, harmonic qualities, dynamics, and anything else you feel is relevant. Does your description correlate with descriptions of the same piece made by other listeners?

3. Having performed the analysis in question 2 above, do you feel confident in holding an opinion about the success of the composition? How do your opinions relate to those of others who have performed the same analysis? How do they relate to those who have not performed the analysis at all?

MODERN: 1900–PRESENT

Gustav Mahler (1860–1911), *Kindertotenlieder; Das Lied von der Erde; Symphony No. 8 in E^b major, Symphony of a Thousand;* Symphony No. 9 in D major. Claude Debussy (1862–1918), *La Mer, Nocturnes, Clair de Lune, Children's Corner Suite.* Richard Strauss (1864–1949), *Death and Transfiguration, Don Quixote, Till Eulenspiegel, Also Sprach Zarathustra.* Ralph Vaughan Williams (1872–1958), Mass in G-Minor; Symphony No. 1, *Sea;* Symphony No. 7, *Antarctica.* Arnold Schoenberg (1874–1951), *Transfigured Night, Pierrot Lunaire.* Charles Ives (1874–1954), *Three Places in New England; Holidays* Symphony. Maurice Ravel (1875–1937), *Bolero,* Concerto in D major for the Left Hand (piano), *Rhapsodie Espagnole.*

Ernest Bloch (1880—1959), *Schelomo*, Rhapsody for Cello and Orchestra. Bela Bartok (1891—1945), *Concerto for Orchestra; Miraculous Mandarin Suite; Music for Strings, Percussion, and Celesta.* Igor Stravinsky (1882—1971), *Firebird: Suite, Petrouchka, The Rites of Spring, Oedipus Rex, Symphony of Psalms.* Edgar Varese (1885—1965), *Deserts, Ionization.* John Cage (1912—0000), *Variation IV, Indeterminacy.* Benjamin Britten (1913–   ), *Young Person's Guide to the Orchestra, War Requiem,* Karl-Heinz Stockhausen (1928–   ), *Mikrophonie I for Tam-tam, 2 Microphones, & Filters, & Potentiometers.* Krzysztof Penderecki (1933–   ), *Threnody for the Victims of Hiroshima, Dies Irae* (Auschwitz Oratório).

Much of the music of the older composers of the modern period, such as Mahler, is close to the Romantics, continuing similar attitudes toward dissonance, rich harmonics, and program music. The younger composers often moved away from a tonal center. They used, like Schoenberg, atonality, an approach which treats all notes of a scale as equal in value, with no tonic, dominant, or mediant notes. Others, like Charles Ives, sometimes employed polytonality, in which melodic lines written in different keys might be sounded together. The effect of having two strong key-based lines operating simultaneously can be very exciting. "July 4th" in Ives's *Holidays* Symphony is an interesting example, with two marching bands playing two different tunes marching toward, then through, one another. This was something Charles Ives once saw when he was a child watching his father's marching bands entertaining an audience in Danbury on July fourth.

Some composers, like Bartók, Stravinsky, and Paul Hindemith (1895–1963), developed a neoclassicism that tried to combine classic formal structures with the expansiveness of the Romantic approach to the use of mythic inspiration and literary sources. Their music has generally been well received, helping us to reevaluate the achievement of the classic composers.

Composers such as Luciano Berio (1925–) and Stockhausen have been working in the medium of electronic music and, sometimes, nontonal sounds. Their work has been difficult for contemporary audiences to appreciate because it seems to break too sharply with the traditions of the past. Some audiences treat their works as if they were not music at all. The absence of not just the strong tonal center but of tonality itself has been enough to make it very difficult for some audiences to respond positively. The timbres achieved by electronic synthesizers have also been difficult for audiences used to the sounds of traditional musical instruments. One of the positive virtues of electronic music is the calling into question the perhaps dogmatic conception of music as having organized tones as its medium. When all sound is at the disposal of the composer, his limits and his ambitions must be considerably different from those of his predecessors, who generally relied upon clearly defined scales and pre-determined structures.

Listen For:

1. Wide variety of tempos, with strong accents and dramatic emphasis; shifts and stops, halts and sudden changes of tempo.

2. Melodic lines which resemble, in many cases, those of the baroque—continuous, restless—and, in fewer cases, those of the classic period.

3. Fragmentation of melodic material in some cases, with themes that do not have the clearly perceptible beginning, middle, and end of traditional music; melodic lines that seem bits and pieces of sound, almost randomly organized, yet obviously linear—or horizontal—in their progress.

4. Considerable interest in timbres, even in the more traditional-sounding compositions, but extraordinary interest in electronic timbres and timbres of objects not ordinarily thought of as musical instruments.

5. Wide variety of structures borrowed from traditional music, but also structures which are not predetermined, which seem to develop and grow in accord with the musical potentialities.

6. Harmonies often similar to those of the Romantics, but much less concern for harmony as such—less reliance on harmony for overall orchestral color or for emphasis and ending.

7. Wide range of dynamics, but a tendency to be more abrupt, to shift dynamics without warning.

8. Preference for percussive effects and an expanded use of percussion instruments in all kinds of compositions.

9. More tolerance for dissonances, even to the extent of using them for the ending points of compositions; consonance does not necessarily resolve tensions nor dissonance create them.

PERCEPTION KEY MODERN MUSIC

1. Choose a piece of music such as the *Firebird: Suite, Ionization,* or *Threnody for the Victims of Hiroshima* and analyze it for its capacity to create, sustain, and resolve tension. What seem to be its resources, in terms of musical elements, for producing tension? Are they vastly different from those of traditional music, or are they much the same?

2. Listen to a piece of music by each of two composers listed as modern. Be sure their birth dates are a generation apart. Compare their treatment of specific musical elements—tempo, melody, harmony, dynamics, timbres, etc. How different are they? How do the chief differences affect your comparative evaluations of the two works?

3. Choose a piece of electronic music and describe its use of musical elements. Are there any musical elements possessed by electronic music which are absent from traditional music? Explain the relative importance of each element used in the composition. Do others agree with your judgments?

OPERA

Claudio Monteverdi (1567—1643), *Orfeo.* W. A. Mozart (1756—1791), *The Marriage of Figaro, Don Giovanni, The Magic Flute.* Gaetano Donizetti (1797–1848), *Don Pasquale, Lucia di Lammermoor, Roberto Devereux.* Vincenzo Bellini (1801–1835), *Norma, La Sonnambula.* Richard Wagner (1813–1883), *Tristan und Isolde, The Flying Dutchman, Tannhäuser, Lohengrin;* the "Ring" cycle—*Das Rheingold, Die Walküre, Siegfried, Götterdammerung.* Guiseppe Verdi (1813–1901), *Aida, Macbeth, Otello, Falstaff, Rigoletto, La Traviata, The Force of Destiny.* Georges Bizet (1838—1875), *Carmen.* Giacomo Puccini (1858–1924), *La Bohème, Turandot.* Scott Joplin (1868–1917), *Treemonisha.* Kurt Weill (1900–1950), *Threepenny Opera.* Gian-Carlo Menotti (1911–   ), *Amahl and the Night Visitors, The Medium.* Krzysztof Penderecki (1935–   ), *The Devils of Loudun.* The Who, *Tommy* (1969).

Because opera depends on a dramatic narrative, which is usually called the "libretto" (little book), it refers to specific events. In a way, the music has a program, but the program is not separate from the composition, as it would be with *La Mer* or any other wordless piece of program music. Opera's program is its story line, which is acted, sung, and sometimes spoken. Most operas are not written in English, so many Americans have trouble following the narratives of Wagner, Verdi, or Bizet, for example. But even operas in English are sometimes difficult to follow, since the musical demands occasionally make clear articulation difficult. The problem can be solved, usually, only by acquainting oneself with the libretto—just as one must acquaint himself with the program of a piece of program music.

The subject matter of opera is more obvious than the subject matter of a piece of nonprogrammatic music. Opera still uses all the basic elements of music, but those elements are closely wedded to the needs of the unfolding drama. Opera usually interprets highly dramatic situations, such as the resolution in face of torture which Grandier displays in Penderecki's *Devils of Loudun* or the heroism Treemonisha displays when she is challenged by voodoo forces in Scott Joplin's ragtime opera, the first opera by a black American. The musical character of great arias often becomes much clearer when one knows the dramatic necessities they are serving—which is to say that the significance of the aria is clearer when we have heard it in the total context of the opera's dramatic spectacle.

The Who's recent success with the rock opera *Tommy*—not to mention similar successes with *Jesus Christ Superstar* and *Godspell*—should serve to remind us that opera is a highly popular art and not something reserved for esoteric tastes. In many European cities opera stars such as Montserrat Caballé, Maria Callas, Joan Sutherland, Sherrill Milnes, and Luciano Pavarotti are cheered like soccer or film stars. Non-European audiences also usually react warmly to opera when they are thoroughly acquainted with the story. This should always be a listener's first step before hearing an opera: read the libretto.

Listen For:

1. Uses of musical elements such as tempo, melodic lines, timbre, harmony, and dynamics which are characteristic of the periods in which the operas are written.

2. Efforts to fuse the musical materials to the text being sung, as in the masses of the late Renaissance and the early Baroque—but now with secular material of a highly dramatic nature.

3. Frequent use of orchestral dynamics to help evoke an emotional response to the dramatic situation on stage—or, if not to evoke the response, to suggest it or interpret it on behalf of the characters.

4. Vocal coloration to express dramatic emotion on the part of the character.

5. Occasional exaggeration of the dramatic situation as an effort to highlight emotional values—sometimes called melodrama (literally, drama with music).

6. Featuring the human voice at its most beautiful, sometimes at the expense of the narrative, as a way of demonstrating the virtuosity of opera's principal musical instrument: the voice.

7. Means of creating tension musically, particularly as moments of tension are timed to the needs of the narrative.

PERCEPTION KEY OPERA

1. Choose a relatively short opera in English: *Tommy*, *The Medium*, or the last act of *Treemonisha*. Acquaint yourself with the libretto. After listening to the opera, identify the kinds of emotions interpreted by the singers. How successful is the opera in clarifying these emotions?

2. In the opera you have chosen, what are the most basic means used to build tension? Compare them with the tension-building means you have discovered in nonoperatic music.

3. After acquainting yourself with the libretto or synopsis of a non-English-language opera, such as an opera of Wagner or Verdi, listen for the ease or difficulty with which it establishes and interprets an emotional situation —in comparison with an English-language opera. Do you find the foreign language an insurmountable difficulty in understanding the emotional interpretations even after you have studied the libretto?

4. Take an opera of a given period—Renaissance, Baroque, Romantic, or modern—and evaluate the ways in which it has used the stylistic resources of that period for the purposes of interpreting a dramatic narrative. Do the resources of that stylistic period lend themselves to the purposes the opera puts them? Does the opera do those resources an injustice? Explain and be specific in referring to the resources in question.

CONTEMPORARY POPULAR MUSIC

This category includes folk, jazz, soul, Latin, calypso, rock, country and western. Since popular music changes very rapidly, our suggestions for this section avoid naming specific groups or albums. The genres of popular music are primarily those named above, but even those are subject to change, as the periodic surfacing and disappearance of rhythm and blues would suggest. It is noteworthy that popular music, like most folk arts, tends to be conservative in its use of the basic elements of music. Most of the music we hear on the radio, for instance, is strong in establishing a tonal center and respecting the implications of a key-based scale. It is also conservative in its use of steady tempos—with some halving and doubling of tempo permitted but little variation of a radical sort. Even the strongly rhythmic Latin music usually establishes a complex rhythmic pattern at the outset and maintains it to the end of the piece. The structure of most popular pieces is also conservative, with precise limits to the number of measures permitted in the verse and chorus of the piece. Building a piece on twelve- or sixteen-bar (measure) units is normal. The result of this is somewhat akin to the result of writing sonnets: sometimes the form will strangle inspiration, sometimes it will intensify inspiration and permit the artist to create "better than he knew."

Listen For:

1. Powerful tonal center with clear and intense cadences leading to rest points and conclusions.

2. Usually a distinct melodic line with a clear and recognizable principal melody and a strongly contrasting subsequent melody.

3. Reliance on the A-B-A form in which the first section is contrasted with the second section, then repeated as a means of reinforcing the conclusion.

4. Occasional disregard for melodic line—as in some modern jazz and "hard" rock—in which the line is not clearly shaped or "memorable," but is reminiscent of the texture of baroque counterpoint: the melodic line pushes onward with vigor, but without much clarity.

5. Various approaches to dynamics, with some pieces totally unchanging and others changing in response to the text being sung or in hopes of offering a contrast to an earlier section.

6. Relatively simple harmonies, usually based on the most clearly delineated chords of the basic key—such as the major triad and the seventh and ninth chords.

7. Various approaches to dissonance—sometimes following the lead of the classic period and sometimes that of the modern period of music.

1. Select a piece of music from a popular style you admire—folk, jazz, soul, or whatever. Clarify its use of basic musical elements in such a way that you are satisfied you are describing the usual characteristics of that particular style.

2. Compare two different popular styles. How do they use rhythm, tempo, melody, timbres, harmony, dynamics, and dissonance? Are the two styles very different from one another, or are they more similar than might first be thought?

3. What kinds of feelings might be considered the subject matter of the pieces you have chosen to discuss? How does the music help reveal those feelings? Do other listeners agree with you?

THE CONTENT OF MUSIC

We began this chapter by suggesting that feelings and sound represented the primary subject matters of music. This implies that the content of music is a revelation of feelings or sound and that music gives us a more sensitive understanding of them. However, as we indicated in our opening statements, there is considerable disagreement about music's subject matter, and therefore there is disagreement about music's content. If music does reveal feelings or sound, the way it does so is still one of the most baffling problems in the philosophy of art.

Even a brief survey of the theories about the content of music is beyond our scope here, but given the basic theory of art as revelation, as we have been presupposing in this book, a couple of examples of how that theory might be applied to music are relevant. In the first place, some music apparently clarifies sounds. For example, John Cage, at times, uses devices such as a brick crashing through a glass. Normally when we hear such sounds, we listen away from them to what they signify, such as an accident or theft or riot. In everyday life it would be strange indeed to listen to such sounds for their own sake, for their intrinsic values. But by putting such sounds into a composition, Cage brackets out the everyday situation and helps us "listen to" rather than "listen through" such sounds. In this way he clarifies those sounds. His musical form organizes sounds before and after the sound of the breaking glass in such a way that our perception of the sound of breaking glass is made more sensitive. Similar analyses can be made of the sounds of musical instruments and their interrelationships in the structures in which they are placed.

Second, there seems to be some evidence that music gives us insight into our feelings. It is not ridiculous to claim, for example, that one is feeling joy like that of the last movement of Mozart's *Jupiter* Symphony, or sadness like the second movement—the funeral march—of Beethoven's *Eroica* Symphony. In fact, joy and sadness are general terms that only very crudely describe our states of feeling. We experience all kinds of different joys and different sadnesses, and the names language gives to these are imprecise. Music, with its capacity to evoke feelings, and with a complexity of texture and structure that in many ways is greater than that of language, may be able to reveal feelings with much more precision than language. Perhaps the form of the last movement of the *Jupiter* Symphony—with its clear-cut rising melodies, bright harmonies and timbres, brisk strings, and rapid rhythms—is somehow analogous to the form of a certain kind of joy. And if so, then perhaps we find revealed in that musical form a clarification or insight about joy. Such explanations are highly speculative. However, they are not only theoretically interesting but may also intensify one's interest in music. There is mystery about music, unique among the arts, that is part of its fascination.

9 DANCE

DANCE AND SUBJECT MATTER

All dance has the subject matter of bodies and shapes in space, and, in this sense, it has common ground with sculpture. Further, dance has the additional dimension of motion—as does kinetic sculpture—which also becomes part of its subject matter. The motion of bodies and shapes and the modulation of spaces between them constitute the primary subject matter of all dance.

Most dances, however, have an added subject matter. Thus the dance may portray a narrative, as does most dramatic literature, which informs us about a human situation. Robert Helpmann's ballet *Hamlet* can be interpreted as having Shakespeare's *Hamlet* as its subject matter. For viewers of the dance who know the play *Hamlet* this might be very important; but for viewers who do not, the subject matter of the dance will be the human situation explored by the dance narrative of Hamlet's struggle. Whether or not we know the play, our insight into the situation will be deepened by the dance itself.

States of mind (including feelings such as moods and emotions) may also supplement the primary subject matter of a dance—or of sections of it. José Limón's dance *The Moor's Pavane* explores the jealousy of Shakespeare's *Othello*. In Limón's version, Iago and Othello dance around Des-

FIGURE 9-1 Judith Black-stone and Paul Sanasardo in *Pain*. Photograph courtesy of Paul Sanasardo Dance Company, New York City.

demona and seem to be directly vying for her affections. Thus *The Moor's Pavane* represents an interpretation of the states of mind Shakespeare treated, though it can stand independently of the play and make its own contribution to our information about jealousy as it was felt by Othello.

The dramatic narrative—the portrayal of a story—is often subordinated in modern dance. Then a more direct attempt to represent and interpret human feelings through bodily movement is possible, as in Paul Sanasardo's *Pain*, in which the dance clearly focuses on a basic human feeling until some of the audience—so it has been reported—virtually begins to feel the pain itself. The still photograph (Figure 9-1) clearly indicates the character of the depiction of emotion.

Like music, dance has a special capacity to interpret states of mind. And like music, the dance is a serial structure unfolding in time and thus cannot be held still for contemplation. The serial character of both arts may be one of the reasons that dance is almost always performed to music. Even silence in some dances seems to imply music, since the dancer exhibits visual rhythm, the rising and falling of stress which we perceive in music. But the interpretation of states of mind is achieved only partly through the elements dance shares with music. The interpretation is achieved more importantly by the motion of the dancing bodies.

By way of experiment, to demonstrate how much most of us know about how body movements can represent and reveal states of mind, the following perception key should be illuminating.

PERCEPTION KEY DANCE AND STATES OF MIND

1. Using as little bodily motion as possible, try to represent a mood or emotion to a group of onlookers. Ask them to describe what you have represented. How closely does their description match your intention?

2. Represent one of the following feelings by bodily motion: fear, love, anxiety, rage, self-confidence, pride, horror. Have others do the same. Do you find such representations difficult to do or difficult to perceive when others do them?

3. Comment on one of the performances in the suggestions above. What were the motions your group used for the above representations? Discuss the distinctive capacity for representing states of mind that bodily motion has.

4. Try to move in such a way as to represent no state of mind at all. Is it possible? Discuss this with your entire group.

5. Representing or portraying a state of mind allows one to recognize that state. Interpreting or revealing a state of mind gives one insight into that state, a deeper understanding. In any of the experiments above, did you find any examples that went beyond representation and involved revelation? If so, what made this possible? What does artistic form have to do with this?

FORM AND DANCE

If the subject matter of dance can be bodies in motion, works of art, human situations, and states of mind, the form of the dance—its textural elements as they function together to organize the structure—gives us insight into the subject matter. But the textures and structures of the dance are not as clearly perceptible as they usually are in painting, sculpture, or architecture. Sculptures, paintings, and buildings normally "sit still" long enough for us to reexamine details. We have time and opportunity to fully perceive and comprehend the textures and their relationships to the structure. But the dance moves on relentlessly, like music or poetry in recitation, preventing us from reexamining its parts. We can only hope to hold in memory a part for comparison with a new part, and those parts as they help create the structure. Therefore, one prerequisite for a thorough enjoyment of the dance is the development of a memory for dance movements. The dance will usually help us in this task by the use of repetitive movements and variations on them. It can do for us what we cannot do for ourselves: present once again textural elements for our renewed consideration. Often the dance builds tension by withholding movements we feel ought to be repeated; sometimes it creates unusual tension by refusing to repeat any movement at all. Repetition or the lack of it — as in music or any serial art — becomes one of dance's most important structural features.

Part of our attention will be directed toward the varieties of dance modes — primitive, folk, social, ballet, and modern — to see how those modes are related to each other and to musical accompaniment. Part of our attention will be directed toward the varieties of textural modes — more specifically, individual dance movements and their character — which constitute a basic "vocabulary" for all dances. We consider first several important kinds of dance, beginning with its origins as perhaps man's earliest art form.

PRIMITIVE DANCE

It has become commonplace to point out that dance is the most original art of all peoples. Since the only requirement for a dance is a body in motion, and since all cultures have this basic requirement, dance, it has been reasoned, probably precedes all other arts. In this sense dance is truly primitive: it comes first.

The origins of dance are probably not strictly artistic (revelatory), in that most primitive dances are connected with either religious or practical acts. Often primitive dance religiously celebrates some tribal achievement. At other times the dance, while still religious, is expected to have a more or less immediate and specific practical effect. In this kind of dance — the Zuni rain dance or the ghost dance of the Sioux, for instance — the movement is ritually ordered and expected to be practically effective as long as the dance is performed properly.

Some primitive dance has sexual origins and often is a ritual of courtship. Since this phenomenon has a correlative in nature — the courtship "dances" of birds and some other animals — it may well be that primitive peoples occasionally imitated them. Certain movements in Mandan Indian dances, for instance, can be traced to the leaps and falls of western jays and mockingbirds who, in finding a place to rest, will stop, leap into the air while spreading their wings for balance, then fall suddenly, only to rise into the air again. Even modern dancers like Ann Halprin of the San Francisco Dancers Workshop, in her recent dance *West/East Stereo*, sent her dancers to the San Francisco Zoo to observe birds, leopards, and other animals in order to represent them onstage. In that sense that particular dance might be thought of profitably in terms of its connection with the origins of dance.

PERCEPTION KEY PRIMITIVE AND SOCIAL DANCE

1. Critics of the social dances of young people occasionally complain that those dances are primitive and therefore unhealthy. Discuss with others, especially young participants.

2. Condemning or praising current social dances as primitive implies a value judgment. Discuss in a group the implications of using the concept of primitive as a basis for making such evaluative criticisms.

Ann Halprin's sending her dancers to the zoo for inspiration points up another interesting fact about dance, whether primitive or not: dance of all kinds draws much of its inspiration from nature: the motion of a stalk of wheat in a gentle breeze, the scurrying of a rabbit, the curling of a contented cat, the soaring of a bird, the falling of a leaf. These kinds of events have supplied dancers with ideas and examples for their own movement. But there is another level of inspiration which comes from the natural shapes of things.

A favorite shape for the dance is that of the spiral nautilus, so often seen in shells, plants, and insects:

This form is apparent in individual movement (see Figure 9-1), just as it is in the movement of groups of dancers whose floor pattern may follow the spiral pattern (see Figure 9-2).

The circle is another of nature's most pervasive and fascinating shapes. The movements of planets and stars suggest circular motion, and, more mundanely, so do the rings working out from a stone dropped in water. The circle and circular motion have been compelling for the primitive dancer, the court dancer in Elizabethan times, and the ballet and modern dancers in our time.

In a magical-religious way, circular dances have been thought to bring the dancers—and therefore man in general—into significant harmony with the divine forces in the universe. The planets and stars are heavenly objects in circular motion, so it was "reasonable" for the primitive dancer to feel that he could make himself congruent with these divine forces by means of

FIGURE 9-2 Spiral plan from
Tanzsynfonia, 1923. (From
Lincoln Kirstein, *Movement
and Metaphor*, Praeger, New

the circular dance. The dance teacher in the Renaissance was thought to have a moral function principally because he helped people put themselves into the requisite harmony with the motion of the most divine objects visible to man. It should be noted, furthermore, that the circular form is powerful in many arts. Many of the illustrations in this book of painting, sculpture, and architecture are evidence of this. Consider also structures in music. And in literature, ending where one began often has an enormous satisfaction to it, acting as a profound release of tension.

THE GHOST DANCE

One of the most fascinating primitive dances we know of was the ghost dance of the Sioux in the late nineteenth century. It was a circle dance performed by men and women lasting for twenty-four hours. Its purpose was to raise the spirits of dead Indians in order to finish off the white man and to reclaim the land for the Indians who remained. In the 1880s a variety of tribes banded together in religious association and began the dancing. A prophet-seer named Wovoca—or Black Elk—declared that if the dance was done properly, the dead Indians would rise.

The dancers, about two hundred at a time, formed a relatively compact circle and chanted as they danced, moving sideways to their left around a center pole. They wore bead-and-bone vests which were called ghost shirts and thought to be impenetrable by the white man's bullets. One of the results of the dancing and chanting for hours at a time was a trancelike state resembling death. The dancer felt he was making communion with the spirit world.

Unfortunately, one of the end results of the faith in the rising of the dead Indian armies was the famous massacre at Wounded Knee in 1890. The dancing unnerved white officials and was disapproved of, but it continued secretly. And those who died at Wounded Knee—at least some of them—fully expected to be invulnerable and to be joined by their spiritual forebears in their struggle.

It should not be thought that the dance was responsible for the death of so many Indians, any more than we should assume that a rain dance is responsible if the clouds above the dancers open. It was only one component in a highly complex situation. The ghost dance was a visible testament of belief and an instrument of action.

THE ZUNI RAIN DANCE

The rain dance is also a religious-practical dance, but its results have not been so unfortunate as those of the ghost dance. Tourists can see rain dances in the American Southwest even today, so the tradition has continued. The floor pattern of the dance is not circular but a modified spiral, as can be seen from Figure 9-3. The dancers, properly costumed, form a line and are led by a priest, who—at specific moments—spreads corn meal on the ground, symbolizing his wish for the fertility of the ground.

The ritual character of the dance is clearly observable in the diagram, with dancers beginning toward the north, then turning west, south, east, north, west, south, and ending toward the east. The gestures of the dancers, as with the gestures in most rituals, have definite meanings and functions. For example, the dancers' loud screams are designed to awaken the gods and arrest their attention, the drumbeat suggests thunder, and the rattles the dancers sound suggest the sound of rain the dancers hope for.

PERCEPTION KEY PRIMITIVE DANCE AND CONTEMPORARY RITUALS

1. Contemporary rituals such as some weddings and funerals involve motion which can be thought of as dance motion. Can you think of other contemporary rituals which involve dance motion? Do we need to know the meanings of the ritual gestures in order to appreciate the motion of the ritual?

2. How much common ground do we share with primitive dancers with reference to our trying to give meaning to our gestures, either in a generally accepted "dance situation" or out of it? Enumerate instances.

3. Do we have dances that can be considered as serving functions similar to those of the primitive dances we have described? Consider, for instance,

FIGURE 9-3 Spiral plan of the Zuni rain dance. (From John L. Squires and Robert E. McLean, *American Indian Dances,* copyright © 1963 by The Ronald Press Company, New York; illustrations by R. McLean.)

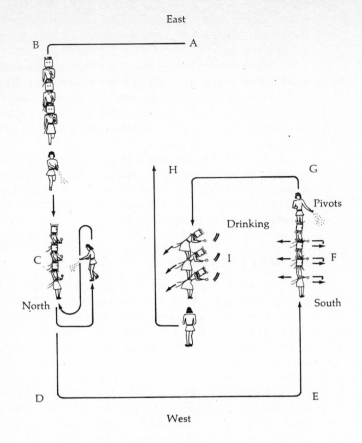

the dancing in the streets that followed the end of World War II. Are there other instances?

SOCIAL DANCE

Social dance is not specifically theatrical, as are ballet and modern dance. Folk and court dances are often done simply for the pleasure of the dancers. Because we are more or less familiar with square dances, round dances, waltzes, and the large variety of contemporary dances done at parties, we have some useful points of reference for dance in general.

COUNTRY AND FOLK DANCE

Unlike primitive dance, social dance is not dominated by religious or practical purposes, although it may have secondary practical purposes which are important to the dancer, such as meeting people or working off excess energy. More importantly, it is a form of recreation and social enjoyment. Country dance—for example, the English Playford dances—is a species of folk dance that has traces of primitive origins, because country people tended to perform dances in specific relationship to special periods in the agricultural year, such as planting and harvesting. The connection now is tenuous, however, since contemporary dancers rarely relate to any specific agricultural subject matter. Now the subject matter seems to be mainly energy and celebration.

Most of the many forms of folk dances that have arisen in Western countries have survived to one degree or another. Folk dances are the dances of the people—whether ethnic or regional in origin—and they are often very carefully preserved in our time, sometimes with contests designed to keep the dances alive. When they perform, the dancers often wear the peasant costumes of the region they represent. Virtually every European nation, as well as Asian and African nations, has its own folk dance tradition. (See Figure 9-4.)

THE COURT DANCE

The court dances of the Middle Ages and the Renaissance developed into more stylized and less openly energetic modes than the folk dance, for the

FIGURE 9-4 Pieter Breugel the Elder, "The Wedding Dance." Oil on panel, 47 by 62 inches. The Detroit Institute of Arts. Purchase, City Appropriation.

court dance was performed by a different sort of person and served a different purpose. Some of the favorite older dances were the volta, a dance which was a favorite at Queen Elizabeth's court in the sixteenth century, and which involved the male dancer hoisting the female dancer in the air from time to time; the pavane, a stately dance popular in the seventeenth century; the minuet, popular in the eighteenth century, performed by groups of four dancers at a time; and the allemande, apparently German in origin, also of the eighteenth century—a dance performed by couples who held both hands, turning about one another without letting go. These dances and many others were favorites at courts primarily because they were enjoyable to do—not because they performed a religious or practical function. Because the dances were also pleasurable to look at, it very quickly became a commonplace at court to have a group of onlookers as large as or larger than the group of dancers. Then it was not long before professional dancers came into demand for more significant court functions, such as the sixteenth-century masques, which were mixed-media entertainments in which the audience usually took some part—particularly in the dance sequences.

PERCEPTION KEY SOCIAL DANCE

1. How would you evaluate rock dancing? Why does rock dancing demand loud music? Does the performing and watching of spontaneous and powerful muscular motions account for some of the popularity of rock dancing? If so, why? Why do you think the older generations generally dislike both rock music and rock dancing? Is rock dancing primarily a mode to be watched or danced? Or is it both? Explain what the viewer and the dancer, respectively, might derive from the experience of rock dancing.

2. If you know any authentic folk dance, arrange a performance. How does the group which watched the performance regard the dance? Discuss the problems involved in doing the dance, and then discuss what might inhibit a full appreciation in viewing the dance.

BALLET

The origins of ballet usually are traced to the early seventeenth century, when dancers performed interludes between scenes of an opera. Eventually the interludes grew more and more important, until finally ballets were performed with no operatic accompaniment. In the eighteenth century, the *en pointe* technique was developed, with female dancers elevated on their toes to emphasize their airy, floating qualities. This has remained the technique to this day and is one of the important distinctions between ballet and modern dance, which avoids *en pointe* almost entirely.

Certain kinds of movements gradually began to be developed and taught for the ballet. Today there is virtually a vocabulary of movements which all ballet dancers must learn, since these movements constitute the textural elements of every ballet. In this sense they are as important as the keys and scales in music, the vocabulary of tones which are constantly employed in musical composition. Figure 9-5 shows a number of the more important positions which ballet dancers use in their compositions. There are many more, but these are the basic ones with which we may begin.

A considerable repertory of ballets has been built up in the last 270 years, with many more ballets lost to us entirely through the lack of an adequate system of notation with which to record them. The same was true of music until an adequate system of music notation was adopted. Today most dance is recorded on motion picture film or videotape, though there is a system—Labanotation—which can be used effectively by experts for recording a dance. Some of the ballets many of us are likely to see are Lully's *Giselle; Les Sylphides*, with music by Chopin; Tchaikovsky's *Nutcracker, Swan Lake*, and *Sleeping Beauty; Coppelia*, with music by Delibes; and *The Rites of Spring*, with Stravinsky's music.

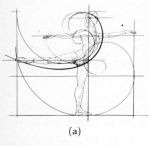

(a)

FIGURE 9-5 Drawings by Carlus Dyer of some important ballet positions. (a) The arabesque spiral. (b) Basic positions of the body. (c) Entrechat quatre. *(Continued on page 326.)*

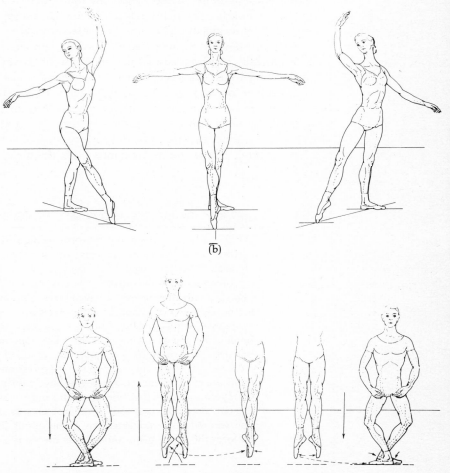

(b)

(c)

FIGURE 9-5 Continued.
(d) Grand plié.

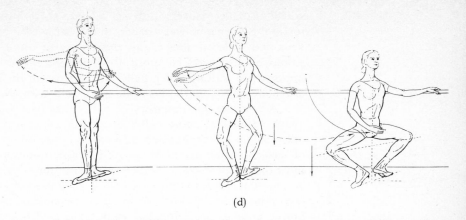

(d)

All these ballets—like most ballets—have a program, which is often called the pretext. The pretext is a narrative line or story around which the ballet is built. In this sense, the ballet tells a story in the medium of bodily motion. The ballet has as its subject matter a story which is interpreted by means of stylized movements such as the arabesque, the bourrée, and the relévé—to name a scant few. Our understanding of the story line is basically conditioned by our perception of the movements which present the story to us. We have little else to respond to, except, perhaps, a printed statement of what the dance represents. It is astounding how, without having to be obvious and without having to resort very often to everyday gestures, ballet dancers can present a story line to us in an intelligible fashion. Yet it is not the story nor the performance of specific movements which constitutes the content of the dance—it is the meld of narrative and movement.

PERCEPTION KEY NARRATIVE AND BODILY MOVEMENT

1. Without training we cannot perform ballet movements, but all of us can perform *some* dance movements. By way of experiment and simply to increase understanding of the meld of narrative and bodily movement, try representing a narrative by bodily motion to a group of onlookers. Choose a narrative poem—a few stanzas from Browning's "Childe Roland to the Dark Tower Came" in our chapter on literature would be quite adaptable for this purpose—or choose a scene from a play which may be familiar to you and your audience. Let your audience know the pretext you are using, since this is the normal method of most ballet. Avoid movements which rely exclusively on facial expressions or simply mime to communicate story elements. After you have presented the narrative, discuss with your audience their views about your success or failure in presenting the narrative. Discuss, too, your problems as dancer and what you felt you wanted your movement to reveal about the narrative. Have others perform the experiment, and discuss the same points.

2. Even the most rudimentary movement attempting to reveal a narrative will bring in interpretations which go beyond the narrative alone. As a viewer, discuss what you felt the other dancers added to the narrative.

Our understanding of what is going on before our eyes in ballet, as in opera, is often conditioned by our knowledge of the pretext or narrative line. Only when we have that knowledge can we be expected to be aware of the meld of narrative and movement which is crucial to ballet. Without that knowledge, our understanding of the dance is restricted to such things as observing the technical exactness of the execution of specific movements or the qualities of the succession of those movements abstracted from reference to specific objects and events. That kind of understanding, of course, has its rewards, as is obvious in the cases of abstract painting and sculpture and music which has no program; but that kind of understanding is related to only a portion of the ballet's perceptible qualities.

SWAN LAKE

One of the most popular ballets of all time is Tchaikovsky's *Swan Lake (Le Lac des Cygnes)*, composed in 1871—1877 and first performed in 1894 (Act II) and 1895 (complete). The choreographers were Leon Ivanov and Marius Petipa, both significant in the history of ballet. Tchaikovsky originally composed the music for a ballet to be performed for children, but its fascination has not been restricted to young audiences. With Margot Fonteyn and Rudolf Nureyev the reigning dancers in this ballet in our time, *Swan Lake* has been a resounding popular favorite on television and film, not to mention repeated sellout performances in dance theaters the world over.

Since the chances of your seeing a performance—live or on film or television—are good, we will offer a brief description of the dance, with a representative photograph (Figure 9-6), as a means of providing some access to the dance experience itself.

Act I opens with the principal male dancer, the young Prince Siegfried, attending a village celebration. His mother, the Queen, finding Siegfried sporting with the peasants, decides that it is time for him to marry someone of his own station and settle into the nobility. After she leaves, a pas de trois—a dance with three dancers, in this instance Siegfried and two maids —is interrupted by the prince's slightly drunk tutor, who tries to take part in some of the dancing but is not quite able. When a flight of swans is seen overhead, the prince resolves to go hunting.

The opening scene of Act II is on a moonlit lake, with the arch magician, Rothbart, tending his swans. The swans, led by Odette, are maidens he has enchanted: they can return to human form only at night. Odette's movements are imitated by the entire group of swans, movements which

FIGURE 9-6 Margot Fonteyn and Rudolf Nureyev in *Swan Lake.*

are clearly influenced by the motions of the swan's long neck and by the movements we associate with birds—for example, an undulating motion executed by the dancers' arms and a fluttering executed by the legs. Siegfried comes upon the swans and restrains his hunters from shooting at them. He falls in love with Odette, all of whose motions are characterized by the softness and grace of the swan. Siegfried learns that Odette is enchanted and that she cannot come to the ball the Queen has planned to arrange the marriage of Siegfried. He also learns that if he vows his love to her and keeps his vow, he can free her from the enchantment. She warns him that Rothbart will do everything to trick him into breaking the vow, but Siegfried is determined to be steadfast. As dawn arrives, the lovers part and Rothbart retrieves his swans.

Act III commences with the ball the Queen has arranged for presenting to Siegfried a group of princesses from whom he may choose. Each princess, introduced in lavish native costume with a retinue of dancers and retainers, dances the dance of her country, such as the allemande, the czardas, the tarantella. But suddenly Rothbart enters in disguise with his own daughter, Odile, who looks exactly like Odette. Today most performances require that Odette and Odile be the same dancer, though the part was originally written for two dancers. Siegfried and Odile dance the famous Black Swan pas de deux, a dance which is notable for its virtuosity. It features almost superhuman leaps on the part of Siegfried, and it also involves thirty-two rapidly executed whipping turns (fouettés) on the part of Odile. Her movement is considerably different in character from that of Odette. Odile is more angular, less delicate, and in her black costume seems much less the picture of innocence Odette had seemed in her soft white costume. Siegfried's movements suggest enormous joy at having found Odette, for he does not realize that this is really Odile, the magician's daughter.

When the time comes for Siegfried to choose among the princesses for his wife, he rejects them all and presents Odile to the Queen as his choice. Once Siegfried has committed himself to her, Rothbart exults and takes Odile from him and makes her vanish. Siegfried, who has broken his vow to Odette, realizes he has been duped and ends the act by rushing out to find the real Odette.

Like a number of other sections of the ballet, Act IV has a variety of versions which interpret what is essentially similar action. Siegfried, in finding Odette by the lake at night, sacrifices himself for her and breaks the spell: they are joined in death and are beyond the power of the magician. Some versions of the ballet aim for a happy ending and suggest that though Siegfried sacrifices himself for Odette, he does not die. Through their sacrifice for one another and through their mutual love, Siegfried and Odette break the evil spell Rothbart has cast over them. In this happy-ending version, Odette, upon realizing that Siegfried had been tricked, forgives him. Rothbart raises a terrible storm in order to drown all the swans, but Siegfried carries Odette to a hilltop, where he is willing to die with her if necessary. This act of love and sacrifice breaks the spell and the two of them are together as dawn breaks.

In the version that does not specifically aim at a happy ending, Act IV concentrates on spiritual victory and reward after death in a better life than that which was left behind. Odette and the swans dance slowly and sorrowfully together, with Odette rising in a stately fashion in their midst. When Siegfried comes, he begs her to forgive him, but nothing can break the magician's spell. Odette and he dance, they embrace, she bids him farewell and casts herself mournfully into the lake, where she perishes. Siegfried, unable to live without her, follows her into the lake. Then, once the lake vanishes, Odette and Siegfried are revealed in the distance, moving away together as evidence that the spell was broken in death.

The late John Cranko produced an even more tragic version with the Stuttgart Ballet. Siegfried is drowned in the rising of the lake—presented on stage most dramatically with long bolts of fabric undulating across the stage. Odette is whisked away by Rothbart and condemned to keep waiting for the hero who can be faithful to his vow. This version is particularly gloomy, since it reduces the heroic stature of Siegfried and renders his sacrifice useless. The hero who can rescue Odette will have to be virtually superhuman.

Clearly the story of *Swan Lake* has overtones of a mythic character much in keeping with the Romantic age in which it was conceived. John Keats, who wrote fifty years before this ballet was created, was fascinated by the ancient stories of men who fell in love with supernatural spirits, which is what the swan-Odette is, once she has been transformed by magic. Likewise, the later Romantics were fascinated by the possibilities of magic and its implications for dealing with the forces of good and evil. Nathaniel Hawthorne, in his *Blithedale Romance*, wrote about a hypnotist who wove a weird spell over a woman, and the story of Svengali and his ward Trilby was popular everywhere, seemingly attesting to the fact that strange spells could be maintained over innocent people. This interest in magic and the supernatural is coupled with the Wagnerian interest in heroism and the implications of the sacrifice of the hero for the thing he loves. Much of the power of the idea of sacrifice derives from the sacrifice of Christ on the cross. But Tchaikovsky—like Wagner, whose hero in the *Ring of the Niebelungs* is also a Siegfried (whose end with Brunnhilde is similar to the ending in *Swan Lake*)—concentrates on the human valor of the prince and its implication for transforming the evil of this world into good.

PERCEPTION KEY SWAN LAKE

1. It may be possible for you to see a production on stage, television, or film of *Swan Lake*. If so, focus on a specific act and comment in a discussion with others on the suitability of the bodily movements for the narrative subject matter of the act.

2. If your cannot see the ballet, phonograph records are easily available; and you should be able to comment on the possibilities for movements which would be effective for specific portions of the dance. For instance, how should Odette and the swans move at the opening of Act IV? How should Siefgried move in his last pas de deux in that same act?

3. Comment on the suggestions for motion apparent in some of the still photographs which accompany this discussion of *Swan Lake*. Which of them seem to suggest the movements of the dancer or dancers most clearly? Can you comment on how any of them may give insight into the narrative of the ballet?

4. Whether or not you have a chance to see the ballet, try to move in such a way as to present your interpretation of a specific moment in the ballet. You might try something as simple as Odette fluttering with the swans in Act II or as complicated as Siegfried or Odette casting himself or herself into the lake in Act IV.

5. If someone who has had training in ballet is available, you might try to get him or her to present a small portion of the ballet for your observation and discussion. What would be the most important kinds of questions to ask such a person? This could be the subject of valuable research.

MODERN DANCE

The origins of modern dance are usually traced to the American dancers Isadora Duncan and Ruth St. Denis. These women rebelled against the stylization of ballet, with ballerinas dancing on their toes and executing the same basic movements in every performance. Isadora Duncan insisted on natural movement, often dancing in bare feet with gossamer drapery that showed her body and legs in motion. She felt that the emphasis ballet places on the movement of the arms and legs was wrong. Her insistence on placing the center of motion at the solar plexus—just below the breastbone—was based on her feeling that the torso had been neglected in the development of ballet. She felt, too, that the early Greek dancers, whom she wished to emulate, had placed their center of energy at the solar plexus. Her intentions were to return to natural movement in dance, and this was one effective method of doing so.

The developers of modern dance who followed Isadora Duncan (she died in 1927) built on her legacy. In her insistence on freedom with respect to clothes and conventions, she infused energy into the dance that no one had ever seen before. Though she was a native Californian, her successes and triumphs were primarily in foreign lands, particularly in France and Russia. Her performances differed greatly from the ballet. Instead of developing a dance built on a pretext of the sort that underlies *Swan Lake*, Duncan took more abstract subject matters and expressed her understanding of them in dance. Her dances were lyrical, personal, and occasionally extemporaneous. Her movements were not stylized, as in ballet, nor were they always predicatable. Since she insisted that there were no angular shapes in nature, she would permit herself to use none. Her movements tended to be ongoing and rarely came to a complete rest. An interesting example of her dance, one in which she does come to a full rest, is recounted by a friend. It was performed in a salon for close friends, and its subject matter seems to be the emergence of man on the planet:

Isadora was completely covered by a long loose robe with high draped neck and long loose sleeves in a deep muted red. She crouched on the floor with her face resting on the carpet. In slow motion with ineffable effort she man-

FIGURE 9-7 Isadora Duncan
in *La Marseillaise*. Dance
Collection, New York Public
Library.

aged to get up on her knees. Gradually with titanic struggles she rose to her feet. She raised her arms toward heaven in a gesture of praise and exultation. The mortal had emerged from primeval ooze to achieve Man, upright, liberated, and triumphant.[1]

Figure 9-7 shows Duncan in *La Marseillaise*.

Martha Graham, José Limón, Doris Humphrey, and other innovators who followed Isadora developed modern dance in a variety of directions. Graham, who was also interested in Greek origins, created some dances on themes of Greek tragedies, such as her *Medea*. Limón, in addition to his *Moor's Pavane*, is well known for his interpretation of Eugene O'Neill's play *The Emperor Jones*, in which a black slave escapes to an island only to become a despised and hunted tyrant. These approaches are somewhat of a departure from Duncan, as they tend to introduce the balletic pretext into modern dance. Humphrey, who was a little older than Graham and Limón, was closer to the original Duncan tradition in such dances as *Water Study*, *Life of the Bee*, and *New Dance*, a 1930s piece which was successfully revived in 1972.

Modern dance can be any one or all of these approaches simultaneously. Today's more innovative dancers, like Twyla Tharp and Meredith Monk, sometimes shock and surprise audiences with dances that often seem to have only bodily motion as their subject matter. Such dances have no recognizable pretext or any recognizable "official dance movements." Both Tharp and Monk are experimenting with abstract movement—as did Duncan—which is not always thought of as appropriate to the dance. However, Monk's ten- or fifteen-acre large-scale panoramic dance entitled *Needle Brain Lloyd and the Systems Kid* (Figure 9-8) does have a general pretext—the settling of America. Dancers enter rowing a boat across a lake, haul the boat out, turn it upside down, and sit in front of it for the entirety of the dance. Meanwhile other dancers play croquet, pitch tents, ride horses and motorcycles, and perform innumerable other movements that have little or nothing to do with familiar dance movements. Isadora's legacy to modern dance is freedom of imagination and invention. Today's dancers have clearly accepted that legacy and today's modern dance can be virtually anything a choreographer can imagine.

PERCEPTION KEY PRETEXT AND MOVEMENT

1. Try a half-minute experiment. Devise a series of movements which will take about thirty seconds to complete and which you are fairly sure do not tell a story. Then "perform" these movements for a group and question them on what they think the pretext of your movement is. Do not tell them

[1]From Kathleen Cannell, "Isadorable Duncan," *Christian Science Monitor*, Dec. 4, 1970. Reprinted by permission from The Christian Science Monitor. © 1970 The Christian Science Publishing Society. All rights reserved.

FIGURE 9-8 Meredith Monk's *Needle-Brain Lloyd and the Systems Kid*. Photograph by Peter Moore.

in advance that your dance has no story. As a result of this experiment, you might ask yourself and the group whether it is possible to create a sequence of movements which will not suggest a story line to some viewers. What would this mean for dances which try to avoid pretexts? Can they?

2. Without explaining that you are not dancing, represent a familiar human situation to a group by using movements that you believe are not dance movements. Is the group able to understand what you represented? Do they think you were using dance movements? Do you believe it possible to have movements which cannot be included in a dance? Are there, in other words, non-dance movements?

ALVIN AILEY'S *REVELATIONS*

One of the classics of modern dance is Alvin Ailey's *Revelations* (Figure 9-9), based largely on black American spirituals and the black American experience. It was first performed in January 1960, and hardly a year has gone by without its having been performed to highly enthusiastic crowds. Ailey, who no longer dances but choreographs for the New York City Center Ballet—as well as for his own company—has refined *Revelations* somewhat over the years, but its basic impact has remained. Favorable response to this dance was heightened considerably in its early years by the presence of Judith Jamison, a striking dancer who took the lead role. But even in her absence it has retained its power to bring audiences to their feet for standing ovations at almost every performance.

Some of the success of *Revelations* stems from Ailey's choice of the deeply felt music of the black spirituals to which the dancers' movements are closely attuned. But, then, this is also one of the most noted qualities of a ballet like *Swan Lake*, which is said to have the richest orchestral score of any ballet. Music, unless it is program music, may not correctly be thought of as a pretext for a dance, but there is certainly a perceptible connection between, say, the rhythmic qualities of given music and a dance which might be composed in such a way as to take advantage of those qualities. Thus in *Revelations* the energetic movements of the dancers often appear as visual, bodily transformations of the rhythmically charged music.

Though it is not possible to describe the entire dance in these pages, we will try to point out certain general qualities of which an awareness—should there be a chance to see this dance in actual performance or on film—may prove useful for refining one's experience of modern dance in general. *Revelations* has a general pretext—that of the black experience as related by the spirituals—and each of its separate sections has its own pretext. But

FIGURE 9-9   The Alvin Ailey City Center Dance Theater, New York. *Revelations,* "Wading in the Water." Photograph by Fred Fehl.

no pretext is as tightly or specifically narrative as is usually the case in ballet. It is usually the generalized situation which acts as pretext.

The first section of the dance is called "Pilgrim of Sorrow," with three parts: "I Been Buked," danced by the entire company (about twenty dancers, male and female); "Didn't My Lord Deliver Daniel," danced by only a few dancers; and "Fix Me Jesus," danced by one couple. The general pretext is the suffering of blacks at the hands of their tormentors, like the Israelites of the Old Testament, but taking refuge in their faith in the Lord. The most dramatic moments in this section are in "Didn't My Lord Deliver Daniel," a statement of overwhelming faith characterized by close ensemble work. The in-line dancers with powerful rhythmic movements parallel the rhythms of the last word of the hymn: "Dań-i-el," with the accents on the first and last syllables.

The second section, titled "Take Me to the Water," is divided into "Processional," danced by eight dancers; "Wading in the Water," danced by six dancers; and "I Want to Be Ready," danced by a single male dancer. The whole idea of "Take Me to the Water" is centered on the concept of baptism, linking the dancers with the Baptist faith and asserting the faith in God that characterizes the source of energy of the black spirituals. "Wading in the Water" is particularly exciting, with dancers holding a stage-long bolt of light-colored fabric to represent the water. The dancers shimmer the fabric to the rhythm of the music and one dancer after another crosses over the fabric, which symbolizes at least two things: the waters of baptism and the Mosaic waters of freedom. It is this episode which featured Judith Jamison in a long gown holding a huge parasol as she danced.

The third section is called "Move, Members, Move," with the episodes titled "Sinner Man," "The Day Is Past and Gone," "You May Run Home," and the finale, "Rocka My Soul in the Bosom of Abraham." In this last episode a sense of triumph over suffering is projected, suggesting the redemption of a people by using the same kind of Old Testament imagery and musical material that opened the piece. The entire section takes as its theme the life of people after they have been received into the faith, with the possibilities of straying into sin. It ends with a powerful rocking spiritual which emphasizes forgiveness and the reception of the people (the "members") into the bosom of Abraham, according to the Bible's prediction. This ending again features an enormous amount of ensemble work and is danced by the entire company, with rows of male dancers sliding forward on their outspread knees and then rising all in one sliding gesture, raising their hands high. "Rocka My Soul in the Bosom of Abraham" is powerfully sung again and again until the effect is almost hypnotically religious in its force.

Such a dance as *Revelations* has at times been criticized as being somewhat slick, somewhat reminiscent of show dance more than of serious modern dance. But for all that negative criticism, there has been much praise. The public—even the public that has little or no dance experience—has always loved it.

The subject matter of *Revelations* is in part that of powerful movement, with remarkable ensemble and solo sections. But it is also more obviously that of the struggle of a people as told—on one level—by their music. The dance has the advantage of a powerfully engaging subject matter even before we witness the transmutation of that subject matter. And the way in which the movements of the dance are closely attuned to the "movement" or rhythm of the music tends to give most viewers a very intense participation, since the visual qualities of the dance are so powerfully reinforced by the aural qualities of the music. Not all modern dance is characterized by this, though it is true that most show dance and most dance in filmed musicals encourages a similar closeness of music and movement.

PERCEPTION KEY   ALVIN AILEY'S REVELATIONS

1. A profitable way of understanding the resources of *Revelations* is to take a well-known black spiritual like "Swing Low, Sweet Chariot," part of which appears on page 282 in the chapter on music, and supply the movements which it suggests to you. Once you have done so, ask yourself how difficult it was to do. Is it natural to move to such music?

2. Instead of spirituals, try the same experiment with popular music such as rock that you feel definitely stimulates motion. Can you comment on the kinds of music that do this? What characteristics does such music seem to have that stimulates motion?

MARTHA GRAHAM

Quite different from the Ailey approach, and probably much more influential for the history of dance in modern times, is the so-called "Graham technique," taught in Martha Graham's own school in New York as well as in colleges and universities across the country. Like Ailey, Graham was a virtuoso dancer—she has only recently retired from dancing—and has become better and better known as her company, for which she constructs her dances, has appeared in America and abroad. After Isadora Duncan, Graham must be counted the most powerful influence in modern dance. Today there is a certain amount of rebellion against her technique, as is natural for any powerful influence, but an understanding of the rebellion depends on an understanding of what is being rebelled against.

Graham technique is reminiscent of ballet in its rigor. Dancers learn specific kinds of movements and exercises designed to be used both as preparation for and part of the dance. Graham's contraction, for example, is one of the commonest movements one is likely to see. It is the sudden contraction of the diaphragm with the resultant relaxation of the rest of the body. This builds on Duncan's emphasis on the solar plexus but adds to that concept the natural systolic and diastolic rhythms of heartbeat and blood-pulse. The movement is very effective visually as well as being particularly flexible in depicting feelings. Further, it is a movement unknown in ballet, from which Graham has always wished to remain distinct.

Graham's dances have at times been very literal, with narrative pretexts quite similar to those found in ballet. *Night Journey*, for instance, is an interpretation of *Oedipus Rex* by Sophocles. The lines of emotional force linking Jocasta and her son-husband, Oedipus, are powerfully accentuated by the movements of the dance as well as by certain props on stage—such as ribbons that link the two together at times. In Graham's interpretation, Jocasta becomes much more important than she is in the original drama. This is partly because Graham saw the female figures in Greek drama—those she interpreted in her dances—as much more fully dimensional than we have normally understood them. By means of dancing their roles, she was able to develop complexities in their character. At other times, Graham has experimented with more abstract subject matters such as states of mind. For example, *El Penitente*, which features a male dancer in loose white trousers and tunic moving in slow circles about the stage with a large wooden cross, is a powerful interpretation of penitence.

ALWIN NIKOLAIS DANCE THEATER

The work of Alwin Nikolais is another important influence on modern dance. For several decades Nikolais has been experimenting with a total dance theater which is an assault on all the senses he can reach. He avoids narrative pretexts for his dance, just as he seems to avoid pretexts which refer to states of mind or emotional situations. He uses challenging music of the ultramodern sort, light shows of the kind that used to be popular at rock concerts, and costumes of a kind that would make most futuristic movies look like antiques. Yet he puts all these ingredients together, with imaginative movements that other choreographers and dancers can rarely copy, into an event that delights those with little as well as those with great experience in dance.

Nikolais often gets his inspirations from the natural world—sometimes from the world of insects. Although insects such as butterflies, caterpillars, and crickets have inspired many dancers, few dancers have been attracted, as Nikolais has, to praying mantises. One of his dances, *Imago* (Figure 9-10), employs odd headpieces and mantislike extensions on hands and feet to achieve an extraordinary suggestiveness of insect life. It is not always clear that this is the subject matter of the dance, since it seems that the abstract movements which are suggested to Nikolais by his examination of the mantis are what interest him most and what attract our attention. However, there is one section, called "Mantis," which suggest that Nikolais is exploring a literal representation. Normally, however, Nikolais's dances are as abstracted from specific objects and events as he can make them. He has been criticized for this as well as for being too technological, thus losing

FIGURE 9-10 Alwin Niko-
lais's *Imago*. Chimera Photo.

the human qualities dance should have. But these seem cavils when one is
in the presence of dances such as *Masks*, *Props and Mobiles*, which has been
produced at the amphitheater in Delphi, Greece, and *Vaudeville of the
Elements* and *Scenario*. Light, props, and movement in conjunction with
sound are handled with great sensitivity and a marvelous sense of humor.
His influence is likely to remain despite his critics.

SOME FINAL COMMENTS

The variety of dance available for us in theaters, television, and films is
overwhelming. For many it can be baffling to see people in motion interpreting a pretext we know nothing about. For others it will be distracting
to think about the pretext when it is the movement itself that is most interesting. But for most of us, one hopes, there will be a happy melding of both.

What is important to keep in mind is the fact that dance has the capacity to transform a pretext, whether the pretext is a story or a state of mind. Our attention must be drawn into participation with this transformation. The insight we get from the dance experience is dependent on our awareness of this transformation. The first step to the achievement of such revelation is that of perceiving the nature of movement in the dance and the narrative or other subject matter on which it is predicated. Once that perception is achieved, understanding begins to grow and our participation with the work begins to deepen.

10 FILM

COMMERCIALISM AND FILM

Film—or movies, or cinema, or motion pictures—is more conspicuously commercial than any of the arts we have hitherto discussed. Because enormous sums of money are involved and huge personal fortunes can be won or lost, it seems there is less possibility of preserving artistic integrity in film than in other arts. As a result of financial pressure, film has been heir to an extraordinary degree of "slickness," a kind of professional, acceptable polish which makes it plausible, entertaining, and not awkward in construction. Because so much money is involved, "slickness" developed early, and today the resultant acceptable level of competence tends to be an ultraconservative force retarding opportunities for innovation in films. Good film makers often will innovate in minor ways in an effort to add something to the artistic excitement of their work, but it is unusual when an artist of considerable innovative talent is permitted to see his own vision brought to completion. His backers rarely permit it. Moreover, the artist can write, direct, and even photograph a film but still not have full artistic control of it. Even when tightly controlled by one dominating artistic talent, films must depend on teams of writers, actors, set men, makeup men, and technicians of all kinds.

SUBSERVIENCE OF FILM

The complexity of the artistic situation is unusual. In the early days of film several giants rose in the industry, both before the cameras, like Charlie Chaplin and Buster Keaton, and behind them, like D. W. Griffith and Serge Eisenstein, and they struggled to make the medium something closer to what they realized it could be. They fought the early tendency to make each film a record of a performance on the dramatic stage, or in the style of the dramatic stage, with the words often printed out and shown on the screen in brief interrupting moments. In this subservience to another medium, the resources of the motion picture were not fully exploited. This is occasionally true even today, though not so much as in the earliest phases of film's development.

Another popular early use of motion pictures was for recording magic tricks which could not be realized on an open stage. George Meliés, a French student of the magician Houdini, made a number of films, often in double-exposure situations in which he would be looking at himself. Other late-nineteenth-century subjects were parades, cavalry charges, dances, and rudimentary travelogues. The motion picture often did little more than duplicate situations which, except in the case of the magicians, could be witnessed in another place at another time.

GRIFFITH AND EISENSTEIN

D. W. Griffith and Serge Eisenstein are unquestionably the great early geniuses of film making. They managed to gain enough control over the production of their works so that they could craft their films into a distinctive rather than a subservient medium. Some of their films are still considered among the finest ever made: *Birth of a Nation* (1916) and *Intolerance* (1918) by Griffith, and *Potemkin* (1925) and *Ivan the Terrible* (1941–46) by Eisenstein are still being shown and are still influencing contemporary film makers. These men were more than just directors. With many of their films they felt responsible for almost everything: casting, choosing locations, handling the camera, directing, and editing.

DIRECTING AND EDITING

Directing and editing are probably the most crucial phases of film making. The director controls the acting. And he supervises the photography, carried out by skilled technicians who worry about such problems as lighting, camera angles and focusing, as well as the motion of the camera itself (some sequences are shot with a highly mobile camera, while others are shot with camera stock still). The editor, usually assisted by the director, puts in order the images or frames once the photography is finished. Pieces of film which represent sequences sometimes shot far apart in time and place are organized into a unity, more or less. The film is usually not shot sequentially, and usually only a small part of the total footage shot is ever shown in a film. The old saying of the bit-part actor—"I was lost on the cutting-room floor"—attests the fact that much footage which was thought of as possibly useful winds up being omitted from a film once the final decisions about editing are made.

THE PARTICIPATIVE EXPERIENCE AND FILM

The question of participation with the film is complex. For one thing, most of us know exactly what it means to lose our sense of place and time in a movie. This loss seems to be achieved rapidly in all but the most awkwardly conceived films. In a film like *Black Orpheus* (1958), shot in Rio, the intensity of tropical colors, Latin American music, and the dynamics of the carnival produce an imaginary reality so intense and vital that actual reality seems dull by comparison. But then there are other films that create the illusion of life itself. Aristotle talked about the ways in which drama imitates life and the ways in which an audience identifies with some of the actors on the stage. Yet the film seems to have these powers to an even greater degree than the stage.

PERCEPTION KEY FILM, DRAMA, TELEVISION, AND PARTICIPATION

1. Observe people coming out of a movie theater. Can you usually tell by their behavior whether the film was comic, tragic, melodramatic, a western, etc? Can you do this as easily with people coming from a drama theater? Or from watching a film on television?

2. Does it make any significant difference whether you experience a film in an empty or packed theater? Compare your experience of a play in a theater. Have you ever experienced, for instance, a comedy performed in a large theater with only a few people present, and did this have anything to do with your sense of the comic? Is laughter somehow enhanced in a crowd? Yet is the humor of a comic film significantly depressed if you see it alone?

3. Are you as explicitly aware of your spatial location in a film theater as in a drama theater? Does the fact that dramas are usually presented discontinuously, i.e., with breaks between the acts, make you more aware of your place in a theater? Are you more conscious of other people in the audience when you are experiencing a film or a drama? Why?

4. Compare your experiences of the same film in the theater and on television. Which presentation engages your participation more intensely? Is the differ-

ence in the sizes of the screens mainly responsible for any difference in the intensity of participation? Or is it, perhaps, the stronger darkness that surrounds you in the theater? Or the commercial breaks that accompany most television presentations? What other factors might be involved?

5. Do you think it would be easier to make a television film or a theater film? What would be the basic differences?

6. What kinds of theater film are most adaptable for television? Conversely, what kinds of television film are most adaptable for theater showing? Or are there really no significant differences between the moving images made for the theater as distinct from television? Discuss.

7. Compare your experience of a drama performed on the stage with your experience of a film version of the same drama made for television. What, if anything, is lost or gained in the filming? Make the same comparisons for the dance.

Participating with a film because of its realism can become the chief artistic criterion we apply to our experiences of the film. We are all familiar with the details of realism—they permeate our lives—and we are quick to respond to any appeal made directly to our images of ourselves and others. For instance, in *The Hustler* (1961), Paul Newman plays a character who represents so many young people in the film's audience that it is not difficult to see why the film had a wide appeal. The audience of would-be "comers" sympathizes with the young hustler, "Fast Eddie" Felsen, and sides with him—*becomes* him in crucial moments of the film. They share his respect and awe of Minnesota Fats, played by Jackie Gleason, and his distaste for the mere gambler-banker, played by George C. Scott. The makers of movies are keenly aware of that kind of response and often play for it because it is an easy way to assure themselves of success. The plot of *The Hustler* is a remake of countless westerns where the young fast gun in town measures off against the legendary old fast gun. Possibly, even deeper, it is a remake of the young man's basic psychological masculine need to prove his sexual potency—which might explain the improbable love interests in these films. Most young men share that need and tend to see themselves as the chief characters in films like *The Hustler*.

But there are problems with that loss of self which is in fact nothing but a veiled appeal to the worship of self. Film can inform us about ourselves, or it can cause a kind of short circuit in which we do not become informed: we simply indulge in hero worship with ourselves as the hero. The other arts may also cause this short circuit, of course, but the temptation is the greatest, perhaps, with film.

There are two kinds of participative experiences in film: one is not principally filmic in nature and is represented by a kind of self-indulgence which depends upon self-justifying fantasies. The other is more specifically caused by the artfulness of the entire film and is unrelated to self-indulgence.

It is the feeling of being removed from self-awareness, of being a part of the medium of moving images, whether it is a case of narrative action or simply the dynamism of images and sound. This second kind of participative experience means much more to us ultimately because it is significantly informative.

Just a word more about the first kind of participation. It is usually referred to as "escapism." "Escape" films give us the chance to see ourselves complimented in a movie, thus satisfying our desire for self-importance. Unhappily, escape films often help us avoid doing anything about achieving something that would *really* make us more important to ourselves. In some ways these films rob people of the chance to be something in their own right. Most television depends on this effect for its success. Maybe it is even true that large masses of people need this kind of entertainment in order to avoid the despair which would set in if they had to face up to the reality of their lives. It may be cynical to think so, yet it is strongly possible that many people who make motion pictures feel this to be a justification of what they are doing.

The fact that film may cause such an intense sense of participation of the wrong kind deadens our perception of the content of the film. We can see a film and know nothing about the finer points of its form and meaning —the nuances that make a film worth experiencing and then pondering over because of its impact on us. There are many mediocre examples, as in any medium, of film making which are hardly worth seeing more than once (or *even* once), while there are others which are rightly called classics because of their lasting qualities, their formal excitement and excellence, and their humanizing achievement. We want to get a sense of how one appreciates what a film can really achieve as it aspires to being a classic.

Questions of criticism, as we hope we established in Chapter 3, are always implicitly operative when we view a film or any work of art. What we are interested in doing is ensuring that our critical faculties will be engaged in heightening our awareness of what the film actually achieves. We are interested in what we do observe in relation to what we can observe. The main purpose of this chapter is to help us be conscious of those qualities which make a film interesting and effective. They are qualities which, for the viewer who has not developed his filmic awareness, might not be noticeable at all.

THE MOVING IMAGE

The starting point in the film is photography, and it is the photography of the image in motion, not the posed or poised image at rest as in still photography. Just as the basically static visual images of still photographs and paintings can move us profoundly by their organization of visual experience, so can the basically dynamic images of film. Indeed, many experts insist that no artistic medium man has ever created has the power to move us as deeply as the medium of moving images. They base their claim not just on the mass audiences who have been profoundly moved but on the fact that the moving images of the film are very close to the moving images we perceive in life. We rarely perceive static images except when viewing such things as paintings. Watching a film closely can help us perceive much more intensely the visual worth of many of the images we experience outside film.

Let us begin with that aspect of the image which is not specifically motion. Many early film makers composed their films by adding single photographs to each other, frame by frame. Movement in motion pictures is caused by the eye's physiological limitations: it cannot perceive the black line between frames when the film strip is moved at a specific speed. All it sees is the succession of frames minus the lines that divide them. The reason the eye is capable of this phenomenon is that it cannot perceive separate images or frames that move faster than $\frac{1}{30}$ second. This is to use the "language" of the camera itself, which can take a picture in much less time than that. Motion picture film is usually projected at a speed of twenty-four frames per second: the persistence of vision merges the images.

Because of this, many film makers, both early and contemporary, attempt to "design" each individual frame as carefully as they might a still photograph. Jean Renoir, the famous French film maker, sometimes composed each frame almost like an impressionist painting, as in *The Grand Illusion*. Eisenstein also carefully framed many of his images, notably in *Potemkin*. David Lean—who directed *Bridge Over the River Kwai* (1957), *Lawrence of Arabia* (1962), *Dr. Zhivago* (1965), and *Ryan's Daughter* (1970)—also pays very close attention to the composition of individual frames. The effect of this can be powerful, but it is not necessarily the best or the only way to make a strong film. Consider the stills which are reproduced with this chapter for their power as fixed compositions: you will see that many of them are not striking by themselves. Some stills, even from the greatest films, are really not effective except in the context of motion. Thus the flawlessly composed still image may not be really exploiting the full advantage of the film medium. Evaluate the stills shown in Figures 10-1, 10-2, and 10-3 from the point of view of their composition, and then try to imagine whether their effectiveness would be enhanced in a sequence of motion. All are from remarkable films.

For some directors, the still moments of the film must be as exactly composed as a painting: the theory is that if the individual moments of the film are each as perfect as can be, then the total film will be a cumulative perfection. This seems to be the case for many films, but it is not so for all. In those films which have long meditative sequences, like Bergman's *Cries and Whispers* (1972), or sequences in which characters or images are relatively unmoving for significant periods of time, the carefully composed

FIGURE 10-1 From Ingmar Bergman's *Seventh Seal*. Photograph from Janus Films, Inc.

FIGURE 10-2 From *Easy Rider*; Wyatt (Peter Fonda), Stranger (Luke Askew), and Billy (Dennis Hopper) arrive at the commune. Copyright © 1969 by Columbia Pictures. Permission to reproduce this photograph furnished by Columbia Pictures Industries, Inc. All rights reserved.

and formally exciting still image will be of real significance. However, most
stills from exciting films will reveal very little of the real power of the entire
film all by themselves: it is their sequential movement that brings out their
effectiveness.

Paying careful attention to the composition of each frame may, nevertheless, pay off. It may not be essential to do what Josef von Sternberg and
Howard Hawks (two directors who paid exceptionally close attention to the
still moments of their film) do—that is, retouch frames or carefully adjust
the lighting to get the most out of a given composition. But usually some
attention to the frames is helpful. Some directors adjust the focus of their
lenses so that the composition is seen first with the foreground in focus,
then with the background in focus and the foreground out of focus. This
can be an effective way of shifting our attention in a static scene without
having to move the camera or the actors. However it is a technique which,
like so many others, is best used in moderation.

From all this, you can see that the motion in the motion picture can
come from numerous sources. The actors or the subjects can themselves
move toward, away from, or across the field of camera vision. When something moves toward the camera it moves with astonishing speed, as we all
know from sitting still while the images of a moving locomotive (the favorite vehicle for this so far) rushes at us and then catapults "over our heads."
The effect of the catapult is important because it is characteristic of the film

medium and is not quite so characteristic of a real-life situation. When a runner approaches the camera, he too will seem to catapult into motion the closer he gets to the focal plane of the film in the camera; the runner approaching you in life does not have the same effect because you are not watching him on a flat screen.

We are used to seeing people move before us the way they move before the camera, but the camera (or cameras) can achieve visual things which our unaided eye cannot: showing the same moving action from a number of points of view, for instance, or showing it from a camera angle the eye cannot achieve. The realistic qualities of a film can be threatened, however, by being too sensational, with a profusion of angle shots and views that would be impossible in a real-life situation. Although such virtuoso effects can dazzle us at first, the feeling of being dazzled can degenerate into being dazed.

Another way the film achieves motion is by the movement of the camera itself. In the 1961 John Huston film *The Misfits*, about cowboys rounding up wild mustang horses to sell for dog food, some amazing chase scenes are filmed with the camera mounted on a pickup truck chasing fast-running horses. The motion itself in the round-up scenes is almost overwhelming because Huston combines two kinds of rapid motion—of trucks and horses. Moreover, the motion of these scenes is further increased because of the limiting focus of the camera. Only the camera records the action. Thus one has the unmistakable feeling that the action, even in that expansive film, is enclosed, that the boundary of the screen we see the action on excludes vision which might tend to distract or dilute the motion we are permitted to see. The screen in motion pictures always constrains us, always controls our attention, even when we imagine the space beyond the screen which we do not perceive, as in instances in which a character moves off the filmed space. By eliminating the space beyond the images recorded by the camera, by refusing to permit our eye to be distracted by anything not of immediate importance to the action we see, the camera causes our attention to sharply focus and fix. And such attention is bound to enhance the visual qualities, such as the motion of the moving images.

PERCEPTION KEY CAMERA VISION

Make a mask with two oblong rectangles, approximately ⅜ inch long by ½ inch wide, as shown:

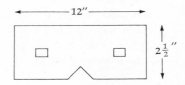

Place the mask so that you can see only out of the slits. This experiment can be conducted almost as effectively by using simple pinholes in place of cutout rectangles. In fact, for those who wear glasses it may be more effective, because the pinholes are actually "lenses" and may permit some people with defective vision to see fairly clearly without their glasses. Obviously, too, pinholes are more like the round lens of the camera.

1. Does the "framing" with the mask or the pinholes make you unusually sensitive to the way things look?

2. What effect does moving your head have on the composition of the things you see?

3. What are some of the differences between using one eye, then both eyes? Which makes you think more of the camera's way of looking?

4. What do you learn from viewing a scene first with one eye, then the other?

5. One very important feature of this experiment which ought to be considered is the analogy with the motion of the camera itself. Be sure that you get a sense of what happens to your visual planes when you move your head in the fashion a camera would move. Moreover, try to consider what kinds of motion you are capable of that the camera does not seem capable of. Are there any?

6. If the camera is the principal tool of the craft of film making, does the director give up artistic control when he has a photographer operate the machine for him? Does your experimenting in the questions above suggest there may be a "camera language" which the director should be controlling himself? Given your experience with film and cameras, how might you define "camera language"?

A final basic way film can achieve motion is by means of the camera lens itself. Even when the camera is fixed, a lens which affords a much wider, narrower, larger, or smaller field of vision than the eye normally supplies will give the illusion of motion, since we instinctively feel the urge to be in the physical position which would supply that field of vision. Zoom lenses which change their focal length along a smooth range—thus bringing images gradually closer or further away—are even more effective for suggesting motion, especially for small-screen viewing of movies on television. One of the favorite shots on television is that of a figure walking or moving in some fashion, which looks, at first, as if it were a normal-distance shot but which is actually revealed as a long shot (from a great distance) when the zoom is reversed. Since our own eye cannot imitate the action of the zoom lens, the effect the lens has can be overwhelmingly dramatic—when used creatively. It is something like the effect that slow motion or stop motion has on us: it interrupts our perceptions of something—something which had seemed perfectly natural—in a way that makes us conscious of the film medium itself.

Technique in this sense, then, has an important shortcoming. Too much of it can make us aware of the film as technique and cause us to lose our sense of participative involvement. Slow motion, rapidly changing focus from foreground to background, and of zooming in and out repeatedly on scenes can all cause this loss. But more and more the sophisticated and experimental film makers delight in making us do "double takes" which points out to us the fact that we are not participating in an experience on the screen but that we are indeed sitting in a darkened room watching an image on a screen. One very peculiar example of this is in the movie *Tom Jones* (1963), in which Tom, after searching for his wallet everywhere, turns and looks at the audience and asks us directly whether or not we have seen his wallet. The effect of an actor on the screen being aware of the audience as an audience and not as a silent participator in the action is really startling. It unsettles the comfortable relationship we have built up for ourselves and forces us into new awarenesses of the meaning of the images. And while this example is not peculiarly technical in nature, it is representative of what many film makers are now doing.

Assuming that the technical aspects of the film do not distract us by making us too consciously aware of them, we may find ourselves participating with the images in motion in a nonescapist way. Then we will be responding to those situations which are unique to the motion picture: the situations created by showing us images in motion. We become participants through the control of artists who give us a form-content that reveals something significant in our lives. If they fail to do that, assuming our sensitivity, we will come away from their film—as we often do—with a feeling of perplexity, of inconclusiveness, of not being fully sure what we have seen is worthwhile.

SELECTIVITY IN FILM

The principle of selectivity, which we will talk about again when we speak about editing, is crucial here. What the director selects and chooses to show us is designed for its impact. When Luis Buñuel shows us the razoring of a woman's open eyeball in *Un Chien Andalou* (1928), he is counting on our personal horror at actually seeing such an act. The scene is artistically justifiable because of Buñuel's careful handling of the scene and its tight integration into the structure. Since then hundreds of film makers have failed with similar scenes because they show sheer violence simply for its own sake, without any attempt to inform. In Roman Polanski's *Macbeth* (1971), for example, many audiences actually began snickering at the final battle scenes in which Macbeth and Macduff fight—partly because they had already been saturated with blood, gore, murder, and violence since the first appearance of the "bloody sergeant," whose head had been gashed and whose eye had presumably been lost shortly before in battle. The line between the exhibition of horror and the interpretation of horror is sometimes easy to miss. A curious phenomenon about experiencing film is that the audience's imagination, left to its own devices, is sometimes a much more reliable instrument for the interpretation of horror than the fully realized visual scene.

As we have suggested previously, it is fairly easy to evoke stock responses from an audience, and such stock responses as laughter, sorrow, repulsion, horror, and smug security are pretty reliable for keeping an audience's attention. But the more complex responses, some of which are as difficult to control as they are to attain, are usually the aims of the most enduring film makers. When Ingmar Bergman shows us the rape scene in *The Virgin Spring* (1959), he does not then proceed to saturate us with horror. He holds off until the final scenes in which the girl's father murders the rapists in turn. And we discover that we still have enough emotional reserve to feel the horror in their violent deaths. But this probably would not have been true if the film had been filled with violence after the rape scene, because then we would have been emotionally worn out by the end of the film.

In any art, control is absolutely vital. We can become emotionally saturated just as we can become bored. The results are often the same: indifference. In talking about violence portrayed on the screen we are also talking about timing and repetition. This is to say, we are concerned with the rhythmic strategy that goes into including scenes or omitting them, into showing similar instances frequently or infrequently, into making decisions which may represent restraint on the part of the film maker.

THE QUESTION OF SOUND

Sound has been a staple feature of professionally made films since Al Jolson's *Jazz Singer* (1927), and its introduction had overwhelming impact on the industry. For one thing, it put those actors out of work who were excellent at pantomime or at broad-style acting but who could not deliver dialogue convincingly. But that was a minor problem in film making. More important was the fact that the people writing films then became more than writers of scenarios—the scenes to be shot. They now had to write films which included dialogue for their progress, much the way most live dramatic productions include dialogue for their progress. Today we take this for granted. What we may not realize is that this change literally revolutionized the entire art. We find in some contemporary films that the entire progress of a film can be given over more to what is said than to what is done on the screen. Numerous films avoid visual possibilities in favor of relatively simple (and sometimes simply dull) solutions with dialogue. Eisenstein feared, and rightly so, that sound might kill the artistic integrity of film. He was afraid that with sound no one would work basically with the images that make film not only effective but specifically filmic, that film would once again become subservient to drama.

Eisenstein knew that images in motion could sustain the kind of dramatic tension which was once thought limited to the dramatic stage. This is a point of consummate importance. A film is, first of all, images in motion. Whatever is added by way of speech, music, or anything else is supplemental. A great film maker will not depend on those supplemental elements for the strength of his film. He may exploit them, but he will never make them the basic ingredients of his film. On the other hand, the mediocre or poor film maker will do precisely the opposite: he will rely on the narrative line of the film almost exclusively, using the camera to do little more than visually record people talking to one another. This almost invariably results in a film of little importance.

PERCEPTION KEY   SIGHT AND SOUND

1. Analyze carefully the next film you see on television. Examine the frames you see for their power as individual compositions, recalling some of the points made in the chapters on painting and sculpture. Decide how strong you feel the film is from this point of view.

2. Does the size and shape of the television screen inhibit intense visual experience? Is your participation with film stronger with television or in the theater? Why?

3. If you have a color set, experiment with the color control and try to produce more interesting color combinations than are provided by the "normal" setting.

4. Turn off the sound entirely. Can you follow clearly what is going on? Is much of importance lost?

5. Tune out the video portion of the program and listen to the sound only. Can you follow clearly what is going on? Is much of importance lost? When you come right down to it, you may find that in all but the more impressive films not terribly much is lost when the images are eliminated. You may have to wait a long while before you find a film in which this is not true. Show a really successful film in class or in a group, and then try the above "modifications" to see how well the film survives.

These experiments probably indicate to you that most contemporary film is a marriage of sight and sound. Yet we must not forget that film is a medium in which the moving image is preeminent. Were we to consider the value of most films we see on this basis alone, we would soon learn the sad fact that the mass production of films has tended to make film makers take the easy way out most of the time. It is rare to see a film which takes seriously its responsibilities to fashion a fine series of moving images. Those that do are memorable. Unfortunately, we cannot always expect such films to be showing in our local theater, but in our discussions here we can concern ourselves with the best films. Whatever we discover about them will, to a lesser extent, be true of other films as well.

THE QUESTION OF STRUCTURE OR FORM

One kind of structure in films is the narrative sequence which orders our experience: a character or characters get into some kinds of difficulties and persist in either worsening their situation or improving it. Such narrative structures seem to have a natural form for most of us. But that form often is, in effect, formula. This is one of the traps—relying on simple formulas which would not honestly represent the complexities that even the simplest viewer would himself have to face in life—that Eisenstein always tried to avoid. Yet it is also true that his own films, like *Potemkin* (1925), were themselves narrative in structure. *Potemkin* opens with sailors on a Russian ship (the *Potemkin*) being badly mistreated. They mutiny and take over the ship, restoring proper justice and humanity. The people of Odessa give them welcome in their harbor. In reaction, the Czar's troops shoot down women and children in Odessa indiscriminately, and gunboats are sent out to sink the *Potemkin*. The Czar's sailors mutiny, however, and will not fire on the *Potemkin*. All this is revealed without audible dialogue. The carefully selected visual aspects of the narrative—the photographed moving images—do the telling simply and economically, without reliance upon formula, and for that reason it is still a powerful film even for those of us who find it difficult to adjust to silent films.

It should be clear that the narrative in this sense is a narrative of outward action: characters performing actions affecting themselves and others. But there are other kinds of narratives. One very popular kind is the narrative of inward or psychological action. Consider, for example, the motorcycle-acid drama, *Easy Rider* (1969): we realize that the organizing elements are not those of *Potemkin* or other films like it. There is action, to be sure, but the sequence of events does not have the same close causal order. The structure is what is referred to in literature as episodic or picaresque: things happen to the protagonist as he goes from place to place. What happens to the protagonist, how he changes and grows because of his adventures, is of principal importance in such structures. Wyatt and Billy are simply motorcycling from coast to coast, from Los Angeles to the East. They are not specifically trying to accomplish anything other than getting their payoff money from drugs safely away. They realize ultimately, however, that what they have done is bad. They are struck by the moral consequences of their action, and when they realize what they are Wyatt says drily—

"We blew it." You might ask yourself what, among the adventures they had and the exposure they had to people of all sorts, good and bad, caused that change of heart. The form of that film, along with many like it, reveals the characters as altered by their experience. The fact that Wyatt is gunned down by rednecks after his moment of understanding is something of a formula, but within the context of this film it is artistically effective. Once one has begun to truly understand himself, as some pessimistic existentialists claim, there is nothing left—death is a blessing, the only rightful conclusion to that narrative structure which is our life. Such a gloomy understanding is rare in life. But art functions to give us a sense of the various possibilities of self-understanding. Certainly the implications of *Easy Rider*, with its enormous popularity, were understood and valued.

The relationship of photography itself to the form of films like *Easy Rider* is sometimes difficult to assess. If we agree that the power of the moving image is central to the effect and to the ultimate meaning of the motion picture, we can see that the most important structural qualities of any good film develop from the juxtaposition of different kinds of images—the texture. Some people place this aspect of film under the term "editing," the process which follows after the shooting of the picture. Sometimes many different versions of a single action will be filmed. The editor and probably the director decide which will be the final mix after they have given thought to each version in relation to the structure they want for the total film. Once they decide on what will be included, the editor does the actual joining of the parts of the film, deciding exactly which frame will end one sequence and which will begin the next. This is a crucial artistic job. The editor usually works very closely with the director because his decisions will have such a powerful impact on the viewer's ultimate responses to the final product.

EDITING

The editor's work gives meaning to the film just as surely as the scriptwriter's and the photographer's. Consider, for instance, the final scenes in Eisenstein's *Potemkin*. The *Potemkin* is steaming to a confrontation with the fleet. Eisenstein rapidly cuts from the inside of the ship to the outside: showing a view of powerfully moving engine pistons, then the ship cutting deeply into the water, then rapidly back and forth, showing occasional anxiety-ridden faces, all designed to raise the emotional pitch of anyone watching the movie. More than that, it gives a clear meaning to the film itself as film. The tension is being portrayed by the moving images—it is being shown to us, not told.

The editing stage of film making can easily be abused. But when it is handled well, it can be profoundly effective, because it is impossible for us in real-life experience to achieve what the film editor achieves. By eliminating the more or less irrelevant, good editing accents the relevant. We cannot "cut" instantly from an airport, where we were watching a hired assassin from Chicago landing at Los Angeles, to the office of the political candidate he has come to kill. Film can do this with ease. The connection or montage—the showing of the psychologically connected but somewhat physically disconnected second scene immediately after the first—can be made without a single word of dialogue. You can undoubtedly recall innumerable instances of this kind of "cutting" and montage work. When done well, this tying together of images which could not possibly be together in real-life experience enhances the meaning of the images we see.

PERCEPTION KEY EDITING

1. Study the next film you see carefully for its use of editing techniques, principally its effort to give meaning to what you see by the conjunction or the disjunction of image sequences.

2. Decide whether the film you are watching is very original in its use of cuts and montages. Or is the editor relying on well-worn clichés?

3. In conversation with others interested in this question, try to see if you can come to an agreement about what is intended by the editing you observe.

CONTENT

The question of meaning is no less complicated in the film than it is in any artistic medium. The fact that we cannot translate filmic meaning into language, any more than we can translate musical meaning into language, should not deter us from trying to understand what meanings are revealed by the technical moves employed by the film maker. In some cases we will be able to approximate a "translation" by describing the connections—emotional, narrative, or whatever—implied by the sequence of images. But there are aspects of that sequence which defy the meanings of language, such as the direct psychological impact of the juxtapositions. Sensitive participants are especially interested in films which explore this kind of "meaning."

When we watch the overturning coffin in Bergman's *Wild Strawberries* (1957), we are surprised to find that the figure in the coffin has the same face as Professor Borg, the protagonist, who is himself a witness to what we see. That there is very significant meaning implied seems quite clear. Yet we cannot translate this scene into language, though we can do a great deal of profitable talking about the power of the scene and its implications for the entire film. The scene, and others like it, achieves full meaning in relation to other dramatic moments in the film. The scene has a certain amount of tension and impact all its own, and yet it is apparent that the full meaning depends on the context of the whole film in which it appears. The relation of part to context exists in every art, of course, but that relation in its nuances often may be more easily missed in our experiences of the film. For one thing, we are not accustomed to permitting images to build their own meanings apart from the meanings we already associate with them. We tend to resist that process. Secondly, we do not always observe the way one movement or gesture will mean one thing in one context while it will mean an entirely different thing in another context or in isolation—that is, insofar as *any* movement or gesture can exist in isolation.

The film maker is the master controller of contexts, just as is the dramatist. In Jean-Claude Brialy's film *Claire's Knee* (1970), a totally absurd gesture, the caressing of an indifferent and relatively insensitive girl's knee, becomes the fundamental focus of the film. This gesture is loaded with meaning throughout the entire film, but loaded only for the main masculine character and us. The girl is totally unaware of what her knee has come to mean to the man. This is absurd, in a way, yet plausible. It is absurd in the strict sense in that the meaning of the gesture is unimportant—except as the gesture is understood in context. It is plausible, however, in that such fixations can occur, even in normal people. But this film is not concerned solely with plausibility; it is mainly concerned with gestures in context that reveal what is unclear in real-life experience. And this is done primarily through skilful photography and editing rather than through a spoken narrative plot line.

PERCEPTION KEY CONTEXTS

1. Examine the next film you watch for its power to give meaning to gesture through the contexts which are established for it.

2. To what extent do the gestures in this film tie the images together (the textural-structural relationships)?

3. To what extent is this film meaningful because of its contextual relationship to the world we ourselves inhabit?

All meanings, linguistic or nonlinguistic, are within some kind of context. Most first-rate films exist in many contexts simultaneously, and it is our job as sensitive viewers of film to be able to decide which are the most important for us. Film, like every art, has a history, and this history is one of the most significant of the contexts in which every film takes place. In order to make that historical context fruitful in our filmic experiences, we must do more than just read about the history. We must accumulate in our experience a historical sense of film by seeing films that have been important to the development of the medium. Most of us have a very rich personal backlog in film: we have seen a great many films, some of which are memorable and most of which have been influenced by landmark films. Further, film exists in a context which is meaningful for the life work of a director and, in turn, for us. When we talk about the films of Orson Welles, Ingmar Bergman, or Federico Fellini, we are talking about the achievements of artists just as much as when we talk about the paintings of Van Gogh or Rembrandt. Today we watch carefully for films by François Truffaut, Alfred Hitchcock, Michelangelo Antonioni, Joseph Losey, and Stanley Kubrick—to name only a few of the most active current directors—because their work has shown a steady development and because they, in relation to the history of the film, have shown themselves in possession of a vision which is transforming the medium. They, in other words, are altering the history of film in significant ways. In turn, we should be interested in knowing what they are doing because they are providing new contexts for increasing our understanding of film.

But these are only a few contexts in which films exist. Every film exists in a social context, in relation to the social system it springs from, portrays, or criticizes. We do not usually judge films specifically on the basis of their ability to make social comment, but if we lived in Russia or China we would probably take it for granted that we judge a film on the basis of its ability to make a positive contribution to the building of a new society. Obviously, the context of the society would then outweigh any context of internal parts: the relation of texture to structure and the meaning of the structure. You can see that our concerns in this book have not been exclusively with one or another kind of context, though we have assumed that the internal context of a work of art is necessarily of first importance to begin with. But no work can be properly understood without resorting to some external contextual examination. A visual image, a contemporary gesture, even a colloquial expression will sometimes show up in a film and need explication in order to be fully understood. Just as we sometimes have to look up a word in a dictionary—which exists outside a poem, for instance—we sometimes have to look outside a film for hints about meaning. Even Terence Young's James Bond thriller movies need such explication, though we rarely think about that. If someone failed to understand the assumptions about Russia and China which such films make, he would not fully understand what was going on. Of course, political conflict is something of a constant the world over, and even if we do not fully understand the nature of the political rivalry of East and West (and it changes all the time), we can still comprehend the struggles we witness in human terms.

EXPERIMENTATION

Because of the vast technical problems involved in film making, a great deal of experimentation has occurred in the film from its earliest days. The fact that many of the original people involved with the medium had technical interests or technical training probably helps account for this experimentation. Today the experimental work is less technical, perhaps, and more a "trying out" of the technical advances. We think of the oddly probing work of Andy Warhol, originally a painter and sculptor, who has done some interesting work in extending the limits of realism. For example, many of us seem to prefer the starkly realistic film to the improbable or unlikely fantasy film. At least many of us say we do, and we undoubtedly think we do. But when Andy Warhol places a figure in front of a camera to sleep for a full eight hours' rest, we may begin to get the message as we watch this monotonous reality: we want a transformation of reality that gives us insight, not reality itself. The difference is really much more important than it may seem because it is the difference between reality and art. We all have reality in front of us most of the time. We have art much less frequently. Realistic art is a selecting of elements which conveys the illusion of reality. When we see Warhol's almost direct transcription of reality on film, we see clearly that the value of selecting, directing, and editing may be greater than we had thought. The power of most striking films is often in their ability to condense experience, to take a year's time, for example, and select its most intense ninety minutes. This condensation is precisely what Marcel Proust, one of the greatest of novelists, expected from the novel:

> . . . Every emotion is multiplied ten-fold, into which this book comes to disturb us as might a dream, but a dream more lucid, and of a more lasting impression, than those which come to us in sleep; why, then, for a space of an hour he sets free within us all the joys and sorrows in the world, a few of which, only, we should have to spend years of our actual life in getting to know, and the keenest, the most intense of which would never have been revealed to us because the slow course of their development stops our perception of them. It is the same in life; the heart changes . . . but we learn of it only from reading or by imagination; for in reality its alteration . . . is so gradual that . . . we are still spared the actual sensation of change.[1]

Some interesting modern films have to do with the question of the film's creation of reality. Antonioni's *Blow Up* (1966), for example, had the thread of a narrative holding it together: a possible murder and the efforts of a magazine photographer, through the medium of his own enlargements, to establish the reality of that murder. But anyone who saw the film would know that the continuity of the narrative was not the most important part of the film. The basic content came out of what were essentially disconnected "moments": a party, some driving around London in a convertible Rolls-Royce, and some unusual tennis played without a ball. What seemed most important was the role of the film itself in creating certain "realities." In a sense the murder was a reality only after the film uncovered it. Is it

[1] Marcel Proust, *Swann's Way*, C. K. Scott Moncrieff (trans.), The Modern Library, Random House, Inc., New York, 1928, p. 119.

possible that Antonioni is saying something similar about the reality which surrounds the very film he is creating? There is a reality, but where? Is *Blow Up* more concerned with film images as reality than it is with reality outside the film? If you have a chance to see this film, be sure you ask that puzzling question.

Some more extreme experimenters remove the narrative frame entirely and simply present successions of images, almost in the manner of a nightmare or a drug experience. The images themselves, like an abstract painting, are capable of establishing their own meaningfulness. Or so the experimenters feel. The fact that we have very little abstract film art may have several explanations. Part of the power of abstract painting seems to depend on its "all-at-onceness" (see Chapter 4), precisely what is missing from film. Another reason may be tied in, again, with the popular nature of the medium: masses of people do not prefer abstraction. There may well be other reasons for the small amount of abstract film making. A recent invention in the field of moving images is Thomas Wilfred's Lumia, an installation that displays shifting patterns of light and color which are totally abstract and always in motion. There is not only no narrative line but no relevant way of adding one, since the moving images are not those of people, places, or things. The success of Lumia has been limited, although Wilfred's *Lumia Suite, Opus 158*, which was opened to the public in 1964 in the Museum of Modern Art in New York City, apparently has become a permanent installation. Most visitors, however, rarely extend their viewings for more than a few minutes. Apparently the public is generally convinced that film, like literature, must have characters, themes, and narrative lines. Thus even filmic cartoons are rarely abstract, even though they are not photographs but drawings.

NARRATIVE AND FILM

It is important to consider, finally, why narrative elements seem so crucial to the film medium. What alternatives can you see for affording meaningfulness to film? Are there any? How excited can you get about them?

PERCEPTION KEY MAKE A FILM

1. For some of you it may be possible to experiment with making a film on videotape. Take the opportunity seriously. Try to invent new ways to give a meaningful unity to the succession of images you photograph. Try substituting another organizing principle for the usual one of narrative.

2. Assuming you do not want to abandon narrative as an organizing principle, try to use narrative "lines" which you do not usually find in films. We all know the normal plot for a western, for instance. Can you free yourself to

some extent from preconceptions about such plots and invent a new narrative principle?

3. Short of making a film, try some editing by finding and clipping from twenty to thirty "stills" from magazines, brochures, newspapers, or other sources. Choose frames you feel have a "logic" to them and arrange them in such a way as to make a sequence that is meaningful to those who view them. How is your sequence affected by rearrangement? This project will be much more interesting if you use or make slides for viewing. Then consider adding a "soundtrack" to heighten interest and to clarify the logic of the sequence.

The experiments of this and some of the other perception keys have been challenging and informative, we hope. Perhaps they may even have stimulated some of you to work in the arts, to become at least amateur artists. They probably have indicated to all of you that making or attempting to make works of art is not an ordinary activity. Artistic creation, for all of its rewards, is usually highly demanding, time-consuming work. But the art that results, we claim, is one of the most powerful of civilizing forces. This is a large claim. We have been trying to support that claim throughout this book, of course, and you may not be convinced. But before you make a final judgment, consider with us in the next and final chapter the impact that we think the arts have on the other humanities. For if we are correct, none of the other humanities could achieve very much without the help of the arts.

11 THE HUMANITIES: THEIR INTER-RELATIONSHIPS

THE HUMANITIES AND THE SCIENCES

In the beginning pages of Chapter 1, we referred to the humanities as that broad range of creative activities and studies which are usually contrasted with mathematics and the "hard" sciences, mainly because in the humanities strictly objective or scientific standards do not usually dominate.

CONCEPTION KEY   CLASSIFYING SUBJECTS OF STUDY

1. Suppose you have been charged with grouping the courses of study at your or some other school. Is it possible to make reasonably clear and defensible groupings? If so, how would you do it? For example, would you place psychology with the sciences? Where would you place sociology? And what about such studies as education and business administration?

2. It seems obvious that literature, music, and painting belong to the humanities. Is there something strange about putting such studies as history, philosophy, and religion in the same slot as the arts? How would you justify such a grouping?

Most college and university catalogues contain. a grouping of courses called the humanities. First, studies such as literature, the visual arts, music, history, philosophy, and religion almost invariably are included. Second, studies such as psychology, anthropology, sociology, political science, economics, business administration, and education may or may not be included. Third, studies such as physics, chemistry, biology, mathematics, and engineering are never included.

The reason the last group is excluded is obvious—strict scientific or objective standards are clearly applicable. With the second group, these "hard" standards are not always so clearly applicable. Thus there is an uncertainty about whether they belong with the sciences or the humanities. For example, most psychologists who experiment with animals apply the scientific method as rigorously as any biologist. But there are also psychologists—C. G. Jung, for instance—who speculate about such phenomena as the "collective unconscious" and the role of myth. To judge their work strictly by scientific methods is to miss their contributions. Where then should psychology and the subjects in this group be placed? In the case of the first group, finally, the arts are invariably listed under the humanities. But then so are history, philosophy, and religion. Thus, as the title of this book implies, the humanities include subjects other than the arts. Then how are the arts distinguished from the other humanities? And what is the relationship between the arts and these other humanities?

These are broad and very difficult questions. Concerning the placement of the studies in group two, it is usually best to take each department case by case. If, for example, a department of psychology is dominated by experimentalists, as is most likely in the United States, it would seem most useful to place that department with the sciences. And the same approach can be made to all the studies in group two. In most cases, probably, you will discover that clear-cut placements into the humanities or the sciences are impossible. Furthermore, even the subjects that almost always are grouped within either the humanities or the sciences cannot always be neatly catalogued. Rigorous objective standards may be applied in any of the humanities. Thus painting can be approached as a science—the historian of medieval painting, for example, who measures, as precisely as any engineer, the evolving sizes of haloes. On the other hand, the beauty of mathematics—its economy and elegance of proof—can excite the lover of mathematics as much as if not more than painting. As was previously mentioned, Edna St. Vincent Millay noted that "Euclid alone has looked on beauty bare." And so the separation of the humanities and the sciences should not be observed rigidly. The separation is useful mainly because it indicates the dominance or the subordinance of the strict scientific method in the various disciplines.

THE ARTS AND THE OTHER HUMANITIES

The artist differs from the other humanists primarily because he creates works that reveal values; that is, he presents them in a context that is clearer than nonartistic reality. The artist is sensitive to the important concerns or values of his society. That is his subject matter in the broadest sense. He creates an artistic form that reveals these values. That is his content. The other humanists—such as the historian, philosopher, and theologian—reflect upon rather than reveal values. They study values as given, as they find them. They try to describe and explain values—their causes and consequences. They may, furthermore, judge these values as good or bad. Thus, like the artist, they too try to clarify values; but they do this by means of nonartistic forms (see Chapter 2).

CONCEPTION KEY   THE ARTIST AND THE OTHER HUMANISTS

1. Explain how the work of an artist might be of significance to the historian, philosopher, and theologian.

2. Select works of art that we have discussed in this book that you think might be of greatest significance respectively to the historian, philosopher, and theologian. Ask others to do the same. Then compare and discuss your selections.

3. Can you find any works of art we have discussed that you think would have no significance whatsoever to any of the other humanists? If so, explain.

The other humanists do not, as in artistic revelation, transform values in their studies. Often they study values independently of the arts. But if they take advantage of the revealing role of the arts, their studies often will be enhanced because, other things being equal, they will have a more penetrating understanding of the values they are studying. This is basically the aid that the artists can give to some of the other humanists. Suppose, for example, a historian is trying to understand the bombing of Guernica by the Fascists in the Spanish Civil War. Suppose he has explored all factual resources. Even then something very important may be left out: vivid awareness of the feelings of those Spanish noncombatants. To gain insight into those feelings, Picasso's *Guernica* (Figure 1-3) may be a great aid.

CONCEPTION KEY   THE OTHER HUMANISTS AND THE ARTIST

1. Is there anything that Picasso may have learned from historians and that he used in painting *Guernica?*

2. Explain how the work of the other humanists might be of significance to the artist. Be specific.

The other humanists may aid the artist by their study of values. For example, in this book we have concerned ourselves in some detail with criticism—the description, interpretation, and evaluation of works of art. Criticism is a humanistic discipline because it studies values—those revealed in works of art—without strictly applying scientific or objective standards.

Good critics aid our understanding of works of art. We become more sensitively aware of the revealed values. This deeper understanding brings us into closer rapport with the artist, and such rapport helps sustain his confidence in his work.

The arts reveal values; the other humanistic disciplines study values. That does not mean that the artist may not study values, but rather that such study, if any, is subordinated to revealing values in a sensuous form that attracts our participation. The other humanists, conversely, study values and communicate their findings in nonartistic forms.

PERCEPTION AND CONCEPTION

Another basic difference between the arts and the other humanities is the way perception dominates in the arts whereas conception dominates in the other humanities. Of course, perceiving and conceiving (or thinking) almost always go together. When we are aware of red striking our eyes, we are perceiving, but normally our brain is also conceiving, more or less explicitly, the idea "red." On the other hand, when we conceive the idea "red" with our eyes closed, we almost invariably remember some specific or generalized image of perceptible red. Probably the infant only perceives, and as we are sinking into unconsciousness from illness or a blow on the head it may be that all ideas or concepts are wiped out. It may be, conversely, that conceiving sometimes occurs without any element of perceiving. Descartes, the great seventeenth-century philosopher, thought so. Most philosophers and psychologists believe, however, that even the most abstract thinking of mathematicians, since it still must be done with perceptible signs such as numbers, necessarily includes residues from perception. In any case, the question of the relationships and interdependence of perception and conception, which has been puzzling thinkers from the beginnings of civilization, still remains open.

CONCEPTION KEY PERCEPTION AND CONCEPTION

1. Think of examples in your experience in which percepts dominate concepts, and vice versa. Which kind of experience do you enjoy the most? Does your answer tell you anything about yourself?

2. Is it easily possible for you to shift gears from conceptually dominated thinking to perceptually dominated thinking? For example, if you are studying intensely some theoretical or practical problem, do you find it difficult to begin to "think from" some work of art? Or, conversely, if you have been participating with a work of art, do you find it difficult to begin to "think at" some theoretical or practical problem? Do your answers tell you anything about yourself?

3. Select from the chapter on literature (Chapter 7) that poem which seems to demand the most from your perceptual faculties and the least from your conceptual faculties. Then select that poem which seems to demand the

most from your conceptual faculties and the least from your perceptual faculties. Which poem do you like better? Does your answer tell you anything about yourself?

4. Which of the arts that we have studied seems to demand the most from your perceptual faculties? Your conceptual faculties? Why? Which art do you like better? Does your answer tell you anything about yourself?

It seems evident that perception without some conception is little more than a blooming, buzzing confusion. Thus all our talk about art in the previous chapters has been a conceptualizing that we hope has clarified and intensified our perception of specific works of art. But that is not to suggest that conception ought to dominate perception in our participation with a work of art. In fact, if conception dominates, participation will be weakened or prevented—we will be thinking *at* rather than thinking *from*. If, as we listen to the sonata form, we name the exposition, development, and recapitulation sections, we will be lowering the sensitivity of our listening. Yet if you were to ask the trained music lover *after* his listening, he probably could easily name the sections and tell you where they occurred. In other words, to experience the arts most intensely and satisfactorily, conception is indispensable, but perception must remain in the foreground. When we come to the other humanities, however, conception usually comes to foreground. The other humanities basically *reflect about* values rather than *reveal* values, as in the case of the arts. Thus concepts or ideas tend to become more central than percepts.

VALUES

A value is something we care about, something that matters. A value is an object of an interest. The term "object," however, should be understood as including events or states of affairs. A pie is obviously an object and it may be a value, and the course of action involved in obtaining the pie may also be a value. If we are not interested in something, it is neutral in value or valueless to us. Positive values are those objects of interest that satisfy us or give us pleasure, such as good health. Negative values are those objects of interest that dissatisfy us or give us pain, such as bad health. When the term "value" is used alone, it usually refers to positive values only, but it may also include negative values. In our value decisions, we generally seek to obtain positive values and try to avoid negative values. But except for the very young child, these decisions usually involve highly complex activities. To have a tooth pulled is painful, a negative value, but doing so leads to the possibility of better health, a positive value. *Intrinsic values* involve the feelings, such as pleasure and pain, we have of some value activity, such as enjoying good food or the nausea of overeating. *Extrinsic values* are the means to intrinsic values, such as making the money that pays for the food.

Intrinsic-extrinsic values not only evoke immediate feelings but are means to further values, such as the enjoyable food that leads to future good health. For most people, intrinisic-extrinsic values of the positive kind are the basis of the good life. Certain drugs may have great positive intrinsic value, but then extrinsically they may have negative value, leading to great suffering.

CONCEPTION KEY PARTICIPATION WITH ART AND VALUES

1. Do you think that the value of a participative experience with a work of art is basically intrinsic, extrinsic, or intrinsic-extrinsic? Explain.

2. Many psychiatrists treat their patients by retraining their sensory receptivity. Dr. J. Samuel Bois in *Art of Awareness* cites the example of a surgeon who came to him for treatment because he was nervous and unsure of himself in performing very delicate operations. Bois discovered that the surgeon conceptualized his operations—i.e., as he cut through the layers of tissue and encountered the various parts of the body, he named each one silently to himself—interfering with the nervous and muscular control of his eyes and hands. Bois prescribed remedial exercises resulting in a decrease in the *conceptualizing* and an increase in the *perceptualizing* processes of the operation. Thus instead of identifying each tissue, vein, artery, and organ by name, the surgeon was trained to identify them by more efficient looking and feeling, through greater sensitivity to nuances of color, shape, texture, size, etc. The treatment worked: the surgeon reduced his nervousness and increased his confidence and effectiveness, so that the time involved in operating was cut in half. Do you think that learning to enjoy painting or sculpture more intensely might have been a part of Bois's remedial exercises? Or might any of the other arts have been helpful to the surgeon? Discuss with others.

3. Dr. Viktor Frankl, a medical doctor and psychiatrist, writes in *The Doctor and the Soul*, "The higher meaning of a given moment in human existence can be fulfilled by the mere intensity with which it is experienced, and independent of any action. If anyone doubts this, let him consider the following situation. Imagine a music lover sitting in the concert hall while the most noble measures of his favorite symphony resound in his ears. He feels that shiver of emotion which we experience in presence of the purest beauty. Suppose now that at such a moment we should ask this person whether his life has meaning. He would have to reply that it had been worthwhile living if only to experience this ecstatic moment."[1] Do you agree with Frankl, or do you consider this an overstatement? Why?

4. It has been variously reported that some of the most sadistic guards and high-ranking officers in the Nazi concentration camps played the music of Bach and Beethoven during or after torturings. Goering was a great lover of excellent paintings. Hitler loved architecture and the music of Wagner. What do you make of this?

[1] Viktor E. Frankl, *The Doctor and the Soul*, Richard and Clara Winston (trans.), Alfred A. Knopf, Inc., New York, 1955, p. 49.

Participation with a work of art not only is immediately satisfying but usually extrinsically valuable because it leads to deeper satisfactions in the future. To participate with one poem is likely to increase our sensitivity to the next poem. Moreover, by enhancing our sensory receptivity, participation with art can sometimes help in our practical activities, as in the case of the unsure surgeon. But perhaps most important of all, the understanding of values we achieve through participating with works of art may be extrinsically very valuable because such understanding helps us face our moral dilemmas with sounder orientation and deeper sympathy for others. And yet again, what about the last question of the last perception key?

CONCEPTION KEY THE ORIGIN OF VALUE

1. Select that work of art discussed in this book that is the most valuable to you. Why is it so valuable?

2. Do you believe that value is projected into things by us, or that we discover values in things, or that in some way value originates in the relationship between us and things? Explain.

Values, we propose, involve a valuer and something that excites an interest in that valuer. *Subjectivist theories* of value claim, however, that it is the interest that projects the value on something. Thus the painting is positively valuable only because it satisfies the interest of someone. Value is in the valuer. If no one is around to project his interest, then there are no valuable objects. Value is entirely relative to the valuer. Beauty is in the eye of the beholder. Jane is not really beautiful. Jane is beautiful only if someone sees her so. *Objectivist theories* of value claim, conversely, that it is the object that excites the interest. Moreover, the painting is positively valuable even if no one has any interest in it. Value is in the object independently of any subject. Jane is beautiful even if no one is aware of her beauty.

The relational theory of value—which is the one we have been presupposing throughout this book—claims that value emerges from the relation between an interest and an object. A good painting that is satisfying no one's interest at the moment possesses *potential* value. A good painting possesses properties that under proper conditions are likely to stimulate the interests of a valuer. The subjectivist would say that this painting has no value whatsoever until someone projects value on it. The objectivist would say that this painting has actualized value inherent in it whether anyone enjoys it or not. The relationalist would say that this painting has potential value; that when it is experienced under proper conditions, a sensitive, informed participant will actualize the potential value. To describe a painting as "good" is the same as saying that the painting has positive potential value. Furthermore, for the relationalist, value is realized only when objects with potential value connect with the interests of someone.

Values are usually studied with reference to the interaction of various kinds of potential value with human interests. For example, criticism tends to focus on the intrinsic values of works of art; economics focuses on commodities as basically extrinsic values; and ethics focuses on intrinsic-extrinsic values as they are or ought to be chosen by moral agents.

CONCEPTION KEY   VALUES AND THE SCIENCES

Since values involve human interests, and these interests are likely to vary from individual to individual, do you think values can be described by the sciences? If so, how?

Values that are described scientifically as they are found, we shall call "value facts." Values that are set forth as norms or ideals or what ought to be, we shall call "normative values." The smoking of marijuana, for instance, is for many a positive value. Much research is being undertaken to provide descriptions of the consequences of the use of marijuana, and rigorous scientific standards are applicable. We would place such research with the sciences. And we would call the values that are described in such research value facts. A scientific report may describe the relevant value facts connected with the use of marijuana, showing, for example, that people who smoke marijuana generally have such and such pleasurable experiences but at the same time incur such and such risks. Such a report is describing what *is* the case, not what *ought* to be the case (i.e., normative values). When someone argues that marijuana should be prohibited or someone else argues that marijuana should be legalized, we are in a realm beyond the strict application of scientific standards. Appeal is being made not to what "is" or to factual value—this the sciences can handle—but to the "ought" or normative value.

CONCEPTION KEY   FACTUAL VALUE AND NORMATIVE VALUE

1. Do you see any possible connection between factual and normative value? For example, will the scientific studies now being made on the use of marijuana have any relevance to your judgment as to whether you should or should not smoke marijuana? Explain.
2. Do you think that the artist can reveal anything relevant to your judgment about using marijuana? Explain.

3. Do you think humanists other than artists might produce anything relevant for your judgment about the use of marijuana? Explain.

There is a very close relationship between factual and normative value. If scientists were to assert that anyone who uses marijuana regularly cannot possibly live longer than ten more years, this obviously would influence the arguments about its legalization. Yet the basis for a well-grounded decision about such a complex issue—for it is hardly likely that such a clear-cut fact as death within ten years from using marijuana regularly will be discovered—surely involves more than scientific information. Novels such as Aldous Huxley's *Brave New World* reveal aspects and consequences of drug experiences that escape the nets of scientific investigation. They clarify features of value phenomena which supplement the factual values as established by science. After exposure to such literature, we may be in a better position for well-grounded decisions about such problems as the legalization of marijuana.

The arts and the other humanities often have normative relevance. They may clarify the possibilities for value decisions, thus clarifying what ought to be and what we ought to do. And this is an invaluable function, for we are creatures who must constantly choose among various value possibilities. Paradoxically, even not choosing is a choice. The humanities can help enlighten our choices. Artists help by revealing aspects and consequences of value phenomena that escape scientists. The other humanists help by clarifying aspects and consequences of value phenomena that escape both artists and scientists. For example, the historian might trace the consequences of drug use in past societies. Moreover, the other humanists can take account of the whole value field, including the relationships between the revealed values of the artists and factual values of the scientists. This is something we are trying to do, however briefly and oversimply, right here.

CONCEPTION KEY TESTING NORMATIVE VALUES

---

1. You probably have made a judgment about whether or not to use marijuana. Was there any kind of evidence—other than the scientific—that was relevant to your decision? Explain.

2. Reflect about the works of art that we have discussed in this book. Have any of them clarified value possibilities for you in a way that might helpfully influence your value decisions? How? Be as specific as possible. Do some arts seem more relevant than others in this respect? If so, why? Discuss with others. Do you find that people differ a great deal about the arts that are most relevant to their value decisions? If so, how is this to be explained?

Factual values are verified experimentally, put through the tests of the scientific method. Normative values are verified experientially, put through the tests of living. Satisfaction, for ourselves and the others involved, is an experiential test that the normative values we chose in a given instance were probably right. Suffering, for ourselves and the others involved, is an experiential test that the normative values we chose were probably wrong. Experiential testing of normative values involves not only the immediacy of experience but the consequences that follow. If you choose to try heroin, you cannot escape the consequences. And, fortunately, certain works of the humanities—Nelson Algren's *Man with the Golden Arm*, for instance—can make you vividly aware of those consequences before you have to suffer them. Science can also point out these consequences, of course, but science cannot make them so forcefully present and thus so thoroughly understandable.

The arts are closely related to the other humanities, especially history, philosophy, and religion. In conclusion, we shall give only a brief sketch of the relationships, for they are enormously complex and require an extensive analysis that we can only suggest.

THE ARTS AND HISTORY

CONCEPTION KEY   HISTORY AND THE ARTS

1. Do you see how works of art might be of great significance to the work of a historian? Explain.

2. Suppose an ancient town were being excavated but, aside from architecture, no works of art had been unearthed. And then some paintings, sculpture, a few musical scores, and some poems come to light—all from that local culture. Is it likely that the paintings would give the historian information different from that provided by the architecture or the sculpture? Or what might the music reveal that the other arts do not? The poems? As you reflect on these questions, reflect also on the following description by Martin Heidegger, the great German thinker, of a painting by Van Gogh of a pair of peasant shoes: "From the dark opening of the worn insides of the shoes the toilsome tread of the worker stares forth. In the stiffly rugged heaviness of the shoes there is the accumulated tenacity of her slow trudge through the far-spreading and ever-uniform furrows of the field swept by a raw wind. On the leather lie the dampness and richness of the soil. Under the soles slides the loneliness of the field-path as evening falls. In the shoes vibrates the silent call of the earth, its quiet gift of the ripening grain and its unexplained self-refusal in the fallow desolation of the wintry field. This equipment is pervaded by uncomplaining anxiety as to the certainty of bread, the wordless joy of having once more withstood want, the trembling before the impending childbed and shivering at the surrounding menace of

death. This equipment belong to the *earth*, and it is protected in the *world* of the peasant women."[2]

The historian tries to discover the *what* and the *why* of the past. He needs, of course, as many relevant facts as possible in order to describe the events that happened. Often he may be able to use the scientific method in his gathering and verification of facts. But in attempting to give as full an explanation as possible of why some of the events he is tracing happened, he functions as a humanist, for here he needs understanding of the normative values or ideals of the society he is studying. Among his main resources are works of art. Often they will reveal the norms of a people—their views of birth and death, disaster and blessing, victory and disgrace, endurance and decline, themselves and God, fate and what ought to be. Only with the understanding of such values can history become something more than a catalogue of events.

THE ARTS AND PHILOSOPHY

Philosophy is, among other things, an attempt to give reasoned answers to fundamental questions which, by reason of their generality, are not treated by any of the more special disciplines. Ethics, aesthetics, and metaphysics or speculative philosophy, three of the main divisions of philosophy, are very closely related to the arts. Ethics in part is often the inquiry into the presuppositions or principles operative in our moral judgments and the study of norms or standards for value decisions. If we are correct, an ethic dealing with norms that fails to take advantage of the insights of the arts is inadequate. John Dewey, one of America's foremost philosophers, even argued "that art is more moral than moralities. For the latter either are, or tend to become, consecrations of the *status quo*, reflections of custom, reenforcements of the established order. The moral prophets of humanity have always been poets even though they spoke in free verse or by parable."[3]

CONCEPTION KEY ETHICS AND THE ARTS

---

1. In the quote above, Dewey might seem to be thinking primarily of poets when he speaks of the contribution of artists to the ethicist. Or do you think he is using the term "poets" to include all artists? In any case, do you think

---

[2]Martin Heidegger, "The Origin of the Work of Art," in Albert Hofstadter (trans.), *Poetry, Language, Thought*, Harper and Row, New York, 1971, pp. 33f.
[3]John Dewey, *Art as Experience*, Minton, Balch and Co., New York, 1934, p. 348.

that literature has more to contribute to the ethicist than the other arts? If so, why?

2. Reflect on the works of art which we have discussed in this book. Which ones do you think might have the most relevance to an ethicist? Why?

Throughout this book we have been elaborating an aesthetic or philosophy of art. We have been attempting to account to some extent for the whole range of the phenomena of art—the creative process of the artist, the work of art, the experience of the work of art, criticism, and the role of art in society—from a philosophic standpoint. We have on occasion avoided restricting our analysis to any single area within that group, considering the interrelationship of these areas. And on other occasions we have tried to make explicit the basic assumptions of some of the restricted studies. These are typical functions of the aesthetician or philosopher of art. For example, much of our time has been spent doing criticism, analyzing and appraising particular works of art. But at other times, as in Chapter 3, we tried to make explicit the presuppositions or principles of criticism. The critic, of course, may do this himself, but then he is functioning more as an aesthetician than as a critic. Furthermore, we have also reflected on how criticism influences the artist, the participant, and society. This too is a function of the aesthetician.

Finally, the aim of most metaphysicians or speculative philosophers, roughly speaking, is to take the results of the various sciences and relate or integrate them with the results of the humanities. A metaphysician who attempts to be adequate cannot reject anything as irrelevant. And then there is the attempt to reflect upon the whole in order to achieve some general conclusions concerning the nature of reality and our position and prospects in it. A metaphysician who ignores the arts will have left out some of the most useful insights about value phenomena, which are very much a fundamental part of our reality.

THE ARTS AND RELIGION

The practice of religion, strictly speaking, is not a humanistic activity or study, for basically it neither creates values in the way of the arts nor studies values in the way of the other humanities. A religion is an institution that brings people together for the purpose of worship. These people share certain religious experiences as well as beliefs about and interpretations of those experiences. Since various people differ especially on their beliefs about and interpretations of their religious experiences, it is more accurate to refer to religions than to religion. Nevertheless, there is a commonsense basis, reflected in our ordinary language, for the term "religion." Despite the differences about their beliefs and interpretations, religious people generally agree that their religious values—for example, achieving in some sense participation with God—are ultimate, that is, more important than any other values. They have ultimate concern for these values. Moreover, a common nucleus of experience seems to be shared by all religious people: (1) uneasy awareness of the limitations of man's moral and theoretical powers; (2) awe-full awareness of a further reality—beyond or behind or within the world of our sense experience; (3) conviction that participation with this further reality is of supreme importance.

Theology involves the study of religion. As indicated in Chapter 1, the humanities in the Medieval period were studies about man, whereas theology and related studies were studies about God. But in present times theology, usually more broadly conceived, is placed with the humanities rather than the sciences. Moreover, for many religious people today, ultimate values or the values of the sacred are not necessarily ensconced in another world "up there." In any case, some works of art reveal ultimate values in ways that are relevant to the contemporary situation. The theologian who ignores these revelations cannot do justice to his study of religion.

CONCEPTION KEY RELIGIOUS VALUES AND THE ARTS

Reflect about the works of art you know best. Have any of them revealed ultimate values to you in a way that is relevant to your situation? How? Are they necessarily contemporary works? Discuss these reflections with others.

Dietrich Bonhoeffer, in one of his last letters from the Nazi prison of Tegel, noted that "now that it has become of age, the world is more Godless, and perhaps it is for that very reason nearer to God than ever before." Our artists, secular as well as religious, not only reveal our despair but, in the depths of that darkness, open paths back to the sacred.

At the end of the last century, Matthew Arnold intimated that the aesthetic experience, especially of the arts, would become the religious experience. We do not think this transformation will happen because the aesthetic or participative experience lacks the outward expressions, such as worship, that fulfill and in turn distinguish the religious experience. But Arnold was prophetic, we believe, in the sense that increasingly the arts would provide the most direct access to the sacred. Iris Murdoch, the contemporary English novelist, describes such an experience:

Dora had been in the National Gallery a thousand times and the pictures were almost as familiar to her as her own face. Passing between them now, as through a well-loved grove, she felt a calm descending on her. She wandered a little, watching with compassion the poor visitors armed with guidebooks who were peering anxiously at the masterpieces. Dora did not need to peer. She could look, as one can at last when one knows a great thing very well, confronting it with a dignity which it has itself conferred. She felt that the pictures belonged to her, and reflected ruefully that they were about the only thing that did. Vaguely, consoled by the presence of something welcoming and responding in the place, her footsteps took her to various shrines at which she had worshipped so often before.[4]

Such experiences are rare. Most of us still require the guidebooks. But one hopes the time will come when we no longer just peer but participate. And when that time comes, then a guidebook such as this one may have its justification.

[4] *The Bell*, by Iris Murdoch, copyright © 1958 by Iris Murdoch. Reprinted by permission of The Viking Press, Inc., New York, and Chatto and Windus Ltd., London. P. 182.

SUBJECT INDEX

Page numbers in *italic* indicate figures.

INDEX OF TITLES

Titles are listed alphabetically under the following headings: Architecture; Dance; Film (& Photos); Literature (& Other References); Music; Painting; and Sculpture. Page numbers in *italic* indicate figures.

ARCHITECTURE

DANCE

FILM (& PHOTOS)

LITERATURE (& OTHER REFERENCES)

MUSIC

PAINTING

SCULPTURE

0-07-040612